£14.95

PICTURING THE PAST

PICTURING THE PAST

◆

THE RISE AND FALL OF THE
BRITISH COSTUME FILM

SUE HARPER

BFI PUBLISHING

791.430941

Media

First published in 1994 by the
British Film Institute
21 Stephen Street
London W1P 1PL

The British Film Institute exists to encourage the development of film, television and video in the United Kingdom, and to promote knowledge, understanding and enjoyment of the culture of the moving image. Its activities include the National Film and Television Archive; the National Film Theatre; the Museum of the Moving Image; the London Film Festival; the production and distribution of film and video; funding and support for regional activities; Library and Information Services; Stills, Posters and Designs; Research; Publishing and Education; and the monthly *Sight and Sound* magazine.

British Library Cataloguing in Publication Data.
A catalogue record for this book is available from the British Library.

ISBN: 0–85170–448–4
0–85170–449–2 pbk

Cover design by Andrew Barron and Collis Clements Associates

Typeset in 9/11 pt Century Schoolbook by
Fakenham Photosetting Ltd, Fakenham, Norfolk
Printed in Great Britain by St Edmundsbury Press Ltd,
Bury St Edmunds, Suffolk

To my mother, Josephine Harper,
whose encyclopædic knowledge of 1940s film culture
and sure instinct for popular taste
have been a real inspiration.

And the poor in their fireless lodgings, dropping the sheets
Of the evening paper: 'Our day is our loss, O show us
    History the operator, the
Organiser, Time the refreshing river.'

W. H. Auden, 'Spain'

CONTENTS

ACKNOWLEDGMENTS

First of all, I should like to thank Vincent Porter, who supervised the PhD thesis on which this book is based. Without his encouragement and intellectual rigour, this whole project would not have seen the light of day.

I am grateful for financial assistance received from the Research Committees of the Universities of Portsmouth and Westminster, and also from the Faculty of Humanities and Social Sciences at Portsmouth.

Staff have been very helpful at the British Film Institute Library, the British Library, the Historical Association Archive, the National Film and Television Archive, the Newspaper Library at Colindale, the Public Record Office at Kew, and the Theatre Museum. I am indebted to Victor Bonham-Carter of the Society of Authors, David Francis of the University of Portsmouth Library, Glenise Mathieson of the John Rylands Library, Dorothy Sheridan of the Mass-Observation Archive, and Jeff Walden of the BBC Written Archives Centre. Roma Gibson at the BFI and David Wilson have been helpful well beyond the call of duty. I should especially like to thank the editor of this book, Pam Cook, who has tempered her criticisms with wit and tact.

Many scholars in the field have been generous with their knowledge, particularly Tony Aldgate, Martin Chalk, Simon Davies, Laurie Ede, Robert Murphy and Linda Wood. I have profited from the very helpful advice of Christine Gledhill, Stuart Hall, Annette Kuhn and Raphael Samuel.

I could not have attempted a map of historical film culture in the period without the help of people who worked in the field, or were involved in it. I am grateful to those who gave so generously of their time in interviews. I should also like to record my appreciation of all my students at Portsmouth, past and present; they have, with great good humour, tolerated my insistence that British cinema was the most interesting topic in the world.

I have been very fortunate in having a network of friends and colleagues with whom I could discuss my work. I owe a great deal to John Moore, who first showed me how to read a film and with whom I have had countless enlightening conversations; he also compiled the index. I am deeply indebted to John Oakley, whose understanding of aristocratic symbolism far surpasses my own. Various draft extracts have been read, and valuably commented on, by Graham Davies, Robert Gray, Verena Lovett, Frank Mort and Betty Owen. Other friends have been unfailingly supportive, and I should like to thank my family in Holland, Russell Baldwin, Peggy Bonser, Vivien Chadder, the Collins family, Monica Davies, Jenny Green, Marj Hales, Adrian Hill, Janet Lowndes, Brendan Kenny, Madeleine Mason, Ady Mineo, Ray Pettitt, Naomi Rivers, Vaughan Ryall, and Jason Smith ('practically the same recipe as Mistress Caroline used to make').

Finally, I should like to thank my husband, Walter Ditmar, whose eye for textual detail has been both my blessing and my scourge. In pursuit of a final draft of this book, he has spent many hours at the word-processor, and has consistently shown grace under pressure.

INTRODUCTION

'If men could learn from history, what lessons it might teach us! But passion and party blind our eyes, and the light which experience gives is a lantern on the stern, which shines only on the waves behind us.' Coleridge's remark from his 1831 *Table Talk* provides a useful focus for analyses of the uses of history. It warns us of the dangers of purism, and invites us to imagine a world in which the lantern of history could swing from the bow as well as the stern, and illuminate the days to come. Such a model interprets the past as a means of prediction as well as explanation, and grants it a vital role in individual consciousness. The historical imagination is crucial to survival; the recognition of the past aids a sense of national as well as personal identity, in that it forces us to distinguish between those transformations which are irreversible, and those which are not. Only then can we make judgments about the real nature of change. But it is crucial to remember that the past *is* another country. On the one hand, it is irrecoverably lost, and its superficial resemblances to our own world should not tempt us into claiming a false kinship with it. On the other hand, the strangeness of the past releases it from the bondage of objective interpretation. History can carry an infinite range of meanings, and societies regularly reformulate it for current use.

This book owes its inception to a walk across a field, many years ago. On a hot day, I found a dry ditch traversing a field diagonally; after scrambling down into it, my head was at the level of the grass. As I progressed, I saw the five feet of earth which lay beneath the grass, and I noted the different textures and colours of soil and rock. Suddenly I realised that both present and past were like the grass, and that an incredibly complex combination of historical elements was hidden beneath the world of cultural forms. To be sure, this was no major innovation, but it was borne in on me with more excitement than had ensued from the perusal of standard works on base and superstructure.

I came to think that the historian ought to produce a geology of culture in a specific period and medium; the various strata of texts which obtained at any one time were not randomly related, but owed their existence to different strands in the historical process. Some 'survivors' were forced to the top by social pressures akin to shifts in the great tectonic plates; some remained buried as fossils, disregarded until an archaeologist sank a shaft or interpreted the layers in a ditch. It seemed to me that such a project, though broad in its implications, had to be narrowly focused to have any credibility. Any geological 'map' of culture had to be specific in its medium and period, and it needed

1

an organising principle. A particularly rich area seemed to be the representation of history; in a whole range of artefacts, it has provided a convenient disguise in which to rehearse debates about class identity and gender definition.

By accident, I then saw the 1945 Gainsborough film *The Wicked Lady*. I knew little about popular British cinema then, and was surprised and exhilarated by the film's flamboyance; it presented a view of the past which challenged more respectable accounts. I had found my subject. The form in question was to be British historical film, because it posed fascinating and hitherto unsolved problems about popular culture. The period was to be that flanking the Second World War, because it was one of acute social change. The medium was to be the cinema, because it was the form which was most responsive to mass taste and popular memory. Film, in the 1930s and 1940s, was an area in which cultural reproduction had become large-scale industrial production, driven by the profit motive. It depended for its success on satisfying consumers' needs, and providing pleasurable avenues for the imaginary positioning of the viewer. What was the role of historical film in providing these pleasures?

This book, then, is concerned with the representation of history. But of late, the word 'representation' has become sullied by careless use. Informed (or misinformed) by ill-digested semiotics and vulgar feminism, a number of writers have laid bare the phallocentrism of advertising images, for example, or the social stereotyping in popular forms. Such analyses can never be more than a statement of the obvious, since the decoding practices they deploy lack any historical resonance. The term 'representation' needs to be redefined, by insisting that analyses of books, films or images are firmly rooted in precise social and historical contexts, and by considering the institutions which framed those texts. Only thus can we avoid being shipwrecked on the wilder shores of psychologism.

I shall consider later, and in more detail, the question of appropriate methods for investigations of this kind. But it needs to be stressed at the outset that, in order to avoid the dangers of a teleological approach, deductive methods will inform this book, even though the sirens of the inductive sing from the shore. That is to say, I shall attempt to do justice to the complexity of the evidence, and to give honest cognisance to findings inconvenient to my own world-view. In a sense, therefore, the aims of this book are modest: to provide a taxonomy of historical film in a particular time and place, and to study the forces which produce images of history and which determine their consumption.

My primary aim is to address the social function of historical film, and to ask why certain periods recur in films in specific patterns; why, for example, the Regency age was deployed more at some times than others, and why historical film flourished as a genre in the prewar period and declined postwar. It is necessary to recognise at the outset that it is inadequate to deal only with films which represent real historical events; we are far more likely to construct a map of popular taste if we concentrate on *costume* dramas. These deploy recognisable historical periods, but not necessarily major events or personages. Historicity is differently nuanced in them, and they fulfil a heterogeneous range of functions. These functions can only be understood by abandoning the expectation that historical film should be judged according to the accuracy of its version of events. Many writers have deployed a reflectionist approach, and have persisted in flaying those films which offend against the criteria of visual or psychological realism. But such critiques are inappropriate; it is far more important to establish the extent to which films provided a coherent symbolism for their audiences, or a set of class alliances. Such films, though they may have had little to do with historical fact, drew on deeply rooted cultural topoi.

Of course, we need to distinguish between popular and less popular films, and much hinges on the means whereby we establish this. Prior to 1937, we have to depend upon fugitive documents in official files, or on piecemeal information which may be gained about the profit-and-loss figures on individual films when presented to bankers or prospective backers. A broad impression can be gained from material presented in trade papers, press books and auto-biographies, but these are not empirically verifiable. From 1937, *Kinematograph Weekly* published an annual survey of box-office takings, broken down into month-by-month figures from 1938. We can also consult *Film Weekly* surveys and *Picturegoer* awards, the work of social historian J. P. Mayer and Mass-Observation; we need to classify the many letters on historical films which were printed in the key film magazines. But there is a paucity of hard-and-fast evidence on popularity, which must temper some conclusions with caution.

It is also important to distinguish between the popular, hegemonic and consensual functions of films. Popular films are those which appeal to mass audiences, and a degree of evidence is available about their profitability; they may have a range of social, sexual and class functions. They provide textual comfort and a sense of optimism for their viewers; they often require more creativity and ingenuity from the audience than is commonly thought. Certain films also play a key role in the hegemonic process; that is to say, in the persuasive and imaginary means whereby dominant forces maintain power. To do this it is necessary to win over, on behalf of the ruling class, those groups on its boundaries. In some films, this is achieved by incorporating such marginal groups into the narrative and according them a symbolic role; they are thus given a sense by the texts that they have a stake in society. Consensual films, on the other hand, secure agreement with a politically centrist position by *excluding* dissident groups or discourses. Such texts work on the principle of discomfiting a fraction which may elsewhere be experiencing profound anxiety: for example, the lower middle classes in the 1930s, or sexual adventurers of any period.

During the 1930s and 1940s, public institutions sought to influence the production of historical film, and attempts were made by the Foreign Office, the Ministry of Information, the Historical Association, the British Board of Film Censors and the British Film Institute. But it is crucial to avoid a reductionist model which proposes that cultural forms are a straightforward proof of conspiracy, in which popular art is particularly complicit. Such views have led some film scholars to an elitist deconstructionism, which often took the form of berating popular texts for not being politically correct. Fortunately, such coercive, puritanical theoreticism can now be safely ignored, in favour of a more considered and catholic approach.

To be sure, official discourses do construct social frames of reference, and

3

these have measurable effects. But audiences can also select out films which permit them to stand at a distance from official realities; and canny producers cater for such eventualities. Of course, a latent sentimentalism may afflict the unwary historian of popular culture, if mass taste somehow becomes the hero in the battle against the forces of darkness. But such an error can be avoided by insisting on two points. Firstly, popular historical films were widely accepted because their audiences were able to decode the complex and sometimes inconsistent messages they bore. Secondly, the field of historical film must be laid out in detail, so as to account for the *lack* of popularity of some films. Only thus can the historian chart a map of pleasure, discriminate between different film types, and show continuities and breaks in taste. Only then is it possible to take account of the range of textual pleasures which obtained in any one period, and we can dismiss the possibility that popular texts simply represent 'false consciousness'. Popular texts are such because, on a symbolic level, they satisfactorily alleviate real problems in the lives of their audience. Gramsci argued that the realm of the individual consciousness contains living 'fossils' or residual deposits from the past, and that one should know oneself as 'the product of the historical process which has left in you an infinity of traces gathered together without the advantage of an inventory'.[1] But culture contains such fossils too, and the 'match' between these and the residual substrata in the individual's mind is what produces the shock of recognition contained in popular texts. The pleasure is in the snug fit, like Cinderella's slipper.

Pierre Bourdieu's work on the sociology of taste has made a major contribution to this debate, but it needs to be handled with care. Bourdieu argues that there is a consonance between 'fields of power', the field of cultural production, and the field of the text. However, the relationships between social power, artistic production and textual structures are neither as predictable nor as regular as he proposes. Often a species of displacement occurs in the process of cultural production, in which disguise or outright cultural banditry can be seen. Bourdieu gives a welcome attention to the consumers of the text, but his account unfortunately privileges bourgeois audiences. 'High' art works apparently require complex deciphering techniques, and 'naïve beholders' are disadvantaged in the decoding process. The invaluable notion of the consumer's 'cultural capital' is deployed. But Bourdieu concentrates on the status conferred on the text by the fact that educational qualifications facilitate the enjoyment of it. Thus his notion of 'habitus' (those social structures internalised in the individual psyche which determine receptivity to types of art) cannot provide an explanatory model of working-class taste.[2] I propose, however, that when the cultural competence of the target audience perfectly fits the requirements of the text, a process is adumbrated whereby a coherent 'parish of belief' is expressed. All popular texts evoke such a parish. It is, of course, absurd to argue that mass audiences or the working classes are culturally bankrupt. If literacy were all, then native tribes with a complex mythology and cosmology (albeit orally transmitted) would be deemed culturally incompetent too.

An exciting area is the relationship between popular memory and artistic taste. Foucault raised the issue in the *Edinburgh '77 Magazine*. For him, popular memory was essentially oppositional; it was a means whereby those

4

excluded from formal historical processes could intervene in official realities. The Popular Memory Group at the Centre for Contemporary Cultural Studies built on Foucault's concept, and they mooted a rapprochement between the discourses of oral history and the languages of fiction.[3] That was as far as it went, however; and some adroitness will be necessary to demonstrate that popular historical films exactly reproduced their audiences' sense of the past. But I shall attempt to address the issue.

So far I have concentrated on the social institutions which attempted to influence historical films, and on questions of audience response. But the role played by a film's producer cannot be ignored. The key issue is that of intellectual control, since a film represents the labours of a wide range of personnel. At one time it was fashionable to praise those heroic director-auteurs who managed to impose their signature on the intractable studio machine; but this approach is particularly inappropriate for an analysis of British film in this period. The delineation of the producer's control does not preclude work on individual directors, and the tensions in a film text can often be accounted for by a vexed relationship between a producer and director. But in the 1930s and 1940s the producer was the determinant in the last instance; the means of production belonged to him, or to the investors he represented. He was responsible for delivering the film to the distributor, who was usually the major investor. I shall attempt to establish the range of influence of key producers such as Alexander Korda, Michael Balcon and Herbert Wilcox.

This notion of producer-authorship should not, however, lead to a crude economic determinism. A base/superstructure model of cultural production can be dangerous if not carefully deployed, since it can fatally relegate artistic style to the role of a decorative excrescence laid on the surface of the 'real' text. Rather, a definition of production control should take due cognisance of the importance of style for a film's popularity. Visual texture is not superficial; it is a site marked by clashes between different cultural cross currents. The relationship between the verbal level of the script and the visual level of the *mise en scène* can differ from one studio to another, and sometimes from one period to another in the same studio. But (*pace* Bourdieu) the cultural competence of a producer always has extensive influence on the broad historical definitions which inform a film.

Of course, the class origins of the producer or director are not straightforwardly replicated in their artistic work. In any case, their education could permit them to partake of any class position. Films (particularly historical films) can be made 'in disguise'; that is, on behalf of any class fraction, representing any class interest. What should concern cultural historians is precisely cases of disjuncture: films where there is a clear misalliance between the position of the text and the class or gender of its progenitors. Such films offer the strongest challenge to the reflectionist argument. For example, it cannot be argued that the aristocracy was historically significant in the period under consideration, nor was it a visible presence in the film industry as such. And yet the aristocracy, and the upper reaches of the gentry class, are the class fractions which work hardest in popular historical films. A species of symbolic substitution is clearly taking place. Raymond Williams's categorisation of texts into dominant, residual or emergent may be efficacious in classifying the different social functions of films.[4] Williams argues that cultural forms may

5

represent existing, fossilised or new social forces, and that this accounts for the lack of homogeneity in any one period. He argues that all texts betray, by the structures of feeling contained within them, their class interest, whether of the status quo, the old order or the new dispensation. This has interesting implications for the study of the cinema. Any map of film culture must take account of residual deposits and real innovation; but the problem with the dominant/residual/emergent paradigm is that, although it provides an explanation for the production of texts, it does not deal well with the question of their reception. Nor does it help us explain why texts dealing with the past were of urgent social concern in some periods and not in others.

The anthropological insights of Mary Douglas may be useful here. Douglas suggests that societies construct ritual forms whereby notions of purity and danger, safety and pollution, are rehearsed. She argues that pollution symbols figure powerfully in cultures with complex taboo systems, and that it is possible to construct symmetrical models of the values which lie beneath rituals of purification and interdiction.[5] Although devised initially for the analysis of tribal cultures, such concepts are invaluable for the cinema. It is an art-form especially predicated upon notions of sexual ratification, and the power of its images of sexuality frequently gives rise to moral panics. Films, like other popular cultural forms, fulfil a quasi-ritualistic function, by endorsing mythic structures of pollution and purity and thus clarifying confusions about moral or social boundaries. The social act of cinema-going mixes complicity in the shared viewing of forbidden acts with an increased sense of group pressure. This approach would enable us to account for the extraordinary power which some films have over their audiences. But insights derived from anthropological concepts must always be carefully historicised. Notions of taboo can change within a short time, and fictional texts adjust accordingly. Moreover, artistic languages, while not autonomous, do have a history of their own, which must be taken into account.

But I have, perhaps, strayed too far into the realms of theory, and I should emphasise that my method will mainly be the evaluation of contemporary journalism, interviews, autobiographies, official documents, studio guidelines and, of course, the films themselves. In analysing those films, I shall deploy the conventional resources of visual composition and *mise en scène*. But no one historical account can be definitive, since so much depends on chance. A crucial document may have been pulped; a key figure may have died inconveniently early; an important film may not have survived; the researcher may have been careless for a day. For example, during an interview with the art director Maurice Carter I was promised access to surviving documents from the Art Director's Guild. These would have been invaluable to me; but it turned out that they had been consigned to the garbage the week before by Mr Carter's wife. I felt rather like Carlyle when he discovered that the manuscript of *The French Revolution* had been used to light the fire. But it was a salutary reminder of the shifting nature of historical evidence, and of the necessity of making the best of one's resources. I began this chapter with one quotation from 1831; and it seems fitting to close it with another, from Mary Shelley's Preface to the Standard Novels Edition of *Frankenstein*. She clearly understood all the problems of intellectual labour and historical research:

Invention, it must be humbly admitted, does not consist in creating out of a void, but out of chaos; the materials must, in the first place, be afforded; it can give form to dark, shapeless substances, but cannot bring into being the substance itself ... Invention consists in the capacity of seizing on the capabilities of a subject, and in the power of fashioning and moulding ideas suggested to it.

1

HISTORICAL FEATURE FILM 1933–1939

POLITICAL CONSTRAINTS

In the late 1920s the British cinema was subjected to widescale scrutiny. But debates were not focused on purely economic issues; from the beginning, the cinema's function in the presentation of a national history and culture was of paramount importance.

Parliamentary debates on the 1927 Cinematograph Films Act provide access to a range of official opinions on historical film. Contributors to the House of Commons debates marshalled historical film straightforwardly into notions of the national interest. Sir Robert Horne noted that 'there is no country with a history or with a scenery which are more adaptable to use in cinematographic exhibition.' The historian Sir Charles Oman thought that British films should 'make available for the public eye all the wonderful stories that lay in the history and romance as well as the folklore of the kingdom.' And Thomas Johnston, who later became the first Under-Secretary of State for Scotland, argued that British films were culpably inaccurate about the national past. He attacked *The Life of Robert Burns* because 'all the captions are wrong, all the history is wrong, and all the life story is wrong ... the mere fact that a man has got a British nationalisation certificate for 25 shillings does not *ipso facto* authorise him to be a director of aesthetic taste in this country.' Individual institutions wished to control cinematic representations of themselves; Admiralty spokesmen wanted to 'see that historical films are as accurate as they can be made, and therefore they think it no harm, indeed they think it right to assist, in the production of such films.'[1]

Clearly, members of the House of Commons had an unproblematical definition of historical accuracy and the national interest, and thought that both could easily be inserted into films. The House of Lords debate on the Act contained more thoughtful interventions. Earl Russell, although he deplored 'these dreadful American films with their mushy sentimentality', thought that the protectionist tactics of the Act would not produce truly 'British scenes'. The Bishop of Southwark considered that interference with free trade was justified if it produced a more nationalistic cinema, reflecting 'what is best in the life and history of the nation'.[2]

Politicians were not alone in such views. The desirability of films that reflected national culture was also mooted in *The Times*, which supported film-maker Ivor Montagu's demand for a 'national studio'. The paper bewailed the fact that the trade did not recognise any responsibility to 'the nation and to the Empire, or indeed to anyone but its own shareholders'. It argued for a much greater degree of government control, in order to encourage exhibitors to discriminate between good films and bad. A sort of quality censorship was being advocated to root out the grosser excesses in popular film. *The Times* argued forcefully that the proposed quota would not produce a more patriotic film culture, and insisted that films without national identity were dangerous corrupters of the public imagination; as such, they had the effect of drugs or 'lying teachers'. A riposte to *The Times* came from the President of the Federation of British Industry, who argued that some sort of quota was necessary in order to resist the Americanisation of British film culture. But *The Times* insisted that priority should be given to cultural quality, and printed letters from those who agreed with its position that 'films should be of and for the British Empire, produced within the Empire, depicting its life history and the high morality for which it stands'.[3] Clearly, those who assumed the position of moral and intellectual arbiters felt that the film industry was ignoring its duty to instruct through pleasure.

Parts of the Establishment, then, had an urgent sense of film's contribution to the ideological formation in the late 1920s and early 1930s. Producers, however, had quite other preoccupations in the period around the implementation of the 1927 Act. They had to make arrangements for the installation of sound; they had to raise capital from new sources; and they had to establish new distribution arrangements. The enormous growth of corporations and cinema circuits from 1927 meant that producers' energies were devoted to marking out territories and capturing expertise, rather than to feeding the ideological hungers of various official institutions. The output for the years 1927–32 showed the results of this politics of expedience. Most films were small-scale entertainments of the adventure type, and producers were resistant to high seriousness.

In March 1927 John Maxwell refloated British International Pictures, and in the same month Gaumont-British was reorganised as a public corporation by the Ostrer brothers, who came from a family of liberal Jewish bankers. The 1927 Act gave rise to a number of vertically integrated combines, in which production, distribution and exhibition were linked. The Act was also responsible for the increase in cinema-building in the early 1930s, led by the launch of the Odeon circuit by Oscar Deutsch, who did not engage in production. It is noteworthy that those producers who were directly involved in the making of films and who also had links on the distribution and exhibition side were particularly interested in the issue of profits abroad. Alexander Korda, Michael Balcon, Herbert Wilcox, John Maxwell and Basil Dean, who made substantial profits for their companies from historical films after 1933, all had a sharp eye for foreign markets. The enormous success of Korda's *The Private Life of Henry VIII* both in Europe and America encouraged emulation by other producers. This film was a definitive innovation in the field, and provides a clear marker of a new cinematic type. It presented history and the monarchy in a domestic and humanised light. Korda's film is crucial in any history of British film culture; but it also stimulated a range of official anxieties, since it was thought to depict authority in a debased manner. The film thus revealed a series of interlocking concerns about verisimilitude and social accountability.

Thus the cycle of historical films which began in 1933 was shaped by a combination of official pressures, institutional constraints, economic determi-

9

nants, market demand, and ideological conditions. What was the range, spread and topology of historical film in the period? S. Craig Shafer uses Dennis Gifford's catalogue in order to construct a statistical description of British film genres in the 1930s.[4] He produces the following results:

Year	Total output	Historical films	% of total
1932	150	0	0
1933	181	1	0.55
1934	183	3	1.64
1935	185	5	2.7
1936	217	7	3.2
1937	211	4	1.9
1938	159	3	1.9
1939	98	0	0

From Shafer's analysis, it would appear that the percentage of historical films was small but that it rose to a peak in 1936. However, there are severe problems with this model, since Gifford's definition of 'historical' is unacceptably narrow and does not conform to the categorisations expressed either by the popular audience of the period or by contemporary trade papers. Gifford defines a historical film as one which is founded on historical fact or involves the representation of real people, living or dead. He does not include costume pictures.

To gain an accurate picture of the proportion of historical films in the overall output, Gifford's definition must be extended to cover all costume films, all historical biopics, and indeed all films set in the past. I have decided to define 'history' here as that which took place at least a generation before; that is to say, for the 1930s one would draw the line at 1914. It is arguable that World War I operated for a whole generation as an index that an older way of life had been superseded. By adapting this broader definition of 'historical', the percentage proportions would be as below:

Year	Total output	Historical films	% of total
1932	150	1	0.66
1933	181	10	5.5
1934	183	10	5.5
1935	185	25	13.5
1936	217	17	7.8
1937	211	10	4.7
1938	159	10	6.3
1939	98	4	4.1

Historical films thus played a larger role in the overall output, and their production peaked in 1935. Moreover, they played a major role at the box office, quite out of proportion to their actual numbers. As I have suggested, the reconstruction of audience taste in the period is fraught with difficulties, mainly the lack of totally reliable figures. But a detailed scrutiny of box-office information is revealing, even though it may be piecemeal.

In 1930 comedy dominated the box office, and film versions of stage plays proliferated since there were few writers experienced in screen dialogue. A survey of exhibitors in 1931 suggested that there were regional differences in the willingness of audiences to respond positively to received pronunciation.[5] But this phenomenon was relatively short-lived. Although Northern audiences did favour Gracie Fields and George Formby in the 1930s, and although Frank Randle only seemed to attract aficionados north of the Trent, film audiences were able to respond positively to a wide range of films, once adjustments to sound had been made.

There is some material available for 1933. Sidney Bernstein conducted a survey with 124,837 returns on the 'best six' films of the year. These were *Cavalcade, The Private Life of Henry VIII, I Was a Spy, The Kid from Spain, Tugboat Annie* and *Voltaire*. Thus half of the top six were historical films. The Bernstein questionnaire allotted the Favourite Actor prize to George Arliss, who had specialised in Hollywood historical films, and it gave high placing to Charles Laughton, the star of *Henry VIII*. Anna Neagle appeared in the 'favourite actresses' list. Everybody's favourite director was Korda, with Victor Saville, Basil Dean and Herbert Wilcox appearing high on the list. On 5 April 1934, *Film Weekly* asked its readers about the British films of the preceding year. *Blossom Time* came first, *The Private Life of Henry VIII* second, *Catherine the Great* fourth and *The Wandering Jew* tenth.

Picturegoer reported another survey on 15 June 1935 asking about viewers' favourite performances in recent British and American films. Again, historical films were very well represented. Laughton came third in *Henry VIII*, Arliss fifth in *The House of Rothschild*, Laughton sixth in *The Barretts of Wimpole Street*, John Gilbert seventh in *Queen Christina*, and Conrad Veidt eighth in *The Wandering Jew*. On the female side, Greta Garbo came first in *Queen Christina*, Norma Shearer second in *The Barretts of Wimpole Street*, Katharine Hepburn seventh in *Little Women*, Elisabeth Bergner ninth in *Catherine the Great*, and Maureen O'Sullivan tenth in *The Barretts of Wimpole Street*.

Historical films, therefore, were popular in 1935, and this was confirmed by film journalism of 1936. *Film Weekly*'s survey of British films on 2 May 1936 suggested that historical films took four of the ten best prizes: *Scarlet Pimpernel* was second, *Nell Gwyn* third, *Jew Süss* eighth and *Scrooge* ninth. *Picturegoer* suggested on 8 August 1936 that seven out of ten favourite films were historical, and awarded first prize to Leslie Howard's role in *Scarlet Pimpernel*. Among the females, Anna Neagle took fourth place with *Nell Gwyn*.

The journalism of 1937 contains some interesting results. *Film Weekly*'s 8 May survey of most successful British films gave the first place to *Tudor Rose*, with *Peg of Old Drury*, and *Rhodes of Africa* jointly in third place. Nova Pilbeam gained first place in the Favourite Actress list with *Tudor Rose* and Neagle came third with *Peg of Old Drury*. Walter Huston and Oscar Homolka came sixth and eighth respectively in *Rhodes of Africa*. The *Kinematograph Weekly* survey on 14 January put American historical films high on the list of successes. Bernstein's 1937 questionnaire on favourite actors gave Laughton third place, with Arliss and Cedric Hardwicke also well placed. Neagle and

Pilbeam also did well in these listings, and Wilcox was highly placed among the favourite directors.

Of particular interest here is the Mass-Observation work done in Bolton in 1937. I shall return later to a detailed analysis of these responses. What is remarkable in an overview of the respondents is the regularity with which *Victoria the Great* was praised. Positive references to *Victoria* far outweighed those to any other film.[6] The significance of this film was endorsed by *Kinematograph Weekly* on 13 January 1937. *Victoria* did very well indeed in its listings of popular films, as did *King Solomon's Mines* and *Under the Red Robe*.

Journalistic material for 1938 shows a distinct decline in popularity of costume pictures. *Film Weekly*'s survey on 24 June 1939 gave first and second place respectively to *Pygmalion* and *Sixty Glorious Years*. *Kinematograph Weekly*'s broader coverage on 12 January 1939 suggested that American costume films made money; *Dr Syn*, *The Return of the Scarlet Pimpernel* and *Sixty Glorious Years* were the only British historical texts mentioned. Material covering 1939 is scanty, as *Film Weekly* combined with *Picturegoer* in that year. The *Kinematograph Weekly* survey of 11 January 1940 featured only two British historical films as profitable – *Jamaica Inn* and *The Four Feathers* – but it did report a large number of American costume films which produced good returns.

So historical films played a significant role in film profits in the 1930s, and production patterns monitored changes in public taste. There were two peaks of popularity and profit: in 1934/5 with Korda's films, and in 1937/8 with Wilcox's royal biopics. Before analysing the significance of specific producers or films, it is also important to trace some determining factors from outside the film industry. For example, in 1933 the British courts awarded substantial damages to Princess Youssoupoff against MGM, for suggesting, in *Rasputin the Mad Monk*, that she had been seduced by him. MGM's appeal failed. This meant that added vigilance was necessary for film producers featuring historical events in which protagonists might still be alive. British law also banned theatrical representations of Queen Victoria. The rescinding of this law on the centenary of Victoria's accession on 20 June 1937 immediately facilitated the production of *Victoria the Great*.

Another constraint on historical films was the British Board of Film Censors. There was a range of personnel there in the 1930s – Lord Tyrrell, the Rt. Hon. Edward Shortt, and the redoubtable Col. J. P. Hanna – who, temperamentally speaking, were not always in accord. In the BBFC's 1931 list of 'forbidden topics' there was no specific reference to historical film as such, but no. 3 forbade 'lampoons on the institution of monarchy, and libellous reflections on royal persons or families, whether British or not'. However, from 1933 a series of comments in the Scenario Reports indicated a more nuanced policy. From 1933 to 1939 the Board expressed an increasing intolerance towards historical inaccuracy and sensationalism. Elements consistently criticised were bad language, 'coarseness', and the impugning of royal reputations past or present. In the 1933 Scenario Reports, the Board dealt with a number of proposals on Jewish historical topics. These were criticised for having too obvious a parallel with contemporary problems. Only two of these projects (*Jew Süss* and *The Wandering Jew*) were subsequently made, and explicit

12

references to modern elements were underplayed in the scripts. The case of *Abdul Hamid* is similar. The Board was concerned that the story could cause affront to the Turks; in the final filmed version called *Abdul the Damned*, care had clearly been taken to reduce references to the details of Turkish politics, to praise democracy, and to increase exotic local colour.

Historical accuracy became a vexed issue for the Board. In its 1933 Scenario Report, it found the proposed *Catherine the Great* factually acceptable but demanded a cut in the unpalatably large number of bedroom scenes. For *Captain Blood* in the same year, it required a full script, because 'manners and conversations 250 years ago were much freer and more outspoken than today, and if reproduced with historical accuracy might easily fail to pass our moral standard.' This was a dilemma which the Board never managed to solve: that historical accuracy was desirable, but that modern audiences needed moral protection from the excesses of real history. This tension can be seen in many of the Board's judgments. An early version of *The Private Life of Henry VIII* was berated by the Board in 1933 for its 'coarseness', and projects were praised which presented the past in an anodyne way. But films which grafted radicalism or atheism on to the past were dealt with severely. One character in a proposed political epic was 'young, enthusiastic, fanatical. In these days we should call him a nasty Bolshie'.[7] The film was not made.

By 1934, the BBFC was permitting a greater range of historical films to proceed untouched. The scripts of *The Iron Duke* and *Me and Marlborough* even received high praise in the Scenario Reports of that year, doubtless due to the hagiographical patriotism of the one and the harmless sentimentality of the other. Two lurid projects (*Mona Lisa* and *Casta Diva*) were passed because they were based on the lives of imaginary people. Even a project on the Tolpuddle Martyrs was permitted, provided it was not made in an inflammatory manner. The Board displayed unworldliness and prurience in its moral judgments; *Anna Karenina* was seen as unsuitable in 1934 because it was 'set in a period when immorality was rife among the Russian aristocracy'. Two areas in which the Board was rigorous were in the representation of the history of India and of Ireland. A proposed film on Sir Roger Casement, for example, was banned outright in 1934.

More relaxation was evident in 1935. The censors displayed a fondness for the popular novels of Rider Haggard, Bulwer-Lytton and Baroness Orczy, and dealt leniently with scenarios of them, with the sole proviso that the eruption of Vesuvius in *Last Days of Pompeii* should not show any horrors. But only certain types of popular novels were encouraged. Films of novels from that Gothic tradition which had always dealt symbolically with sexuality were robustly rejected. Of course, the Board did have a preference for certain types of historical films. *Tudor Rose* and *Rhodes of Africa* were the only historical scripts to receive outright praise in the 1935 Scenario Reports. These were films with a clear propaganda direction, and, to the Board, they were clearly of greater significance than films about Sweeney Todd. The Board protested about the latter; but it is hard to see how the film could have been made without any reference to the barber recycling his customers into pies.

In the 1936 Scenario Reports, BBFC assessors had concluded that the mass audience wanted, or should be educated into wanting, 'historical accuracy and not the fictional story'. Accuracy was particularly demanded when an

13

individual or an institution was described, such as Nelson or the Foreign Office. Of course, Col. Hanna was exigent on the matter of historical military uniforms. But accuracy when describing imaginary characters was no longer such a burning issue, and there was also a distinct relaxation of standards vis-à-vis the representation of unhappy marriages or adulterous relationships in the past.

By 1937 there were two historical issues on which the BBFC was expressing strong opinions. The first was on the necessity of a positive interpretation of the Empire's history. A. E. W. Mason's book *The Broken Road*, when submitted for assessment of suitability, prompted the reply in the 1937 Scenario Reports that it 'seemed to bear out the truth of the well-known Kipling saying that East is East and West is West and never the twain shall meet', and as a project it was duly approved. The second issue was a fierce defensiveness towards the British royal family and its antecedents. Both an American and a British film on aspects of Queen Victoria's life were dealt with sternly.

Of course, the 1937 change in the law on the theatrical representation of Victoria forced a reassessment of the Board's policy. Lord Tyrrell, then President of the BBFC, argued that the cinema must be bound by the same laws as the theatre.[8] The consequence was that the Board could not object to the fact of representation, only to its manner. Thus the Board's Scenario Reports for 1939 dismissed a film on Disraeli because it was 'insensitive' in its handling of the Prince Consort.

There remains the question of the Board's veto of Korda's proposed *Lawrence of Arabia* in 1939. Jeffrey Richards and Jeffrey Hulbert have provided thorough documentation of this case.[9] This example shows that the BBFC was much less subtle in its dealings with foreign bodies than was the Foreign Office, and that it was subject to the FO's directives. Korda had a distinct taste for dealing with those in the top echelons of power rather than in the middle. For him, therefore, a rapprochement with the FO was possible but one with the Board was not. Col. Hanna and Lord Tyrrell *appeared* to be instrumental in putting a stop to the film, and this permitted the reputation of the FO to be left intact. Here the BBFC operated as a rather ham-fisted errand boy of higher government bodies.

We can assume, therefore, that the BBFC had a role in fine-tuning and nuancing historical films in the 1930s. It gradually abandoned its coherent policy of accuracy; it was forced to relinquish its chivalrous championing of royalty. Some films, such as *Tudor Rose*, *Rhodes of Africa* or *Victoria the Great*, were accorded leniency because they were consonant with the Board's own notions. Other productions never saw the light of day. Some producers managed to circumvent the Board. But its influence was subject to other government bodies: it had to be responsive to recommendations on historical film by the Secretary of State for India and by the Admiralty.[10] We should not overestimate the power of the BBFC. It was severely trounced by the case of Herbert Wilcox's project on Ireland, *Dawn*; it banned the film, but Wilcox managed to get it shown by the London County Council, which caused an uproar in Parliament.[11]

The BBFC, then, did not realise its desire to censor the portrayal of historical reality. It played a *negative* role, since it had no sense of compensating moral values as the American Hays Office did, and it was subject to the

Home Office, the Colonial Office and the War Office. But the Foreign Office could play a *positive* role in the production of historical films, since it had to be supportive of British film-makers in their overseas relations. It attempted, often successfully, to intervene in film production, distribution and publicity, and it gave priority to the issue of history.

The Foreign Office correspondence files at the Public Record Office have been extensively weeded. Many entries in the index of correspondence are absent from the files themselves. In addition, the denizens of the FO were cautious about showing their hand on propaganda matters. Nonetheless, from material that is extant, it is possible to trace a development in FO thinking on the uses and significance of historical film.

One cannot discuss the Foreign Office without mentioning Sir Robert Vansittart. He was Permanent Head of the Foreign Office from 1930, and his major preoccupation was the folly of appeasement. In 1938 he was 'kicked upstairs', to become Chief Diplomatic Advisor to His Majesty's Government, a post which he held until 1941.[12] He had a particular interest in psychological rearmament; indeed that was the chief business of the Vansittart Committee which produced its influential Report in 1939. Vansittart had a high regard for the propaganda value of film, and was reputed to have produced some of the dialogue for *The Four Feathers*. He was certainly credited with advice on the dialogue of *Victoria the Great*. Vansittart had a particularly close relationship with producer Basil Dean, and he used his influence to alter the status of historical films (to 'charities') in order to facilitate overseas showings.[13] With the approach of war, Vansittart campaigned for a more central organisation 'to ensure that the needs of national publicity are taken into account in newsreels, feature films etc.'[14] He attempted to circumvent bureaucracy by asking for £100,000 directly from the Prime Minister, to the fury of those government bodies then hatching the embryo Ministry of Information. Chamberlain called Vansittart's request for a National Films Council 'a very astonishing document, and entirely personal to the writer'.[15] Roars of rage ensued from bureaucratic functionaries over his high-handedness.

Although Vansittart was Permanent Head of the FO at this time, his 1938 actions were untypical of the usual FO mode of procedure. It may well have been a matter of style. Vansittart was a flamboyant personality, but the usual FO mode was covert. Officials would encourage producers privately and intervene indirectly in order to further policies. To break cover as Vansittart had done meant incurring the wrath of other government agencies; this 1938 event was no doubt the origin of the antipathy on film business between the FO and the MoI. But we should now turn to the development of FO film policy on a broader level.

In 1933, the FO presented a studiedly neutral face to some supplicants for its patronage. The Central Information Bureau for Education Films attempted to enlist FO support for its attack on the 'mental pabulum' of those images of history contained in popular literature and film. Privately, FO officials dismissed this attitude as 'bumph'. But in its public reply the FO maintained a seeming even-handedness on the high art/mass art debate.[16] Because it was well-apprised of the usefulness of low as well as high culture to those in power, the FO was catholic in its range. In its list of preferred speakers on historical topics, the FO was prepared to take those from both the left and the right of the

15

spectrum.[17] Covertly, however, the FO did have clear preferences in the area of film. In 1933, it favoured *The Private Life of Henry VIII* and disfavoured Herbert Wilcox.[18] Rex Leeper, who had a distinguished career in the FO from 1929, was a key figure on cultural policy. He insisted to Vansittart that 'it is always best for the FO to remain behind the scenes as guide, philosopher, and friend'.[19] But Leeper himself made determined overtures to entrepreneur Stephen Courtauld, who was then heavily involved with Basil Dean's enterprises, about the desirability of British feature films that would celebrate the historical aspects of British culture abroad. Vansittart took the advice and directed funds to be allocated accordingly, albeit in a discreet manner.[20]

So from 1933 the FO maintained a public image of masterly inactivity on the film and cultural front, while making its preferences known covertly and directing influence accordingly. It was prepared to cast its net wide, and thought that films promoting British culture need not necessarily be made in Britain. Such a view was anathema to British producers and to other government departments. The FO accepted the view of the British Library of Information in New York (effectively an undercover British propaganda and intelligence organisation) that the American-made *Cavalcade* had been efficacious 'since the objection of propaganda might have been raised had it been made in England'.[21] Indeed Austin Haigh, a senior attaché at the FO, expanded this into an issue of policy:

> I have always regarded the American production of a British theme with British actors as the most successful combination, and we are lucky indeed to have found a propagandist in so great an artist as Mr. Coward, who can scarcely be accused of political motives.[22]

This tactic remained a favourite with the FO, and one which it later deployed to effect with the wartime *Lady Hamilton*.

The FO had high hopes of Gaumont-British as a company which would fulfil its behests. Its chief advantage for the FO was that it had unparalleled access to foreign designers and cameramen who could produce films which were technically acceptable by international standards.[23] Gaumont-British had acquired some foreign distribution rights to *The Private Life of Henry VIII*, and when the FO heard that it had not been credited as a British film it took the unprecedented step of writing to David Ostrer, then head of the corporation, to advise him how to maximise company interests in the film. It also congratulated Ostrer on the quality of Gaumont-British's productions and, especially, their 'exportability'.[24]

The FO did not agree with the chorus of disapproval of *Henry VIII* which ensued from some respectable quarters. The British Library of Information liked the film, as did Neville Kearney, who was a key figure in the Travel Association, the embryo British Council.[25] Lord Cottenham, in the *Daily Telegraph* on 20 November 1933, had argued that the film was bad foreign publicity for Britain since it presented a British king as a 'dissolute buffoon'. Cottenham opined that 'those who love the empire contemplate with anger and disgust the world-wide distribution of a vulgar travesty of history such as this.' He thought the film 'subversive'; but at least one British Ambassador disagreed, and thought the film was 'first class ... but then I have a certain

16

delight in strong and Rabelaisian meats'.[26] His view was that *Henry VIII* could have a mass market abroad as well as at home.

By 1934, Rex Leeper was arguing for greater financial latitude for the FO so that favoured films could receive help with distribution to crucial foreign countries. Leeper noted that 'ill-considered enthusiasm can do as much harm as indifference'. It was a question of style; Leeper urged that the FO should be discreet above all, but that it should encourage studios to make films of which it approved, 'and to let it be known that they have our approval'.[27] Clearly, both Korda's London Films and Gaumont-British fell into this category, and the FO indirectly championed their productions. Gaumont's *Jew Süss* is a case in point. It was banned in Austria because of the unrest it was claimed to have caused, and the authorities there suggested that the film be cut to make it less likely to arouse Nazi ire. But the FO, advised by its Austrian embassy, refused to pressurise Gaumont; it argued that the film was acceptable to British audiences and should not be altered to placate Nazis.[28]

The maintenance of a low public profile on film was an FO priority, and it advised its diplomats accordingly.[29] We should not assume that there was complete unanimity of taste; Leeper, for example, found the propaganda value of *Henry VIII* roughly equivalent to that of the Girl Guide movement.[30] But taking an overall view, the FO certainly approved of *Henry VIII* and championed it quite vigorously. The embassy in Peru was instructed by London to act swiftly when it was advertised as a United Artists and not a London film, and later they were told to complain again when the London Films trademark was incorrectly used. London Films was duly grateful, and the FO noted that 'in the interests of national propaganda we ought not to miss any opportunity to show film people what to do'. The FO also encouraged the Tokyo embassy to defend the film when it was seriously criticised in Japan. They noted that 'any films dealing with Royalty in a way which does not conform to the Japanese concept of the dignity inherent in Royalty will always be banned', and argued that, even if *Henry* could be regarded as having a 'louche morality', it should be stoutly defended nonetheless.[31]

Korda's other films were also treated preferentially by the FO. Goebbels requested that *Catherine the Great* be withheld from showing, supposedly because of public protests about the Jewish star, Elisabeth Bergner. The FO instructed the Berlin legation to defend the film on the grounds that the public had a right to see it, even though they privately held the view that Bergner was 'anaemic'.[32] The affair led to a Parliamentary question in the Commons on 14 March 1934, and Vansittart prompted the Federation of British Industry to write to the Reichsfilmkanzler. The Federation's letter is interesting, given that it had the full backing of the FO:

> We venture to suggest that the photographic portrayal in a film of an historical character by an individual artist who is not *persona grata* is scarcely likely to bring about a breach of the peace in an enlightened community.[33]

The film was banned in Germany nevertheless. The FO was doubtless partially moved to champion *Catherine* by the enthusiastic reports from the British Library of Information in New York. It was the perception there that the

British could turn out superlative historical films, 'even though foreigners have to be employed on the technical production'.[34]

By 1934, then, FO officials and their consular representatives were acting defensively on behalf of the producers of historical features; the files do not indicate that non-historical feature films received this attention. The FO was becoming increasingly ready to accept propaganda help from historical films from America. It welcomed the American film *Lafayette* because it could 'make up sentimental leeway and bolster up hitherto existing institutions'.[35] The FO was in close contact with the Department of Trade on the film issue, and agreed with its view that, for overseas consumption, 'richly staged historical plays' were of the greatest efficacy for the image of Britain.[36]

In its relations with the British Council (set up under its own aegis), the FO proceeded to prod gently on the issue of history:

> It might be quite amusing to take from time to time short films on histori-
> cal events, not specially dramatised for the purposes of the screen but as
> faithfully reconstructed as the present state of historical knowledge
> permits.[37]

In 1935, the FO also undertook considerable groundwork for BIP's film on the history of George V's reign. It gave advice on the publicity for the film and its orientation towards foreign audiences, and made detailed suggestions on narrative style and shot length. FO officials noted that BIP 'will do almost anything we like in regard to cuts'. The FO had chosen BIP's *Royal Cavalcade* as 'by far the most substantial of the Jubilee films, and we have been prepared to give it a certain amount of support as such'. As usual, they were too cautious to give it any official imprimatur. But they did defend the film when it was attacked by foreign journalists.[38]

In its early days the British Council committed the cardinal error of showing its hand, and began to forge links with Conservative Party film workers.[39] The FO objected to such overt methods. This mismatch of approaches doubtless produced the tensions in the Joint Committee on Films which was set up in 1936 between the FO, the British Council and the Board of Trade. This committee, which was Vansittart's brainchild, produced a list of seventy-two 'approved' documentaries which represented British culture. Eight of these – quite a high proportion – were purely historical. On the feature side, history was also well represented. The committee drew up film programmes for embassies during Coronation week. *Rhodes of Africa* was the favourite film, and *The Scarlet Pimpernel* second.[40] Clearly the FO was playing both sides against the middle: the two films represented opposite views of the uses of history.

From 1937 the FO discreetly championed the use of historical documentary and feature films. At an English Speaking Union dinner, FO representatives supported the production of such films for the New York World's Fair. In its advisory work on film, the FO sought to encourage a match between the film text and the competence of the audience, sometimes with a fine sense of irony. One propaganda debacle led it to reproach the British Council: 'Anyone could have told them that as there were no railways in Albania it was hopeless to send this country *Night Mail*.'[41]

18

In the immediate prewar period, the FO had an emollient relationship with Korda's London Films. It offered supportive advice when *Knight Without Armour* was banned in various countries for its supposedly political bias, and Korda made cuts specifically on FO advice.[42] When problems were experienced abroad with *The Drum*, the FO intervened to smooth things over on behalf on London Films, who in turn were eager to comply with the FO's suggestions.[43] I have already mentioned the case of Korda's *Lawrence of Arabia*. What is notable about the PRO material on this project is the conciliatory attitude of the FO towards Korda, of whom it clearly had a very high opinion. Korda was seen as 'reasonable and handsome' in his attitudes, and 'there is great force in all his points ... indeed they are unanswerable'.[44] In all its dealings on film matters, the FO displayed a sophisticated, catholic approach which was critical of bourgeois narrowness. This is perhaps not unrelated to its recruitment pattern in the 1930s and earlier, which drew primarily from the upper classes.

Film producers of historical features in the 1930s, then, had a variety of determinants and constraints. They had to respond to changing patterns of audience taste, and various censorship demands were made. The Foreign Office had particular views on historical films, and could facilitate or discourage films at will. Moreover, the industry experienced considerable instability in 1936, and severe financial difficulties in 1937; the lure of the American market was not an unmitigated blessing, and attempts to exploit it were unpredictable in terms of profit. Historical films were more expensive to make, because of scenery and costumes, and thus were more susceptible to market fluctuation. The success of *The Private Life of Henry VIII* had encouraged some industry expansion, largely facilitated by loans from insurance companies, but this did not produce a stable situation. We should now turn to the work of producers in the period, in order to assess the methods they used to balance these pressures and determinants – official, economic and cultural.

2

KORDA AND BALCON

ARISTOCRATIC AND BOURGEOIS SYMBOLISM

Clearly, *The Private Life of Henry VIII* was a significant cultural innovation. Korda was the major presence in historical film in the 1930s, and he was treated with special favour by the Foreign Office. Little attention has been paid to his thinking on the use of history. In part, this is because Korda was an instinctive rather than a theoretical film-maker. In addition, to isolate Korda's thinking on historical film may have an unbalancing effect on consideration of his oeuvre as a whole. For example, an analysis of *The Girl from Maxim's* could add a useful perspective to a study of the sexual politics of *Henry VIII*, and one cannot assess the significance of *The Four Feathers* without considering *The Drum*. It is nonetheless possible to delineate a policy in Korda's historical films. He was a foreigner, with extensive cultural competence, a strong historical sense, and High Tory sympathies; these put him in a unique position to predict and respond to popular taste.

Before the appearance of *Henry VIII*, Korda had developed a film theory which eschewed realism. He argued that grand opera and Shakespeare could give pleasure to mass audiences, and that it was fatal to condescend. He insisted in *Film Weekly* on 23 August 1933 that historical films should not be 'characterless' in an international way, but firmly located in British culture: 'the more typically national a film is . . . the more general its appeal will be.' He noted that historical films were 'not favoured by the film trade, but are a bold venture' and that sexual desire should be abundant in such films so as to maximise profits. In the same journal on 4 May 1934, Korda argued that costume films were profitable because audiences could instinctively decode the language of the genre; it was easier for a producer to create a coherent world in a historical than in a modern setting. Moreover costume films were more efficacious in feeding visual hungers; and 'men, in particular, look ten times handsomer in the more colourful clothes of other ages.' For Korda, the target audience for costume films was female, and he held that such viewers disliked 'historical exactitude – where can it be found?' Historical films provided a better opportunity for showing a wide social spectrum, thus increasing the possibility of audience empathy.

In 1935, Korda proposed a film on the life of Christ. It was not permitted, but this gave him the opportunity to attack the censorship system, whose chief error was to underestimate the audience. Korda thought that the mass audience was receptive to ideas and 'creativity'. *Film Weekly* attacked Korda for his flamboyance and his overestimation of audience acumen. But Korda persisted: 'People are not as unintelligent as the newspapers make out. They want their entertainment to be both progressive and cultured.'[1] The role of historical film was to render service to the cultural life of the whole of the British Empire. Korda was intellectually eclectic, arguing that 'the whole of history and the whole world is there for the taking'.[2] But there were radical aspects to his theory. He espoused a type of liberal utilitarianism, arguing that the notion of the greatest happiness of the greatest number could be profitably applied to the cinema, where the people, for once, had choice and 'power of veto', and where the final arbiter was not 'some elegant Petronius, but the man in the street'. For Korda, the 'lowest common multiple' was also the 'highest common factor'.[3] In addition, he displayed a sustained interest in the language of the psyche and in different types of repression: he attempted to set up a film of Freud's *Interpretation of Dreams*, but it proved impracticable. Korda's radicalism was never discussed by the Right, and only rarely appreciated by the Left. The *Daily Worker* suggested that his historical films contributed to mass worship of royal profligates. Unaligned left-wing papers such as *Tribune* were scathing when Korda films were re-released in 1948. Only the *Millgate Monthly*, a Co-operative Society journal, showed an awareness of the potential radicalism of Korda's view of history, praising his delineation of the complexity of the historical process.[4]

How were Korda's theories deployed in his historical films? *The Private Life of Henry VIII* was the first and in many ways the most significant example. Korda's choice of scriptwriters was interesting. One of them was Lajos Biro, who had written thirty plays in his native Hungary and whose later dramatic work concentrated on the mythical and archetypal aspects of

The Private Life of Henry VIII

21

history. Biro had some scriptwriting experience, and he had a taste for periods and texts that were 'florid in attire'.[5] His collaborator was Arthur Wimperis, a dramatist and lyricist who held firm views on the subordinate position of the author. For him, 'the director is the whole works', Korda was the 'architect in chief', and the cast-iron shooting script should contain no scene longer than a minute; 'the slogan on the screen is speed'.[6] This team was a potent combination of forces, and when the script of *Henry VIII* was published a debate ensued about its artistic status, which was a 'first' in the field of film criticism. The issues of quality, authorship and popular culture were raised in the context of the film.[7]

The Private Life of Henry VIII cost £93,710 to make, and its first world run netted £500,000. It was the most modestly made and the most profitable of all Korda's costume films.[8] The publicity material concentrated on the enigma of Henry's personality: 'Was he a tyrant, was he a monster, concerned with nothing but his own lascivious pleasures?' Cinema managers were not advised to foreground the historical elements. Certainly the film avoids reference to political crises of the time, and to the establishment of the Church of England. Instead, Henry is presented as a victim of feminine wiles. Thus Anne of Cleves and Catherine Howard are both unfaithful to Henry in different ways, and Catherine Parr dominates him ruthlessly. Those wives who did not fit into this paradigm are omitted from the script. The dynamics of the film are fuelled by the contrast between the public figure and the private man in the undignified pursuit of various appetites. The film quotes a range of historical sources – the Holbein painting, Henry's own songs, the practice of falconry – and combines them to show how individuals may be transformed into icons. Thus it provides the audience with a method of interpreting the monarchy, shown as a double-edged sword which confers power on the bearer but inhibits his capacity for fulfilment. Sexual desire is foregrounded, but its affectionate consummation is prevented; the energy thus generated can only be unleashed by the violent consumption of food. Henry's lack of 'table manners' was the chief burden of complaint of many conservative critics of the film. But Korda was showing the means whereby the psyche will replace one unassuagable hunger by another that is more amenable and convenient.

So the past was deployed in *Henry VIII* as a language in which to address the damaging effect of state power on the individual. The mode of address adopted towards the past was one of confidence. It was not a site of mystery, but of familiarity, where the audience was invited to recognise contemporary similarities; the film showed the audience that their ordinary passions were *more* likely to be satisfied than those of their rulers.

Released in August 1933, *Henry VIII* instigated a major debate on historical film in general. But specific critical responses to the film were also significant. Lord Cottenham spearheaded the opposition in the *Daily Telegraph*. He argued that the King's 'revolting habits' were the 'acme of bad taste'; the Tudor heritage was one of 'growth, of consolidation, of magnificence', which the film defamed. Korda replied that a film was not a treatise, since one had to omit 'certain facts and emphasise others'. Cottenham returned to the vexed issue of table manners, and other letter-writers bewailed the 'cheap and tawdry' aspect of the film. One historian attempted to scotch the issue by 'proving' that Henry had bad table manners after all. But the *Telegraph*'s film critics had already distanced themselves from such views. They argued, 'Whether this is Merrie England is a matter on which dons may differ. It is certainly first-rate cinema.'[9]

Other negative responses to the film had a clear class or political bias. *The Times* found the modern parallels in the film a 'dangerous device'. The *Weekend Review*, a quality paper, remarked that 'to those who know no history, it probably contains elements of suspense'. The *Spectator* found its mixture of modes 'distressing'. The historical inaccuracy annoyed *Country Life*. Two ultra-right journals, *The New Age* and *New Britain*, panned the film for its suggestiveness. The *Sphere*, a conservative journal, argued that 'the less educated public will swallow a great deal more accuracy.' The *Era*, a radical journal of the same political colour, agreed.[10] We may conclude that the film's populist sentiments were anathema to members of the intellectual Right.

Such negative views were not shared by other critics. Very positive reviews were given by a wide range of papers, many critics praising *Henry VIII* as a film which gave unproblematical access to Tudor England. A review in the popular *Evening News* on 4 November 1933 merits attention. In an article entitled 'Messing About with History', the anonymous reviewer argued that with *Henry VIII*

> the childish imaginings in dusty schoolrooms have been suddenly and warmly brought to life, and what is wrong with that? Of course it is an emotional and ignorant picture of the past, and it would never do for an honours school ... but we are most of us pretty ignorant, really, about the past.

The author argued that the muse of cinema was the cap and bells rather than the cap and gown. For the latter, real history was 'an ugly, uncompromising affair', whereas film history produced 'an essential satisfaction of spirit in each beholder'. Such a view neither absolutely reflected nor directly influenced the opinions of its readers; the relationship between polemicist and audience is a complex one. Nonetheless, the foregrounding of the pleasures of historical texts and of the irrelevance of accuracy is of note at this early date.

The success of *Henry VIII* was such that an extra 500 prints had to be run off. Its progress abroad was widely reported. The film's profitability had knock-on effects: a play about the Tudor court (*The Rose Without a Thorn*) did extremely well in the West End. There was a widespread increase in demand for books on Henry and his reign. A special edition of the King's letters was published, dedicated to Laughton, which sold very well. An MGM subsidiary made a burlesque in 1935 called *The Public Life of Henry the Ninth*.

Korda's next historical film, *Catherine the Great*, was released in January 1934. This coincided with the first British showings of Sternberg's *Scarlet Empress*, and the similarity of subject matter preoccupied many critics. Korda's film was based on a play, *The Czarina* by Lajos Biro and Melchior Lengyel, but the film's authorship was the subject of a lawsuit in 1937. London Films was sued for breach of copyright by the playwright Puznansky, who wrote *La Petite Catherine*. London Films argued that Catherine was 'almost a legendary figure' like Napoleon and that no author could have sole rights over representations of her. The trial broadened out into a debate about historical film, in which the defence argued that the film was not intended to be accurate. The first draft was called, significantly, 'The Eternal Feminine'. Korda argued that historical films were his greatest interest, but

> one did not want perfect historical detail in films ... film producers had to falsify history as Shakespeare did, and had to make Catherine a character who would gain the sympathy of the millions of people who would see the film.[11]

The case was dismissed, as no copyright breach was found.

We may conclude from this suit that *Catherine* was eclectic in its historical sources, and that the analysis of femininity was a key aspect of its meaning. Certainly the publicity material suggested that the female audience was the target. Managers were advised to advertise the film with 'wolfhounds and negligee as a good ballyhoo combination', which produced a 'new fashion silhouette from Russia'. The film was angled to appeal to female masochism: 'The more pain and cruelty he inflicted on her, the more fiercely she clung to him.' *Catherine* was also proposed as an 'ideal feature for classroom study', but this was a secondary consideration.

Paul Czinner, Elisabeth Bergner's husband, directed the film and was probably influential in some of the laundering of Catherine's image. Certainly one cannot imagine Bergner's gamine whimsicality being responsible for the headless bodies of the real Catherine's discarded lovers, which were regularly found floating in the Neva. This cinematic Catherine believes in true love: 'I don't care about governing Russia, I only care for the Grand Duke.' The film reproduces the structures of feeling of the Gothic novel, where the vulnerable heroine struggles against the causeless moods of the hero; Peter, played by Douglas Fairbanks Jnr, foregrounds capriciousness and rapacious sexuality.

Because of the laundering of Catherine, the film's more explicit debates about female power and sexuality are carried by Flora Robson as the old Empress. The script characterises her as 'the most shameless rake who ever wore a petticoat', and as one who 'if she weren't on the throne, would be on the streets.' Her own remarks indicate a feminist world-view: 'Women can rule and men can't', and 'Every beast of a man begins to want you when he thinks you belong to another beast of a man.' The power of Robson's performance balances out the 'purer' Catherine. The visual style of the film is extremely opulent. Vincent Korda's decor, as befits the period, is ornate, the male costumes are as sumptuous as the female, and the narrative structure is cumulative rather than episodic as in *Henry VIII*.

Catherine had a big society premiere. The reviews, however, were extremely mixed. The film was attacked by C.A. Lejeune in the *Observer* for having 'no national feeling', and the *Daily Express* ironically noted that 'as an essay in interior decoration, *Catherine* is a great film'. A range of papers of different orientations criticised the film for its extravagance.[12] The positive reviews were similarly mixed; journals with little in common praised the film for its 'intelligence'. There was no consonance of views, as with *Henry VIII*.

The Private Life of Don Juan was Korda's next historical film, which he directed himself and which he influenced in both the cutting and the photography; he cast Douglas Fairbanks in the lead role. *Don Juan* was the only one of

Korda's costume films to be a serious loss-maker. This was doubtless because its presentation of sexuality was unpalatable to its target audience, which, on the evidence of the publicity material, was again predominantly female. The fashion aspects of the film were in evidence here, and it was suggested that what 'the modern girl' looked for in her own Don Juan was the ability to wear clothes well. The film itself indicates that Juan's amatory success is due to his high opinion of women. To a tedious husband he remarks, 'You just owned her like a monkey a fiddle.' The film's script has a liberal sense of 'the eternal hunger of women for love. Every woman must have a sense of gratitude for the man who brought love to so many of her sisters.' Had the film continued along those lines, it would have been a success; but instead it concentrates on Juan's declining vigour. His wife remarks that 'You've no money, no looks, not very much brain and you're no chicken.' Humankind cannot bear very much reality, especially not about the cessation of desire. The rueful tone of the film ('My poor husband was so much bigger') and the way it presents marriage as a sort of pipe-and-slippers of the spirit were doubtless reasons for its failure. In addition, the critical response was unrelievedly negative. There had been advance notice of the film's sumptuous sets; but no one liked them.

However, Korda's next historical film, *The Scarlet Pimpernel*, which was released early in 1935, had positive responses from all the critics. The *Sunday Times* noted that 'in every respect it constitutes a triumph for the British film world ... the settings rejoice one with their beauty and accuracy', and C. A. Lejeune in the *Observer* argued that it had 'a background of authority and a certain moving dignity of expression, that the original never knew.' Other papers were equally complimentary.[13] But good reviews alone cannot guarantee a film's box-office success. *The Scarlet Pimpernel* was profitable for three reasons: for the potency of the Regency theme in British culture, for the established popularity of the Baroness Orczy novel on which the film was based, and for the way in which the hero, played by Leslie Howard, was directed so as to teeter between masculine and feminine characteristics.

The film is set in the latter years of the French Revolution, and portrays a Britain where aristocratic culture still flourishes and succours French members of its tribe. Arguably the Regency, and the years immediately prior to it, was the last period in which the aristocracy may be said to have attempted a hegemonic role. The aristocracy and the upper reaches of the landed classes were under extreme economic pressure because of corn prices, bad harvests, changing patterns of industrialisation and middle-class investment. The landed interest in this period responded to the crisis by asserting itself forcefully on the cultural level, in the areas of literature, architecture, and interior and landscape design. The Regency preoccupation with style should be interpreted as a coherent aristocratic attempt to supersede middle-class dominance. The phenomenon of the Regency Corinthians and Dandies is part of this process.

The Regency rapidly became an important source for those writers who wished to analyse a successful class fraction in the last years before its decline. The later work of Byron, and some of the novels of Bulwer-Lytton and Thackeray, are evidence of this. In the twentieth century, the Regency was a site for those romantic novelists (usually female) who wished to explore the boundaries of sexual licence and to evoke pleasure by delineating the surface of a

25

The Scarlet Pimpernel

confident class. The works of Doris Leslie, Barbara Cartland, Georgette Heyer, Lady E. F. Smith, Norah Lofts, Baroness Orczy, Ouida and others are examples. Of course, in both nineteenth and twentieth-century literary culture, the aristocracy functions not solely as itself but as a symbol of repressed desires or inexpressible social fears. As a class, the aristocracy has always been prone to symbolic substitution in this way.

It is vital to bear this in mind when interpreting cinematic representation of the Regency, *The Scarlet Pimpernel* in particular. Too often critics have behaved as though the cinema, in its creation of mythologies, was isolated from the paradigms of popular literary culture. Korda was particularly alert to the fertility of the Regency topos, and went on to make *The Return of the Scarlet Pimpernel* in 1937; in 1950 he produced *The Elusive Pimpernel*. It was obviously a theme that gave him stimulus and latitude. Some contemporary critics of the 1935 film recognised the crucial aspect of the Regency/aristocracy themes, which were foregrounded in the press books and in the advance publicity for the film.[14] *The Scarlet Pimpernel* represents Regency culture as the apotheosis of style. The interiors and the costumes connote an aristocracy which is able, *in extremis*, to rise to the occasion. Sir Percy Blakeney is able to deploy the full resources of disguise because, sufficiently at ease in his own culture, he has the confidence to don the accent and aspect of other classes (and the other gender) when expedient. The original novel does not present these elements with the same degree of intensity. The film script, and Howard's performance, combines in one figure different aspects of Regency behaviour

26

which were recognisably separate in contemporary practice. He is at times a narcissistic Dandy, concerned with fine surface appearance; at other times he is a Corinthian, muscular in riding boots. The film's appeal to female viewers resides in the way the hero combines male and female personae. He is a lover who combines feminine sensitivity with masculine vigour.

There were problems with the script, because of the difficulty of discovering a spoken register which would combine a sense of period with modern informality. However, it had the advantage of being based on a well-loved novel. Orczy worked intensively with Korda in the pre-script stage, and rejected any attempts to make the text more 'highbrow'. The success of the film also led to an enormous increase in the novel's sales.[15]

The Scarlet Pimpernel was successful because it combined a female orientation with cultural themes deeply embedded in British culture. Korda's next historical film was *Rembrandt*, which appeared in late 1936. The film featured well in the 'favourite performances' list. Clearly Laughton made a welcome return to historical films. His performance in *Rembrandt* was sufficiently compelling to prompt *Picturegoer* fans to draw portraits of him in the role as late as 7 May and 9 July 1938. However, the film was not an outright success like *Henry VIII* or *The Scarlet Pimpernel*, although it was claimed that it grossed £400,000, and received very respectful reviews over a broad spectrum.

Korda directed the film himself and foregrounded the issue of an artist whose creativity is at odds with society's desires. The film deals unflinchingly with the autonomy of the art-object, and with the artist as a holy fool. Such concepts would have been assimilable by a mass audience had they been set in a British context, since they could have drawn directly on the Romantic tradition. But the combination of a high-art debate with a foreign setting was not compelling for the mass audience. Korda did structure the film so as to emphasise the importance of the female principle. Rembrandt apotheosises woman thus: 'a creature half-child, half-woman, half-angel, half-lover ... when one woman gives herself to you, you possess all women.' But the world of female experience offered to the audience is a dreary one: repression, sickness, housework, exploitation. In order for historical films to please their target audience, the past had to be presented as a site where either pleasure or power could be experienced vicariously.

Korda's next historical film was *Fire Over England*, which was released early in 1937 and dealt with the defeat of the Spanish Armada. Korda had long intended to deploy the Tudor period again, and having chosen an international team and fixed the details of the script, he left it to them. Erich Pommer owned the production company, and he attempted to produce a text which would 'have the unique power of appealing equally to the popular and the highbrow audience'.[16] William K. Howard, the American director, was worried that it was 'far more academic than anything I have ever done', and his fears were shared by the *Film Weekly* critic.[17] These anxieties were well founded. The film did not appear on any popularity lists, although it was clearly seen as a Korda vehicle. Good reviews did not help, nor did the fact that it was based on an A. E. W. Mason novel. The problem was that the film's politics were before their time. Pommer claimed that 'I stress the importance of a strongly armed and invulnerable England.'[18] But such pro-rearmament views needed to be differently expressed in early 1937. *Fire Over England* was clearly recognised

27

as a fiercely pro-British film in spite of its foreign production team. But the style of its patriotism was not assimilable until the war years, when part of Elizabeth's Greenwich speech were used in Korda's 1939 *The Lion Has Wings*. The script of *Fire Over England* emphasises the importance of vigilance; but warnings against invasion were untimely, and the film is unbalanced by the weak love interest. A comparison with *Henry VIII* is instructive. That film argues that emotional unfulfilment is an inevitable accompaniment of political power. But *Henry VIII* has a male hero, and his unhappiness is expressed in terms of activity and anger. The Robson heroine in *Fire Over England* displays her frustrations by a hatred for her own mirror-reflection. If Korda was attempting to appeal more to the female audience, then such a pattern was liable to discomfit them.

However, with the release in December 1937 of *The Return of the Scarlet Pimpernel*, Korda once again found his form. I have indicated that this film was profitable, doubtless because it reworked the gentry topos, and once again deployed a popular Orczy novel. Lazar Meerson, the film's art director, worked for Korda as before, and his opulent style was appropriate to the themes of pleasure and aristocratic disguise. However, *The Return of the Scarlet Pimpernel* differs significantly from Korda's first *Pimpernel* film. Two opposing types of females are contrasted. Marguerite, the wife of Sir Percy, is pregnant and thus purified. On the other hand, Theresia, the 'polluted' woman, betrays Sir Percy. In the first *Pimpernel* film, the two different elements were combined in the same character. Their separation in the second film permits moral categories to be drawn with greater clarity. In addition, the script is more overtly political than Korda's first *Pimpernel*, foregrounding the issues of individual liberty much more, and mooting justified rebellion against unjust leaders. Robespierre is compared by Tallien (James Mason) to an English politician: 'I have seen the army of the new Cromwell, and I have come with a dagger to plunge into his bosom.' Implicitly, a Cavalier rather than Roundhead interpretation of history was being preferred.

Korda's last historical film before the war was *The Four Feathers*, which appeared in the *Kinematograph Weekly* list of box-office successes. It was based on an A. E. W. Mason novel about a man's undercover exploits to disprove a charge of cowardice during Kitchener's 1898 Sudan campaign. Korda gained the approval of Mason for his radical alterations to the original. But in contrast to *Fire Over England*, this tale of war had a topical poignancy, and the theme of courageous self-sacrifice had a new relevance; many contemporary critics noted the modern parallels in a favourable way. *The Four Feathers*, set in the Edwardian period, deployed the resonance of the chivalric ideal in order to promote confidence in British traditions. Although many of the film crew had not read the original novel, they considered that its spirit was faithfully reproduced.[19] The film had the fullest co-operation of the Governor-General of the Sudan, where much of it was shot. And when the old officers who had commanded at Omdurman were invited to the premiere, they thought it was 'better, my dear fellow, much better' than the real thing.[20]

As usual, Korda's respect for verisimilitude was tempered by his desire for visual splendour. The 'correct' blue uniforms were changed to red ones in order to deploy Technicolor to the maximum effect. The film's props list indicated, however, that a degree of naturalism was sought. Great care was taken

The Four Feathers

to ensure that tattooing kits and dogcarts were of exactly the right period.[21] The final shooting script contained significant revisions, and indicated that problems were experienced with the representation of Empire. One proposed gambit had an old statesman arguing that 'we are continually pressed by Mr Cecil Rhodes to burden ourselves with useless possessions in South Africa. England would be far happier if she could rid herself of half her colonies.' This was cut from the final version; in the last instance, Korda wished to highlight personal bravery and the chivalric code of honour, rather than force a too overtly political reading of events. The final script suggests that humanitarian feelings, rather than the desire for Empire, should be presented as a motivating force: 'There should be some sympathetic reference on behalf of the officers to the cruel work of the natives.' The script also profoundly alters the nature of Harry Faversham's rebellion by having his father die before he resigns from his commission. 'When he died,' says the film Harry, 'my duty towards him was done.' But in the novel the father and his values live on, and Harry's hubris is thus much greater.

We may draw a number of conclusions from Korda's 1930s historical films. First, although patterns of critical response were of cultural and social significance, there was no automatic effect on film profits. Secondly, his two outstandingly successful films (*Henry VIII* and *The Scarlet Pimpernel*) deployed historical periods so as to exploit their cultural resonances to the full, while foregrounding the issues of sexuality and pleasure. Thirdly, Korda's historical films displayed an awareness of the resources of aristocratic symbol-

29

ism, and he used that period as a shorthand connotation for confidence and bravura.

The personality, production style and intellectual orientation of Michael Balcon formed a strong contrast to Korda. He tended to be rather conservative intellectually, and felt at a disadvantage to the charismatic Korda.[22] He expressed an early dislike of technique for its own sake, and a preference for simple narrative structures.[23] Balcon was head of production at Gaumont-British from 1931 to the end of 1936, when he was responsible for many non-historical films such as *The Good Companions* and *The 39 Steps*. He also produced *Jew Süss* (released October 1934), *The Iron Duke* (January 1935), *Me and Marlborough* (August 1935), *Rhodes of Africa* (March 1936), *Tudor Rose* (May 1936) and *King Solomon's Mines* (July 1937). Balcon's later adherence to a species of realism and lower middle-class audience orientation has been widely noted. Two of the above films were explicitly preoccupied with Empire, since Gaumont-British wanted to 'bind it together by bringing the old country to the farthest of our far-flung kinemas'.[24] As I have already indicated, Gaumont had an intimate relationship with certain government departments, and although the films may in no sense be regarded as officially sanctioned, they should be interpreted as texts with some degree of access to government thinking.

Balcon exerted considerable producer-power, as he did later at Ealing, and he used *Rhodes of Africa* and *Tudor Rose* in particular to develop his unit production system whereby favoured individuals were encouraged so long as they concurred with his world-view: 'We find, develop, and train young men capable of taking complete charge of a film unit.'[25] At Gaumont, Balcon encouraged the production of historical films which would be morally improving. He noted in *Film Weekly* on 11 August 1933 that they could play a crucial role in 'the safeguarding of public morals.' Balcon encouraged directors to use the standard realist device of empathy; for example, he argued in the *Daily Telegraph* on 1 July 1935 that *Rhodes* should humanise the 'bleak and austere' hero. Predictably, Balcon had a greater respect for historical verisimilitude than Korda; he supported *Me and Marlborough* for its authenticity, although its burlesque mode made it an unlikely candidate for the honour. Later, Balcon attacked Basil Dean's *Whom the Gods Love* (1936) for its 'falsification' of historical fact.[26] His most important intervention in the debate about historical accuracy may be found in his letter on *Rhodes* to *The Times* on 29 April 1936, when he insisted that any minor tampering with historical fact was only undertaken with a reverent cognisance of the true spirit of history.

We may conclude that realism, accuracy and moral improvement were important criteria for Balcon in this period, and that he attempted to insert these qualities in historical films made under his aegis. Of course, a producer's stated intention may often be undercut by a director, and, as I shall show, Victor Saville and others sometimes exceeded Balcon's remit. But Gaumont's historical features from 1934 to 1937 should be interpreted as an attempt to deploy the past as a means of recuperation for certain middle-class values which Balcon held to be under threat.

Jew Süss was based on the successful novel by Lion Feuchtwanger, which was published in an extremely popular translation in 1926. The novel's five-part narrative structure permitted a politically radical interpretation of socially marginal groups. No attempt was made in the film to reproduce this plurality of class interest; the film's politics are more obviously partisan. Script, art direction, casting and acting style all combine to produce unambiguous sympathy for the oppressed Jewish group. Moreover, an overwhelming majority of the film's personnel were of Jewish extraction. The script foregrounds the oppression of the ghetto and, implicitly, modern parallels in Hitler's Germany. It argues that if atrocities were permitted in 1730, then 'they can do it in 1830 and they can do it in 1930'. Interestingly, the film concentrates, with an intensity absent from the book, on the compensations for a lack of official status. It ends, quite rarely for its period, with a caption pleading for religious tolerance: 'Perhaps, one day, the walls will crumble like the walls of Jericho, and the world will be one people.'

Jew Süss cost over £125,000 to make, which was relatively expensive for the time.[27] Forty-seven sets were built, and it was claimed that there were a thousand different lighting operations each day. A quarter of the total outlay was spent on costumes and settings, which was a high proportion.[28] No expense was spared on the decor and camera set-ups. Visually, the film was complex, with inventive camerawork; the art direction by Alfred Junge was expressionist in style. In *Jew Süss*, the past is not presented as a site of visual pleasure, but of insecurity and pain. The palace interiors are opulent, to be sure; but the use of unbalanced compositions and chiaroscuro inculcate a sense

Jew Süss

31

of dread. Lothar Mendes, the director, suggested to *Film Weekly* on 12 January 1934 that for him it was 'essential to dominate' other workers on the set if the film was to capture an international market. But it is clear that the film was the result of a number of preoccupations shared by the administrative workforce rather than a straightforward reflection of the director's aims.

Jew Süss did extremely well in both Britain and America, although there is no information on exact profit margins. It had a good critical reception across a wide span of journals. Many critics emphasised the moral necessity of supporting the film. The *Sunday Referee* argued that 'it is your duty to see it'. The *Spectator* praised its sincerity, since 'but for Hitlerism, this film would never have been made'.[29] But all critics implied that to see *Jew Süss* was a painful duty rather than a pleasure. Of course, international disquiet on the Jewish question fuelled the positive responses to the film.

Victor Saville made two films under Balcon's aegis, *The Iron Duke* and *Me and Marlborough*. Saville held liberal views on explicit sexual material in historical films, favoured texts which were oriented towards the audience rather than critics, and defended poetic licence in historical features.[30] Further light is shed on Saville's attitude to historical film by the report in *Today's Cinema* on 16 May 1935 of a ribald parody 'trial', when he was arraigned on a charge of misappropriating history. The 'jury' found the trade as a whole and Saville in particular not guilty. It argued that cinematic history should be divided into Ancient Times (with 'the consumption of lions specially doped for the purpose'), the Age of Polygamous Monarchy and the Age of Arliss. Saville himself proposed Mae West for the role of the Queen of Sheba ('excellent for cleavage') and Sonny Hale, in Saville's defence, suggested that Henry VIII invented the phrase 'and so to bed'. Beneath the ribaldry, however, lay a serious defence by the film trade of historical inaccuracy for the purposes of popular art. It is clear from this spoof trial that Saville was seen (or presented himself) as part of the film trade's assault on academic notions of accuracy. This would, of course, put him at odds with the more puritanical and rigorous Balcon.

The Iron Duke was released in January 1935. It purported to show aspects of the life of the Duke of Wellington, but it was presented primarily as a vehicle for George Arliss. Arliss had already made his name with a series of Hollywood historical biopics – *Disraeli*, *Voltaire*, *The House of Rothschild* and *Cardinal Richelieu*. The problem was that Arliss's screen persona had developed as a genial, wily valetudinarian of advanced years and minimal sex appeal, and this accorded ill with the demands of the script of *The Iron Duke*, which requires the hero to display military prowess and sexual charisma. The Prince of Wales attended the London premiere, and the film was re-released in 1942 by Gaumont-British Instructional as part of their task of reviving historical films for educational purposes.

The idea of the film had first been mooted in America by Zanuck, who shelved it because 'any Duke of Wellington who didn't look like Aubrey Smith would not be accepted in the movies'.[31] When Saville accepted the project, the scriptwriters and star were made aware of the danger that surviving relatives might sue. This ensured that the finished result would be anodyne; and Arliss was encouraged to enter into an emollient correspondence with Wellington's kin, ostensibly to ensure accuracy but in fact to head off any likely litigation.

The press book is valuable in establishing the studio's intentions. The main selling point was Arliss himself, who was presented as 'Always the Master ... with Men ... with Women!' Sketches were provided of him in rheumy dalliance with dewy-eyed young women. The written material emphasised the film's accuracy: 'Old prints were unearthed, musty engravings pored over.' The period and military advisers were given considerable credit, since their efforts maintained 'a realism that must be the secret of success if any great historical event is to live before our critical eyes'. This indicated that the opinions of academic historians were beginning to be heeded by some parts of the film trade; and it is significant that these arguments were first met not by Korda's studio, but by Balcon's. Gaumont's publicity material for *The Iron Duke* presented it as a historical parallel to the modern issues of appeasement and rearmament. In order to give *The Iron Duke* greater respectability, the studio commissioned the historical novelist Philip Lindsay to write a book-length version of the film, and arranged for a new print run of Philip Guedalla's *The Duke*. Clearly, a literate audience was being addressed.

Although Alfred Junge was the art director for this film, its visual texture is less expressionist than his previous *Jew Süss*. The compositions of *The Iron Duke* are statically organised within the frame, and pictorial values do not predominate. Unlike *Jew Süss*, which deployed close-ups to great effect, *The Iron Duke* has a plethora of medium-length shots, which give a stagey effect. This is augmented by the stiff body language of Arliss and other leads, which in turn reduces any potential erotic charge. The film has an authoritarian voice-over, which reduces the audience's interpretative space. The crowd is never individualised; Wellington calls them 'dangerous cattle. They'll eat out of your hand one day and bite your fingers off the next.' Inevitably, therefore, increased importance is accorded to the middle classes by the script, which also makes clumsy comparisons between past and present. Wellington claims that 'Our reward will be found in the attainment of the purpose for which we fought the peace of Europe and the salvation of the world from unexampled tyranny.'

The Iron Duke's overt propagandism, its middle-class orientation, and its avoidance of the erotic were the result of Balcon's overall studio control. Certainly Balcon supervised and approved the casting and structure of the film, according to *Picturegoer* on 28 July 1934. As I shall show, Saville's *The Dictator*, made in the same period but without the same zealous production control, had none of these characteristics. Significantly, *The Iron Duke* satisfied those critics eager for more respectable historical features. However, there were some interesting attacks. The *Observer* suggested on 2 December 1934 that Saville's direction was 'a study in masterly inactivity'. The *Sphere*, a journal which was rigorous about history, attacked Saville on 15 December for making a film which contained 'as much truth about Wellington during the Waterloo campaign as does a pantomime of Dick Whittington about the history of a great mayoralty'. There was no critical unanimity, but *The Iron Duke* clearly aroused debates which were different from those which Korda's films provoked.

Saville made one other historical film under Balcon's direct aegis. *Me and Marlborough* was a Cicely Courtneidge comedy vehicle, which Saville intended for the burlesque mode. The narrative dealt with Kit Ross, who donned male clothing to follow her husband to Marlborough's army in

Flanders. The use of the cross-dressing motif was a continuation of Court-neidge's music-hall work. But although the film is a comic version of historical events, the emphasis during production was upon realism. Battle scenes were reconstituted on Salisbury Plain with serving soldiers as extras. Even the farmyard sets were liberally provided with manure to provide an authentic aroma. As in *Jew Süss*, modern parallels were drawn with a heavy hand. The opening caption proclaims that 'Three times in three centuries Flanders has been crucial: to Marlborough, Wellington, Haig ... Not for the first time in our history, political cowardice now threatened to throw away the fruits of military action by an ill-timed and inconclusive peace.' This and similar remarks in the script indicate that the film's politics were anti-appeasement. Saville, when left to his own devices, did not foreground politics in this way, as *South Riding* and *The Citadel* show. We may surmise that the politics of *Me and Marlborough* have a family likeness to those of *Jew Süss*, and that Balcon was the cause.

In any case, the film was a financial failure. Its proletarian humour accorded ill with its grave theme, and musical interludes assorted oddly with the full-bottomed wigs. The film received universally bad reviews. In the case of *Me and Marlborough*, the combination of Saville's light touch and Balcon's high seriousness was unfruitful.

Before returning to other historical films produced under Balcon's influence, it is worth mentioning Saville's only other period film, *The Dictator*, which was set in the Danish court. This film was an independent project produced by Ludovic Toeplitz, and was made for Gaumont-British release. Saville had to replace the original director at a week's notice. Toeplitz played an active role, and seems to have outmanoeuvred Balcon since the film bears none of the latter's characteristic signatures. Toeplitz was anti-fascist in his politics, and was more oriented towards the international 'prestige' market than Balcon. *The Dictator* permits a comparison between Saville's historical work under different producers. It is visually opulent, the art direction by Andrejev and camerawork by Planer being inventive and expensive. The script deals with aristocratic excess and with sexual pleasure. But it was a box-office failure, probably because the manner in which it presented court intrigues was not palatable to the mass audience.

Jew Süss and *Me and Marlborough* were the result of a relationship between director and producer in which the values held by the latter were much more in evidence. *Tudor Rose*, the next Gaumont-British history, was directed by Robert Stevenson, with whom Balcon had a less stressful relationship than with the more combative Saville. Stevenson had been trained as an engineer and had minimal film experience; he was initially hired by Balcon as scenarist to the project. As Balcon's protégé, Stevenson was unlikely to challenge his judgment. An interesting article in *Cinema Arts* in September 1936 described their relationship in *Tudor Rose*. Balcon 'didn't give the scenarist the chance to write new footnotes to history' and he appointed Stevenson director because the latter had a 'deep-seated respect for accuracy'. Balcon exploited Stevenson's suggestibility, and *Tudor Rose* should be interpreted as a product of Balcon's authorship.

The film deals with the last year in the life of Lady Jane Grey, and ends with her execution in the Tower. A special premiere was arranged there, and

Tudor Rose

the *Daily Telegraph* noted on 8 May 1936 that government representatives co-operated enthusiastically with the event. *Tudor Rose's* publicity material suggested that it was intended as a corrective for earlier, lewder historical films. Balcon's copy of the script gives important indications that a major theme was the state's vulnerability to exploitation by intellectuals. Lord Dudley is accused by Edward VI of being one such, 'who care nothing for England; nothing for the people; only for your own power.' Although Jane is opposed to 'building your greatness on the graves of others', her execution is presented as inevitable. The script demands a conformity to the notion of historical necessity, and it adduces 'duty' as its agent. Jane and her husband must be sacrificed, since they have colluded (albeit unknowingly) with a corrupt intelligentsia. It is a bleak view of the historical process.

The *Tudor Rose* script also gives some scholarly directives about accuracy. The art director (Vetchinsky) was instructed to furnish an early Tudor room fifty years out of date, in order to locate Jane's family precisely in terms of their lack of status. A model shot in a later scene was to be based on a 1543 drawing. As with *The Iron Duke*, there is little interest in pictorial composition, although the editing by Terence Fisher is varied. Symbols such as released doves or spilled wine are used in order to avoid explicit presentation of an execution or a sullied reputation.

Balcon deployed Tudor England for quite other purposes than Korda. Three years on from *Henry VIII*, *Tudor Rose* describes the period as one of painful repression, in which dogged acceptance of one's duty is the only salvation and the greatest danger comes from disaffected aristocratic intellec-

35

tuals. Gastronomic, sartorial and sexual pleasures are absent. And yet this version of the past found significant favour; it appeared in various popularity lists and Nova Pilbeam won the coveted *Film Weekly* award for her role as Lady Jane. The film probably appealed to those who saw themselves as a cut above the 'vulgarity' of *Henry VIII*'s champions; *Tudor Rose*'s bourgeois historiography and its visual restraint made it a text of higher status.

Critical responses bear this out. *Tudor Rose* had a much more positive critical profile than any of Korda's films, and debates about it had different parameters. The *Era* argued on 6 May 1936 that it was

> the best historical film ever made, bar none ... there is no distortion or burlesque, and it makes a gesture to the public's intelligence. Not the slightest deviation is made for the purposes of a cheap laugh at history. On the contrary, the film goes out of its way to suggest that life was very grim.

This was praise indeed, and other quality journals responded similarly. Popular papers welcomed the film's more 'subtle' approach to Tudor history, while trade papers praised it as an example of a native British school of history-making.

Clearly, Balcon's attempt to reorient historical film in line with a middle-class ethic managed to win over the majority of critics and a significant part of the cinema audience. *Rhodes of Africa* reveals how he developed this approach. One of the film's directors was Bernard Viertel, who had worked at Paramount with Murnau before being brought to Britain by Balcon in 1934. In his writing on *Rhodes*, Viertel expressed a bleak theory of historical necessity very similar to the one in *Tudor Rose*. For him, Rhodes was merely 'an instrument of progress' who was 'representative of progressive capitalism spreading modern civilisation'.[32] Geoffrey Barkas directed the location scenes, and in his account of the film's production, he, like Balcon, roundly castigated those who objected to the telescoping of historical events. Barkas argued, in exactly the same terms as Balcon, that the bias of the film conformed to the spirit of historical accuracy.[33] Barkas displayed an awareness of the atrocities of Rhodes and his followers, but he never criticised the acquisitive spirit which motivated them. Rather he expressed irritation that the Matabele massacre scenes had to be toned down. Since the film's premiere coincided with the Abyssinian war, it seemed tactless to include long scenes of natives with assegais being mown down by whites with machine guns. The *Rhodes* project as constructed by Balcon had no room for liberalism on the native issue. A comparison with Korda's *Sanders of the River* is apposite. Sanders is condescendingly paternalist, but the blacks' welfare is considered and they are being groomed for a limited independence. The only future offered to the blacks in Balcon's film is the barrel of a gun and a burning kraal.

Balcon had clearly developed a talent for selecting compliant directors. But the use of two directors for *Rhodes* produces an uneven texture, in which the exterior shots are picturesque but the interior scenes are turgid, and are not enlivened by the clumsy inclusion of a love-interest in the casting of Peggy Ashcroft. Rather, the film is given coherence only by the script, which argued in favour of *Lebensraum*. Rhodes remarks:

Houses full of people and towns full of houses – that's England. And I came over here, for many months I travelled in an ox-cart and I only discovered a corner of the country – vast, empty, magnificent. You realise the immense possibilities? England must expand or perish.

Such an argument was advanced in England throughout the nineteenth century by influential bourgeois philanthropists, as a means of alleviating the miasma of proletarian living conditions; it would therefore be well assimilated into the common sense of a later period. It was also a view that would appeal to uprooted Europeans with nothing to lose and everything to gain. The ideology of Empire as expressed in *Rhodes* was structured so as to ensure a very wide catchment area.

I have suggested that the film enjoyed a fair popularity in Britain, and that Walter Huston was particularly esteemed by audiences for his role. It is noteworthy that *Rhodes* stimulated a public debate about Empire, realism and artistic responsibility. *The Times* praised its accuracy and its programmatic structure: 'This is a most useful technique for the historical film. The scenes are like diagrams and as instructive.' The *Daily Herald* reported the High Commissioner of Rhodesia as appreciative of the film. A warning note was sounded by Sir Archibald Weigall, head of the Royal Empire Society and chairman of the Conservative Party's film propaganda committee. He argued that the inclusion of massacre scenes was untimely: 'I deplore that this will be seized on as a peg for propaganda at this particular moment in history.'[34] Balcon had already attempted to preclude this, but his excisions were not enough for Sir Archibald.

The film was criticised in a letter to *The Times* on 18 April 1936 by a representative of Rhodes House, the administrative centre of Rhodesian affairs. He felt that it had too British a bias, and his letter was accompanied by one from Sir Archibald, who reiterated that the film should not 'tamper with the accuracy of the general picture'. It was this two-pronged attack which stung Balcon into his defensive reply of 29 April. Positive responses to the film's treatment of Empire were expressed by a wide range of journals.

We can conclude that, for Balcon, *Rhodes* was a means whereby he could expand his analysis of historical entrepreneurism. His last historical film for Gaumont was *King Solomon's Mines*, which gained a significant success in the *Kinematograph Weekly* ratings. But this colonial epic was based on a well-known novel by Rider Haggard which was not amenable to radical reworking; Balcon's freedom to manoeuvre was limited.

Balcon's copy of the script is significant. He appears to have chosen as the final shooting script the version by Roland Pertwee. This nuanced the novel in an interesting way. The novel's symbolic field is dominated by two mountains called Sheba's Breasts: 'On the top of each was a vast round hillock covered with snow, exactly corresponding to the nipple on the female breast.' The most taxing of the heroes' feats is to ascend this 'nipple' and descend down the other side to the land of mythical wealth. We should interpret these mountains as symbols of that female principle which inspire terror in the protagonists. Not for nothing did Haggard dedicate the book to 'all the big and little boys who read it'.

The film handles and displaces the female principle in a specific way. The sexual resonances of the landscape are removed; instead, a female protagonist is introduced, played by Anna Lee, who was then married to Robert Stevenson, the film's director. Lee's screen presence lacked sexual charisma, and it is unlikely that she could symbolise the Eternal Feminine necessary to Haggard's original disposition of elements. The script also maximises the grotesque appearance and power of the witch Gagool. In the novel she merely represents dark native forces; the script converts her into a source of sexual terror and disgust, and it suggests that shots of a severed mummified head be used to heighten dread when she appears. This should be interpreted as a symbol of male castration fears.

The script, then, presents a field of forces in which the female element is both weaker and more feared than in the novel. The male characters are altered correspondingly. Quartermain in the novel is a crusty, self-doubting figure. But the script insists that he is 'dry, reliable and a realist' who is powerfully poised 'on the boundary between inhabited territory and the bush'. He is directed to act with 'unexpected firmness'. Similarly the black Umbopa, a noble savage, plays a minor part in the novel; the script increases his importance, and his stature was augmented by the casting of Paul Robeson in the role. Balcon's final Empire epic for Gaumont was aimed specifically at male audiences, and presented the past as a place where their sexual fears could be addressed.

Balcon was responsible for the development of a body of historical features that was qualitatively different from that of Korda. In all the Gaumont-British histories, the past was presented as a site of pain and struggle. The grim repressions of history, it was implied, had to be endured; but Balcon's films all celebrated an entrepreneurial spirit which could facilitate survival. Typically, the historical films made at Gaumont in the 1930s addressed themselves to middle-class audiences or issues, whereas Korda had deployed the resonances of the aristocratic ethic while at the same time celebrating popular taste. Balcon's intention was more overtly didactic, and he aimed to improve the audience's awareness of the similarity between past and present by a more explicit propagandism and a more accurate surface texture. He also privileged the male audience, whereas Korda had been primarily interested in female visual pleasure. Balcon's production methods ensured that directors and scriptwriters were more than usually compliant, whereas Korda's flamboyance and inspirational mode of control reduced the predictability of his historical product. Both producers managed to make history profitable, though they appealed to different parts of the mass audience.

Korda and Balcon thus represented two poles of historical representation. Korda's histories deployed the aristocracy as a source of symbolic power, and celebrated visual and sexual pleasure. Balcon's historical films had didactic aims, focused on the middle classes, and they supported a revised puritan ethic. Other film-makers in the 1930s negotiated these two poles in different ways, and we should now see what patterns emerge from a broader map of production.

3

DEAN, WILCOX AND OTHERS

THE POLITICS OF THE MARKETPLACE

The construction of an overall map of historical film production in the period is fraught with problems. Although there is material on producers such as Alexander Korda and Basil Dean, perhaps because of their zeal for self-advertisement, there is a paucity of evidence on figures such as Julius Hagen of Twickenham Studios. Lack of material may make it difficult to assess the popularity of some films, simply because they were not made by well-known figures, or because the work of the production companies was undocumented.

But it is possible to establish important absences in the field, and to recognise differences between American-financed and British-financed films and between different types of British production. Korda was linked to United Artists and Balcon was head of Gaumont-British, so they both had substantial backing for their enterprises. But historical films were risky ventures for smaller companies, since they were expensive to produce. One failure could have serious consequences for a small unit; *Don Quixote* lost £100,000, which resulted in the bankruptcy of Nelson Films in 1935. Many historical projects never got off the ground at all; a large-scale production of *The Private Life of Lord Byron* was halted by its Greek backer. Many of Korda's historical proposals did not leave the drawing board.

American production companies based in Britain had no advantage in the British market. Paramount's British Crusader company released *Flame in the Heather* in 1935, but its version of the Jacobite rebellion is merely picturesque. Fox's British operation attempted two 'quality' productions in 1936 – a Bergner version of *As You Like It* and *Wedding Group*, an inspirational tale about the Crimean war – but neither gained critical or popular attention. In the same year United Artists was responsible for *A Woman Alone*, which dealt with Imperial Russia, but it made no mark. Criterion, Douglas Fairbanks Jnr's company, attempted to redress the record for American-owned products in 1936 with *The Amateur Gentleman*, based on a popular Jeffrey Farnol novel set in the Regency period. Both these elements should have worked in the film's favour, but it appeared on no popularity lists, and was not mentioned in the extensive historical debates in *Film Weekly's* correspondence columns. It had the good offices of the Assistant Keeper of Costumes at the Victoria and Albert Museum; but the production was dogged by acrimony, and the writers sued the company.

The British-based companies commissioned by MGM to fulfil their quota requirements had little success either. Hammer (not the later company of that name) produced the 1935 Gothic *Mystery of the Mary Celeste* with Bela Lugosi. Fitzpatrick Pictures made *David Livingstone* in 1936, *George Bizet, Composer of Carmen* and *The Life of Chopin* in 1938. The company known as George King (MGM) specialised in sensationalised remakes of Victorian melodrama; *Maria Marten, or the Murder in the Red Barn* (1935) and *Sweeney Todd, or the Demon Barber of Fleet Street* (1936) both starred Tod Slaughter, and the company released *John Halifax, Gentleman* in 1938. The stilted visual style of these quota vehicles indicates that American production companies did not invest much effort into these cheaply made historical films, since for the Americans quota film production was merely a legal obligation; whereas to Korda, Balcon, Dean, Wilcox and others, history was a means whereby film could take its rightful place in the mainstream of national culture, as well as being a valuable source of revenue abroad.[1] But the American quota vehicles deployed aspects of the past which were residual; they frequently used nineteenth-century texts or myths that had become stripped of any class resonance.

However, a range of British companies did produce some historical features which were recognisably different from those of Korda or Balcon. British International Pictures (BIP), for example, under the aegis of Walter Mycroft, produced historical films with marked similarities: *Blossom Time* (August 1934), *The Old Curiosity Shop* (December 1934), *Abdul the Damned* (April 1935), *Royal Cavalcade* (April 1935), *Mimi* (May 1935), *Drake of England* (June 1935), *The Student's Romance* (July 1935), *Invitation to the Waltz* (September 1935), *I Give My Heart* (November 1935), and *Marigold* (November 1938).

British International Pictures, originally led by John Maxwell, had aimed to establish links with European production companies. Under Mycroft's leadership, it specialised in two types of costume films: light operettas, and historical heavyweights. The former were all cosmopolitan in tone. *Mimi* was based on Puccini's opera *La Bohème*, and though it starred Douglas Fairbanks and Gertrude Lawrence it made no critical or popular impact. *I Give My Heart* is an uneven version of the operetta *The Dubarry*. *The Student's Romance* is a series of duelling scenes set to music. *Invitation to the Waltz* combines musical interludes with nineteenth-century German politics. The only one of BIP's operettas to make an impact on the box-office was *Blossom Time*, which came first in *Film Weekly*'s list of viewers' favourites for 1934. *Blossom Time* is a romanticised biopic of Schubert (played by Richard Tauber). The portly tenor is shown encouraging his true love to run off with a virile soldier, while he solaces himself by singing 'Ave Maria' surrounded by cuddlesome choirboys. *Blossom Time* was particularly popular with female audiences.[2] This was possibly because of the appeal of the wounded hero; certainly Paul Stein, its director, suggested as much to *Film Weekly* on 24 August 1934. In any event, the film did well because it created an anodyne version of high culture and emphasised the romantic aspects of the past.

But BIP made more determined assaults on the serious historical market by employing directors such as Norman Lee and Thomas Bentley. Lee held that films should present history as more than 'battle, murder and sudden death' and he was given his chance to prove it in *Royal Cavalcade*.[3] Bentley, who had an impressive array of directing credits, was employed as supervising director. *Royal Cavalcade* was a coup for BIP, since it was the only company to produce a full-length feature film celebrating the reign of George V. The film had substantial support from the Foreign Office. The original idea for *Royal Cavalcade* was Maxwell's, and he gave Mycroft unlimited funds.[4] The publicity material celebrated the active co-operation of 'the War Office, the Admiralty, the GPO'; the film used 'current tunes, dances and catch-words' to hold the 25-year narrative together.

Royal Cavalcade is an attempt to combine official and popular realities, but the narrative device deployed for the task is too slender. The vicissitudes of a single penny are followed throughout the King's reign 'to symbolise national stability at a time of financial crisis', according to the publicity material. But it is a cumbersome film, whose flashbacks to speeches of Elizabeth I, Henry V, Charles II, Wellington and Nelson attempt to provide a rousing hymn to the monarchy.

Mycroft encouraged his directors to present history as the site of respectable pleasure. *The Old Curiosity Shop*, directed by Bentley and adapted by Margaret Kennedy, interprets Dickens' novel as an expressionist nightmare which educated the audience's moral sensibilities. The film is painterly, and the sets an intelligent attempt to reproduce the grotesque aspects of Dickens' style. Bentley deploys the gestural resources of melodrama and music-hall in his direction of the actors, but these aspects of popular culture are raised to a higher level by alterations to Dickens' text. Kit Nubbles is gentrified; Nell's death occurs in the middle of a history lesson; and 'the old coaching days' are presented as quintessentially English. BIP's publicity material suggested that cinema managers emphasise the film's respectability and verisimilitude. Neither of these qualities are strongly evident in Dickens' original text.

The Old Curiosity Shop's attempt to move Dickens socially up-market won praise from a wide range of critics. Mycroft and Bentley collaborated in 1938 on one further historical film with similar ambitions. *Marigold* deals with the vicissitudes of a young Edinburgh girl in 1842. But female autonomy in the film can only be granted by Queen Victoria; Marigold appeals directly (and successfully) to her. *Marigold*, in the wake of *Sixty Glorious Years*, presents the monarchy as a means whereby female pleasure can be controlled; and the studio stressed its indebtedness to government authorities.

Mycroft's two other historical vehicles for BIP were similar. *Abdul the Damned* was a co-production with Capitol Films and it was staffed by émigré Germans well aware of the dangers of political dictatorship.[5] Set in Turkey in the Gladstone era, the film deals with the overthrow of a tyrant. The script contains some lighter touches, such as 'What *can* he do with 300 wives?' and 'Do you think you look like a Sultan sitting there with your mouth open like a dog catching flies?' But it is really a rigorous analysis of the ruthless Machiavellianism encouraged by an autocratic system. The film's politics are tempered by opulent local colour. Karl Grune, the director, argued in an interview with *Picturegoer* (23 May 1936) that historical film should also show how past oppression has contemporary parallels.

Mycroft appointed Arthur Woods to direct *Drake of England*, which was released in May 1935. In its treatment of the Tudor period, the film provides a corrective contrast to Korda's *Henry VIII*. It celebrates the vitality of the monarchy, and suggests that the buccaneering exploits of Drake are acceptable because they 'opened the gates of the sea and gave Elizabeth the keys of the world'. A succession of short scenes ensures a swift-moving scenario. An air of authenticity was attempted by using Dr Charles Beard as director of historical research for the film. Some critics from right-wing papers noted that *Drake* was more patriotic than *Henry VIII* and could be more easily accommodated within a defence of Empire.[6]

Under Mycroft's aegis, then, BIP developed a species of historical film which had a strong moral undertow but little class analysis. This contrasts strongly with the productions of Korda and Balcon, and also with other popular films such as *Dr Syn* or *Under the Red Robe*, in which the class element was of paramount importance. BIP's historical films earned some critical acclaim, but there is no evidence that they performed well at the box-office; they were respectable but did not address contemporary anxieties or provide new symbolic resolutions for them. Mycroft's insights on history, such as they were, lacked the conviction to inspire his team.

There are interesting contrasts between Mycroft's case and that of Julius Hagen at Twickenham Film Studios. Hagen founded this small-scale independent operation in 1927, and made a fair profit in the years 1931–4 from quota films and from studio rental. Twickenham's most popular films in the early 1930s were low-budget melodramas which received critical opprobrium. Hagen borrowed extensively to expand the studio, and in 1937 he was declared bankrupt and the studio was closed. As Head of Production, Hagen made a range of historical features: *The Wandering Jew* (released in November 1933), *The Rocks of Valpré* (January 1935), *D'Ye Ken John Peel* (January 1935), *Scrooge* (August 1935), *Spy of Napoleon* (September 1936) and *The Vicar of Bray* (May 1937). Hagen was a shrewd businessman who was wary of the historical genre, thinking it ambitious and risky.[7] Nonetheless he wished to emulate the profitability of other costume films; he based his own films on popular novels, and he sold *Scrooge* to American backers on very favourable terms.

The Wandering Jew was directed by Maurice Elvey; it was opulent, but its structure and subject matter militated against popular appeal. Hagen then attempted to recoup his losses by deploying H. Fowler Mear, a rather lurid novelist, as his scriptwriter. *The Rocks of Valpré* was based on Ethel M. Dell, and is devoid of any class interest. Hagen's next historical effort, *D'Ye Ken John Peel*, is an 1815 highwayman romp. *Picturegoer* suggested on 27 October 1934 that it, *The Iron Duke* and *The Scarlet Pimpernel* constituted a new cinematic type: 'Three costume films, and important ones at that, dealing with approximately the same period! I don't suppose that has ever happened in British studios before.' But the difference is that the Twickenham film does not foreground problematical areas of Regency culture as the other two films do, since it presents the social outsider as a figure of timeless allure. The same flattening out of class elements is evident in Hagen's next historical film, *Scrooge*. This is based on Dickens' *A Christmas Carol*, but it eschews the story's Gothic aspects and substitutes hymn-singing and the national anthem. *Scrooge* is much less expressionist than *The Old Curiosity Shop*, and its sets and ghosts display poor imaginative resources.

The Spy of Napoleon, also directed by Maurice Elvey, attempted an increased artistic quality which finally cost the studio dear. The film deploys class elements in an uninflected way, the Orczy novel on which it was based being less overtly political than her *Pimpernel* books. Moreover, the novel had only been published in September 1934, and so the film could not draw upon an established reputation. *The Vicar of Bray* was a Stanley Holloway musical set in Cromwellian Ireland, which appeared after Hagen's bankruptcy. The publicity material suggested that the film's charm resided in the way it presented Charles II as a social catalyst, and it proposed the 'homely humour' of Holloway as a major selling point. But the film has an uneven tone, which does not conceal its political dubieties. The working class is shown as boorish and noble by turns; the monarchy is both despotic and flexible. Cromwell is presented as benignly 'reorganising the nation's affairs', but he is also revealed as a tyrant. *The Vicar of Bray* attempts to defuse these contradictions by the use of songs which implicitly propose a popular resolution, but they are too slight a means for the job in hand.

Clearly, Hagen's historical films did not proceed from any urgent sense of the topical relevance of the past. Nor did they deploy particular classes, historical periods or cultural topoi with any consistent resonance. Hagen was a producer whose entrepreneurism was untempered by any specific intellectual tastes. He simply tried anything on, to see if it would fit. Other producers of the period, such as Balcon or Dean, had a more complex awareness of historical resources.

Some enterprises, like British Lion Studios at Beaconsfield, were too small to develop a coherent policy on historical features. British Lion was hampered by its own limited studio space; whereas Capitol GFD, the production company of the German impresario Max Schach, always rented space from

The Vicar of Bray

others. Capitol leased space at Denham, Elstree and Shepperton for its various enterprises. It produced only thirteen films, but four of these may be categorised as histories: *Koenigsmark* (released in October 1935), *When Knights Were Bold* (February 1936), *The Marriage of Corbal* (June 1936) and *The Lilac Domino* (July 1937), all produced by Schach. They display a sophisticated lightness of touch, and they all foreground the aristocracy. *Koenigsmark* is a Ruritanian fantasy whose visual style is resonant of the silent work of Stroheim. *The Lilac Domino* is a musical set in Budapest in which aristocrats attend masked balls; it is, again, sumptuously produced. *When Knights Were Bold* is a musical farce about the heir to a castle (Jack Buchanan) who imagines himself in mediaeval times. It had extremely good reviews, and the critics recognised that the lightness of tone was intimately connected with the confidence in handling class matters. *The Marriage of Corbal*, too, overtly displays its class symbolism. It concerns a deputy in 1790 France who loves and succours an aristocrat. Significantly, the film was praised by many critics for the subtlety of its handling of the cross-class theme.[8] Others, however, castigated the film's overt intellectualism.[9] Capitol's historical films coherently demonstrate the complexity of the aristocracy's role, but critics (and possibly audiences) were hostile to a style which they perceived as excessively continental.

Some of the smaller film companies, then, evinced a coherent attitude to historical representation. There is no evidence that any of their costume films gained more than a modest popularity, though this does not preclude their cultural significance. There remains the case of Hitchcock's *Jamaica Inn* (1939). This was made by Mayflower Pictures, which was owned by Erich Pommer and Charles Laughton; it appeared in the popularity lists of 1940. *Jamaica Inn* had oddly assorted personnel: Tom Morahan and Harry Watt did the art direction and the special effects respectively, and since they were both committed to realist methods, they felt uncomfortable with Hitchcock and Pommer. The first script was deemed unsuitable by the Hays Office because the parson was the real villain, and Sidney Gilliat and J.B. Priestley rewrote it with the squire as the culprit. This script, and Laughton's masterly performance, were probably the reasons for the film's success. The squire was played as a decayed Regency aristocrat who, in the face of post-Revolutionary desires for democracy, insisted on style à la Pimpernel. The novel presented him as a villain; but in the film his dying words include a significant quotation from Burke's *Reflections on the Revolution in France*: 'The age of chivalry is gone.' This famous passage contained Burke's powerful defence of the *ancien régime*, and was subsequently well assimilated into conservative discourse. *Jamaica Inn*'s success may be partially attributed to its evocation of well-established cultural topoi.

We should now turn to the more developed ideas of Basil Dean, and examine the role of historical films in a larger production company. Dean completed three historical films at Associated Talking Pictures – *Lorna Doone* (released in January 1935), *Midshipman Easy* (October 1935) and *Whom the Gods Love* (February 1936). An adaptation of *The Mill on the Floss* was made under his aegis and released in January 1937. None of these appear in the popularity lists, although Dean asserted that *Midshipman Easy* was 'a rip-roaring success' and that *Lorna Doone* also did well.[10] Dean had made his reputation with *The Constant Nymph*, and with Gracie Fields vehicles like *Sing As We Go*. His historical features may seem untypical in terms of his overall output, but they are the logical extension of the cultural ideas which he developed in the 1920s and 30s.

Prior to his historical films, Dean's personal popularity was low. His attitudes to culture and his handling of actors were widely criticised.[11] By 1927 he had 'to a great extent lost my faith in the response of the public to good work.'[12] He mounted a campaign in the early 1930s for the production of films of Shakespeare plays.[13] This didactic undertaking stemmed from Dean's desire to protect the cinema from cultural dereliction by transforming it through the theatre, and his views gained some support. But Dean espoused a particularly narrow definition of Englishness: 'A country has but itself to give to the screen.'[14] He argued that British culture should avoid internationalism in style, and the public's taste for American films should be reformed.[15] And he insisted that historical film could play a crucial role in this process. However, Dean had a folkloric notion of history. He argued that ideal film subjects were Robin Hood – 'the genuine Romance of our English history' – and characters like eighteenth-century squires who 'lived in those spacious days before women were emancipated'.[16] Films should celebrate national icons: 'Who shall say that the glorification of English national heroes is not a fit subject for screen presentation, and that those who make such pictures are not entitled to their just reward?'[17] Dean oversimplified the issue of audience identification with historical characters in a way Korda and Balcon never did, and he had a straightforward notion of the way texts could suggest a congruence between past and present. He continued to deploy history in this way in the street pageants he organised during the war for ENSA, and also in his work for the Festival of Britain.

Dean's ability to produce successful historical films was hampered by his reverence for prestigious novelists and playwrights. He squandered much energy attempting to persuade writers like George Bernard Shaw, John Galsworthy and John Drinkwater to participate in historical and other projects.[18] The *Yorkshire Evening Post* of 12 February 1935 reported a proposed collaboration between Dean and Drinkwater which was to be 'an instructive and elevated picture of Victoria and her times ... not à la Arliss, but with historical accuracy'. Despite the respectability of his connections Dean was unable to realise this project.

Early in 1935 Dean met Sir Robert Vansittart, then Permanent Under-Secretary for Foreign Affairs. It is clear from unpublished letters (in the John Rylands University Library) that this meeting quickly developed into an intimate friendship, in which they gave each other Alsatian dogs as a sign of mutual esteem. Dean arranged charity concerts for Vansittart's wife, and Vansittart smoothed over immigration difficulties for Dean's French cook. The extent of their friendship may be seen from the letters about Vansittart's plays. Vansittart followed in every particular Dean's advice about alteration, and Dean, who was then in an influential position in London stage management, facilitated stage production. Of particular interest is Vansittart's intervention to ensure the smooth passage of Dean's film about Mozart, *Whom the Gods Love*. Dean, stressing that the film was made 'with the collaboration of the Austrian Government', asked Vansittart to give the film official diplomatic blessing at its showings abroad: 'Any little push you can give this scheme to help it along would be deeply appreciated, as always.'[19] Vansittart complied at once. (Of course, the 'little push' had to be paid for; Vansittart tried to persuade Dean to put on one of his own plays.) Vansittart's championing of the Mozart film doubtless increased its status. He helped Dean over its location problems; Austrian government officials were convinced that the film would 'do good' because Dean was empowered to act as a sort of unofficial ambassador of British culture. His way in Austria was prepared by Vansittart, who was assiduous in sending personal letters of introduction.[20]

Dean, then, clearly had powerful connections, which he did not scruple to use to promote the Mozart film and doubtless other projects as well. But even the support of such a powerful ally as Vansittart could not guarantee popular success for a historical film if it did not deploy history in the right way; nor could Dean make profits in an intractable financial situation. The economic situation at ATP was dire before and during the production of the Mozart film. There were acrimonious arguments over policy and frequent changes in the board of directors.[21] ATP were working on very small profit margins, and the greater cost of costume films was more than they could carry. Problems with the distribution company exacerbated the difficulties of *Lorna Doone*; Dean noted that the company was 'a very hungry child that has got to be fed', even though *Lorna Doone* was 'a big subject'.[22] *Lorna Doone* was begun without adequate funding, the scriptwriters could not be paid, and the location team 'lost all sense of proportion' in their zeal for realism.[23] Their search in Devon for dialect coaches, local folklorists and thirty men of unusual height to play the Doones gained much publicity.[24] The film had bad reviews for its folkloric sentimentality. It was a box-office failure, although Dean defended it: 'We have come to regard *Lorna Doone* as a disastrous blunder, whereas in fact it proved to be nothing of the kind. Its excessive cost was due to other causes ... it is quite possible for even the more expensive pictures to tumble down disastrously at the box-office.'[25] He noted that Gaumont and Korda had also had their costume failures. The distinction was that Dean's was a smaller operation, and with different cultural capital.

The problem was that Dean combined an attempt at surface accuracy with a mythopoeic approach to history, and the two methods were ill-assorted. The publicity material for *Lorna Doone* indicated this. On the one hand it insisted that 'every effort was made to secure authenticity', with 'Devon and Somerset music'; on the other hand, it suggested that the film be sold through the appeal of the 'wassail in the great oak-beamed kitchen'. The film presents Old England as a picturesque place in which to consume roast swan, and the camera is most active when focused on the detailed peasant interiors. By the use of costume and decor, the film suggests that the peasantry are doughty Puritans and the gentry effete Cavaliers. The robber Doones are clearly the gentry principle writ large. This type of political analysis was absent from the original novel. Dean's *Lorna Doone* celebrates a peasant culture which still adheres to Cromwellianism, and where archetypal images prevail. The miniature of the farm should give 'a Christmas card effect', according to the script, which emphasises the ritual elements of harvest. Womanliness is symbolised by images of a duck with ducklings, manliness by images of sickle and blunderbuss. The acting style of both protagonists is wooden. Dean's insistence that

Lorna Doone

the role of Lorna be played by his then wife, Virginia Hopper, was clearly misguided.

History in *Lorna Doone* is presented as a place where organicist values can be celebrated, with a surface accuracy which conceals a deep conservatism. The same politics were evinced in Dean's next historical film, *Midshipman Easy*. Dean remarked that he was first drawn to Marryat's book because it glorified 'the days when Britain's wooden walls ruled the seas'.[26] *Midshipman Easy* was Carol Reed's first film as director, and its pace is swift; the art direction, by Edward Carrick, is expressionist in tone, and the editing, by Sidney Cole and Thorold Dickinson, is crisp. The script was by Anthony Kimmins, who was well qualified for the naval topic.[27] The film had excellent reviews but no mention in the popularity lists. Competently crafted though it is, it was handicapped by its exclusive address to a young, male audience. The combination of a boy's adventure story with a historical background was not appropriate. By this stage in the 1930s a historical film had to address particular class or sexual issues to capture a mass audience. *Midshipman Easy*'s target audience was too small to make a profit. A further contributing factor to the film's failure was that it reproduces, with tiresome regularity, the ideas of the protagonist, who is a believer in Godwin's principle of Necessity. This was

47

recognisable to the original readers of Captain Marryat in 1838; it was less appropriate for the film audience of 1935.

Dean's next historical enterprise, *Whom the Gods Love*, had its path well prepared and its status confirmed by Lord Vansittart. But despite these good offices, Dean's film failed to appear in any popular listings. Acute financial problems dogged the production. There was a shortfall of £9,500 early in the shooting process, problems with the Electrical Trades Union, and anxieties about Dean's obsession with authenticity.[28] But for Dean the Mozart film was his big production, in which his ideas about high culture could finally be expressed. He admitted a great emotional commitment to the project, and was aggrieved when it was curtailed.[29] But the critics did not share his enthusiasms; the film was universally slated for its ponderous authenticity. The shooting script by Margaret Kennedy did not encourage the viewer to experience the past confidently; the surface details of history are displayed in an antiquarian way, but the viewer is prevented from understanding its causes. There is no exploration of the processes of Mozart's creativity, or even of the way in which the operas were staged; a spectacle is provided, but no explanatory model. Thus the high culture so painstakingly recreated appears mystifying, and the script's attempt to broaden its appeal by having workmen exclaim 'It's our Mozart!' seems ludicrous. Moreover, the structure of the narrative is halting and unbalanced. The image of history and high culture in *Whom the Gods Love* pleased Dean, Vansittart and Margaret Kennedy, but it is doubtful whether it gave much pleasure to anyone else.

However, Dean was nothing if not persistent, and returned to the fray again with *The Mill on the Floss*. Once again there was a frantic attempt to recreate historical local colour, with location shooting and expensive sets. Once again he attempted to deploy his notion of authorship, this time by giving John Drinkwater sole rights over the adaptation of George Eliot's novel. Clearly Drinkwater was convinced by Dean's ideas, since he now argued that 'in any work of art, what is essential is the unifying effect of a single mind. It should all bear the stamp of a single mentality.'[30] There are no records of the film doing well at the box office; the book's concern with the repression of female adolescents did not translate successfully into film. Nor could the 'Red Deeps' of the written text, which symbolise the female body, be appropriately dealt with under the censorship conditions of 1937.

Dean's historical films, then, were shaped by a number of elements: the economic plight of ATP, his own theories of authorship, his crusading attitude to high culture, and his concern with an accurate but folkloric history. The films are of significance in the overall map of historical film in the 1930s, since they reveal the persistence of elitist notions of culture held by some intellectuals, and the difficulty which they had in translating those ideas into cash.

But there were other films of the late 1930s which did make history a profitable business. For example, *Under the Red Robe* and *Dr Syn* appeared in the *Kinematograph Weekly* popularity lists of 1937 and 1938. The first was made by New World Pictures, which belonged to 20th-Century Fox – the only American-owned subsidiary to make a popular historical film in the period. However, material in Board of Trade files indicates that circumstances were rather more complex. New World had a very close relationship with Korda's London Films, and a distribution contract with him which stipulated that only films 'fit for international release containing an international cast' should be made. The Home Office viewed New World's *Under the Red Robe* and *Wings of the Morning* as 'important and expensive films' which were significant earners of revenue.[31] It seems likely that New World was technically a Fox property but with very strong Korda alliances; personnel were paid by London Films through the covert agency of Rock Pictures. The screenplay of *Under the Red Robe* was by Biro and Wimperis, who had scripted Korda's period films. The photography was partly by Georges Périnal, who had also worked on those films. The film was made at Denham, using many of Korda's workforce. In addition, the foreign personnel drafted in were of the highest calibre: Victor Sjöström directed, and James Wong Howe collaborated with Périnal on the photography.

The film was based on the popular novel of the same title by Stanley Weyman, which dealt with court intrigues in early seventeenth-century France; the film emulated the novel's stylistic richness. However, the script makes important alterations from the novel. The narrative structure is altered by the scriptwriters so as to scatter textual gratifications throughout, rather than deferring them to one cathartic crisis as in the novel. Greater emphasis is given to the female protagonist and to the romantic element. The heroine asserts, in a tone absent from the novel, 'What do I care what you have been? It's your hands, your eyes, your courage that belong to me.' Another important alteration is that the style and power of the monarchy is emphasised. The film ends with a paean to the king, who is not in shot, but who erases the power of Richelieu. Taking the king's point of view, the camera enters through a row of

Dr Syn

courtiers in a finale which reflects the film's sumptuous production values.

The success of *Under the Red Robe* was due to a number of factors. It was shot in a lively manner; it deployed personnel experienced in the Korda school of history; it was based on an established historical novel, and it celebrated the monarchy in a compelling way. Gaumont-British's *Dr Syn* was a box-office success for different reasons. Balcon had left the studio in 1936, and the head of production was then Maurice Ostrer, from the financier family which owned the company. Ted Black, an efficient but rough-and-ready organiser, was in charge of the day-to-day running. According to Bill Slater and Dennis Mason, who worked at the studio, Black enforced rigorous control. It seems very likely that the seeds of the wartime costume blockbusters at Gainsborough were sown during the late 1930s. *Dr Syn* may therefore be interpreted as the earliest prototype of such films as *The Wicked Lady*.

Dr Syn deals with the exploits of a pirate who disguises himself as a clergyman to avoid detection. It is based upon a popular novel by Russell Thorndike. The film reproduces the book's narrative structure, which contains exciting events at regular intervals. The non-realist visual style also approximates the literary texture, which is ornate and archaic. The piracy of Dr Syn and his comrades symbolises their social marginality. Parson and squire in *Dr Syn* are beyond the pale of polite society; the officers of the army and the law are stupidly gullible. The film thus defends a sort of popular lawlessness, and is implicitly anti-authoritarian. The film's stars operated in its favour: George Arliss, hero of so many costume films, played the lead, and John Loder the romantic role. Graham Moffatt took a comic part, and Margaret Lockwood an ingenue role. Gaumont-British's publicity material suggested that cinema managers should 'get co-operation from teachers in running contests among pupils, requiring them to write essays on famous pirate chiefs of history'. But it hedged its bets by suggesting that another selling point was the film's similarity to adventure tales like *Treasure Island*, another 'blood-curdling, tingling narrative'.

Dr Syn was popular because it evoked the continuity of a lawless adventure tradition, and because of its narrative structure and star values. But it should be interpreted as an eccentric text in its period. It was far outnumbered in the late 1930s by historical films which endorsed institutions and authorities. The most important producer of these was Herbert Wilcox, whose films about Queen Victoria had a well-documented popularity. Wilcox made five historical films in the 1930s: *Nell Gwyn* (August 1934), *Peg of Old Drury* (August 1935), *Victoria the Great* (August 1937), *Sixty Glorious Years* (September 1938) and *A Royal Divorce* (December 1938). There is little information on Wilcox's intellectual tastes, since he lacked the flair for self-publicity of other producers. His autobiography suggests a conservatism about artistic form, a preference for texts with 'a beginning, a middle and end', and a vague sense of the contemporary relevance of the Victorian films.[32] He was opposed to melodramatic expressivity, and told *Picturegoer* on 26 January 1935 that 'the English race is reserved and not given to emotion.' Wilcox had an instinctive sense of the controversial, as his *Dawn* attests. But he appears to have been unimaginative, unctuous and slavishly impressed by the Establishment. Moreover, his uxorious devotion to Anna Neagle caused some serious errors of casting.

Nell Gwyn

Nell Gwyn deals with the relationship between the eponymous heroine and Charles II, until his death. The credits claim that the script was taken verbatim from the words of the King, Nell and Samuel Pepys, and it opens with pages from Pepys' diary and shots of the Lely portrait. These clearly signal authenticity, and the voice-over insists that the Restoration monarchy is a combination of mercy and vigour which should take a high priority in public memory. The film suggests that the Restoration provided the materials for modern popular culture; the theatre is indicated as the origin of the music-hall and the cinema. Moreover, it presents the argument that the crucial class alignment is between the aristocracy and the lower classes; this negotiated alliance effectively excludes the middle class.

Nell Gwyn is unusual in Wilcox's output in that it foregrounds sexual desire. The heroine, in a grossly metonymous manner, sucks the monarch's finger after the remark 'When will you show me how much you can please me?' Her body language throughout is broad, sensual and expressive, and a series of voluptuous eating scenes functions as an implicit disguise for the consumma-tion of other hungers. The decor presents the physical surface of the past as dense and interesting. Controlled camera movement tells what the script could not; one scene shows Nell waking, and the camera follows her glance over to the space in the bed recently vacated by the king. The film avoids moralising; as 'Duchess of Greenwich', Nell walks from the King's deathbed in a dignified manner. Of course, the American censor objected to the film, and demanded alterations which made its American release problematical.[33]

Nell Gwyn took third place in *Film Weekly*'s survey of 1935's most popular films. Neagle also took fourth place in the *Picturegoer* list for her performance. The film pleased audiences because it duplicated the images of social structure, pleasure and history contained in *Henry VIII*. The critics' response to *Nell* was significant. A widespread attempt was made to recuperate the film in terms of a respectable cinematic history. On the face of it, *Nell* is a curious ally for the accuracy/decency school of historical representation, since it is a particularly salacious film.

Very positive reviews appeared in a wide spectrum of journals. Significantly, there were a number of attempts in 1934 to reduce the impact of *Nell*'s raunchiness. *Film Weekly* ran an interview with the scriptwriter Miles Malleson on 21 September 1934, in order to prove that the film was respectably based on documentary evidence, such that the dead 'are able to come to life once more and speak the actual words they spoke in real life.' On 3 October 1934, the *Daily Express* interviewed Cedric Hardwicke, who played Charles II, and reported him as emphasising that for the audience it was 'their first introduction to history ... it behoves us to be conscious of our responsibilities.' Others suggested that *Nell* represented a popular strand of historiography.[34] Of particular interest was a long letter in *Film Weekly* on 18 January 1934, purporting to be from a filmgoer. The writer argued that

> History and its protagonists have this peculiar fascination for the mass of people, who, without knowing or caring very much about accuracy of detail, like to feel that history is being recreated before their eyes – not gibed at or illuminated, but brought to life ... that characters have all the vivacious vulgarity and good nature, all the wisdom, wit and charm with which popular tradition has endowed them.

This is perhaps the nearest we can get to a common-sense view of history in the period; or at least a journalist's perception of it.

Nell was able to accommodate a wide range of different critical positions. As a reason for its popularity, the *selection* of historical period was at least as important as the *manner* of its representation. The Restoration plays a peculiar role in British popular culture. It is widely perceived as a period of popular monarchy when fixed sexual morality was shaken loose by the licence of the king. Whether or not this is an accurate interpretation is irrelevant, though doubtless an awareness of sustained pockets of Puritanism and the severe economic difficulties of Charles II would contradict this image of the period. The function of the Restoration period in the cinema from the mid-1930s was probably to permit the audience to rehearse the possibility that efficient systems of power could also be florid and permissive. By implication, the forgiveness extended to the king's peccadillos could also be accorded to one's own.

Nell Gwyn was able to draw on a rich seam of popular memory, just as *Henry VIII* did. Wilcox then attempted to repeat his success with *Peg of Old Drury*, and did so.[35] The film deals with the life of Peg Woffington, an eighteenth-century actress who was Garrick's mistress. Wilcox took great care over the production; he was reputed to have spent £5,000 on retakes alone. He was made aware by his theatrical adviser that in the eighteenth- century theatre Peg would have worn contemporary dress; but he chose to ignore historical accuracy, since 'the cinema-going public were not all, perhaps, quite as well-versed in the niceties of theatre history.'[36]

Peg had very good reviews, especially from the quality papers. Particularly interesting was the *Sunday Times* on 1 September 1935, which was quite prepared to accept the film's historical liberties: 'Not strictly in accordance with historical fact perhaps, but maybe the better for that. Who would want to see Peg die an old withered hag, as she did?' The film's popularity owed much to the way in which Wilcox duplicated the mood of *Nell*. But *Peg* also succeeded because it debunked received wisdom about the Augustan period. The early eighteenth century is generally held to epitomise balance and bourgeois rationality. *Peg* presents it instead as a period in which roistering took place, and where the by now familiar liaison between high and low life could circumvent the power of the middle class.

Peg and *Nell* can be interpreted as films which used the past as a means of celebrating female desire and the vitality of popular traditions. This certainly was not the case with Wilcox's two Victoria films. Both took a stern view of pleasure, and were politically conservative. They both did very well at the box office.[37] Wilcox suggested that he had direct encouragement for *Victoria* from Edward VIII and Mrs Simpson, and he described how he heard the announcement of the king's abdication in the early planning stages of the film.[38] The timing of the two Victoria films was crucial; they could be interpreted as an attempt to allay public anxiety about the abdication crisis, and to assert, via history, the desirability of Victorian values. They were also part of the celebrations of the centenary of Victoria's accession.

There was enormous advance publicity for *Victoria the Great*, much of it

Victoria the Great

emphasising the film's accuracy and respectability. Most reviewers were extremely complimentary; according to the *Daily Telegraph* of 20 September 1937, *Victoria* was superior to *Henry VIII*, whose 'peers were gangsters and queens were wantons'. *Victoria* was the first film to be wholeheartedly recommended by a teaching magazine: 'There were standards of conduct and she stood for them,' said *Teacher's World and Schoolmaster*.[39] The film also scored another 'first' when a whole number of *Film Weekly* was devoted to it on 22 December 1937; its special authorisation from the royal family was emphasised.

Of course, *Victoria* is politically biased. The film besmirches the orderly protests of Chartism by connecting them with regicide riots; the Queen and Albert are supposedly 'on the side of the people', while the efforts of liberal intellectuals of the period are ignored. The intervention of the royal pair in British-American relations is exaggerated. The use of intertitles gives *Victoria* a dated look, and its pace is ponderous. The tone of the film is unctuous, and the structure of the narrative, with the change-over to colour towards the end, throws positive emphasis on to the theme of Empire. Victoria appears finally as a static icon, the 'grandmother of the great family of mankind'. Britain is presented as the only source of 'democracy, tolerance and freedom', to the tune of 'Land of Hope and Glory'. *Victoria* has a markedly old-fashioned air when compared to the more innovatory costume films of the 1930s, but its politics are unusually aggressive and close to the surface. Unlike in *Henry VIII* or *Tudor Rose*, the film's political message is forcefully displayed, rather than disguised. In *Victoria*, there are no tangential, metaphorical or implicit meanings.

The same arrangement of politics and narrative structures obtains in *Sixty Glorious Years*, which appeared in September 1938. This film, too, was very popular. On the face of it, *Sixty Glorious Years* is a remarkable phenomenon: a reworking of *Victoria the Great* which reproduces its turgid propagandism. Yet the 1938 film fulfilled a very different ideological function. *Victoria* dealt with the anxieties produced by the abdication crisis; the later film addressed the dangers posed to Britain by the international situation. For help with the script, Wilcox approached Vansittart, who was now in a much more advantageous position than he had been in the mid-1930s. Then, his pro-rearmament position had been supported by few; now his anti-German views seemed reasonable to many. Vansittart persuaded the King to allow shooting at Windsor and Balmoral. The King offered Wilcox the loan of the Windsor Greys, encouraged the Princesses to watch the filming process, and prompted Lady Antrim to coach Anna Neagle in the body language of the real Victoria.[40]

Vansittart's intervention in *Sixty Glorious Years* was well publicised. Wilcox implied that he operated as a sort of *eminence grise* during the production, and Vansittart's script certainly presents history in a quite different way from *Victoria*. Quotations from well-known writers were used to fuse unwieldy material; selections from Dickens, Tennyson, Browning and Kipling locate the action firmly in cultural history.[41] The Queen's German relatives, who were obtrusive in *Victoria*, are conveniently less visible in Vansittart's script. Instead, static pageantry and long shots of buildings proliferate. There are clear signs of Vansittart's authorship in the passages on General Gordon at Khartoum. Victoria noted with anguish that 'we may be too late. That is the danger to which this country so often exposes itself. One day it may be our undoing.' This clearly derives from Vansittart's own views on rearmament.

In general, the presentation of the monarchy is much more forceful than in *Victoria*. History is the site of a warning and a lesson. *Sixty Glorious Years* was extremely well received by a wide range of journals. Two significant reviews foregrounded the extent to which the film was assimilable into respectable discourse. Canon Wilkinson argued that the producers of films like *Sixty Glorious Years* operated in the way scholars used to. Such was their success that now 'The almost delicious pleasure of seeing the past revealed in action on the screen is the passion of the multitude.'[42] The *Weekly Illustrated* argued that hitherto all historical films had 'caricatured and falsified history so as to make it palatable', but this was now rectified by *Sixty Glorious Years*.[43]

Wilcox was extremely flexible in dealing with history. He was able to deploy the insights of Korda with *Nell* and *Peg*; with the Victoria films, he could respond to political change, and could produce films which easily took the impression of official favour. The key issue here is the representation of the monarchy. With no firm views of his own, Wilcox could run through a wide gamut of class symbolism, allying the monarchy with the masses (*Nell*) and with solid bourgeois values (*Victoria*), from one film to the next. Some part of the audience of 1937 and 1938 was clearly in need of the naked, undisguised certainties offered by the Victoria films. But the audience was not homogeneous in its tastes, as the success of *Dr Syn* and *Under the Red Robe* shows.

Patterns of production were not homogeneous either. Clearly, though, two things were necessary for success in the market of historical films. One was the scale and resources of the operation. Small outfits found it difficult to gain entry into the new market, because sheer costs were prohibitive. But secondly, and more importantly, the cultural capital of the larger producers was a major determinant of the popularity of historical films. In the 1930s, the emergence of a recognisable position on class was predicated on visual style; a film's symbolic system could be carried within its decor or its star. Producers of historical film could be categorised by the extent to which they bolstered their class arguments with supporting ones of gender idenfication. Korda, Balcon and Wilcox held radically different views on the uses of the past, but what they had in common was a readiness to combine class analyses with debates about sexual pleasure, albeit variously defined. Hagen and Dean were unable to reproduce this combination of class and sexual elements. This was because of the intellectual alliances of the latter, and the gross entrepreneurialism of the former. And American companies were too imprisoned within fossilised cultural forms to produce innovatory texts.

However, films are received as well as made. We can only begin to evaluate them fully when we analyse what they meant to the societies they addressed. To this end, we should now turn from the production context of historical films to the history of their reception, remembering always that audiences, too, are divided along the axes of status, class and gender.

4

LOWBROW AND MIDDLEBROW RESPONSES
IN THE 1930s

All the evidence of audience response in the 1930s has gone through some type of filter; letters to magazines have been selected and possibly amended, and Mass-Observation material may be coloured by the bias of the interviewer. But a representative selection of material can be made, so long as different kinds of journals and geographical regions are covered. In the study of public opinion on any issue in the period, it is helpful to divide material into highbrow, middlebrow and lowbrow respondents and journals. This terminology does not, of course, exactly correspond to social distinctions between the upper, middle and lower classes, nor to political orientation. It has to do with status, intellectual pretensions, and definitions of culture. A middle-class writer like R. J. Minney could be robustly lowbrow in his orientation and interests; and a letter writer to *Film Weekly* could be working-class by origin but middlebrow in terms of attainment and taste. This chapter addresses lowbrow debates on historical film, and then assesses a range of middlebrow opinion. The next chapter examines attempts by quasi-official, highbrow bodies to influence ideas on historical film.

Henry VIII clearly constituted a real innovation in the field. Popular journalism gave little attention to historical film before *Henry VIII*'s release. Some hostility was expressed to American censorship of British historical films, and disquiet was felt about the BBFC's control over historical representations.[1] But on the whole it was the furore surrounding *Henry VIII* which raised the level of debate.

Many writers asserted that *Henry VIII* was valuable in establishing a popular historiographical style.[2] Throughout 1934, it was argued that British historical films were more accurate than American ones; and if British producers were tempted into exaggeration, it was forgivable.[3] In 1935, popular journals continued a spirited defence of British uses of history.[4] Of particular note was the *Daily Mirror's* comment on 27 November 1935:

> As to films with facts in them (like fish with bones in it), we try to like them. We don't always succeed. There's something about a fact more depressing than it has a right to be. How boots are made, how toads live ... still, you can see all that if you like. If you don't like it, just don't worry or don't see it. Make for the romantic, the delusional film as hitherto. For undoubtedly most people go to the cinema palaces not for self-improvement, but to escape from themselves.

Here an argument about artistic licence was combined with a defence of popular taste and a rejection of documentary realism.

However, popular journals soon began to retreat from their defence of cinematic inaccuracy. The *Daily Herald* was an early champion of historical accuracy from late 1934; very few journals took a more liberal view. In general, a sharp increase in pro-accuracy views was evident in popular journals from 1936. A rash of comments on accuracy drew attention to a range of offending phenomena: anachronistic whiskers, hairstyles, dance routines.[5] On 22 October 1937, the *Daily Mail* attacked the selectivity of British historical films, and wondered why films on Cromwell or the industrial revolution did not appear.

Many male critics suggested that the poor quality of historical films was because they were aimed at a female audience. The *News of the World* saw history as a mere excuse for selling 'beauty aids', and a range of journals emphasised the fashion potential of historical dress.[6] The tie-in advertisements carried by film magazines from 1935 are of interest. *Picturegoer* contained recommendations for 'Nell Gwyn Skin Food', and *Film Weekly* ran a series of advertisements for 4711 Toilet Water, 'chosen by beauties since before Waterloo'. It also argued the emergence of 'a new form of entertainment which relies largely on the support of women for its existence'. Male history was to be 'confined to the schoolroom or the study'.[7]

Film Weekly and *Picturegoer*, the two major lowbrow film journals, developed coherent theories about historical film and printed a wide range of readers' letters on the subject. Other less popular journals raised the issue only in a limited way. There are some publication figures available for *Film Weekly*, and it is clear that although it was phenomenally popular more than half its readership came from London and the South East.[8] On the outbreak of war the magazine amalgamated with *Picturegoer*. From early 1933, *Film Weekly* had mounted a spirited defence of the visual competence of the mass audience, arguing on 30 June 1933, for instance, that 'the public is much more discriminating than highbrow critics would have us believe.' Throughout the 1930s, the magazine celebrated popular taste and educated its readers about the way films were made; it also acquainted them with recent critical debates. The one issue which it consistently foregrounded between 1933 and 1939 was that of history.

Film Weekly had a rigorous definition of periodisation and of the historical. The key date was 1918, because after that time popular memory of clothes and mores did not necessitate that 'infinity of research' that marked a serious film project.[9] Editorial policy was subtle on the question of accuracy, and, in balancing popular taste against academic qualms, frequently played both ends against the middle. The editor, when comparing Korda's *Catherine the Great* with Sternberg's *Scarlet Empress*, noted on 13 October 1933 that academic research proved that the real Catherine had several chins. Such information was dangerous, since it abandoned hapless producers to the rage of historians: the editor could 'already hear the barrage of criticism which will be set up by the meticulous and pedantic'. Academic objections were unfounded because 'history is not copyright'. However, *Film Weekly* provided a refined gloss on its populist position by attempting, on 26 January 1934, a taxonomy of historical films. It also frequently reproduced historical portraits alongside film stills, in order to endorse the work of well-meaning producers and to widen the experience of the readers. *Film Weekly* claimed that it was simply responding to audience taste on the issue.

Throughout 1934 and 1935 *Film Weekly* gave a high profile to history, and printed sumptuous spreads on important films. Two articles in 1935 were of particular interest. It endorsed an 'unsolicited letter' on *Nell Gwyn* on 18 January which argued that

> History and its protagonists have this peculiar fascination for the mass of people, who without perhaps knowing or caring much about accuracy of detail, like to feel that history is being recreated in front of their eyes not gibed at, or illuminated, but brought to life.

An editorial on 28 June suggested that popular histories were 'miracles of accuracy', that 'slavish realism' was counterproductive, and that 'trifling errors seldom have any bearing upon the artistic merit of a picture'.

Until mid-1936, then, *Film Weekly* was an enthusiastic champion of popular history. Thereafter, the journal changed its policy. It suggested on 4 July 1936 that producers should embrace 'the equally vivid drama much nearer to the hearts and thoughts of their patrons'. On 15 May 1937 it asked Korda to neglect history and 'do something for ordinary people'. The editor printed a letter on 6 November 1937 from 'simple country folk' bewailing historical films, and he commented: 'Costume films are admirable in some ways. But very many people are apt to overlook that few films claim to teach the facts of history and too literal an acceptance of their stories can breed a lot of misapprehension.' *Film Weekly* then organised a 'tribute luncheon' for *Victoria the Great*, showing that, as a matter of policy, it now supported a more respectable type of history. Finally, on 9 April 1939, it concluded that filmgoers wanted not fantasy but 'history as it really happened', whereas producers would merely 'fiddle history to suit their purpose'.

This shift in orientation may be accounted for by *Film Weekly*'s intellectual pretensions. It may have been convinced by the position of the Historical Association's *History Teaching Films*, which I shall describe later. The ideological clout of the Association's argument made it difficult for anyone to defend popular history and claim any intellectual status.

The letters of *Film Weekly*'s readers may have been filtered or selected, but they indicate a range of attitudes which did not always reflect editorial opinion. There were some 65 letters on historical film from 1933 to 1939; very many had no gender identification, and readers sometimes described their own class in a haphazard way. It is difficult to differentiate between male and female views of history from this evidence; and it is dangerous to attribute too much sociological weighting to readers' utterances, since the very act of writing to a magazine made them unusual. However, there is much of value. Readers expressed an intense interest in history, and provided an endless stream of suggestions for possible projects: another film on Disraeli, films on Florence Nightingale, Madame Tussaud, the Tower, the Borgias, Napoleon, Nelson, Hereward the Wake, Byzantium, Scott, George IV.[10] All proposals were for films about individuals or places; not for issues or periods. Taste either closely followed the lead given by popular producers or (more likely) the most astute film-makers colluded with what they imagined was their audience's interpretation of history.

Some of the letters argued in favour of greater historical accuracy. There were quibbles on accents, geographical knowledge, behavioural style and incorrectly cropped dog's ears; but all these were criticised with humour and a lightness of tone.[11] They decreased dramatically after late 1936. Pro-accuracy views were far outweighed by assertions of the irrelevance of accuracy. Many writers argued that successful historical films conformed to popular rather than academic notions of the past.[12] An interesting letter on 12 October 1934 claimed that 'knowing nothing, I enjoy everything. I leave the cinema delighted and happy because I do not know any history ... the screen whets my appetite for finding out what really happened. I enjoy the fiction and am learning the facts.' Very many letters praised the genre as a whole.[13] Readers were well aware of the ease with which historical film could be co-opted for propaganda, and there were a few letters in favour of realism. But the majority of *Film Weekly* letter writers were passionately in favour of historical spectacle, and it is they who were probably the 'opinion leaders' in their own locales.

Film Weekly letters did not follow the shift in editorial orientation; they stoutly maintained an interest in historical spectacle until 1939. A slightly different pattern obtained for *Picturegoer*. Its editorial policy turned away from historical film earlier than *Film Weekly*'s, and it did not foreground history as an issue with the same intensity. On 5 August 1933, *Picturegoer* printed a key article championing the genre as 'a fine branch of vital screen entertainment' in which 'strict historical accuracy is not the important thing'. But from the beginning *Picturegoer* had stressed the educative aspects of historical film; on 2 September 1933 it printed an article by the historian Sir Charles Oman which argued that 'there would be a popular interest in history films if only history were carefully and faithfully portrayed'. By 7 October 1933 editorial policy had changed; the historical cycle would 'make the long winter evenings longer for film-goers'. A series of articles in 1934 bewailed the costume boom as 'really getting beyond a joke'.[14] By 1935 *Picturegoer* rejected the whole genre. Historical films could express in disguised form emotions which might be censored, but their time was past. The only *Picturegoer* article of the period to defend popular histories was, significantly, by R. J. Minney, on 7 September 1935. Minney had written *Clive of India*, and he went on to mastermind the Gainsborough bodice-rippers of the 1940s. For him,

Until now, men and women who to the average mind were merely something sandwiched between the dates which denote birth and death have been and are now being recalled from the printed tombs in which historians have buried them ... the films, with their magical power of illusion, can build the characters of world figures into something human, and this stirs renewed interest in them.

By 1935, Minney already had an unerring sense of popular taste.

Picturegoer's letters praised British historical films on the patriotic grounds that Britain had 'a history second to none, world renowned authors, beautiful scenery'.[15] The pleasures of history for *Picturegoer* readers were those of empathy; one writer on 14 March 1936 wanted films in which 'the big men of the past really spring to life before our eyes.' On 2 May 1936, one reader cared little for seeming anachronisms: 'Surely the Cagneys and the Thelma Todds have not been solely confined to this era? Surely it is a fallacy that only the twentieth century has tough he-men lovers and wise-cracking gold-digging femininity?' Readers were full of suggestions: Greek and Norse myths (but without 'highbrow phraseology'), the history of Windsor Castle, the Boer War, the Tolpuddle Martyrs, the War of the Roses, were all advanced as topics.[16] This was a different range from that of *Film Weekly* readers. But *Picturegoer* readers shared with them a defensive attitude towards popular historical inaccuracy: 'Political intrigue and Acts of Parliament do not appeal to the general public', according to one writer on 13 March 1937. In the teeth of the experts, some readers praised popular histories for their educative value. Clearly, *Picturegoer* readers were not impressed by *History Teaching Films*. There were a few pro-accuracy letters after 1937, but they were signed by professional teachers or historians and so are unrepresentative of the mass readership.[17]

Film Weekly and *Picturegoer* letters are signs of resistance by the mass audience to the blandishments of respectable gatekeepers of opinion. For other evidence of audience taste, J. P. Mayer's books are useful. His 1946 *Sociology of Film* was based on research done during the war, but many respondents referred to the 1930s and the pleasures of those historical films were stressed. 'History and geography can live, instead of being a succession of dates and rivers and towns', said one female government inspector. An engineer praised earlier historical films because past events were 'brought before us forcefully, vividly, in all their glory'. An old gardener had spent time in the East and valued *The Four Feathers*, because it was 'acted *True* and in the Native Locality'.[18] Many writers claimed that historical films had stimulated their reading. Mayer's 1948 book, *British Cinemas and Their Audiences*, also contained interesting material. In general, respondents most admired the costume elements of 1930s historical films.[19] One woman's response to *King Solomon's Mines* is noteworthy: 'I have a savage exultant feeling, and I want to dance to the beat of native drums. The thud-thud of tom-toms always shakes me to the depths.'[20] It is significant that all the answers foregrounding visual and sensual pleasures in historical film were by women. However, Mayer also printed a woman's letter criticizing *Catherine the Great* as 'the supreme example of twaddle. Anyone who knew the bare facts of Catherine's life and her marriage with Peter must either have blushed or giggled hysterically at such a ridiculous film!'[21] Such views pleased Mayer, who held profoundly elitist views and thought that popular histories were analogous to the circuses of Ancient Rome.

Mass-Observation's investigation of cinema-going in Bolton in 1937 contained some relevant material. Its statistics suggested that historical films came third as overall favourites, and that women favoured them more than men.[22] Women also placed a higher priority on the visual ('seeing beautiful things'), and less priority on realistic representation ('more people like you and I'). *Victoria the Great* was the outstanding favourite with both men and women. Individual letters praising *Victoria* were roughly half male, half female. Both sexes attributed a vital role to historical film in the maintenance of support for the Empire. It is interesting that the most elaborate considerations of the genre were by men. One noted: 'Historical Films or Films of Books by Famous Authors educate the people tremendously. The working classes who are the bulk of your patrons haven't the time to read or delve into Historical Books.'[23] Another wrote: 'There are far too few historical films ... until recently the working class public does not seem to have appreciated this type of film.'[24] In *Mass-Observation at the Movies*, Richards and Sheridan suggest that this material contains much information about the self-image of people in Bolton in 1937. It is predictable that the men in this particular culture had greater confidence. But female silence on the topic in the Bolton material does not mean that the debate was irrelevant to women. Of course, those organising Mass-Observation material had their own views on the function of history, which may well have been at variance with those of the respondents.

The response of the mass audience to historical film in the 1930s is accessible only through a number of filters which may skew the original utterances. None the less, a significant proportion of the audience maintained a robust resistance to official and 'quality' critics' promulgation of accuracy in historical film. The question of differing gender taste is a vexed issue. Only the Bolton material draws clear distinctions. Clearly, Herbert Wilcox's *Victoria the Great* instigated a shift in popular taste. In the event, this was short-lived; as I shall show, audiences during World War II returned with a vengeance to inaccurate spectacle like *Lady Hamilton* and *The Wicked Lady*.

We should now turn to the constitution of middlebrow taste in the 1930s. From 1932, disquiet was expressed by some intellectuals about the public's debased taste for historical spectacle. Hugh Griffith argued that a quality cinema based on verisimilitude was the only corrective.[25] The Royal Empire Society mounted a debate in which speakers insisted that British historical films should reform the perceptions of those 'who were not interested in literature, who did not read history'.[26] Left-wing writers also bewailed the brutalising effect of inaccurate spectacles on the masses.[27] Some socialist intellectuals suggested that historical films should be expressly made to enlighten the masses about their heritage.[28] One definition of historical accuracy in films was, therefore, Marxist; but it did not have major currency in the debate, which was dominated by right-wing attitudes.

In *Cinema Quarterly* in Winter 1933, a sharp exchange between the historical novelist Philip Lindsay and the history teacher Thomas Simms demonstrated the range of middlebrow conservatism. Lindsay suggested that historical films should be more accurate in order to improve the character and behaviour of audiences: 'Instead of lads striving to be Cagneys, they will wish to be d'Artagnans.' But he had been responsible for some of the historical detail in *Henry VIII*, and so he was writing in self-defence. Thomas Simms dismissed Lindsay with a vigorously puritanical polemic: 'Of what importance to us is finesse in love-making – the deceptions of an immoral game of sex played among the dust-smeared gilt of baroque sensibilities?' By 1934, middlebrow opinion on the issue was becoming cohesive. *The Times* argued that producers should not 'mix imaginary characters with real ones', and it printed a range of letters calling for more classical history in film.[29] The London School of Economics mounted a series of debates in the form of mock 'trials'. In one of these, recorded in the *Era* on 23 May 1934, Philip Guedalla, as Prosecuting Council, accused film producers of having 'been responsible for the falsification of the past'. He argued that Basil Dean should be in the 'dock', and claimed to be operating on behalf of the Manchester Watch Committee, Lord Reith, the Historical Association, and Princess Yousoupoff. The event was a light-hearted one; but Guedalla was an influential historian who was to become a powerful figure in the British Council, and the 'trial' is indicative of some strength of feeling in key intellectual coteries.

Inaccuracy continued to be a middlebrow shibboleth throughout 1934. The *Sphere* argued on 17 November 1934 that 'the less educated public will swallow a deal more accuracy.' The *London Mercury* blamed Dumas and Lytton Strachey for the moral crisis in historical film.[30] Even *British Film Reporter*, an up-market journal for workers in the industry, attacked the costume film on 30 June 1934 as 'an obsessive and treacherous master'. Campbell Dixon in the *Daily Telegraph* expressed more liberal views in the mid-1930s. But he was in a minority; middlebrow opinion on the issue was fixed by 1934. Individual writers then began to use historical films as an excuse for a *jeu d'esprit*. Alistair Cooke mocked the 'cardboard castles and kingly wink' of British efforts.[31] Graham Greene excoriated DeMille's *Crusades* because it had 'the air of being made by the Oxford Group', and in a key essay on 'The Middle-Brow Film' he satirised the histories of Korda and Balcon.[32] He led the way for James Agate and other 'quality' journalists to attack the notion of popular history.[33] *The Times* also threw its weight heavily behind this position in 1936. It printed letters on 18 April claiming that cinema falsified history, which caused 'much resentment to the historian and the reasonable layman', and that historical film should 'give the world authentic studies of the Empire's achievements and ideas.'

The intensity of the controversy and the currency of middlebrow notions of accuracy is indicated by the brief debate in the House of Lords in late 1936 on historical film. Viscount Mersey proposed the motion that the government should vet the historical accuracy of films, and should be particularly vigilant about cinematic representations of the Tudor period, which could damage the 'proper understanding' of the young. Mersey was opposed by Lord Moyne, who argued that the quality of historical films could be raised without state intervention. The Marquis of Dufferin took a more liberal view, arguing that 'what matters is not mythical incidents or accuracy, but whether the public get a wrong perspective of past events'. Persuaded by these arguments, Lord Mersey withdrew his motion.[34] It is possible that this debate was covertly prompted by the powerful lobby of the Historical Association; but Mersey would not have acted without the expectation that moderate opinion would support him. It is more likely that the debate was prompted by the groundswell of middlebrow opinion.

It is predictable that there was no radical change in middlebrow opinion after the publication of the Historical Association's *History Teaching Films* in 1937. In a sense, middlebrow opinion could be said to have taken the initiative; the more highbrow polemic of the Historical Association could have been a reactive response. After 1937, middlebrow critics continued a vigorous prosecution of popular historical films.[35] Three collections of essays published after 1937 indicated the solidity and confidence of the middle ground. In *Cinema Survey*, Robert Herring bewailed the vulgarity of spectacle, and Bryher (a woman critic) was offended by historical films: 'Learning is being deflected from its true purpose, if a knowledge that is intended for the exceptional few be applied as a general standard to hundreds of thousands.'[36] In *Footnotes to the Film*, John Betjeman attacked period films with inns 'bulging with beams'.[37] And in *Cinegram Preview*, one writer remarked: 'We have learned at school that a certain person was a scoundrel or a weakling yet in a film he will be glamourised ... there ought to be a law against it.'[38]

By 1937, middlebrow opinion was consistent. Many letter writers to major papers attacked inaccuracy in historical film, and no letters were published expressing an alternative point of view.[39] The key issue was the potential harm to the working class. Even Campbell Dixon changed his opinion; in the *Daily Telegraph* of 16 December 1937, he quoted a letter supposedly from a working-class correspondent in which spectacular historical film was described as 'like smothering every dish in syrup. In time, the appetite for plain wholesome fact, like the appetite for plain wholesome food, is lost.' A case of what we may call 'class ventriloquism' may have been taking place, in which the proletariat was a dummy mouthing its supposed desire for verisimilitude. It was a recurring phenomenon in the period; an Indian critic insisted that the masses really preferred realism in history.[40] A letter to the *Daily Telegraph* on 17 December 1937 insisted that workmen preferred historical films which showed 'what really happened', while only epicene solicitors foolishly spurned realism.

History, control, realism, moral improvement of the masses – it is a familiar paradigm. Middlebrow debates on popular historical spectacle were, perhaps, informed by the work of Leavis and the *Scrutiny* group in the 1930s. Certainly a Leavisite (and Arnoldian) sense of the enobling effects of high culture, and an urgent awareness of the supposed dangers of popular texts, had a wide currency in the film debates of the period. The central ground was captured by middlebrow puritans; and highbrow institutions such as the Historical Association attempted to raise the discussion to a higher level.

5

HIGHBROW INTERVENTIONS

THE HISTORICAL ASSOCIATION AND ITS FRIENDS

The Historical Association was the first national institution to make concerted attempts to reform historical feature film. The Association was organised for teachers of history, and it had a central nexus informing local groups. Those at the centre were eminent figures such as professors; those on the periphery were teachers or local historians. The Association's structure enshrined deeply authoritarian attitudes, which inevitably coloured the texts it produced.

The Association's early publications displayed a mistrust of historical fiction and its picturesque pleasures.[1] In July 1932 the influential Catherine Firth argued against historical film in the Association's journal *History*: 'It cannot but seem an unkind blow that the enemy which is being ousted from the textbooks should appear in a more formidable disguise in the film.' According to another key Association member, Dorothy Dymond, influential members pressed in the early 1930s for a conservative policy on historical films. In a collaboration between Miss Dymond and three other members of the Films Committee it was argued that academic historians should promulgate linear historical representations and the abandonment of fictional elements.[2]

The importance of the Association's ideas in the 1930s may be demonstrated by the high regard in which it was held by the government's regulatory body, the Board of Education. The Board accepted the view that 'real history is an adult study'. It complied with Association requests to include Empire history in syllabuses, and it urged a closer relationship between its own inspectors and the Association.[3] The Association's wartime status was unassailable. A Crown Film Unit project on democracy followed the Association's position in every particular, as did a later film on prehistory. The Ministry of Information thought so highly of a 1941 Association pamphlet that it ordered 120,000 copies to be distributed to the troops.[4] The Ministry insisted that the pamphlet remained under the imprimatur of the Association, which attests to the reliability of its image. The pamphlet's Toryism was broader than that of the Conservative party, and it was doubtless attractive to the MoI because it could not be inconveniently identified with the interests of any one political group. Ministry and Association support for the pamphlet encouraged the BBC in 1942 to seek the advice of its author, and to act on it, in radio treatments of British-Indian relations.[5]

The Association's pronouncements became increasingly confident towards 1945. Clearly, proponents of old-style Toryism felt secure in this niche, and from it they made assaults on the excesses of mass culture. A. L. Rowse noted on behalf of the Association:

64

If there is one thing worse than novelised history, it is history on the films ... the grossly unhistorical legends woven by them around such figures as Gladstone, Parnell and Rhodes cannot be unimportant evils, if truth be an important good.[6]

The Association was a respectable body with an established journal, a solid organisation and a conservative executive. It was under this 'umbrella' that a consistent aesthetic of historical feature film was developed in the 1930s and 1940s. This aesthetic was backed by intellectual status and institutional experience. The Association's strictures on historical film, and the subtlety with which it manipulated the British Film Institute, had the effect of making historical feature film even less respectable to the intelligentsia.

Professor F. J. C. Hearnshaw, Emeritus Professor of History at the University of London, was President of the Association from 1936 to 1938. He was particularly interested in film, and was a skilled polemicist. In a letter to *The Times* on 4 April 1936, he argued that historical film was poised between 'meticulous accuracy' and 'dramatic intensity'. He said that it was handicapped by its need for a story and by the limitations of the audience, and considered it impossible to reform their taste for historical inaccuracy; the only hope lay with educational films, and even they were 'too imaginative, doubtfully accurate, and too colourful'. He insisted on a rigid categorisation of discourses, implying that no one could watch a feature film and expect to learn good history.[7]

Hearnshaw exhibited a distaste for modern Conservatism, and a passionate loyalty to 'the saints and heroes of the past'. The real popular culture of England did not reside, he argued, in republicanism or puritanism but in the 'old sports and peaceful hamlets' of a rural society. Hearnshaw was primarily offended by Socialism because it gave a voice to atheists and sensualists. The only conservative politicians that Hearnshaw deemed worthy to inherit the mantle of Burke were the Younger Pitt, and Disraeli with his 'profound dislike of middle-class mercantilism'.[8] It is surely no accident that biographical films of these two politicians received considerable official support during World War II.

However, the Association's film work had a longer history. It inaugurated its Films Enquiry Committee in 1929, appointing Frances Consitt as its investigator into historical films in schools. The report was financed by the Carnegie Trust, which also funded *The Film in National Life* in 1932. The Films Enquiry Committee was dissolved on the publication of Consitt's report, and the Trust distributed 10,000 free copies of the abstract. Much of the Association's energics in the early 1930s were given to publicising Consitt's *The Value of Films in the Teaching of History*. It urged that her report be adopted as government policy, and it invited all branch members to provide scenarios along the lines recommended by Consitt.[9]

Consitt's book contained far-reaching comments which were ignored by its sponsoring body. Consitt argued that history was a humane study productive of 'loving kindness', to which cinema, with its emphasis on empathy, was particularly adaptable.[10] Consitt's was a mystical conservatism, yet she valued popular memory and argued that the layman's history – Alfred and the cakes, Henry VIII and his wives – was stored unconsciously; the pleasure which popular films produced was due to the shock of recognition from the unconscious.

Naturally, Consitt insisted on visual accuracy. But she also argued that historical feature film was more effective for working-class children, since they had greater visual competence. The Association never referred to Consitt's suggestion that film viewing was a creative act. She had given a voice to junior historians with their preference for 'battles, Miss!'. But this implicitly challenged the control of the professional historian, and so was ignored. Only the most traditional elements of Consitt's work were selected as guiding principles of the Historical Association's Films Committee. This committee was set up in 1934 and immediately began negotiations with the British Film Institute. The dangerous 'falseness' of historical feature films was a major topic at the Association's 1935 Annual Meeting, and a resolution was passed that

> This meeting of the Historical Association is gravely concerned at the effect on children and adults of film purporting to represent historical personages which are being shown in picture palaces, and considers that steps should be taken to assist teachers and others to estimate the accuracy of such films.

There are no extant records of the meetings or membership of the Films Committee; the documents were pulped in the 1950s when the Historical Association moved its archive. The Chairman was Mr G. Hankin, a figure of some adroitness. Hankin was the husband of Mary Field, who from 1934 was a leading film-maker at G-B Instructional; at her behest, the company planned to allow Hankin to direct a film. Hankin was aware of the desirability of acting under disguise. He thought that the Association was the only body with sufficient intellectual status to confer the stamp of respectability. He himself operated on a number of fronts, although his main function was as a chief HMI in history at the Board of Education.[11] Hankin was held in high regard at the Foreign Office, and had access early in the 1930s to Home Office thinking on educational film.[12] He was respected by the BBC, and by the late 1930s was Chairman of the BBC History Programmes Sub-Committee for Schools.[13] Hankin fully deployed his wide-ranging influence to promulgate his own views of historical representation. He termed himself a 'democrat' and believed that historical films should celebrate important freedoms.[14] But he also believed in tailoring texts to suit audiences. He suggested that 'we want to avoid the middle-class point of view' in historical plays so as not to alienate the masses.[15] But the working class were inferior: 'They have a limited background and vocabulary ... they are accustomed to a very simple type of spoken word.' Historical films for them required both 'verisimilitude and local colour'.[16] Hankin expressed rightist views which gradually became more extreme. By 1949 he was suggesting that it was the chief business of historians to 'stem the tide of Bolshevism'.[17]

By 1934, when he was appointed to the chair of the Historical Association's Films Committee, Hankin was the chief link between the Board of Education and the Association. He saw his work for the Association as a means of consolidating the Board's position, and his suggestions to the Association followed the Board's views in every particular.[18] But although Hankin was the

Board's chief HMI in history, it was the Association, not the Board, that he represented at important conferences on film and education; he was even the Association's spokesman on one of the Board's own advisory councils.[19] This seems Machiavellian; but the Board did not wish to make its views on historical film explicit, and preferred instead that Hankin should use the Association and thereby filter down official views through respectable but unofficial channels.

Hankin was extremely critical of the British Film Institute. He insisted in 1935 that Board of Education members should 'get as near the centre as possible' to influence the BFI secretly.[20] He may well have been instrumental in promoting the relationship between the Association and the BFI as a way of keeping the latter under control. He felt that *Sight and Sound* was dangerous, since it gave undue prominence to leftist intellectuals; he attempted to enforce the reorganisation of the *Monthly Film Bulletin* by putting it more firmly under government control. Hankin saw the BFI in its unreformed state as a waste of public money.[21] He wanted the BFI's committees to be vetted by seemingly 'neutral' bodies. The Board of Education was duly gratified when Hankin became Chairman of the BFI's Inspectors panel. The Board was particularly troubled by the BFI's History and Arts Committee, and in 1935 asked Hankin: 'The mixture of Arts and History is curious and rather suggestive of the entertainment film world. Do you think History should have a separate representative?'[22] Clearly Hankin did; a strong Historical Association presence was evident on the committee. The pamphlet it produced (*History Teaching Films*) represented the Board's views as well as the Association's. Hankin energetically promoted this pamphlet; it was 'the best and most scientific enquiry into the value of films for History teaching that has yet appeared'.[23]

Hankin's various roles show that the Historical Association's work on historical film enjoyed considerable government support. It was this which lent such confidence to the Association's pronouncements. In a classic case of power by substitution, it used such organisations as the BFI and G-B Instructional to ensure that its beliefs would have effect.

In the years prior to *History Teaching Films*, the Association made itself the official arbiter on historical films. But it was extremely narrow in the range of advice it was prepared to give. It would not advise on likely profit or aesthetic value; only historical accuracy, or lack of it, could be guaranteed. The Association clearly felt that it was in a monopolistic position.

After the publication of *History Teaching Film*, there was a steady decline in the work of the Association's Films Committee. Hankin had moved on to the BFI's History and Arts Committee, and there were no Films Committee reports for 1938 or 1939. The Association proceeded to further its views on the BFI Education Committee; but this gave insufficient priority to history. Rachel Reid suggested that 'the Association must find some other way of insisting on the production of suitable films'.[24] The BFI was being blamed by the more rigorous historians for the continued production of 'worthless' historical features; they felt that it was recommending and encouraging seditious and educationally unsound films. It is possible that the odium in which the BFI was held by several government departments had seeped through to the Association and made its members uneasy about its partner. In any case, historical accuracy in films was no longer a burning issue after 1945; the BFI had no control over feature film production, and was too flaccid to exert any real pressure.

There was a clear decline in the Association's interest in historical film. The high point of its involvement in the issue was the contribution it made to the 1937 *History Teaching Films* via the BFI's History and Arts Committee. There are no extant records of the workings of this group. Its rationale must be reconstructed from BFI Annual Reports, from a study of its personnel, and from analysis of its publications. The History and Arts Committee was chaired by Sir Charles Petrie, and comprised Hankin, F. Wilkinson, Mary Field, Arthur Bryant and Rachel Reid. The group recommended that a historian, a teacher and a 'technician' should jointly ratify feature and educational histories. After *History Teaching Films*, the committee had little success with its projects. And by 1941 it was no longer on the list of BFI committees.

Sir Charles Petrie, the Chairman of the History and Arts Committee for the crucial years of 1934–9, was an interesting figure. He was engaged in diplomacy and in 'quality' right-wing journals such as *The English Review*. He was an important forces lecturer during the war, and received honorary degrees. Petrie defined 'Englishness' as the ability to throw a civilising gloss on to the tastelessness of capitalism. He termed himself 'a Tory, not a Conservative', and, like Hearnshaw, his favourite politicians were Disraeli and Pitt. The business supporters of the Conservative Party were anathema to Petrie, who thought they lacked style. But he reserved his most bitter invective for the middle classes, since they represented 'the unpleasant side of the English Nature, an active jealousy of the happiness of others'. As a staunch anti-socialist, he thought the MoI was 'hand in glove with the communists'.[25]

The Board of Education, as I have indicated, was worried about the History and Arts Committee. The Educational Panel expressed satisfaction that Petrie had the public status necessary for the chairmanship.[26] Someone like Hankin could work 'under cover', whereas a more flamboyant figure like Petrie could express different class values. Petrie's was a Burkean conservatism, defensive of the values of the older landed interest. Indeed he attempted to be a spokesman for that fraction. He mourned that, at the end of World War II, 'rarely in history has a governing class at the end abdicated its position so quickly or so readily'.[27] Those supporting that interest had limited access to media expression by the mid-1930s; proponents of this type of conservatism had perforce to take cover where they could, and snatch the opportunities offered by seemingly apolitical institutions. It is of great significance that this class interest should have become visible in the area of history and its dissemination.

Petrie's cultural politics were already formed before he came to chair the History and Arts Committee. His views on historical film were echoed in *History Teaching Films*; he was clearly a persuasive chairman. In 1935, Petrie had attacked historical novels and popular historical films; he argued that studios should submit themselves to academic vetting, so that history should not appear as a series of sensational episodes but as a painful process. He suggested a return to silent films in order to put history more firmly within the teacher's authority. Orthodox opinion could thus be more firmly enforced.[28]

For Petrie, the chief problem with film was its mass audience; it was intellectually dull, and could not see that *Battleship Potemkin* was actually socialist propaganda. Since the British audience was incapable of reading film thus, it should be prevented from viewing such dangerous texts at all.

The Chairman of the History and Arts Committee, therefore, was culturally elitist. I have already described the ideas and influence of G. T. Hankin and Frances Consitt. Another member of the Committee, F. Wilkinson, had already argued for control by academic historians over film production, and he suggested that historical film offered an ideal means of separating mental from manual labour.[29] He did not, therefore, dissent from the views of Consitt and Petrie. Nor did Mary Field, who was hardly likely to offer strong public opposition to her husband, G. T. Hankin. At the time of her appointment to the History and Arts Committee, she was on the Board of G-B Instructional. Field insisted that the masses cared little for history, and argued that, as a palliative to the cinema's hypnotic effect, feature films should be consciously aimed at the most intelligent members of the audience.[30]

Another member of the group, Rachel Reid, had been on many Historical Association committees, particularly those concerned with film. She too was a prestigious figure; she was subsequently elected Honorary Vice-President of the Association, and became Director of Historical Studies at Girton. But Reid's version of history was as partial as Petrie's; she wished schools to concentrate on 'the revival of learning and the birth of individualism'.[31] Reid's views were extreme even by the standards of the Historical Association; she finally became notorious for her obsessive views, and was disowned by an Association spokesman in 1946 for her 'usual perhaps too narrow view of historical accuracy'.[32]

The other historian on the Committee was Arthur Bryant, who offered a different perspective; he was a popular rather than an academic historian. He had equated Englishness with 'the sweet and lovely breath of conservatism', and celebrated 'the old cottage folk of England' whose sturdy yeomanry repulsed reform.[33] Like other Association writers, Bryant's favourite figure was Disraeli. But what marked Bryant off from the others was the broader role he permitted to fiction. He insisted that accounts of the past were lamentably narrow if they failed to take account of such writers as Keats, Traherne or Scott.[34] Bryant probably tempered the austerity of the other members by his attention to the 'readability' of historical texts.

The body which produced *History Teaching Films* had a remarkable homogeneity of opinion. The Toryism held in common was quite different from that of Conservative Central Office. It was a far right, retrospective belief which had successfully sought an appropriate niche for itself. There was a general paucity of outlets for such theories about elites and representation; and the combined History and Arts Committee of the BFI and the Historical Association provided a place of refuge. It is also certain that official voices spoke through the Committee, and that it was unwittingly acting at the behest of a government department.

History Teaching Films had two aims. Firstly, it was defensive, attempting to refurbish the intellectual forces of Toryism; secondly, it was offensive, attempting to reform public opinion on a matter of cultural politics. It was presented to the Governing Body of the BFI in 1937. The main thrust of its argument owed much to Consitt's earlier text, but it concealed some of her radicalism. Consitt had rejected the feature film as an adjunct to teaching; *History Teaching Films* also insisted that all the trappings of fiction – actors, plot, settings – be abandoned in educational histories, since there were no actors 'with the appropriate humility' for historical personages. Indeed, such were the ills ensuing from films such as *The Private Life of Henry VIII*, it suggested, teaching films should eschew well-known personages altogether. Thus the pamphlet's suggestion that historical films should deal with the life of the people instead of their leaders was less progressive than it appeared.

History Teaching Films preferred plain documentary style. Lavishness encouraged the audience into 'an excessive admiration for the inessential and trivial'. For Petrie's committee, the 'inessential' element was pleasure, whether gastronomic, sartorial or sexual. The report constantly shifted its ground from feature to classroom film, but insisted throughout that educational film must present a moral improvement on features if cultural anarchy were not to prevail. But here an interesting paradox emerged. *History Teaching Films* rejected the procedures of fictional narrative; but by its insistence that stylised selection and broad coverage be sacrificed, the possibility that films could present a chain of causes was also lost. Hence the texts which would be produced could not carry the desired historical interpretation. The report gave a caricatured account of the split between profit and culture. The commercial director, in thrall to the box office, produced 'a sin against truth'; the educational director on the other hand had 'ideas which he will not sacrifice to popularity'. In between these two extremes, the Committee proposed itself as a gate-keeper intervening at two stages: pre-production, to avoid falsification in the script, and post-production, to give a ratified seal of quality.

Of course, the Committee's view of history was not neutral. It wanted films about manorial organisation rather than about industrial relations. It wanted a film about Canterbury, framed by captions from Chaucer and illustrating the probity of mediaeval life. The fact that Powell and Pressburger went on to make such a film in 1944 is an index of the enduring fertility of such ideas. The mediaeval period was a suggestive one for artists as varied as Hurd, Keats and Morris, since it can carry a range of political meanings. But *History Teaching Films* saw the Middle Ages as the apogee of craftsmanship (an interesting comparison may be made with the radicalism of Morris) and it praised the feudal system underpinning such practices. *History Teaching Films* set its face against the practices of contemporary social historians, and suggested that left-wing bias had ensured that 'we know of Wat Tyler the rebel, but we know less of Wat Tyler in his trade, the house he lived in, the food he ate, the clothes he wore'.[35] This is, of course, a misleading version of the state of mediaeval scholarship at the time.

When publicising the pamphlet, Petrie emphasised feature film. He suggested that historical features were a major resource of cultural value, which was too important to be left to the studios. In a letter to *The Times* on 16 December 1936, he argued that pressure groups should 'overcome evil with good' by 'creating popular support' for accurate historical films rather than for 'box-office travesties'.

History Teaching Films was the product of a number of intellectual crosscurrents. The members of the History and Arts Committee, and those who invisibly advised them, were making a subtle attempt to redirect public opinion in the area of history. But the response of the trade papers was cool. Most producers, suggested *Today's Cinema* on 17 December 1936, 'just won't take advice or dictation from the outside world'. Hostile responses came from papers on the radical or intellectual Left.[36] *The Freethinker* highlighted the partisan nature of the tradition to which the pamphlet belonged: 'Who in authority ... wants the truth about Drake and Hawkins, those Elizabethan heroes, salutary though it would undoubtedly be? ... Distortions and lies have always been elements of British history as taught in the schools.'[37] Irish writers also recognised the selective nature of 'official' history, and Scottish critics took a jaundiced view, objecting to the authoritarian celebration of a metropolitan culture.[38] But the sharpest criticism of *History Teaching Films* came from one 'John Gilpin', whose 'Shakespearean Blood and Thunder' was printed in the northern newspapers. It was a blistering account: 'It seems as though we shall have to make a choice between Shakespeare and the British Film Institute, and I for one feel inclined to plump for Shakespeare.' Ben Jonson's turgid *Sejanus* was wittily instanced as the type of text which the History and Arts Committee would promulgate.[39]

Clearly, then, hostile responses to *History Teaching Films* came from two sources: firstly, from those marginal groups most alert to the authoritarianism of 'official' history, and secondly, from those areas which had most to lose from a metropolitan cultural machine. Favourable reports came from Conservative papers and educational journals.[40] None of the positive reviews argued out the complexities of the case. *History Teaching Films* endorsed current theories of cultural elitism but it did not redefine them. The opposition to the pamphlet by groups marginal to dominant cultural forms is, paradoxically, an index of its ideological strength.

History Teaching Films did have some impact on the production of educational films: Mary Field made films at G-B Instructional which were fully consonant with the report. But as I have shown, Field had direct access to Board of Education thinking through her husband; the head of the company, H. Bruce Woolfe, clearly valued government input and argued that educational films should be kept free from 'propaganda', by which he meant vested interests outside state bodies.[41] But by 1947, Bruce Woolfe was disappointed with the History and Arts Committee; following their advice, G-B Instructional had used diagrams and cartoons, but the resulting films were lacklustre and unprofitable.[42]

Under the pressures of war, G-B Instructional reissued feature films such as *The Iron Duke* for educational distribution. Such procedures had been vetoed by the Historical Association, but Gaumont-British was nearing the end of its involvement with them by the mid-1940s. There are only two available viewing copies of historical films produced by G-B Instructional, which is too small a sample on which to base a firm judgment; but *Mediaeval Village* (1936) and *The Development of the English Town* (1942) display identical attitudes. The former describes a village in which the allocation of land has remained unchanged since 1630. The film praises the farmers for 'clinging stubbornly to methods from before Robin Hood'. Although 'great men' had declined, rural crafts remained unscathed. The advisers for the film, H. Beales and R. S. Lambert, were interesting. Beales was a well-known educationalist and Lambert was the editor of the *Listener*, who detested the venal films of the free market.[43] In *Mediaeval Village*, visual pleasure is nil. This also holds good for *The Development of the English Town*: all information is carried by a voice-over, which insists on the evils of progress, and no argument is developed about historical causality. The British Council, the Ministry of Works and the Foreign Office put some pressure on Field to produce a less pessimistic film, but to no effect.[44]

The History and Arts Committee, then, had a clear influence on Gaumont-British Instructional; moreover, its ideas were given considerable space in BFI publications from 1934 to 1942. Reviews in the *Monthly Film Bulletin* bore the Committee's imprimatur of 'accuracy'. Historical films with radical politics were rejected. Predictably, authenticity was not neutrally defined. *The Iron Duke* was praised because it embodied a high Tory interpretation of history; *The Scarlet Pimpernel* was acceptable in its portrayal of the real moral probity of the aristocracy. The Committee was forced to make aesthetic sacrifices in the cause of accuracy. The salacious *Nell Gwyn* was perforce praised because of its documentary reliance on Pepys' diaries, while *Rembrandt* was summarily dismissed for its overtly artistic qualities.

In its work for the *Monthly Film Bulletin*, the Committee's major criterion was homogeneity of tone and high seriousness. Naturally, sexual material reduced a film's 'seriousness', and Gainsborough costume melodramas were summarily dismissed. The Committee preferred films about rural societies, especially if they celebrated the landed interest. Overtly patriotic films such as *Victoria the Great* were automatically praised. But such patriotism had a political cost. Only those films which displayed the working class as a brutal minority were termed 'plausible' by the Committee, a conservatism that led it to praise a British Council film for 'ambiguity' but to castigate the Workers' Film Association for the same quality.[45]

In the *Monthly Film Bulletin*, then, the History and Arts Committee expressed an extreme purism. *The History of the Wheel* was rejected for showing actors dressed as Stone Age people, while *The Beginnings of History* was praised for its integrity in showing an empty screen; if nothing could be absolutely established about a period, then it was clearly best to show nothing at all. But *Sight and Sound* was also used by the Committee as a more extended platform for its arguments. One article stressed that historical films should cease to be 'a self-conscious posing in fancy dress'; another blamed female audiences for their lack of historical accuracy.[46] Space was provided for peevish scholasticism: 'Why was the execution of Queen Anne furnished with a German two-handed fighting sword of 1500 and not the proper headsman's weapon?'[47] During the war, Rachel Reid contributed three important articles to *Sight and Sound*, as a member of the History and Arts Committee. In autumn 1941 she reviewed *Lady Hamilton*, whose chief offence was its celebration of female pleasure. The real Lady Hamilton was 'vain and shallow, self-centred and self-seeking, illiterate, common and quite amoral'. Reid extended her argument in the summer 1942 issue, when she attacked commercial cinema because it presented history 'tricked out with sentimentalities, and packed with anachronisms'. And in autumn 1942, she recommended *The Young Mr Pitt* since it was a factual text devoid of pleasure and was 'excellent propaganda, stressing ... the necessity of giving all for the country to which we owe all that we have and are.' The case can rarely have been put with such clarity: that history should be tamed until it was the tool of the dominant class, that the audience should be deprived of those visual pleasures in which they were most competent, and that scripts should enforce the production of a past which was turgid and painful.

The collaboration between the Historical Association and the British Film Institute gave rise to a theory of historical representation which was of unparalleled narrowness. It had hardly any precedent in the educational field. Before the publication of *History Teaching Films*, very few teachers or professional bodies were taking a comparable line. A range of books had been published in 1935 on film and education which were much less pessimistic about popular historical film.[48] Prior to *History Teaching Films*, educational journals also expressed quite liberal views on historical spectacle.[49] And institutions took a softer line on accuracy in the pre-1937 period. The BBC was also not rigorous on the issue of history and education. Rhoda Power, chief scriptwriter for children's historical programmes from 1935 to 1945, held that children were better taught by excitement than by realism. Her letters to the BBC insisted on the power of legend and myth, and her completed plays had a mixed texture, with music, crowds and multiple narrators. She viewed excessive accuracy as pusillanimous.[50] But Power's work fitted in to a coherent BBC policy; historical plays for adult audiences were predicated on entertainment qualities.[51] The BBC remained unimpressed by *History Teaching Films*; during the war it criticised such narrowness, arguing that 'reality' should be transformed through narrative pleasure.[52] The audience's need for 'brisk and vigorous action' rather than meticulous accuracy was monitored by careful research. And until 1949 the BBC was arguing that 'our historical programmes are all in a dramatic form. An element of interpretation is of course implicit in the selection of material.'[53] Clearly the BFI/Historical Association arguments could not convince the BBC, which held more experimental views. In wartime historical features for radio, the Association view was rebuffed; writers were urged to write historical programmes in 'a vivid popular style which would make them attractive to a majority audience', and subjects were chosen that celebrated popular culture.[54]

Prior to *History Teaching Films*, then, very few institutions were taking a line which could have influenced the Historical Association or the BFI. *History Teaching Films* was a major innovation, yet its progenitors were remarkably isolated in the intellectual community. The BBC, engaged with aural historical representations for mass consumption, rejected the narrowness of the pamphlet. But because of the institutional status of the Historical Association, and because government bodies acted 'in disguise' on the History and Arts Committee, *History Teaching Films* had an extraordinary ideological strength. However, it was deleteriously affected by the fact that the BFI was an immature and culturally insecure body which sheltered beneath the greater experience and intellectual coherence of the Historical Association.

The British Film Institute was set up as a quasi-autonomous body with government funding, in order to enhance the status of film. At the outset it made the educational potential of film a priority and it wanted to issue 'vouchers of approval' of a film's value and historical accuracy.[55] The connection with the Historical Association, which was inaugurated in 1934, was an attempt to strengthen its position. For the BFI, 'quality' was ineluctably bound up with high culture, and it compiled a list of recommended historical films, divided according to rigid gender patterns.[56] A particularly conservative interpretation of British society was enshrined within the Institute's praise for films like *West Riding* and *Owd Bob*. In the late 1930s it attempted to found a cinematic archive of old rural customs.[57] It did not volunteer to save records of co-operative crafts; only the individualistic and entrepreneurial were held to be worth preserving. Throughout the 1930s the BFI attempted to operate as the Establishment voice of educational film; but it was, in fact, held in deep contempt by a number of government bodies.

The energy fuelling the BFI's activities during the late 1930s must be attributed to Oliver Bell, who was appointed as General Manager in 1936 and subsequently became Director until he left in 1949. Bell was General Secretary to the Magistrates' Association, had taught history at university level, and was rumoured to have been drafted in from Conservative Central Office. Bell certainly had a High Tory interpretation of the relationship between history and culture. Since, he argued, audiences were only capable of reading historical films on a literal level, powerful gatekeepers were necessary for this portal of the national heritage.[58] Bell wanted the BFI to advise those in intellectual power, but he underestimated the extent to which such members of the clerisy insist on having their own way. Bell thought the BFI could function as an intermediary: 'Like our offices in Tottenham Court Road, we are a half-way house between busy Wardour Street on one side, and the ascetic calm of the British Museum on the other.'[59]

Right from its inception, the BFI attracted a degree of hostility. An important public opponent was Walter Ashley, a formidable liberal figure who was acute enough to see that the BFI's attempt to 'clarify' historical films entailed an undue collusion with state power.[60] More crucially, however, government departments covertly expressed hostility towards the Institute. It was clearly the Historical Association, with the good offices of G. T. Hankin, that was the enabling force which permitted the Institute to play a public role. As early as 1934, the Treasury did not consider the Institute a suitable body to manage funds. The Home Office wished to prevent the Institute from poaching its own preserves. The Board of Trade advised Buckingham Palace in 1935 not to favour the Institute with any Royal patronage: 'We doubt whether the Institute is yet ripe for the honour of the attendance of the Prince at their annual dinner this year.' The Privy Council met unofficially in 1936 to discuss the BFI's inadequacies, and it thought that Bell was 'not the right type.'[61]

But it was the Board of Education that was most critical of the BFI, considering it intellectually 'indeterminate' and insisting that 'the separate panels will do the more effective work'.[62] The Board of Education (on which, we should remember, G. T. Hankin was the chief History HMI) insisted that the Institute's reliability was vitiated by its close relationship with G-B Instructional, and asked its members to keep a watching brief on the BFI that was 'definite even if not direct'.[63] The Board so mistrusted the Institute's judgment that it made separate researches into the accuracy of educational films.[64] The Board did have joint conferences with the BFI, and gave limited public support to BFI pronouncements. But the BFI's Education and History and Arts Committees were the only ones the Board thought 'worth bothering with'.[65] It disliked the Institute's visible bias because it thought that class interests in the teaching of history should be concealed, and it dismissed the BFI as a sort of minority pressure group.[66]

During the 1930s, then, the BFI was disliked by important government departments, and this impeded the dissemination of its ideas. However, during the exigencies of wartime the Ministry of Information was prepared to use the despised Institute for its own convenience. In order to facilitate the certification of education films for the USA (and in order to conceal their propaganda intention), the MoI suggested that the British Embassy liaise with the BFI alone. It was to be a 'deodorising agency', in the words of the Ministry, and this was possible because the Institute was not an arm of the government.[67]

The wartime reputation of the BFI was irreparably damaged by its loutish behaviour towards the British Council. Bell attended Council films uninvited, and brought companions hostile to Council film policy.[68] He enraged the Council by publishing critical opinions of its films, which doubtless prompted its refusal of the BFI's distribution offers.[69] The nadir of relations between the two bodies was reached over the issue of historical accuracy. Rachel Reid mounted a ferocious attack on the Council's film *Market Town*, insisting that it was liable to produce 'a loss of faith in the film as a record of truth.' Bell attempted to smooth matters over by privately discrediting her. Neville Kearney, Head of the Council's films section, noted that Reid's outburst 'was scarcely calculated to encourage the Council to continue with the experimental films that it had agreed to undertake, largely at the insistence of the BFI.' Kearney then snubbed the BFI by requesting the Board of Education to vet its films instead.[70] Clearly the ill odour in which the Institute was now held meant that even Historical Association 'accuracy' was now irredeemably tainted. The Council continued to persecute the BFI. It refused to sanction the preservation of films by Mary Field because they were particularly recommended by Bell, and it campaigned against the BFI's taste: 'They have excluded all the good films, and listed all the duds.'[71] The Council then excluded the Institute from its committees, and effectively outmanoeuvred it.

As the war progressed, then, the BFI became increasingly insecure. It had an acrimonious relationship with the British Council and was regarded with disfavour by the Board of Education. This meant that its activities on historical film (an issue dear to the heart of the hapless Bell) were doomed to failure. Increasingly, too, the MoI disapproved of the BFI's ideas. Bell had a simplistic view of 'John Citizen' – 'It is quite easy to give him a dose of moral tonic.'[72] But the theory of propaganda at the MoI was much more sophisticated. Bell insisted that the MoI should take overtly critical positions on American representations of British history.[73] The Ministry, however, preferred covert manipulation, and did not scorn to deploy popular historical features for its own ends. As early as 1940, Ministry personnel expressed the utmost contempt for Bell, whose suggestions were 'ponderous ... inept ... obvious ... platitudinous'.[74] Duff Cooper's 1941 letter to Bell displayed considerable rancour. In a clear attempt to inspire alarm, Cooper (then Minister of Information) noted that *Sight and Sound* had been disloyal: 'It is doubtful whether this publication, in its present form, serves any useful purpose.'[75]

Throughout the war, Bell continued to commit the BFI to impossibly grandiose schemes of centralisation. The Institute wanted historical films in which British errors were rendered invisible; but the MoI instead encouraged films which contained seemingly open audience options. The Institute wanted a series of historical films to be made by the Ministry on 'the exploits of great men of the past'; this was loudly ignored. Bell proposed a film about the history of the steam engine; this was eviscerated piecemeal by the Ministry's Arthur Elton.[76]

With the 1945 Labour victory, the BFI's attempt to be the authoritative body on historical and educational film was a lost cause. The new Ministry of Education recalled the old scandals – the Institute was 'much too closely allied to Mr Rank's organisation' – and Labour personnel did not see it as 'a body that would give a lively direction to the new developments we are seeking'. In 1946, the Treasury accepted Ministry of Education reservations about the Institute, and it too saw the History and Geography Committees as 'the only ones of any use'.[77]

In a 1946 Treasury meeting on the future of the BFI, the Privy Council, doubtless acting on advice from the Ministries of Information and Education, suggested that the Institute's educational work be severely curtailed. Since the BFI had not won the confidence of government departments, a new official body was proposed which would pronounce on issues of film and education. Instead of making history a paramount issue, as the BFI had done, the new body would encourage the production of films on 'current social behaviour'. The Home Office now took a publicly hostile view of the Institute.[78] This was doubtless a deciding factor in the 1948 recommendations of the Lord President's Committee, which insisted that the BFI should no longer certificate educational films.[79] The new government body was the EFVA (Educational Foundation for Visual Arts) and was intended to improve on the BFI's performance. The EFVA gave far less prominence to the issue of historical film than the BFI had done.[80] It also kept the old animosities alive; in 1948 it asked the Chancellor to undo the harm the BFI had caused, and it was still calling attention to the 'delicate' position of G-B Instructional.

The Historical Association was a confident, culturally secure body in whom the Board of Education and the Ministry of Information had confidence. Its polemic on films, elitist though it was, gained a public platform because of its institutional status and because its leaders represented an older Tory parish of belief which still had currency. *History Teaching Films* expressed views on historical films which were agreeable to the government, largely through the good offices of Hankin. The Historical Association exerted its power through a form of disguise and substitution which, in the end, had a very high cost. It chose to use the British Film Institute as the enabling agency for its views; but this organisation was less culturally secure, and it manifested a type of cultural conservatism which was too brash for a government that preferred more Machiavellian cultural politics. The strength and spread of Association influence through *History Teaching Films* was severely limited by its association with the BFI; an old-style Toryism was vitiated when it offered shelter to a more shrill entrepreneur in the field of culture. The BFI was outmanoeuvred by a variety of government departments, and the priority which it gave to historical accuracy was, after 1945, simply a bit of the wreckage. But the Historical Association's influence in the field of film was also part of the shipwreck.

6

OFFICIAL HISTORIES IN THE WAR YEARS

Government attempts to influence historical feature film increased in urgency and intensity during World War II. A deep intellectual rift occurred between the Foreign Office and Films Division of the Ministry of Information; the usefulness of history for propaganda purposes in film was an issue on which much acrimony was expended. The Foreign Office maintained a continuity with its earlier historical theories, and these policies were developed through the British Council. Both the FO and the Council objected to the utilitarian attitudes towards history enshrined within MoI directives.

In 1939, the Ministry of Information stressed the usefulness of a historical perspective in its general approach. It encouraged the BBC to increase the proportion of historical material in its series of radio plays *Great Occasions*, and verbatim speeches from Disraeli and Pitt were accordingly inserted into the scripts.[1] MoI personnel were attracted by the findings of the International Propaganda and Broadcasting Enquiry, which argued that propaganda bodies should 'in a stratified society, persuade the dominant group', and should note that 'trappings and pageantry inherited from the past form valuable propaganda for stability.'[2] The Ministry tempered this conservatism by suggesting that historical texts should also stress the long progress towards democracy. Since this was to be a 'people's war', the working class were the main target of propaganda.

MoI posters in 1939 favoured historical elements but deployed them clumsily. A long-bowman from the Hundred Years War was chosen for one design because 'the archers, who provided the mainstay of the English Army, were drawn from the lower classes. The dress of the archer should make this point clear.'[3] Historical posters from World War I were redeployed. Small cards quoting encouraging words by Queen Victoria were distributed.[4]

Clearly the Films Division needed a less lacklustre approach than this, but it was hampered by the Ministry's stubborn refusal to deploy existing propaganda expertise. The British Psychological Association provided the Ministry with a register of appropriate personnel, some of whom could have been informative on the uses of history, but this was ignored. Professor F. Bartlett was eminent in the propaganda field and his work took account of class-specific discourses, symbolism, subliminal messages and the sporadic nature of emotion, but the MoI rebuffed him savagely.[5] Instead, it favoured the ideas of Dr Edward Glover, largely because he dismissed 'the more morbid aspects of the science of psychoanalysis'. Glover's views on propaganda were mechanistic; he insisted that subjective elements in the audience were subordinate to 'real' empirical ones, and this approach effectively removed gender as an item worthy of attention.[6] By favouring Glover's methods, the Ministry effectively banished subjectivity, gender and the tools of psychoanalysis from its repertoire. This impoverished its resources, for the uses of history and elsewhere.

So the Films Division was working under broad Ministry directives which assumed that gender or class-specific languages were unimportant; and it was convinced that the population should be roused by methods precluding attention to subjective desires. In the early stages of the war, the Films Division's lack of nuance was remarkable. Notions of 'Englishness' and 'the common man' were simplistically conceived.[7] Films which concentrated on spiritual or intellectual issues were rudely dismissed.[8] Straightforward past/present parallels were encouraged. Of course, the MoI had its own preferences and adjusted its patronage accordingly. The Ministry facilitated the re-release of historical documentaries such as *Mediaeval Village* because they represented 'what we are fighting for'.[9] Historical feature films from the 1930s which showed 'the heroic achievements of the British past' were given subsidies to induce cinemas to show them again at a low charge.[10]

During his brief term of office as head of the Films Division, Kenneth Clark promoted films 'illustrating various liberties of the British subject' and their histories.[11] He was implementing the Policy Committee's paper, in which it was argued that films glorifying 'histories of national heroes' should be promulgated by the MoI. This had suggested that British society 'should be treated historically. It might be possible to do a great film on the institution of British liberty and its repercussions in the world.'[12] History was thus blandly presented as an unambiguous lesson to the present about the superiority of British cultural forms.

During 1940, the Films Division made a number of spirited forays to protect its own narrow definitions of history. Not only did it trounce the BFI and the hapless Oliver Bell; it also mounted a series of louche attacks on the film trade. Clark was unperturbed by finer ethical points: 'We should first endeavour to get power and then the question might arise of our own arrangement.'[13] The trade's protestations of patriotism were met with a jaundiced eye by the MoI, as 'little more than the timely use of an unusual opportunity of getting something for nothing'.[14] There was considerable opposition to government attitudes from producers and critics; but in 1940 the Films Division cared little for anyone else's views on matters of history or national culture. Jack Beddington was Head of the Films Division from May 1940, and he consolidated his team by installing writer Dallas Bower in a post of intellectual control, as leader of creative planning. In a classic case of the separation of intellectual from administrative labour, Colonel Bromhead was given charge of budgets and schedules because he was old enough 'to have known every member of it [the film trade] since they first entered his office as page-boys'.[15] Thus the very hierarchy of the Films Division was a calculated assault on those commercial producers who had any claims on popular taste or memory.

Clarification of the MoI's early position on history may be gained from an analysis of Arthur Elton's riposte to Oliver Bell. The latter had proposed a scenario on the invention of the steam engine. Elton, as a historian, insisted that the project lacked 'background', and he inserted the following patriotic interpretation:

> Owing to the explorers of the sixteenth and seventeenth centuries, the standard of life began to rise. People were demanding more and more commodities and ornaments. Eighteenth-century prosperity produced a feeling of security ... [but] we are not blinded by temporary fashions as are the Germans, for example, who wanted to scrap everything the moment somebody discovered something new.[16]

This view of cultural innovation was evident in all Ministry pronouncements on history in the early years of the war.

Throughout 1940 and early 1941 history was a priority for the Films Division and for the Ministry as a whole. In its dealings with the BBC, the MoI urged that 'British history is full of stirring speeches on the subject of individual freedoms and more or less dramatic struggles for the freedom of speech'.[17] It encouraged BBC playwright Rhoda Power to use stories like Alfred and the cakes because this was the best way 'to organise cultural and educational propaganda to neutral countries'.[18] And it instilled into the educational sections of the BBC the desirability of a more nationalistic curricular history.[19] The BBC's entertainment plays also bore the signs of detailed MoI intervention. *Napoleon Couldn't Do It* in early 1941 suggested that 'It might be the story of contemporary events ... history repeats itself, that is all. The same factors which overthrew the dictators of 100 years ago will inevitably bring about the destruction of his modern but infinitely less imposing imitators.' An internal BBC memo noted that the project was 'very acceptable to the Ministry', and the MoI argued that the opinion 'here' was that the public needed to be persuaded that 'Napoleon could not do it, so Hitler won't be able to.'[20]

Of course, the Ministry had its favourite historical characters, who were most useful for its propaganda purposes. Rhodes was one, Disraeli was another. When the BBC mounted a series called *Great Commoners*, the MoI only displayed interest in the Disraeli programme, and urged that John Gielgud should play the part. The final script, approved by the MoI, showed marked similarities to Thorold Dickinson's film *The Prime Minister*.[21]

The MoI, then, placed quite a high priority on history until mid-1941. After that, its stance shifted; it increasingly focused on American audiences, assuming that history could usefully promote British ideas and goods. The role of history was narrowed down to teaching the lesson that 'in human history Britain has the special contribution of fair play.'[22] The change may be attributed to two factors. Firstly, the MoI was smarting from rebukes from the Foreign Office that its film efforts left the American public unmoved; a key American journal found MoI films 'too parochial, or too poorly produced, or both, for American audiences ... and acted in the manner of amateur theatricals.'[23] Secondly, Brendan Bracken, who had taken over as Minister of Information from June 1941, had been very closely allied to Churchill's interests, but his Machiavellianism did not, by all accounts, extend to intellectual matters; he rarely showed subtlety in propaganda issues.

Certainly, some residual interest in the past was evident after 1941. In 1942, Dallas Bower pushed the BBC to produce a programme on Christopher

79

Columbus, and the BBC was still gamely following MoI precepts on Queen Victoria.[24] But the trade papers, at least, were well aware of growing MoI apathy on historical matters. *Kinematograph Weekly* noted on 30 July 1942 that the Ministry now only wanted films 'which were not nostalgic for the old ways and old days ... but realistic films of everyday life'. By 1943, MoI policy papers did not present history as an issue at all. Historical films which were too jingoistic were an embarrassment, since 'we may be the benefactors of the human race, but to rub it in can easily cause irritation.'[25] By 1945, Beddington was actively expressing hostility towards the use of historical films; in the delicate post-war world they 'might give rise to ill-will between nations by a tendentious or biassed representation of the facts.'[26] Indeed, in spite of the machinations of the BFI, Beddington succeeded in removing the word 'history' from the film proposals for UNESCO. Instead, only films 'of a scientific or cultural orientation' were recommended. For MoI purposes, history was dead.

There were, however, a few historical documentaries backed by the Ministry. The 1943 *Guy Fawkes* made rather clumsy parallels: 'Methinks 'tis a crime most horribly wanton to destroy so much goodly fuel.' Lest any dunderheads missed the point, 'Be A Good Guy: Don't Waste Fuel' was flashed on the screen. *Houses in History* (1944) praised the bourgeoisie as 'the class which displaced the old fighting nobility', and warned that people's love of the antique made them vulnerable. *The Beginnings of History* was started during the war but only completed in early 1946.[27] It appeared as respectable as possible by eschewing actors, music and visual pleasure; the only mobile inhabitants of the Neolithic village were 'a few attractive goats'. These were purist views of historical representation, and they were echoed in the memos concerning the MoI's proposed film on the history of democracy. In the 1944 draft, history was represented as the site of remorseless oppression which could only be alleviated by a meritocracy: 'There was a time ... when the dictatorial powers we have voluntarily and temporarily given to the Home Secretary under regulation 18b) were involuntarily and permanently invested in the small ruling class.' Gradually the drafts became less historical. Novelist John Mortimer was instructed to write a new script which would 'leave history and political science in the background'.[28] There was thus a clear consonance between MoI theories of history and the few historical documentaries it sponsored.

A narrative of official views on historical film would be incomplete without reference to the wartime work of the Foreign Office and the British Council. The Foreign Office had a catholic and permissive view of the uses of history. It influenced commercial production covertly, succoured its favourites, and had a marked disinclination for showing its hand. In all these aspects, the FO was opposed to the style of the MoI, which was puritanical and less discreet. Bad relations between the two bodies began in September 1939, when Lord Lothian, Britain's Ambassador in Washington, castigated MoI film efforts to influence American audiences. Lothian was liberal-minded and cultured.[29] He complained to the Foreign Office that the MoI was puritanical and instrumentalist in its propaganda efforts; he particularly disliked its 'condensation and presentation of the story of England into narrow limits'.[30] Lord Vansittart, who had been crucial in raising the FO's profile on historical film in the 1930s, was now its permanent head; and he responded to Lothian's initiative by insisting that the MoI was incapable of producing films that could 'get at the feelings'. What was most needed was a 'big film', and Korda, he argued, was the most appropriate man for the job.[31] It seems very likely that *Lady Hamilton* was this 'big film', and that Vansittart encouraged Lothian to facilitate the film in America. Lothian certainly emphasised the potency of British history for Americans, 'because Britain, owing to ancestral tombs, Magna Carta, the Bill of Rights, Shakespeare and Milton and so on, is able to exercise a profound influence over [American] feelings.'[32]

The FO kept a nervous eye on the proceedings of the America First Committee, fearful that British propaganda efforts would be blown. FO representatives in America were fully apprised of the politics of historical representation:

> Whether or not all history is written with a partisan purpose, it seems at least clear that there is a group of allegedly serious historians in the USA ... which seeks, under the cover of a dispassionate view of the past, to influence the future in a sense directly antagonistic to the interests of Great Britain.[33]

But as usual the FO sought to operate covertly. When Warner Bros approached them, rather than the MoI, with offers of propaganda help with feature films, their proposal was enthusiastically received.[34] The *Hornblower* débâcle was an interesting indication of the difference between FO and MoI approaches to historical film. The author of the Hornblower novels, C. S. Forester, approached the FO through the Washington embassy, proposing (on behalf of Warners) a *quid pro quo* arrangement whereby the FO would guarantee British support for the project and receive some profits. The FO was enthusiastic: 'The Captain Hornblower trilogy would make a very useful film, and useful to Britain.'[35] Forester was prepared to trim his novel to suit FO demands: 'The novel itself had a slightly pacifistic flavour, which of course I was prepared to eliminate.' But the MoI scotched the project, ostensibly because it was too complex to unfreeze Warners' British receipts. The Ministry carelessly argued that Warners would make the film anyway, and some propaganda benefits might accrue to Britain. But the real reason for the veto was doubtless that the MoI could not endure that the FO had got there first.

Until America's entry into the war, the FO proceeded to intensify its campaign on history and to irk the MoI. It professed itself at a loss to account for the MoI's choler: 'The Ministry are convinced that our sole concern is to obstruct them.'[36] As the war progressed, the policies of the two bodies became more distant; and the ground on which the differences were rehearsed was that of history and national culture. The MoI eyed the FO's international work jealously, attacking its ideas as elitist and retrospective:

> By 'culture' in this context is meant much more than art galleries, museums, and old country houses. A people's life and culture cannot be presented as something separate from its daily life and thought ... we do not want to present our culture as a ... venerable survival from the past.[37]

The key body in the quarrel between the two institutions was the British Council. It was originally the Foreign Office's creation, and its task was 'the projection of Britain', primarily overseas, via different media. The Council had given a high priority to history in the 1930s; this was predictable, given its parentage.[38] With the outbreak of war, the MoI seized the opportunity of routing its only rival in the field of cultural politics. The FO could not be decimated, but the British Council might be. Accordingly, high-ranking Ministry personnel began chipping away at the Council's film remit. In early 1940, Kenneth Clark attempted to limit the Council's films. He insisted to the Head of the Council, the historian Philip Guedalla, that the MoI would deploy its right of veto over Council films. Guedalla recognised that the future of the Council Films Section was at stake, and noted that 'the essential thing is to maintain in the Council's hands continuity of those operations which will be desirable after the war.'[39] Council personnel had already recognised that the Ministry was in a temporarily weak position, since they then had very few films of their own for distribution. The MoI was ready to expand, however: 'At present the best hope of extending the exhibition of British films seems to lie in the encouragement of the British Council's cultural documentary films.'[40] For 'encouragement', read 'take-over'.

At a key meeting in June 1940, Beddington proposed to Neville Kearney, Head of the Council's Films Section, that MoI films should deal with the political and the contemporary and Council films with the cultural and historical. Kearney found this overschematic, but they agreed on an uneasy compromise: 'The Ministry was putting a little more water in its wine, whereas we were putting a little more wine with our water.'[41] To Kearney, history was the life-giving water; but the MoI at once started laying down conditions for the Council's historical films. Kearney astutely recognised that 'they are trying to get everything in their hands so that at the end of the war there will be no-one to carry on but themselves.' Nonetheless, he and his staff continued to attempt to produce films in which the past was invested with an intrinsic value. But the MoI wanted them instead to make films about Shakespeare's handwriting, which reduced the usually mild Kearney to ferocity: 'This is the sort of *slime* the MoI would like us to produce.'[42] The MoI scorned the Council's use of history in its *Queen Cotton*: *'This* is supposed to be our all-in war effort.'[43] Kearney was well aware of the difficulties of maintaining a distinction between culture and propaganda. The MoI, however, persisted in simplifying the issue, with ludicrous results. At the end of the war, both bodies wished to make a film about the wool trade. The Council struggled to differentiate its effort from the Ministry's: 'We shall not deal with *Commonwealth* wool, nor shall we advertise wool as a fabric.' It envisaged a history of British wool, with 'the effects of sheep-raising on the social life of England'. The MoI would deal with international wool, but not with wool culture.[44]

By mid-1941, the MoI had the confidence to approach Churchill directly to request 'unity of command' on film matters. Churchill wanted the Council closed in any case ('There are no doubt a number of influential people who have ensconced themselves in this organisation') but was persuaded against closure by Anthony Eden, then Foreign Secretary.[45] This meant that the views held by Kearney, liberal though they were, had little institutional clout. But he persevered, overruled Oliver Bell's view that 'reconstructed history always seems to be phony history', and heretically welcomed films containing 'old men with false beards'. He was in favour of deploying overtly fictional narrative techniques.[46] Such views were anathema to the Ministry, and the Council was forced to marshal support from the unlikely bodies of His Majesty's Stationery Office and the hated BFI.[47]

Meanwhile, with Brendan Bracken now in charge of the MoI, there was a chorus of complaints that Council films, being too historical and cultural, did not show the impact of the war on the people. Given the Council's remit, this was impossible. The MoI wanted films which were 'simple, direct and man to man'. In the event, the Ministry could impose its views on the Council. It forced a change in a film about the social services: 'The facts and circumstances of the war made it clear that the longer historical perspective would be out of place ... only essential references to earlier history have now been retained.'[48] And it won the day when the Council complained about its tactics to the FO. The MoI argued, 'When we make a film, we design it as war propaganda, whatever the subject matter may be'; the Council riposted, 'We know better than they do what should be the subject of cultural films.' Guedalla added his complaints to the uproar; but the Council lost its claim to be regarded as a body equal to the Ministry.[49]

In fact, the Council's Films Section had offended its parent Foreign Office, which began to hedge its support. In 1945, the FO threateningly remarked:

> The fact that the Council has decided to reconstitute the Films Committee and almost to abolish Government representation on it without first consulting the Government departments, and that it assumes that the FO is only interested in films where 'political issues' are raised, shows how far the Council is at present from appreciating how its work is linked with that of other departments. This is an ominous sign of what may happen if the Council's relations with the FO are not soon clearly defined.[50]

They were 'defined' out of existence; and in the postwar Labour administration, the Council's film work, full of historical probity though it was, gradually came to an end.

The British Council did sponsor some historical documentaries during the war. *English Inns*, produced in 1942, was much disliked by the MoI for being 'too remote from the war' since it was exclusively historical in orientation.[51] The 1943 *Development of the English Town* was directed by Mary Field for the Council. The MoI intervened on the script, insisting that it should reflect the Ministry's own ideas on the past.[52] Much may be learned, too, from the abortive *Magna Carta* project, which was first instigated by Guedalla in 1942 and was still acrimoniously unmade in 1946. Guedalla was a liberal historian, as his books show.[53] From Kearney he demanded 'the minimum of false beards'; but Kearney thought the audience needed all the interest it could get, beards or not. Many scripts were commissioned, none of which pleased everyone. Meanwhile Kearney enraged his chief by minute attention to the wrong sort of detail. Poor Guedalla then turned to Rank, and experienced 'the hankering of old Wardour Street hands for the greatest possible number of barons saying "by my halidame" with false beards'. Rank seriously proposed to make the film as a cartoon, 'along Disney lines'.

The MoI finally put paid to *Magna Carta*. Jack Holmes, the Ministry documentarist, noted:

I don't know that history as such interests cinema audiences much, unless it is a bastard kind of dress-up story of some picturesque characters, with all the historical effects suitably distorted and with plenty of love-life thrown in for seasoning. Most people can easily be made interested in contemporary life.[54]

The MoI position can rarely have been expressed with such clarity. Holmes put an embargo on the historical imagination, and encouraged a script which foregrounded the middle classes. *Magna Carta* was never made.

The British Council, then, followed its parent Foreign Office, in that it had a historical theory which was catholic and which dealt with popular as well as polite culture. Its past was a site of pleasure, while the MoI's was the site of instruction. But the Council could not withstand the institutional power of the MoI, which after 1942 argued that history was a nightmare from which the middle classes should awaken. Certainly the documentarists gained a dominant role in the MoI as the war progressed. It may well have been as a result of their influence that MoI policies became predominantly contemporary; the Council's attraction to history increased proportionally. But because of its failing relationship with the FO, this was a fatal attraction.

What of the historical feature films made under the aegis of the different Ministries? The official documents suggest that the Ministry of Information and the Foreign Office had radically opposed notions of history and culture, and that the ill feeling between them was fought out through the British Council. Is it therefore possible to trace the effects of these differing policies within actual film texts?

It took some time for commercial producers and the MoI to come to terms, and the film-making process was cumbersome so that films addressing particular morale problems frequently missed the boat. Nonetheless, some films were made which closely corresponded to MoI precepts on history. There is evidence of some direct MoI intervention, as with *Thunder Rock* and *Henry V*. *Thunder Rock* was released in September 1943, and appeared in the *Kinematograph Weekly* list of modestly popular films; it was based on a popular stage play by the American Robert Ardrey. The trade papers thought that 'such fantasy is not for the hoi-polloi'; it was 'only a tip-top offering for the best halls, for those with a mind above song and sex'.[55] This, of course, chimes in with the MoI notion that the best propaganda would, 'in a stratified society, persuade the dominant group'. Certainly, the Ministry evinced considerable interest in the original play, and those responsible for troop and factory entertainment used extracts from it in 1941. Both film and play were held in very high regard by the British Council and the National Film Library.[56]

MGM backed *Thunder Rock*, which was made by Charter Films, owned by the Boulting brothers and Bernard Miles. Charter preferred to make highbrow films with 'political, religious, philosophical subjects'.[57] John Boulting suggested that *Thunder Rock* was made at the direct behest of the Ministry of Information:

At the suggestion of Duff Cooper, Roy and I were released to make *Thunder Rock* ... Though in retrospect philosophically naive, as a film it was way ahead of its time ... *Thunder Rock* matched the need and mood of everybody.[58]

The film dealt with Charleston, a *déraciné* intellectual in self-imposed exile in a Canadian lighthouse. To alleviate his solitude, Charleston peoples the lighthouse with the ghosts of nineteenth-century European refugees whose ship foundered. But the 'ghosts' come alive and demand that Charleston accord them their full complexity; in return, he persuades them to abandon their cowardice and return to their own problematic period. Clearly the project was favoured at the MoI because it foregrounded the issues of morale and commitment, and because it presented the relationship between past and present as hortatory and inspirational.

But *Thunder Rock* also addresses the issue of the artist's autonomy. Charleston is in retreat, and only from the periphery can he experiment with the notion of subjective reality. This is a position deeply embedded in romantic culture. Only after the lighting of the lamp (a potent symbol) can the alienated hero unleash his creativity. He constructs history as the site of miserable oppression. But the problem with *Thunder Rock* is that it both celebrates and criticises intellectual labour. The refugees, who are Charleston's artistic creation, rebel against his authority, and he finally consigns them to oblivion. This put the highbrows, at whom the film was aimed, in an uncomfortable position.

Roy Boulting attempted to resolve the problem by purely visual means. His description is worth quoting:

> My problem was that Charleston creates them twice, first as he sees them and the second time when they take over and he is forced to see them truly. In my first creation I had to show them as unreal and untrue ... I talked the problem over with Duncan Sutherland and my lighting cameraman, Max Greene. After some days Max found the solution. He said, 'Why don't we build the set at an angle for the first creation of the characters, and drop it down foursquare when Charleston recreates them as they were?' With the set at an angle of 12 degrees and the camera at a similar angle, the set appeared to be quite level, but the characters moving about on the set were obliged to respond to the laws of gravity, and although completely normal and three-dimensional in appearance, they seemed to swirl across the screen at extravagant angles in relation to the set ... It was an innovation at Denham known as Boulting's Folly, but it worked like the dream it was supposed to help achieve.[59]

Such techniques were of course a far cry from popular expressionism, and indeed from orthodox realism. *Thunder Rock*'s visual methods encouraged the audience to mistrust the products of the psyche. The comforting angles of normality are resumed only when the inhabitants of history choose to self-destruct.

Thunder Rock could not hope to address the issue of *political* neutrality, since America had now entered the war; it deals instead with moral and intellectual neutrality. The Boultings' adaptation of the original play inserts a pessimistic flashback about Charleston's journalistic career, in which he expresses his mistrust of mass culture. Typewriters, books, lectures – all the accoutrements of democratic self-expression – are shown as futile. Charleston proceeds to a passionate espousal of Churchillian leadership via a hatred for the masses. In a key scene, the camera pulls back during Charleston's final encomium, to show stupid and largely female listeners. This shot precisely replicates a later one of the cinema audience, which is presented as comatose and lustful; it is guilty of the cardinal sin of inattention to documentary films. The individual psyche is encouraged to transcend the errors of history and bad taste. *Thunder Rock* suggests that these two are the same thing.

The Boultings' film thus espoused emergent, middle-class values, and it deployed visual techniques which verged on the avant-garde. Mass-Observation evidence suggests that audiences associated the film with a degree of status; consumption proved one's patriotism and high cultural competence. The same can be said of *Henry V*, which also had the support of the MoI. *Henry V* was released in December 1944 by Two Cities, and was aimed at an audience for whom victory was in sight; it addressed the definition of 'a land fit for heroes', and its emphasis on an accommodation between victor and vanquished. Shakespeare's play had previously lent itself to nationalist fervour – the Old Vic produced it every year from 1914 to 1919 – but from then until 1937 it was little performed. It was used for a number of official purposes immediately prior to the outbreak of war.[60]

The germ of the idea of re-using *Henry V* was Dallas Bower's. He had written a radio script for a putative broadcast of the play in 1939, and, when appointed to the MoI, he urged the project anew but in film form. Bower was instrumental in obtaining the Army release of key personnel, but experienced initial problems:

> The situation regarding *Henry V* has become more complicated ... We appear to be surrounded in this country by past masters in the art of mismanagement. However, I think we shall be in production eventually, but the battle has been a dreadful one for me.[61]

Bower had already developed an elitist theory of film. In 1934 he had expressed contempt for popular cinema and especially for the female audience: 'Being a woman, the average woman, she is not very interested in ideas.'[62] Bower's attitudes partially informed *Henry V*. He left the MoI for the BBC in late 1942, and when Filippo del Giudice accepted his ideas for the film, he joined Two Cities.

Del Giudice financed the project, and Rank baled him out when the film encountered problems. Del Giudice retained artistic freedom under Rank, Bower was an associate producer, and Olivier, who chose most of the technicians, was released from the Fleet Air Arm for *Henry V* and *The Demi-Paradise*. The Treasury was approached for direct financing of the battle scenes on location in Ireland, but it declined; Stafford Cripps was reportedly very sympathetic to the project and may well have encouraged bankers to give initial loans. So although there is no direct evidence of government sponsorship, there are plenty of suggestions that the film enjoyed official support. Certainly the French government saw the film as the expression of official views.[63] *Henry V* was dedicated to 'the commando and airborne troops of Great Britain'. But the other and more crucial part of the target audience, as I shall show, was the school audience. *Henry V* appeared in *Kinematograph Weekly*'s listings, and won a range of awards.

Henry V

A large part of *Henry V*'s budget went on sets. The film made considerable demands on the decoding abilities of the audience, which was expected to recognise mediaeval iconography and Elizabethan perspective, perhaps like the ideal Historical Association spectator. The art director Roger Furse suggested that

> the audience will allow these liberties to be taken and will respond to the dramatic effects without quibbling about details of background ... Distortion of actual scenery will not be resented by the audience, but they will be sensed psychologically and will add to the dramatic effect of the film.[64]

The skills required from the audience are quite other than those needed for popular historical spectacle, and *Henry V* has three distinct styles: the anti-illusionist one of the Globe, the realist one of the battles, and the illusionist one quoting the Duc de Berri manuscripts. In all of these, the film celebrates an emphatically phallic vigour. The soldiery are consistently robust and uncultured, compared with their fellows in *A Canterbury Tale*, who are men of finesse and mysticism.

The final script is extremely selective; omitted passages are the more complex philosophical speeches, the negative aspects of Henry's character, and the positive aspects of the French. Also missing are the suggestions about internal dissent, and the paeans to Divine Right. This means that the film can concentrate on the issue of leadership, without the inconvenience of metaphysics. *Henry V* evokes the maximum emotional response by narrowing and intensifying definitions of national culture.

The studio's publicity material suggested that past/present parallels be foregrounded, and that fifteenth-century maps be laid alongside those of 1944 in cinema foyers. The material was strongly slanted towards churches and schools. The film's moral irreproachability was stressed as a selling point for Christian audiences, and art students and schools were to be alerted to the film's value: 'Work through the schools. You have the historical element in your favour for one thing.' Strenuous efforts were made throughout the country to arrange early 'special screenings' for children. In Brighton, the Education Committee paid for thousands of children to attend the film as part of the curriculum. Similar arrangements were made elsewhere. The 'hard sell' to schoolchildren paid off, in so far as *Henry V* was still being instanced in 1947 as children's favourite historical film.[65]

Henry V's critics stressed its 'official' aura. The left-wing *Commonweal* noted that 'the English are again praising themselves and shooting their tops off about their own wares.' The *New Statesman* and other radical papers savaged its too visible patriotism.[66] The film seriously irked some American reviewers. The influential *Boston Post* noted that 'the voice is the voice of Shakespeare, but the hand is sometimes the hand of Brendan Bracken.'[67] Such writers recognised that *Henry V* was being sold as a major status item by the studio and, covertly, by the MoI. In fact, *Henry V* presents the past as the site of masculine display, bellicosity, and unflattering haircuts; history is a bran-tub, and every prize fumbled from it is a proof of English superiority.

Two American-financed films, *The Prime Minister* and *The Young Mr Pitt*, also displayed an extraordinary consonance with MoI views; there is no firm evidence of their parentage, but they are sufficiently different from straightforwardly commercial products to encourage us to categorise them as 'official' histories. *The Prime Minister* was made by an all-British team at Teddington and was released in March 1941; it dealt with the career of Disraeli. Warner Bros had developed a strongly anti-isolationist stance during the early years of the war. Jack and Harry Warner were subpoenaed by the America First Committee in 1941 for being over-zealous in their defence of the British position in their films. Harry Warner argued that it was studio policy to 'aid in the defeat of the Nazi menace', and suggested that all recent Warners' films, even historical ones, covertly supported this view.[68] In the light of this, it seems likely that Warners would have consulted the MoI in order to ensure government approval for *The Prime Minister*, especially after the débâcle of the *Hornblower* project. The film's director, Thorold Dickinson, noted that the film had a very high quota rating, and that reckless expenditure was encouraged; for example, a complete House of Commons interior was constructed, even though only a few members were in shot.[69] Dickinson had a strongly Ministry-oriented career during the war, and he was closely allied with Dallas Bower of the MoI at the time *The Prime Minister* was made. The finished film echoed MoI precepts in its celebration of intellectual labour, its rejection of revolutionary politics, and its views of leadership.

Warners' publicity material indicated that they saw *The Prime Minister* as a major prestige vehicle, and it stressed the similarity between Churchill and Disraeli, arguing that the two shared a mercurial style of conservatism.

The film contains some interesting disjunctions, since the verbal and visual discourses are at odds from the outset. Disraeli is described by the script as a connoisseur who only produces books for the gentry; he can easily 'sacrifice the things that came easily'. But the first image of the novels is via a long, mobile shot down a street, through a window, and along a row of richly tooled vellum tomes. It is a seductive representation of intellectual life, which is further complicated by the manner of Gielgud's performance. He is directed so as to lack conventional masculine traits, and constantly fusses with his hair, face and gloves. His intellectualism is expressed through feminisation. This could work in the *Pimpernel* films, and even in the popular *Lady Hamilton*, because the heroes there also expressed strength and control. *The Prime Minister* lacks that, which vitiates its attempt to delineate a virile leadership.

The film's politics are contradictory. The script shows Disraeli rejecting the upper classes: 'Our kings are a race of half-wits and debauchees, our aristocracy a brood of Tory farmers fighting the industrialists for the market.' The working class is displayed as a howling mob. The vacant space between the two class extremes should properly have been filled by a vigorous defence of the middle classes; but this is impossible because the film is concerned with personal rather than class politics. It was a clear attempt to invoke confidence in Churchill, via historical parallel. Disraeli's shift to the Tories is presented as an apostasy to a higher creed; by implication, this neutralises Churchill's own earlier party shift from the Liberals. *The Prime Minister* expends considerable energy in upholding the viability of a 'mature' leader. Disraeli might give the appearance of doddering; but he knows 'these dictators, these men of blood and iron. They're always in a hurry.' The film thus attempts to evoke confidence in masterly inactivity. It had indifferent reviews, and did not do well at the box office, probably because of its slow pace which, along with its ambiguities about masculinity and leadership, scuppered it as a propaganda enterprise.

The Young Mr Pitt, however, could cloak its dubieties, and it appeared in the *Kinematograph Weekly* listings for 1942. It also pleased the Foreign Office. Great interest was evinced by FO officials when a detailed report on response to the film came from the Soviet Relations Division. The film had been much admired in Moscow, and British officials were gratified when 'an intelligent Russian girl said that we had taken liberties with history for propaganda purposes "just as we do."'[70] Material in this FO file indicates that the British government were happy to have *The Young Mr Pitt* represent its position. Moreover, the film had government co-operation during its production; Maurice Carter and Vetchinsky, as art directors, were allowed into Churchill's study in Downing Street during a trying period of the war. Churchill watched patiently from his desk while they made measurements to ensure maximum verisimilitude. The American backers of the film insisted that it expressed the official British position that 'Britain is most unbeatable when, to the outside world, she is most likely to be beaten.'[71] *The Young Mr Pitt*'s publicity material suggested that its quasi-official status should be used as the main selling point.

The Gainsborough team commissioned to make the film was largely the one which was to produce the bodice-ripper cycle. But *The Young Mr Pitt* displayed a different visual style from (say) *The Man in Grey*, and this was

The Young Mr Pitt

probably at the behest of the production company. Flamboyant opulence was absent from the film. Instead, sobriety and attention to detail were evident. The reconstructed House of Commons was painstaking, but devoid of visual pleasure; and real *objets d'art* were hired from private collections, which resulted in unduly high set expenditure.[72] *Pitt*'s script was the dominant discourse, preoccupied by the issue of leadership and implying that a popular leader may manipulate national institutions with impunity; but, conversely, he must sacrifice domestic happiness. Pitt claims that 'We must put aside all personal affairs, leisure, family, even sleep, for this one imperative duty.' His less creditable actions (such as the trial of Warren Hastings) are played down, and the Jacobin aspects of the period are absent.

The script thus presents the past as a lesson about correct leadership. But according to Launder and Gilliat, Viscount Castleross's dialogue was archaic and unwieldy ('had I but known, I would have flown to my William on wings of love') and they were also in dispute with Carol Reed and Robert Donat, the star, who insisted on a 'whitewash job'.[73] Reed generally preferred to work on a script for three months before shooting, and to shoot in sequence; but with wartime exigencies this was impossible. However, Reed's style of direction concealed such problems. He had directed *Kipps* for Fox in 1940, and knew how to trim a text to a producer's wishes; one critic noted that he 'understood American sympathies and worked accordingly'.[74] Moreover, Reed was at that time in high favour at the MoI, who were pressing hard for him to be taken out of active army service and into feature films with strong propaganda elements.[75]

Thus the influence of the MoI on historical film was complex and indirect. Historical features which enjoyed the discreet approval of the Ministry argued that history's propaganda usefulness was temporary, and that the lessons of history were less relevant as peace approached. High expenditure (however obtained) was thought necessary to give the impression of quality and to distance the product from cheaper, more sensational histories. Indeed, with *Thunder Rock* and *Henry V*, the MoI took no risks at all, since the texts on which they were based had secure propaganda value. In MoI-backed films, a range of historical interpretations *seemed* appropriate, but ultimately the films endorsed one favoured view. They presented the past as a cycle of misery and oppression from which the audience should learn to value the present and its liberties. The films often had a narrow target audience, such as intellectuals or children, and they all endorsed charismatic leadership and a broadly conservative interpretation of history. Because of the cumbersome nature of the MoI's methods of encouragement and permission, there were examples of 'slippage'; films were made exemplifying an MoI perspective on history well after the MoI had shifted its views.

But what of the Foreign Office and the propaganda usefulness of history? The FO preferred to work covertly, and it felt that its own aims could be fulfilled by American-made films. In reply to Lord Lothian's attacks on the MoI, Vansittart had proposed Alexander Korda as the best man to make the 'big film'; this would use history in order to 'get at the feelings'. Accordingly, *Lady Hamilton* (US title: *That Hamilton Woman*) was made in Hollywood with a largely British workforce, and was directed by Korda with his own production company. Korda preferred historical figures who could attain mythological status, and who could tap a range of audience feelings about national identity, class composition, and sexual pleasure. *Lady Hamilton* was the only wartime film with any covert official backing that deployed a historical figure in this way. It was phenomenally popular on its release in August 1941.

Evidence from *Lady Hamilton*'s scriptwriter, R. C. Sherriff, endorses the suggestion that the Foreign Office promoted the film:

> The sort of pictures that they had in mind would relate to valiant episodes in Britain's none-too-distant past that would serve to counteract enemy propaganda and do a lot of good in neutral countries, provided they didn't wave the flag too ostentatiously and had good entertainment value.[77]

The range of government support for the film should not be underestimated. The Minister of Information, Duff Cooper, had made encouraging noises to Olivier.[78] And Churchill's own interest in Korda and in *Lady Hamilton* is well documented.[79] Korda had been in America to make pro-British films from June 1940 to January 1942, and he received hostile press coverage for his supposed defection. It is now widely accepted that Korda's production offices in America were used for British Secret Service activity, and that he himself was involved in such work. But most importantly, Korda had been in high favour with the Foreign Office since the 1930s, and this relationship continued throughout the war. The British Library of Information in New York was a covert arm of the FO, and it reported that hostile American critics of *Lady Hamilton* should be ignored, since 200,000 Americans had seen it in three weeks 'and some of them must have accepted the historical lesson which Mr Korda apparently was trying to teach.'[80] When the ultra right-wing film critic Mrs M. Robson assailed the FO with demands that *Lady Hamilton* should receive no more official support, she was met with masterly official inactivity. She thought that the film should not be used as propaganda to Russia; clearly the FO did not agree.[81]

Lady Hamilton was made in Hollywood at a period when the political situation was tense. Once made, it was a prey to isolationist groups. The America First Committee prompted a Senate Committee inquiry in September 1941, and subpoenaed Korda to defend *Lady Hamilton*. America's entry into the war in December 1941 demolished the isolationist case, and Korda returned home unscathed. However, the Senate papers merit some attention since they indicate the degree of anxiety produced by Korda's film. The committee's aim was to establish whether the film industry was exerting undue influence on American audiences about the war issue. The main assault was led by Senator Robert Nye, who objected to foreign directors and suspected Victor Saville of being a spy.[82] He and Senator Clarke reserved particular scorn for *Lady Hamilton*, since it was unfairly well-made. Clarke noted that 'historical facts were being distorted. They injected a speech that Nelson was supposed to have made to the British cabinet, which of course he never made at all.' A journalist, Mr Flynn, was called to judge *Lady Hamilton*. But as chairman of the America First Committee he was hardly unbiased, and anyway he thought that history was bunk; the past was simply something 'that occurred hundreds of years ago and which we have all stopped fighting about'. He too

Lady Hamilton

denounced Nelson's speech as 'a regular 1941 war speech. He delivers it to the Admiralty, but he is actually delivering it to the audience. He is ostensibly talking about Napoleon and the events of that particular period, but he is actually addressing it to the times.' The Committee expressed its displeasure with Korda's 'whispering campaigns' to publicise *Lady Hamilton*, and with the involvement of British consular officials in discussions with Korda about the historical importance of Emma Hamilton.

Lady Hamilton clearly had extensive Foreign Office support, and this rattled the Americans. Sherriff was initially refused a visa by Washington bureaucrats. He and Korda had strained relations with the Hays Office, and frequently had to work all night to satisfy Breen, who refused the first draft since it presented adultery as pleasurable: 'Being historic doesn't make it any easier.' To comply with Hays Office demands, Sherriff was forced to restructure the film as a flashback from the perspective of a dissolute Emma.[83]

Nonetheless, the final script contains some radical sexual observations. Emma is compared to a Greek statue raised from the mud, 'changing hands every year until it comes to its rightful place in the hands of someone who understands the true glory of its beauty.' On one level, this realistically suggests that a woman's worth is relative to the value placed on her by men. But on another, it implies that the more variously a woman is loved, the greater her significance; she is not besmirched by sexual exchange. Emma also makes an interesting remark on marriage. Her husband argues that there are three kinds of husband: those born to be deceived, those ignorant of the fact, and those who no longer care. She ripostes that a fourth kind have cold hearts, and deserve all they get. This exchange has similarities to *The Wicked Lady*, which also displays cynicism towards monogamy. Both films clearly address the change in wartime mores of their female audience.

But the key language in *Lady Hamilton* is the visual one. The pleasures of sight and touch are emphasised, and erotic aspects foregrounded; Korda insisted that the sets should be primarily 'a bedroom'. The techniques used stimulate the eye. The line of vision is frequently broken up to produce a serpentining, 'picturesque' perspective appropriate for the period represented, and the decor is richly evocative. One volatile scene has a smouldering Vesuvius in the background; the foreground shows, at right, a painting of Emma which gazes left towards the real Emma, who also looks left towards a naked female statue, in turn gazing left at a shadowy, half-hidden male figure. Such procedures make maximum use of cultural codes, and show attention to detail; for example, Lady Nelson's body language, braided hair, tight collar and preference for unbuttered toast, all connote sexual frigidity.

Indeed, *Lady Hamilton* celebrates female desire and examines its arousal by male vulnerability. In mainstream pornography for men, women are habitually displayed as powerless. But in texts intended to arouse female desire, male protagonists are feminised: they bleed. This is a motif deeply embedded in literary culture; with Heathcliff and Mr Rochester, male wounding is an erotic symbol. In *Lady Hamilton*, Emma's desire is not aroused until she witnesses Nelson's eye and arm. He too is 'damaged goods', and this fuels the dynamics of the affair.

The film presents to the female audience the possibility of a freer mode of libidinal life. But significantly the sexual message of *Lady Hamilton* is compounded with the political one. It is Emma who can negotiate her way through any class dialect, and who can teach Nelson to inhabit the opera and the public house with equal ease. In the balcony scene on Nelson's return the only reciprocal gaze is between Emma and the crowd; she *enables* Nelson's identification with popular naval tradition, which is most marked in the rendering of popular songs such as 'Hearts of Oak'.

Lady Hamilton, then, suggested that the only real aristocratic leadership was one which symbolically represented popular aspirations. But it linked that argument with a persuasive one about female pleasure; its publicity material proposed that 'the great lover' rather than 'the great man of history' was a selling point, and ideal tie-ups were with local beauty shops. This lack of serious emphasis may well have accounted for the film's unpopularity with quality critics; the *Observer* suggested on 3 August 1941 that 'these are not the days when we have much patience for looking at history through the eyes of a trollop'. The mass audience disagreed.

Lady Hamilton did not present history as a form of coercion, but of pleasure, and it attempted to merge a political populism with an erotic appeal. The cultural competence it evoked was quite different from those histories which came under the MoI aegis. The FO's interest in the history debate went back to the 1930s; the MoI's was perforce of a more recent date, and its films were more narrow and puritanical in their views. A different class symbolism operated too. MoI films celebrated middle-class perceptions of progress, whereas the FO film re-presented the aristocratic and proletarian alliance in a compelling way.

7

COMMERCIAL FILM PRODUCTION AND
HISTORY 1939 – 45

The range of uses to which history was put in commercial film raises interesting problems. What were the intellectual resources available to producers and directors in wartime? Is it possible to establish that any one historiographical practice was dominant? If so, how was that filtered through to film production? There was a variety of cultural resources at the disposal of film entrepreneurs, who were eclectic in their methods.

Academic historians put their subject to a range of wartime uses. A. L. Rowse argued that Britain was more likely to win the war because Churchill was a historian; an awareness of the past in wartime should inculcate pride in the British character.[1] G. M. Trevelyan's popular *English Social History* celebrated a broadly based popular culture. Academic historians with more explicitly socialist leanings, such as G. H. Cole and Raymond Postgate, were productive during the war.[2] More conservative academic historians represented the past as an uncomfortable place where elite groups and brutal majorities subjected the favoured middle classes to recurring cycles of threat. The wartime work of Herbert Butterfield and Lewis Namier should be interpreted in this light.[3] Arnold Toynbee was important here; his six-volume *A Study of History* was adapted for radio during the war, and was so successful that it was abridged into a very popular one-volume edition. Toynbee argued that the middle-class intelligentsia should reform the proletariat, partially by encouraging 'that faculty called mimesis'.[4] He reserved particular scorn for spectacular cinema, which he held responsible for the process of proletarianisation.

Academic histories during the war, then, had a broad political range. But there were also many popular historical texts which attempted to recuperate the past for the present crisis by highlighting its 'heritage' aspects. H. V. Morton's *I Saw Two Englands*, for example, was phenomenally popular.[5] Its celebration of Canterbury cathedral, pilgrims, blessings and tea-shops was remarkably similar in tone to Powell and Pressburger's *A Canterbury Tale*. Morton suggested that the war had a positive outcome: it gave the population a renewed sense of a communal past. This point was also implicitly made in Collie Knox's profitable anthology, *For Ever England*.[6] Other popular writers suggested that history had mystical powers which could be invoked *in extremis*. Arthur Mee urged the Americans to share 'the deep sense of something mysterious' in English history.[7] And Arthur Bryant, too, celebrated a pre-capitalist culture.[8] Some histories attempted more radical or revolutionary explanations.[9] But they were marginal in terms of popular historical production as a whole.

Those versions of the past which were produced for a mass audience are difficult to quantify. Army education, for example, did not appear to give a privileged role to history at all, and indeed the education section was called the Army Bureau of Current Affairs. The popular magazine *Picture Post* had an interesting profile on the issue; prior to the outbreak of war, its editor Edward Hulton argued that 'It was not in the immense dominions of the Great Kings of Persia and their attendant satraps that ancient civilisation flourished. Its fairest flowers grew in the tiny but free city states of Greece.' Significantly, Hulton praised the role played by the aristocracy in British history; in a formulation which becomes increasingly familiar, he noted that, before 1832, the most fruitful alliance had been between the aristocracy and the working class.[10] *Picture Post* went on to deal in an informative and politically liberal way with history, arguing that there had been no 1848 revolution in Britain because 'the people, or rather the middle classes, who were everywhere the mainspring of the Revolution, had in England gained these rights long before, in 1688 and in 1832.'[11] It suggested that after 1848 'socialism was still a vague idea ... and when Chartism collapsed, middle-class England felt more established and more eternal than ever before.'[12] *Picture Post* clearly offered its readership a radical reinterpretation of the past, arguing that only social history, with an emphasis on mass culture and lifestyles, could ensure that 'man's long story could be presented as a whole'.[13] Articles proliferated about past/present parallels: France in the 1870s, Greece in the 1820s, the history of the bayonet. The readers were thus encouraged to see their plight in the context of recurrent cyclical themes.[14] And historical films were frequently celebrated for the labour which was entailed in the process of capturing the past.[15]

The historical novel was, for our purposes, perhaps the most important mediation of history in World War II. In 1940, Sir John Marriott wrote an innovatory critique of the genre.[16] This was succeeded by a qualitative change in the historical novel itself. A cycle of 'bodice-rippers' by women novelists became best-sellers and appealed to a specifically female readership.[17] These historical novels all celebrated marginal groups, such as gypsies, aristocrats or libidinous women, and examined them for signs of social pollution. They evoked the past as a pleasurable place where refugees from common sense could temporarily reside. These novels were not concerned with accuracy, and their style was opulent, dense and metaphorical.

During World War II, then, a rich patina of historical interpretation was available to film producers. There was a range of academic histories of different political persuasions, and another range of popular histories of a more conservative cast. Popular journalism and a new species of historical novel gave a more radical reinterpretation of the past. On the face of it, film producers selected quite broadly from the spectrum. Ealing histories seem to have drawn sustenance from conservative academic historians; Gainsborough costume melodramas were derived from the new 'bodice-ripper' novels and from popular radical history. The inspiration behind MoI historical films seems to have come from liberal academic historians. And the films of British-National and Powell and Pressburger's Archers company appear to owe most, intellectually speaking, to conservative popular histories. But such suggestions must remain tentative until confirmed by close textual analysis.

First, however, the producers' responses to official precepts merit consideration. Government intervention in film was met with mistrust throughout the war by those in close touch with audience taste. A *Kinematograph Weekly* article on 11 January 1940, 'Do Propaganda Films Pay at the Box-Office?', quoted the owner of two Plymouth cinemas: 'People do not want films dealing with war and its horrors or propaganda films which preach at patrons who pay to be entertained.' A cinema manager, who saw himself as a 'lineal descendant of the barker', held the same view. *Kinematograph Weekly* published an article on 11 January 1945 attacking 'the higher cinema being prattled about by the Higher Brows'. The British RKO sales manager felt that 'uplift' was incompatible with audience pleasure and studio profit.[18] The attitudes of the MoI towards propaganda and the audience enraged Walter Mycroft of Associated-British, who berated 'intellectuals who have attached themselves like limpets in decorative clusters to film production.' He argued that 'outwardly untutored people react instantly against anything phoney, anything pretentious.'[19] John Baxter of British-National insisted that overt war stories were inefficacious, and that entertainment films left audiences 'with propaganda seeds planted in their mind to gain fruition later'.[20] Even Arthur Lucan's Old Mother Riley was 'a great character for propaganda purposes'.

Other producers and directors expressed a degree of resistance to MoI attitudes. Gabriel Pascal argued that wartime conditions prompted the audience's need for non-realist entertainment.[21] Filippo del Giudice suggested to J. Arthur Rank that historical and spectacular films were 'of the greatest artistic and cultural or propaganda value'.[22] Bernard Miles insisted that the cultural homogeneity demanded by the MoI could not lead to a popular national cinema.[23] And, at the end of the war, Maurice Ostrer noted that 'costume melodramas pack the box-office. I suggest that this is an escape from the drabness of the present-day world of clothes coupons and austerity.'[24]

Throughout the war period, influential figures in the film industry championed popular spectacle and expressed hostility towards the more puritanical behests of the MoI. But that was on their own account; the *corporate* behaviour of the British Film Producers' Association, as a public body, was more conciliatory. The Minutes of the Executive Council are of great interest. When Michael Balcon, a doughty supporter of MoI propaganda policy, attempted to resign as Chairman of the Association in 1940, strong opposition was voiced since his resignation might reveal to the government the extent of the producers' disagreements; he was persuaded to remain.[25] He was also required to abstain from public statements on Association policy without prior consultation. These minutes show the extent to which the producers were prepared to combine to lobby the government and to operate restrictive practices. They also indicate important areas of disagreement with the MoI. The producers accepted Brendan Bracken's offer to release key male stars from active service. But they (especially Maurice Ostrer) were critical of the Ministry's Ideas Committee and its definition of entertainment. Jack Beddington was reported as saying that 'propaganda films could be made outside those dealing with the present war. In this connection he mentioned the work of Mary Kingsley and her life on the Gold Coast, which portrayed past events connected with the

97

foundation of the British Empire.' This suggestion was loudly ignored by the producers, who prevaricated instead about the availability of jute.[26] Beddington also suggested films about historical changes in the role of women, and stories of past Greek heroism to chime in with the Crete campaign. But such overt uses of history as a lesson were anathema to the producers, who again appeared to be stricken with mass deafness.

As the war progressed, the BFPA became increasingly hostile to MoI suggestions. The President's yearly address for 1942 criticised the Ministry and noted that the public 'was asking for films which took their minds off the tragedy now taking place'. The Association responded negatively to an MoI memo which argued that special support should be given to films dealing realistically with everyday life. On the realism issue, Balcon appeared to be isolated from the Association. The other producers were not unpatriotic; but as entrepreneurs they resented the blandishments of MoI intellectuals whose profession had not been the prediction of public taste.

The producers had a more anodyne relationship with the British Board of Film Censors than with the MoI. The BBFC was of course subject to the MoI, and the scale of its operations was reduced. There was a considerable wartime liberalisation in censorship attitudes on sexual and some social matters, largely at the instigation of the Home Office. However, such relaxation did not obtain in the area of historical film. Colonel Hanna and Mrs Crouzet, who were still working at the BBFC as they had in the 1930s, zealously defended innocuous representations of history. A proposed life of William IV was permitted in the Scenario Notes of 1941 because the script gave a purified version of 'the somewhat coarse and crude atmosphere of the period'. The censors were particularly vigilant about the recent history of the Royal family; a proposed life of Kaiser Wilhelm was vetoed because Edward VII might somehow be implicated. A narrow moralism was evident; *Boule de Suif* was deemed totally unsuitable. For Colonel Hanna particularly, historical accuracy and 'quality' fiction were coterminous, and the preferred image of the past was one that was cleansed of sensuality and republicanism. In the 1942 Scenario Notes, Hanna encouraged the producers of *Thunder Rock* by praising its 'backbone'; the script corrected those 'who had suffered poverty, persecution, etc., and had not stood up to their troubles, but had run away from them'. The producers' relationship with the BBFC was less astringent than with the MoI, because the latter had more power and because Hanna's views on history did not represent any one powerful constituency.

British commercial production during World War II dealt extremely selectively with disruptions to conventional procedures. Crises in morale were concealed or indirectly addressed, and films such as *Millions Like Us* displaced anxieties about industrial work and repositioned them in the context of familial experience, where they could be resolved. An official 'moral panic' was brought about by changes in female sexual behaviour. Some films displaced, exaggerated, concealed or falsified this change; others celebrated female pleasure by deploying metaphors or symbols which were outside conventional signifying systems. Some used the motif of 'gypsyness' as a means of addressing new sexual and social mores.

In the context of this overall production pattern, it is possible to delineate a rudimentary map of historical film from 1939 to 1945. Twenty-seven historical features were made during this period; about twenty-one were made out-side the aegis of any official body. There were two American-financed vehicles, *Kipps* and *Hatter's Castle*, and some ambitious but unprofitable films from British-National. There were also 'non-aligned' histories, such as *The Great Mr Handel* which attempted an idiosyncratic approach to propaganda. History played an important role in the Archers' *Life and Death of Colonel Blimp* and *A Canterbury Tale*. Most importantly, the war saw the inception of two cycles of histories, one from Ealing and the other from Gainsborough. The latter's bodice-rippers dominated the market. As usual, there are 'speaking absences' in the overall output. Some historical periods were deemed inappropriate for film production; other films never got off the drawing board. Bernard Miles made strenuous attempts to produce a film about the Tolpuddle Martyrs, for example, but was unable to get any support from Bevin at the Ministry of Labour.[27]

Which of these historical feature films were popular at the box-office? *Kinematograph Weekly*'s monthly breakdown is invaluable, although without hard box-office data we have to rely on Josh Billings's interpretation. In 1939, Billings indicated that historical films were not resoundingly successful. *The Citadel* was the overall winner, and *The Four Feathers* was the only British history film to appear in the box-office listings, though a range of American costume films found favour with British audiences. Historical films did moder-ately well in 1940; *Rebecca* was the overall favourite film, but *Gaslight* was quite profitable and a range of American histories appeared in the list. The biggest winner for 1941 was *The 49th Parallel*, although *Lady Hamilton* was a close runner-up. For 1942, the overall winner was *Mrs Miniver*; but *Hatter's Castle* was classified as a British runner-up. *The Young Mr Pitt* was popular, but no other historical films, British or American, appear in the list. However, a marked change was evident in 1943. *In Which We Serve* was the favourite film, but *The Life and Death of Colonel Blimp* was third runner-up and *The Man in Grey* did very well. It is significant that for the first time Margaret Lockwood, James Mason, Stewart Granger and Phyllis Calvert appeared in the Favourite Actors list; they had clearly made an enormous impression in *The Man in Grey*. *Thunder Rock* also appeared in the listings. The success of the Gainsborough melodramas was repeated in 1944, when *Fanny by Gaslight* was second runner-up to *This Happy Breed*, and *Love Story* was also very profitable. The reissued *Lady Hamilton* and *A Canterbury Tale* were also very popular, as was a range of American historical films. In 1945, *The Seventh Veil* was the most profitable film, but a number of historical films were in Billings's listings: *I'll Be Your Sweetheart*, *Waltz Time* and *Henry V*. *Madonna of the Seven Moons* did extremely well, and *I Know Where I'm Going* was a reason-able performer. We should also consider films made at the end of the war, which appeared in the listings for 1946. The biggest box-office attraction was *The Wicked Lady*, and two other Gainsborough histories, *Caravan* and *The Magic Bow*, did extremely well in that year. *Caesar and Cleopatra* was men-tioned by Billings, as was the reissue of *The Private Life of Henry VIII*. Several American historical films were profitable.[28]

So although historical films were a relatively small part of British film output as a whole, they found significant favour with the mass audience during the war. Some with covert official backing were popular, such as *The Young*

Mr Pitt; but the Gainsborough histories constituted a spectacular melodramatic cycle, which was innovatory in many ways. As always, it is also necessary to analyse those historical films which did not find popular favour, if a coherent sociology of film culture of the period is to be attempted.

I have already discussed American-financed historical films which had the blessing of the MoI. There were two other American-backed period vehicles: *Kipps*, made by Twentieth Century Productions and released in March 1941, and *Hatter's Castle*, Paramount British, November 1941. These differ interestingly. The latter was mentioned in the *Kinematograph Weekly* listings, while the former was not. The films made quite different use of their original literary texts. *Kipps*, directed by Carol Reed and based on H. G. Wells's novel, was made at Shepherd's Bush, using the Gainsborough team hired for *The Young Mr Pitt* and which then made the bodice-ripper cycle. *Kipps* displayed the craftsmanship of the workforce; the camerawork and editing was deft, and the art direction and costume design stylish. The film was directed so as to emphasise the rhythm of the narrative structure, and the acting was both purposeful and restrained.

Why, then, did *Kipps* make no impact at the box-office? It starred Michael Redgrave, and it had extensive pre-release publicity and uniformly good reviews. A report by the *New York Times* on 25 May 1942 was astute: 'The English are an imperturbable race. During the heaviest struggle in Britain's history, they have the mental tranquillity to make a gently satirical portrait of Victorian caste and snobbery ... This is not a film for the present moment.' Precisely; the use of the past in *Kipps* is neither consolatory, exhortatory nor distracting. The press book insists that a nostalgic evocation of a period atmosphere is crucial to the film's meaning, and that the pleasure of 'croquet flannels and weird neckties all contribute to the authenticity of untroubled England of long ago'. But the past in *Kipps* is a place of discomfiture, especially for the eponymous hero; his negotiation of the social minefield is clumsy, and he returns thankfully to the bolt-hole of class familiarity.

Embarrassment, whether in protagonist or audience, is a sure index that something important is afoot. *Kipps* focuses on an individual poised not between two class fractions (which is common in film and literary culture), but between four: the upper and lower working class, and the upper and lower middle class. The textual embarrassment comes from the overload. The nuances of the different class registers are unusually extensive; and each class fraction in *Kipps* experiences a profound crisis of confidence, from which it does not recover. Wells's original novel was structured differently; it enunciated, albeit in a mocking manner, the coherence and homogeneity of the lower middle class.

The position offered to the mass audience in *Kipps* is impossibly inconsistent. Moreover, all social groups in the film suffer agonies of cultural insecurity, and the past is a retreat for the dogged and glum. In order to be profitable, history in wartime had to offer a workable pattern of class identification, and a coherent theory of the past; it also had to provide pleasure or encouragement. *Kipps* did none of these, either because of the demands of the production company, or because it represented a stage in Reed's directorial career which was crucial for his development but not for the audience's.

But *Hatter's Castle*, made by Paramount-British, another American production company, was a popular success. Carefully located in Scotland in the 1870s, it deals with a paterfamilias who exerts his authority excessively. *Hatter's Castle* was scripted by Paul Merzbach and Rodney Ackland and directed by Lance Comfort – an experienced team. It was based on A. J. Cronin's best-selling 1931 novel, which figured heavily in the publicity material. This suggested that the novel was a primitive *ur-text*, by a writer with 'no pretensions to technique, no knowledge of style or form'. This was a gross misrepresentation of Cronin, whose style here and elsewhere was chastely subdued. But the production company needed to disabuse the audience of any suspicion that realism was an issue.

Hatter's Castle is a melodrama, and was recognised as a successful example of the genre by quality critics.[29] But it was a melodrama of a recognisably *Gothic* type, in which the visual style displays explicit debts to expressionist practice, and in which masculine authority is ruthlessly exacted on weaker female victims. The father figure was played by Robert Newton in his familiar florid style; he is supplanted by the daughter's doctor lover, James Mason. The hapless female duplicates one kind of control with another more amenable. Significantly, for the 1947 re-release the press book displaced authoritarian excess from the father to the lover. By this time, Mason had played Gothic villains in *The Seventh Veil*, *Fanny by Gaslight* and other melodramas. The re-released *Hatter's Castle* was advertised thus: viewers would learn

> of men who teach women the terror of cruelty and mad obsession, and of women who know the sting and insult of a man's hand ... Ever since James Mason cracked Ann Todd's knuckles with a cane in *The Seventh Veil*, the Mason fans, a sizable segment of the movie-going population, have become insatiable in their demand for more of their hero's special brand of cruelty.

How are we to account for the popularity of *Hatter's Castle* in the light of this evidence? It seems clear that the film was angled at a female audience, and that it fed important psychic drives in the same way that *The Man in Grey* and *The Wicked Lady* were to do. Tania Modleski suggests that literary Gothics

> perform the function of giving expression to women's hostility towards men while simultaneously allowing them to repudiate it. Because the male appears to be an outrageous persecutor, the reader can allow herself a measure of anger against him; yet at the same time she can identify with a heroine who is entirely without malice and innocent of any wrongdoing.[30]

This could well apply here, especially given the changing gender composition of the wartime film audience. *Hatter's Castle*, like other melodramas which are Gothic in their emotional structure, addresses the female Oedipus complex. Here as elsewhere, the female protagonist is recognisably separate from the mother-figure; she confronts male power, and then develops beyond it. En route, the male principle is split into two opposing halves because of the ambivalence of the heroine and the female audience towards the male.

In the exigencies of wartime, therefore, one American production company was able to use history as a profitable means of addressing those gender relations which were then acutely at issue. When the past was used for these purposes, class elements were of secondary importance. Some British studios, such as the Archers, Gainsborough and Ealing, combined class and gender elements in their historical films. Others used period settings, but found it difficult to develop a consistent studio practice. For example, *Crimes at the Dark House*, directed by George King and released by Pennant (British Lion) in February 1940, made minimal impact. British Lion had not been organised in the 1930s so as to give rise to a consistent policy on history, and George King had specialised in sensational remakes of Victorian melodramas for American production companies. The 1940 film was a version of Wilkie Collins's *The Woman in White* and, on the face of it, might have been successful since it was a Gothic melodrama; the publicity material suggested that a board be displayed 'as vividly as possible with stills showing the star strangling one of his female victims'. Female identification is hampered, however, by the fact that the heroine is seriously insane. *Crimes at the Dark House* appears to have had an untimely combination of terror and humour; the real horrors of war probably made studio gore seem superfluous.

Pennant–British Lion was fixed in a residual and fossilised use of history. So was Butcher's, which produced *Variety Jubilee* in March 1943. Butcher's had specialised in musicals in the 1930s, and in the comedies of variety performers Gert and Daisy during the war; *Variety Jubilee* was an unusual departure for them. The publicity material suggested that it was a 'star-studded romance of music hall history', and its selection of extracts from the acts of George Robey and Marie Lloyd Jnr doubtless accounted for the film's re-release in 1945 after Ealing's 1944 *Champagne Charlie*. All we can assume is that *Variety Jubilee* evinced a nostalgia for the 'good old days' of music hall.

The Great Mr Handel (1942) attempted a loftier definition of culture. The film was directed by Norman Walker, and was produced by Gregory, Hake and Walker Ltd., a company owned by J. Arthur Rank, who took a strong interest in the film. The composer was played by the renowned tippler Wilfrid Lawson, who kept losing his script. As the press book suggested, 'dignity should be the keynote'. Enormous efforts were made to draw in an appropriate audience. The film was made in Technicolor, the distributors financed a concert by the Handelian Orchestra at the Leicester Square Theatre, and Novello's were persuaded to publish a new selection of Handel's work; the standard Handel biography was reprinted, and HMV issued special records in connection with the film. The publicity material argued that these arrangements were necessary in order to 'bring to the cinema a vast audience that do not usually patronise this form of entertainment'. But to no avail; the film had poor reviews, and made no profits.

There were several problems with the film. It had an inconsistent attitude to culture. Handel's oratorios were nicely performed, but the film was punctuated by a series of popular ditties, presumably in an attempt to weld together polite and popular culture, and the two levels jarred. Secondly, the film foregrounded a type of religious piety which was unfashionable. Thirdly, the question of royal patronage of the arts was hardly a burning issue in 1942. *The Great Mr Handel* was an idiosyncratic celebration of high culture. But the mass audience would prefer the piano-playing in the later *Love Story*.

British-National, another independent company, gave history a certain priority, producing *Gaslight* (May 1940), *This England* (March 1941), *Penn of Pennsylvania* (August 1941), *When We Are Married* (March 1943), *Waltz Time* (July 1945) and *Latin Quarter* (November 1945). Only *Gaslight* and *Waltz Time* were mentioned in the *Kinematograph Weekly* or other lists of box-office successes. British-National had been set up by Rank and Lady Yule in 1933, and John Baxter joined the company in 1939. The studio had been unambitious in the 30s, but Baxter was energetic and changed its orientation. He described himself as a 'lowbrow', and in *Kinematograph Weekly* on 8 January 1942 criticised prestige pictures: 'There is neither time, labour, nor space for these film Forsyte sagas.' Baxter's fellow film-maker at British-National, John Cor-field, had similar aims but was more intellectual in his approach.[31] The studio's profile on history was varied.

Gaslight (directed by Thorold Dickinson) had the last gala premiere of the war, but it was released during the height of the Blitz, which of course affected takings. Nonetheless it appeared in the *Kinematograph Weekly* listings, and it received extraordinarily good reviews; it suited a very wide range of critical tastes. Even the usually churlish critic of the *Daily Worker* was impressed, commenting on 4 June 1940 that it showed 'the monstrosities of Victorianism ... all the cruel conventions of the middle-class mind of the period, and indeed of our own times.' MGM was so impressed with the reaction of critics and public that it bought the film in 1944, and destroyed (as it thought) all extant copies so as to facilitate its own remake. This made any British reissue imposs-ible.

Gaslight deals with a hapless heroine driven to near-insanity by her husband; it accords precisely with the characteristics of Gothic melodrama described earlier. Indeed the studio printed a handout in Gothic script, fore-grounding these elements of the tale. Despite the declared intentions of Baxter and Corfield, and despite Dickinson's competence with official nostrums, it was impossible to recruit *Gaslight* into a propaganda argument. *Gaslight* rep-resents history as the site of misery; its world is claustrophobic, and the heroine's escape from it, though cathartic, has a dreadful cost. The film is an uncomfortable experience, since it combines an analysis of patriarchy with a rigorous scrutiny of middle-class hypocrisy. The success of *Gaslight* had less to do with British-National's aims than with Dickinson's artistic preoccupations of quality and craftsmanship.

British-National's next film, *This England*, was more consistent with studio intentions. It deals with the continuity of British rural ideals across a spectrum of periods: the Norman invasion, the Armada, the Napoleonic Wars, and the two world wars. Each period shows an identity of interest between landowner and farm labourer; in each, the female protagonist is a disruptive influence. Indeed, in the Tudor tale, she appears as an exotic witch or gypsy, prefiguring the Margaret Lockwood harridans of post-1942. *This England* had extremely bad reviews, and there is no evidence that it did well. What should be stressed is the extreme cultural conservatism of the film; its central gentry/labour relationship is negotiated in a spirit of expedience. History is rep-resented teleologically as a series of crises, each of which was a foregone conclusion; and important members of the film's target audience (women, the

middle class, the urban working class) are marginalised. The popular historical films of the 1930s had evoked the continuity of 'human nature'; more
importantly, they had stressed the *strangeness* of the past, and evinced an
awareness of the changes in the surface texture of people's everyday lives. *This
England* insisted instead that the past was the *same* as the present, and thus it
could not propose a dialectical relationship between the two. This was not the
case with *The Young Mr Pitt*. Historical propaganda films backed by the MoI
were at least coherent in their audience address, and the proposed relation
between past and present had elements of vitality. Privately backed propaganda efforts often managed the issue more clumsily.

British-National's *Penn of Pennsylvania* was another sorry venture. Set
in the Restoration, it deals with the tribulations of the Quaker William Penn.
The film shows how the persecuted Penn was dispatched to America and
founded Pennsylvania. En route he commits acts of inhuman piety. *Penn* was
conceived as an attempt to encourage Anglo-American feeling. The publicity
material claimed that the producer, Richard Vernon, had been fired by one of
Roosevelt's speeches, and that he and the director, Lance Comfort, made the
film for 'a time when Britain and America are more closely bound together
than ever before in history, and when co-operation and mutual understanding
between the two countries were never more essential.' But there were four
problems. Firstly, if an affectionate relationship between two countries is to be
inculcated, it is hardly tactful to present one as a bolt-hole from the atrocities
of the other. Secondly, the Restoration had by now become the symbol in film
culture of aristocratic tolerance and sexual largesse, and *Penn* instead
presents the period as one of repression. Puritanism, and by implication
Cromwellianism, was not ideologically central enough to carry the weight
placed on it by the film. Thirdly, it is hampered by leaden pace and dialogue.
Finally, excessive goodness is not interesting, in films or elsewhere.

British-National then filmed J. B. Priestley's *When We Are Married*, with
the Baxter/Corfield team. Priestley's play had already had extensive exposure,
and his BBC *Postscripts* had enormous currency. The studio exploited Priestley's status to the hilt. But *When We Are Married* was a case of overkill, rather
like making a film of *The Mousetrap*. Moreover, it was leadenly directed and
received few good reviews. The problem is that its comedy relies on sexual
politics which were no longer appropriate. It deals with the dismay of solid
burghers who discover that they are not legally married after all. But this was
of minimal interest to many of the mass audience, who were by that time
experiencing a sexual bonanza, and who probably did not care to be reminded
whether their unions were ratified or not. The war period was one of profound
reorientation and some liberalisation in sexual matters. Historical films which
attempted to redraw sexual boundaries in an explicitly conservative way stood
no chance at all. British-National had got it wrong again.

However, their *Waltz Time*, which was released at the end of the war, did
appear in the *Kinematograph Weekly* listings. This film is a lavish musical set
in a Vienna sufficiently historical to erase memories of the *Anschluss*. It deals
with the masked cavortings of the portly Richard Tauber and the warblers
Anne Ziegler and Webster Booth. The film was savagely (and hilariously)
reviewed, with one critic suggesting that Tauber was 'the rabbit the Elstree
python just can't swallow.'[32] But the critics failed to recognise that *Waltz Time*

combines a number of winning factors. It derives from a solid tradition of Ruritanian musicals; it deals exclusively with a heavily frilled aristocracy; and it has a script rife with sexual innuendo. For once the studio publicity machine recognised that the audience needed a past in which 'the ballroom is ringing with melody and romance.'

British-National's last historical film of the period was *Latin Quarter*, set in 1890s Paris and dealing with a mad sculptor who kills his wife and puts her in a statue. He is subsequently unmasked by a psychic. On the film's re-release in 1951 the studio foregrounded the occult elements, suggesting that cinema managers should 'arrange a screening for the various psychiatrists in your town and ask how the murder was committed.' We saw with *Crimes at the Dark House* that excessive violence and gore were not well received in wartime. Moreover, mass audiences of the period only liked films about *female* neurosis, such as *Madonna of the Seven Moons* or *The Seventh Veil*. Other films with serious occult elements were not successful; neither *Halfway House* nor *Dead of Night* did well. In spite of good reviews, therefore, *Latin Quarter* did not appear in box-office listings. Its brand of *grand guignol* was out of joint with the times.

So British-National's historical film production was, intellectually speaking, a ramshackle affair. *Gaslight* did well because of its stylish direction and its deployment of culturally assimilated Gothic elements. *Waltz Time* was only successful because the audience liked tenors and frills. But British-National's other period films provide an interesting lesson about the relationship between history and propaganda in wartime. The ethos of the studio and the orientation of the producers meant that propaganda elements were inserted into the films with too heavy a hand. Moreover, there was no consistent class position embedded in the films. Clearly, a recognisable studio orientation on class matters was one way of producing a stylish and coherent body of texts, which then stood more chance of pleasing a popular audience or of winning a particular constituency of audience experience. Ealing and Gainsborough were two cases in point; the lower middle class and the working class were addressed in their historical films with competent discourses and coherent symbolism.

We should not assume, however, that large cinema audiences could not enjoy film texts whose politics were elitist. It is sentimental to suppose that mass audiences in wartime were naturally drawn to films which enshrined radical politics. Film in World War II did not have that simple relationship to the 1945 Labour victory. A more appropriate metaphor for film culture in this or indeed any period is that of the patchwork quilt. The whole is composed out of fragments of different political colours and different cultural/historical orientations. There may be a dominant colour in any one period; but the 'quilt' is composed and indeed held together by the fragments from earlier modes of perception or from politically marginal positions.

It is within this framework that we should interpret some of the wartime films of Powell and Pressburger, who were engaged in the defence of elite groups and cultural conservatism. Their backgrounds meant that they had different competences: Powell was trained in a wide variety of cinematic crafts, whereas Pressburger's brand of Continental romanticism was focused on his scripts. Nonetheless, they were intellectually deeply compatible. Once Rank's financial umbrella relieved them of anxiety, they were able, as The Archers, to take artistic risks. Many of their Archers films contained a strong historical element: *The Life and Death of Colonel Blimp* (released May 1943), *A Canterbury Tale* (May 1944), *I Know Where I'm Going* (November 1945) and *A Matter of Life and Death* (November 1946). *Blimp* and *A Canterbury Tale* appeared in the *Kinematograph Weekly* list of successes. *A Matter of Life and Death* was named by Josh Billings as a 'notable box-office attraction'. All these films pleased a considerable proportion of the audience, though they were not smash hits like *The Wicked Lady*.

Blimp's vexed relationship with the MoI has been well documented.[33] The project was opposed by a number of government figures; Churchill, Beddington, Bracken and James Grigg, the Secretary of State for War, are all on record as discouraging the film. Nonetheless it was made, and the tide of wartime events meant that by mid-1943 it was no longer seen as a threat to official images of the Army. What should be emphasised is the major role played in *Blimp* by the defence of the past. Clive Candy is a relic of a superannuated old order; but that is shown to be more dignified, humane and liberal than its modern counterpart, which is brutally contemptuous of the rules of conduct. The overall tone of the end of the film, particularly the scene where Candy contemplates the withered leaf, is elegiac. The representation of the pre-World War I period in *Blimp* is of great interest. It is thoroughly consonant with the chivalric code and its emotions are in the high romantic mould. Candy's pursuit of *das Ewig-weibliche* is cunningly displayed by the device of using the same actress for the three female roles. The audience is presented with the spectacle of a European history held together by an officer class whose forte is loyalty and honour, and whose only fault is pomposity. Thus the past world is presented as one in which a small elite group operates as the cement of society's disparate values.

Such a resonant use of the past is also evident in *A Canterbury Tale*. History is presented with a materiality of expression; the manner in which the film is made calls attention to the complex nature of historical cause and effect. The cut from mediaeval hawker and bird to modern soldier and weaponry, the change of lighting on Eric Portman's face as he lectures on 'those ancient people', the aureole round his head in the railway carriage, and especially the use of music throughout, all attest to the necessary dependence of the present on the past. This interrelatedness is signalled by cinematic methods which avoid realism at every turn. Great narrative weight is carried by Colpepper the Glue Man, played by Portman. He is of minor gentry stock, and his attitude to the land is one not of ownership but of temporary stewardship. However, he is deeply flawed, since he displays a fear of the female principle and a fastidious dislike of the messiness of sex. The glue operates as a sign of moral interdiction; but it is also clearly a symbol of semen. Neurotic and misogynistic though Colpepper is, he is vitally necessary to the other three major characters and by implication to the rest of the fighting force; in order to obtain blessings, they need his good offices, because he is the vital conduit through which a sense of history can flow.

The meaning of *I Know Where I'm Going* is also structured round the urgent relevance of history and elite groups. In this film, the major symbolic issue is *rent*. The virile, charismatic Torquil is the rightful owner of the Scottish isle; since he has no portable property or surplus value, he is forced to rent it to the unseen industrialist. A contrast is drawn between the laird's erotic charge and the industrialist's implied impotence; the latter can only buy a wife. *I Know Where I'm Going* is a continuation of literary debates about the exiled aristocrat as the bearer of history; Burke, Byron, Austen, Bulwer-Lytton, even Yeats, all rehearse the same theme. It is no accident that the phrase which required the famous twenty-two takes concerns rent: 'Money isn't everything.' The heroine asks Catriona why she and Torquil do not sell their patrimony. Catriona replies with the disputed phrase. Powell demanded the retakes because 'there's only one way to say it, and that's the right way.'[34] The Herculean efforts required to find 'the right way' are akin to a stammerer struggling to articulate a crucial word. It is difficult because it is important.

In *I Know Where I'm Going*, Powell and Pressburger also approach the complexity of history through erotic power. Torquil is denied access to his real past because the castle is taboo. In an arousing scene, he opens the door and gains access to the labyrinthine passages and sunny courtyard within. Of course, this is a metaphor for the recesses of the female body and for the fulfilment of heterosexual love. Erotic pleasure and the possession of the past are coterminous.

This theme is further elaborated in *A Matter of Life and Death*, which appeared in the *Kinematograph Weekly* listings of 'notable attractions'. The film was first mooted by Jack Beddington, when in 1944 he invited Powell and Pressburger to make a 'big film' which would build on improved Anglo-American relations and prepare audiences for the postwar international situation. He thought they would be adept at this type of propaganda because they could, in his words, 'put these things in the way that people understand, without understanding.'[35] Because of the difficulties in obtaining the Technicolor stock Powell wanted, the film was late in production. But such was its ideological significance that it was given a Royal Command Performance in November 1946.

A Matter of Life and Death is a fantasy in which the everyday scenes are shot in colour, while the world after death is filmed in monochrome. According to Powell, audiences responded positively to this device, but the relationship between the two worlds preoccupied critics in the 1940s and has continued to do so. The Robsons, right-wing critics of the earlier period, saw the monochrome heaven as a metaphor for Hitler's New Order, which they presumed was endorsed by the authors. More recently, Raymond Durgnat has claimed that the monochrome world represents a rejection of socialist bureaucracy. Nicholas Pronay has argued similarly that the film celebrates an untidy individualism.[36]

What should be stressed is the priority which Powell and Pressburger gave to the issue of history, and the complexity and coherence of their case. *A Matter of Life and Death* represents a bid for intellectual power on behalf of a small intelligentsia. The authors attempt to elucidate, for old-style Tories, a strategy for possible postwar reforms. They summon to their aid the resources of the English Romantic movement. In their attitude to subjectivity, history and art, Powell and Pressburger precisely replicate the ideas of Wordsworth, Burke, Keats and especially Blake, for whom 'man is a garden ready planted and sown. This world is too poor to produce one seed.' *A Matter of Life and Death* deploys these writers, who are well assimilated into British cultural life, but gives them an additional conservative gloss. Peter Carter's subjectivity is structured so as to embrace the whole of culture and human history. With the closing of his physical eye before the operation, the audience is granted access to his mind's eye, which contains both Technicolor and monochrome worlds, as well as the collected wisdom of Plato and Bunyan. The film displays Peter's unconscious as the fertile location of that individual psychic power which provides social cohesion. Its propaganda aim was to suggest that what bound the British and the Americans together was their common history and their shared definition of culture. From material in the Foreign Office correspondence files at the Public Record Office, and from information obtained from prominent diplomats, it is clear that the propaganda intentions of *A Matter of Life and Death* were not revealed to British representatives abroad.[37] Its extravagant conservatism and multi-layered use of history may well have been an embarrassment to the new Labour government.

Powell and Pressburger's later films did not use history to any significant degree. We can assume that the exigencies of wartime prompted them to foreground the past, and to deploy it as a means of political intervention on behalf of a small social group. But for a fuller account of wartime and immediate postwar historical film, we should turn to the work of Ealing and Gainsborough Studios.

8

A MIDDLE-CLASS VIEW OF HISTORY

EALING 1939 – 49

I have suggested that the delineation of the producer's cultural competence is a valuable method of analysis. The historical output of Ealing and Gainsborough studios in the wartime and postwar period raises the issue of visual style and production control. Ealing was committed to the principle of realism, and Gainsborough to visual flamboyance. The two studios present a strong contrast in managerial approaches, and they produced two cycles of historical films which differ in every way. Broadly, Ealing's historical films, made under the aegis of Michael Balcon, displayed a continuity with his historical work at Gaumont-British in the 1930s; the Ealing histories were preoccupied with probity and respectability. Gainsborough costume melodramas have certain similarities to Korda's 1930s histories, since they foreground both visual and sexual pleasure. Gainsborough bodice-rippers, as I shall show, had a particular arrangement of style and class, which permitted the representation of history as a place where sexual and social fantasy could be fruitfully rehearsed. The important difference between the two studios' historical films is that only two of the Ealing films (*Scott of the Antarctic* and *Nicholas Nickleby*) were mentioned in the *Kinematograph Weekly* popularity charts, but almost all the Gainsborough ones were.

The historical films produced at Ealing in the wartime and postwar period were *Young Man's Fancy* (release date, August 1939), *Champagne Charlie* (August 1944), *Fiddlers Three* (October 1944), *Pink String and Sealing Wax* (December 1945), *Nicholas Nickleby* (March 1947), *The Loves of Joanna Godden* (June 1947), *Saraband for Dead Lovers* (September 1948), *Scott of the Antarctic* (December 1948), *Eureka Stockade* (January 1949), and *Kind Hearts and Coronets* (June 1949).

In the 1930s Balcon had conducted experiments with a form of unit production at Gaumont-British, and had encouraged favoured individuals so long as they concurred with his world-view. He developed a category of historical film in the 1930s in which realism, accuracy and moral improvement were major criteria. There is a clear continuity between Balcon's work at Gaumont-British and Ealing. At Ealing, a large administrative staff and a small creative elite followed the intellectual leadership of Balcon; a rigorous control was exercised, and little autonomy was granted to separate units at the studio. It is a truism frequently uttered by historians of, and workers at, Ealing that it had a 'family atmosphere'. But it was a notion of family predicated on an authoritarian father.

The managerial arrangements which obtained at Ealing partially accounted for the intellectual conservatism and sexual puritanism of its output. Balcon was isolated from his fellow-producers in his enthusiastic support of MoI propaganda aims. During the war, he was certainly liked by the British Council; he and Robert Stevenson were termed 'intelligent men', useful for official purposes.[1] This may well have stemmed from the Foreign Office's fondness for Gaumont-British in the 1930s. It is likely that, unpopular though he may have been with some of his peers, Balcon enjoyed the good opinion of official bodies during World War II. He was, however, frequently testy about MoI hamfistedness, and thought he could make better propaganda pictures than they could.[2] He certainly expressed vigorous views on the necessity of patriotism in the cinema, which gained considerable popular support, and he thought that national identity could be unproblematically foregrounded.[3] Interestingly, Balcon held views about feature film control which were far in excess of those of his peers. He was the only enthusiastic supporter of a Board of Trade attempt (ultimately abortive) to establish a National Controller of Film Production.[4]

Historical films produced under these intellectual and management conditions are likely to have certain characteristics in common, but a zeal for symmetry should not make us overlook important distinctions between film texts. *A Young Man's Fancy*, for example, is nuanced differently from the three other historical films produced at Ealing during World War II. It was directed by Robert Stevenson, and, like his *Tudor Rose*, concerns itself with the role of the aristocracy. The film is set in the 1870s, and deals with two lovers from different classes who are trapped in Paris by the advance of the Prussian army. Class hostility is foregrounded; the girl's proletarian father insists that 'Me veins have been sucked dry by the capitalist classes', and the boy's aristocratic father argues that 'Between the honest workman and the gilded plutocrat, understanding is impossible.' But such tensions are defused by the comic element in the script, which suggests that the peer should appropriate the squeaker from the Punch and Judy show and speak with it in his mouth, and that the heroine's chief charm is her performance as 'The Human Cannonball'. History is deployed in *A Young Man's Fancy* as a means of facilitating this joyous conciliation between warring class fractions. En route, popular culture is celebrated. But the vigour of the circus and music hall is presented with a wistful sentimentality which marks an outsider's perspective. The publicity material celebrated 'those plaintive and saccharine numbers that made all London weep, from duke to dustman'.

Champagne Charlie also displays this interpretation of popular culture, although made by a different director, Cavalcanti. It deals with the rivalry between warring performers in the 1860s music hall. Interestingly, the final version omits any mention of working-class deprivation. A draft script paid attention to the mining background of the hero, George Leybourne, and to the seditious content of some of his songs.[5] But these elements were removed, doubtless because they conflicted with the anodyne version of popular culture which Balcon deemed appropriate. *Charlie* had excellent reviews, but appeared on no popularity lists. The reason for its lack of broad appeal appears to be the *manner* in which the past is presented. Tommy Trinder and Stanley Holloway, both popular stars, engage in lively musical banter; moreover, such national symbols as jellied eels and boiled beef are prominent, and female thighs are displayed. But the narrative structure of *Champagne Charlie* is too episodic to engage the audience's imagination, and it should be compared in this regard with the successful Gainsborough film about show-business history, *I'll Be Your Sweetheart*. Here, a carefully placed catharsis ensured empathy. Another reason for *Champagne Charlie*'s lack of popular success was probably its lack of visual pleasure. Cavalcanti was at this time primarily interested in a type of documentary realism which specialised in persuasion and detail, and this accorded ill with the demands of the popular historical film, which required spectacle and sensuous visual textures. It is possible that Cavalcanti was slightly at odds with Balcon on the definition of realism. Certainly *Champagne Charlie* displays the past as a cramped, miniature place, in which a robust entertainment industry provided the only respite from discomfort. There is minimal attention in the film to the aesthetics of composition.

The nineteenth-century music hall was a fertile source of material during and after the war: *Variety Jubilee*, *I'll Be Your Sweetheart*, *Champagne Charlie*, *Trottie True* and others. It was a means whereby popular culture could be assessed and recuperated. Those working on *Champagne Charlie* certainly thought that they were giving an accurate account of music-hall history.[6] In fact, the film was extremely selective. Peter Bailey has demonstrated that Leybourne was a sophisticated virtuoso, while Vance was of lesser importance and versatility. The Ealing film instead presents Vance (Holloway) as the experienced figure, and showed Leybourne (Trinder) as a working-class innocent who lacks confidence in his ability to manoeuvre his way through different class and entertainment codes. Bailey suggestively argues that the 'swell song' inaugurated by Leybourne exploits the tensions generated by social and sexual ambiguities. It is a song of 'male exploit and display; in both, its historic and contemporary models are aristocratic or upper class though the style is never merely imitative, but rather an appropriation.'[7] The Ealing film, rather, deploys the swell song as a means of demonstrating working-class insecurity, since Leybourne is prompted by anxiety and competition.

Champagne Charlie, unlike *A Young Man's Fancy*, shows history as a place where a culturally insecure working class had to learn to imitate the codes of its superiors. This argument is achieved under the guise of celebrating the vigour of a popular tradition. A similar pattern obtains in the next Ealing history, *Fiddlers Three*, which deals with two sailors and a Wren who are magically transported to Roman times. This ruse affords numerous anachronistic gags: Stonehenge is 'another government housing scheme', Poppaea is 'the girl who invented glamour'. The two sailors are significantly differentiated. Sonnie Hale is a university lecturer whose specialism is Anglo-Saxon land tenure, which 'fairly pulsates with drama'. Tommy Trinder works in the Caledonian Market; he has Neanderthal intellect, but gets the girl. In a series of key scenes, Trinder feigns a trance in order to relay historical information whispered to him by the 'Professor'. Comedy is used as a means of endorsing a type of class ventriloquism, in which the ignorant (though physically adept) proletariat needs the prompting of intellectuals in order to survive.

Fiddlers Three had appalling reviews, in which the ponderous decor was the chief offender. Visually, the film is taxing without being pleasurable, since accurate details are piled on with no sense of meaning or proportion. The art direction is by Duncan Sutherland, who also worked on *Pink String and Sealing Wax* and *The Loves of Joanna Godden*, and who conformed to the Ealing practice of realism. Harry Watt directed *Fiddlers Three* because he was tired of 'sweaty heroes on the skyline' in quasi-documentaries, and he wished, 'after the Calvinism of the GPO and Crown, to surround myself with lovely dames'.[8] But Watt was misguided in expecting the puritanical Ealing to provide sensual bliss.

Once again, an Ealing history dissected a proletarian character and simultaneously celebrated his vitality and displayed his inadequacies. The last historical film made in the studio during wartime was *Pink String and Sealing Wax*. Great care was taken to render the claustrophobic surface of the period, but pleasurable visual details were not stressed. The film was directed by Robert Hamer, who, unusually for Ealing, favoured the mode of melodrama. The problem was that cinematic melodrama had by now become female territory. Women expected the genre to celebrate their pleasure and power, albeit fleetingly; and *Pink String* presented a stern retribution for erring females, who were shown to be implacably evil. *Pink String*, like Hamer's *It Always Rains on Sunday*, implicitly discomfited the audience at which its genre was aimed. The Gothic mode could fulfil important psychic drives in female audiences by permitting them to imagine and challenge male power. But the expression of patriarchal excess in *Pink String* is markedly uninflected, and the resolution at the end is unconvincing, since the softening and unbending of the tyrannical father is only shown by one shot of a static photograph. Hence the position of the female viewer is split between helpless victim (the wife and daughters) and hopeless criminal (Googie Withers). The latter is beautiful; but in a very long shot at the end her suffering prior to her suicide is constructed as a spectacle.

It is instructive to study the script's advice about the presentation of this character, Pearl. Hers 'is a hard loveliness, and the essential coarseness of her nature is always in danger of breaking through'. A revealing aside on the *mise en scène* suggests that she is sitting on 'a pile of dirty underclothes and old corsets'. A frisson of sexual disgust is prompted by the film, which is absent from the original play. The advertising also stressed the *femme maudite* theme: 'The story of a bad woman who loved shamelessly, who murdered ruthlessly.' A *Picturegoer* 'conversation' on the film on 5 January 1946 is revealing. A husband and wife discuss the repressions suffered by the women in the text and in the period in general. They then defend Pearl:

> We both liked Googie Withers. Though while I didn't believe for a moment she could have poisoned her husband the way she did, Sally didn't think she could have kept that lovely, creamy white complexion the way she was knocking half-glasses of whisky back every time the potman had his eye off the till.

Journalism it may be; but it is a classic case of 'reading against the grain', in which the respondents insist, in the teeth of the textual evidence, on a positive interpretation.

During the war, then, Ealing used history so as to discomfit women and

112

the working classes. Given that these groups constituted the mass audience at that time, it is predictable that the films were not popular. Perhaps surprisingly, Balcon and his directors did not emulate the propagandist uses of history promulgated by the MoI and others. Ealing's postwar historical productions constituted a different intellectual enterprise. Rather than concentrating on the historical relations between classes as it had done hitherto, the studio in its postwar films deployed history as a means of examining the constitution of the middle classes and the moral codes appropriate to them.

Nicholas Nickleby, for example, imposed a considerable class homogeneity on the original Dickens tale. The film should be compared in this regard to David Lean's *Great Expectations* and *Oliver Twist* from the same period, in which care was taken to replicate the complexity of Dickens's class coverage. The Ealing *Nickleby* attempted, by accent, dress and body language, to flatten out original class distinctions; it thus ushered in a celebration of a middle class which, though it contains villains, also has compensating heroes. Smike, for example, instead of being a deformed idiot from the residuum, gains a personable exterior and 'received pronunciation.' Miss La Creevy, the Crummles and the Cheerybles are all moved up the social register from ambiguous positions to ones firmly within the middle class. Dickens's novel provides a panorama of hopeless greed and mutual predatoriness; the Ealing film instead displays a middle class whose finer instincts are all aimed at domestic achievements.

Cavalcanti directed *Nickleby*, and his documentary inclinations are again evident in the narrative structure, which is in equally sized, linear scenes,

Nicholas Nickleby

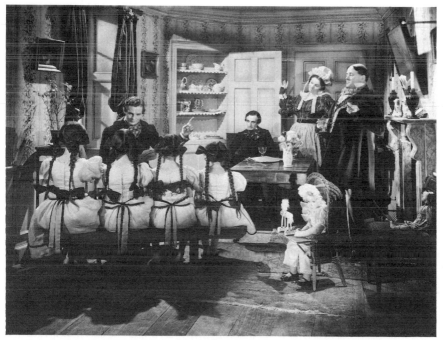

113

punctuated by montage cuts. Michael Relph was the film's art director, and his orientation is displayed in the credit sequence, which deploys the original book illustrations; the visual tone of the film is antiquarian, and it uses blocks of light and shade in a symmetrical way. *Nickleby*'s script provides a plethora of details about period accuracy. Relph suggested to me in an interview that in *Nickleby*, as elsewhere, the studio ethic of realism was encouraged. What 'realism' meant in this context was a consonance between the different discourses within the text; that is to say, the respective languages of script, music, decor and costume endorse each other, rather than providing dissonance or contradiction as in Gainsborough or Archers films. But a realist aesthetic is inappropriate for Dickens, whose style is defined by the grotesque element in his social observation. His mode of caricature permits the aristocracy and the working classes to have a symbolic and sometimes positive function; but the Ealing version, foregrounding domesticity and class exchange, eschews such resonance. All the reviewers used the original novel as a touchstone for their often quite stringent criticism.

A similar rigour and narrowness obtains in *The Loves of Joanna Godden*, which was based on a 1921 novel by Sheila Kaye-Smith. This describes the vicissitudes of a vigorous woman farmer on Romney Marsh in the 1890s, who courageously decides not to marry the father of her child; the end of the novel is a celebration of female independence. The Ealing version shows farming disasters, social pressures and loneliness impinging on the heroine (Googie Withers), such that she allows herself to be side-tracked by true love in the muscular form of John McCallum. Once again, the social range of the original text is curtailed; the book has a broad spread of social attention, but the film concentrates on small landowners. Charles Frend, the director, suggested in the publicity material that this narrowness and local colour added to the film's charm. But the reviewers did not agree and were uniformly unkind about the attention lavished on sheep husbandry.[9] Visually, *Joanna Godden* presents the past as uncomfortable, dirty and labour-intensive, although this is marginally undercut by some landscape shots of lyrical intensity and by the Vaughan Williams score. The script suggests that at a key moment there must be 'shots, each of which must be carefully composed, of a solitary tree, a twisting dyke, a row of elms.' But it also insists that this was a male perspective, and that, in order to appreciate it, Joanna has to see the marsh through the eyes of the hero. The script reminds the female audience with some sternness of the desirability of traditional sexual roles, and argues that Joanna is 'a mare who ain't never been properly broke in, and she wants a strong man to do it.' *The Loves of Joanna Godden* shared its sexual politics with *Nickleby* and *Pink String*; and they all suggest that the past was a nightmare for the middle class, from which it should be pleased to wake.

The later historical films concentrated on the construction of an appropriate code of behaviour for the governing class, which had by now become firmly identified (albeit optimistically) as the bourgeoisie. *Scott of the Antarctic* was a major status project, with location shooting, Technicolor and a Vaughan Williams score. It appeared in the *Kinematograph Weekly* list of box-office successes and was also chosen as a Royal Command Performance film. *Scott* can be interpreted as a celebration of the heroism of the new bourgeois officer class, rather than as an examination of its failures. Certainly most of the narrative

114

time is taken up by celebratory shots of comradely grit, and by an explanation of group loyalty in the face of absurd odds. *Scott* could be easily assimilated into a coercive morality.[10] But most of the critics, undecided though they were about the film's artistic merit, were certain that its 'realism' and its non-aristocratic morality would be key factors in coming to a decision.

What no one noticed was the film's preoccupation with masculinity. The script constructs male identity as a speechless but inexorable yearning towards one's own kind. At the end Scott 'looks affectionately at his companions. Then he moves so as to be alongside Wilson, and throws his left arm over Wilson's shoulder.' Expressivity is taboo, however; in an important speech, 'emotion is washed out of it [his voice] for this passage.' And the utmost unease is evinced about women. One of the heroes can see 'the place where the letter's going to, I mean, where she is; but her face is always misty.' The female face is absent, and the female body is a source of male anxiety. In a key scene, Ponting delivers a music-hall rhyming monologue. The one selected is about the difficulties of wriggling into his fur sleeping bag: 'So the fur side is the outside and the skinside is the inside.' This could be interpreted as a covert metaphor for female genitalia – a site of danger and distaste if the manner of the verse's delivery and the explorers' sniggering response is read aright.

We can conclude that *Scott*'s liberal class politics are underpinned by a profound misogyny. This pattern is replicated in *Eureka Stockade* (1949), which is also concerned with the 'grace under pressure' of male middle-class ethics. It is set in an Australian mining town in the gold rush of the 1850s, and its view of the locale in particular and the past in general seems to accord with Captain Scott's 'Great God! This is a dreadful place!'. Enormous care was taken to replicate clay pipes and borrow old weapons in order to ensure an authentic historical texture. But the film concentrates on morality and social codes. Those who rebel against unjust authority *become* the people, and take over the symbolic functions of the middle class. *Eureka Stockade* defines the freedom to buy land as the *sine qua non* of liberal politics, and contemporary critics found this aspect of the film unpalatable.

Kind Hearts and Coronets (1949) could also carry such a reading of class politics. The hero, after all, initially lives within the bourgeoisie; his campaign against the d'Ascoynes can be interpreted as straightforward class revenge. He appropriates the aristocracy's codes, and finally one of their women, with aplomb; the film has a sophisticated veneer which masks a real sense of social hunger. The class message is underpinned by the Oedipal sexual politics. Loyalty to the mother, and rage at her maltreatment, fuel Louis' desire to destroy the family, who all have the same face. However, *Kind Hearts and Coronets* is markedly more radical and experimental than other Ealing histories, particularly in its witty espousal of an amoral style and behaviour. This must be attributed to the influence of its director, Robert Hamer. By all accounts, he and Balcon were in serious disagreement about the film's moral provenance; Balcon attempted to tone down the sexual elements, and he finally 'encouraged' Hamer to seek his artistic fortunes elsewhere.

Finally there is *Saraband for Dead Lovers* (1948), a film which does not obviously conform to the paradigms described above. This film deals with the doomed love affair between Count Königsmark and Sophia Dorothea, wife of George I and mother of George II. *Saraband* was expensive, and the studio

Saraband for Dead Lovers

attempted to increase its production values by making it on location at Blenheim and by hiring tableware of the period from the Goldsmiths' Guild. The film was a failure at the box office, probably because of the idiosyncratic choice of historical period; it is difficult to see how the corrupt Hanoverian genealogy of the British Royal family could be of interest to the audiences of 1948. Nonetheless, the British Board of Film Censors insisted on removing some of the grosser remarks in the script, cautiously noting that 'as our reigning King is a direct descendant of George Louis, it is unfortunate that his profligacy and repellent German attributes are stressed and underlined.'[11] The censor was aware that mistresses had semi-official roles in the Hanoverian court, but suggested that this be played down for reasons of propriety. It was also suggested that the script make the audience more aware that George I's claim was impeccable, in that he was descended from James I and was supported by the 1689 Bill of Rights and the 1701 Act of Settlement. Thus the BBFC used its position to augment the celebration of legitimacy. Its critical response to the original Ealing script was unusual; its attitude towards *Scott of the Antarctic* and *Eureka Stockade* (and other Ealing films too) was congratulatory.[12]

Saraband for Dead Lovers was the result of attempts by both the producers and the workforce to achieve a complete integration between the different narrative languages. Alan Rawsthorne was the composer, and his copy of the script shows how painstaking were the efforts to obtain a close match between dialogue and score.[13] The practice of Ernest Irving, Music Director at Ealing, can be valuably compared with that of Louis Levy at Gainsborough, who often used music contrapuntally so as to heighten emotion in a different

116

way from the script.[14] Another important area of consonance in *Saraband* is between the costumes and the script. In the original novel, Sophia Dorothea only remains chaste by accident, and there is a hint of an incestuous relationship.[15] Yet all four available scripts of *Saraband* insist on her purity, and this is endorsed by the manner in which her period costume is adapted so as to flatten and de-eroticise her figure.

However, the intentions of the art department went slightly askew. Michael Relph, the film's associate producer, has suggested that *Saraband* was intended to be realistic and to conform with the practice already established by him at Ealing with Duncan Sutherland and Tom Morahan; the latter insisted that art direction should be 'functional, in that the setting had to be completely authentic, being integrated into a design which no longer had to be larger than life.'[16] One script, however, suggests that the decor should be 'grandiose and forbidding, suggestive of the ruthless ambition of the Hanoverians'. Another describes a castle interior with a baroque staircase which is 'devious, ornamental and vaguely erotic'. So the art department was caught between two conflicting desires: to be soberly realistic, or sumptuously symbolic. Another complication is that the use of Technicolor in *Saraband* is particularly gorgeous, and the sets are unrestrained in their use of crimson. Thus the colour red operates as an alternative sensual pleasure to the dry intrigues of the Protestant Hanoverian court. By implication, it could signal a commitment to Catholic, Stuart values. But in mainstream British culture Catholicism has often been symbolic of unknown terrors, and so a hopelessly contradictory message is being transmitted to the audience. In the official publication accompanying *Saraband*, Relph and the cinematographer Douglas Slocombe suggested that the painterly use of colour carried narrative values which the audience would be able to appreciate.[17] The film was praised for its colour and art direction by most critics. But its failure at the box office indicates that, skilled though the audience was at decoding the decor of the lurid bodice-rippers from Gainsborough, it was resistant to the respectable pleasures of *Saraband*. Critics' blandishments that the film was 'the mixture as before, but mixed at the Balcon rather than the Ostrer laboratories, by the new and tasteful chemistry of Messrs Basil Dearden and Relph' were to no avail.[18]

Saraband was reputedly Balcon's pet project. The studio publicity material suggested that he was the motivating force and had been 'the foremost in developing the technique of factual backgrounds which has become the hallmark of Ealing productions.' I suggest that Balcon's influence on the film is most clearly seen in two areas: female sexuality and the legitimisation of the monarchy. Women are split into two types: pretty, vapid celibates like Sophia Dorothea, or rapacious, ugly harridans like Countess Platen. The toils and privations of the monarchy are foregrounded, and its members complain that they 'marry for politics, bear children for politics, and lose them for politics.' The whole package is marked by an urgent sense that the audience should be acquainted with the real facts of history, whether these are palatable or not.

The problem with *Saraband* was that, firstly, it offered a horrid set of alternatives to the female audience, who, as I shall show, habitually used historical films as a means of stimulating imagination and desire. Secondly, the probity of the monarchy did not need endorsement in 1948. The dynasty was assured, the traumas of the abdication were forgotten, and the Royal

Family was, under a Labour government, beginning to develope a populist façade. Thirdly, in spite of (or because of) the blandishments of intellectuals on the desirability of historical accuracy, mass audiences had long demonstrated that they cared nothing for facts. In the 1930s, as I have shown, Balcon's costume films achieved a modicum of popularity because there was a definable constituency for his type of history. But he had lost that parish of belief by the time he made his cherished *Saraband*.

The wartime histories at Ealing put the working-class audience in a marginal position; the postwar histories, except *Saraband*, concentrated on the constitution of the middle class. Detailed attention to the historical films of Ealing shows that a very wide range of fractions from the middle class was examined. Its past miseries were pitied; but a taxonomy of the class was provided, whereby the complexity and coherence of the bourgeoisie as a whole was celebrated. The historical films allow us to recognise that Ealing's interests were not modestly confined to one class fraction, but were an ambitious attempt to locate the whole middle class at the centre of the cultural debate, and also implicitly to endorse a bourgeois value-system. Coincidentally, Ealing histories also located male characters at the centre of their narratives, and these heroes had a primarily moral function. A strong contrast can be drawn with the Gainsborough histories, which were oriented towards women and the working class.

9

HISTORY AND THE WORKING CLASS

GAINSBOROUGH 1942–50

The Gainsborough costume cycle was quite extensive: *The Man in Grey* (release date, July 1943), *Fanny by Gaslight* (May 1944), *Madonna of the Seven Moons* (November 1944), *A Place of One's Own* (March 1945), *I'll Be Your Sweetheart* (June 1945), *The Wicked Lady* (November 1945), *Caravan* (April 1946), *The Magic Bow* (October 1946), *Jassy* (August 1947), *The Bad Lord Byron* (March 1949), *Christopher Columbus* (June 1949), *Diamond City* (October 1949), *So Long at the Fair* (May 1950). The popularity ratings of most of these Gainsborough histories are impressive; except for *A Place of One's Own*, they did extremely well up to and including *Jassy*. After that they ceased to dominate the market, following changes in studio management style and possibly also in audience composition.

Until late 1947 Gainsborough costume films all have a rich visual texture, and deal with the upper gentry class; they contain female protagonists, often with gypsy blood, who seek sexual pleasure and who are ritually dispatched. As I shall show, there were contradictions between the verbal level of the script and the non-verbal discourses of decor and costume. Gainsborough provided a site for a carefully costed expressionism whose practitioners had been unhappy working in the theatre or other studios because of the dominance of a realist orthodoxy; it was through this visual expressionism that the audience's fears or desires could be rehearsed.

Balcon had founded Gainsborough in 1924, and left it in 1936. It was then acquired by the Ostrer brothers, a family of liberal Jewish entrepreneurs. From then until the end of 1941, Maurice Ostrer and former showman Ted Black ran the company. J. Arthur Rank then bought it, and interfered little in the organisation until late 1946 when he appointed Sydney Box as Head of Production. During the period of Gainsborough's greatest profitability, from 1942 to 1946, Rank was preoccupied with other production companies in his empire. In any case, his lack of cultural capital ('Who is Thomas Hardy?') meant that, until his finances became pressing, he allowed free rein to Gainsborough producers.[1] From 1942 Maurice Ostrer was Head of Production, and, as joint producers, he appointed veteran cost-cutter Harold Huth and writer R. J. Minney, who had co-scripted the Hollywood success *Clive of India*. Ted Black, as an Associate Producer, was also prominent until late 1943, responsible for the day-to-day running of the studio. Thus with Gainsborough we see a quite different type of production control than obtained at Ealing or The Archers. Under the Ostrers, and under Rank until 1946, those owning the studio had no firm intellectual position; they abrogated that responsibility to men who were firmly rooted in the industry, and who were experienced in teasing out the different strands in mass film culture. Thus uniquely at Gainsborough a space was opened up in which various practitioners were given their head, and were permitted to experiment as long as it proved profitable.

Black and Minney had an unerring sense of popular taste. Black was the first to notice that Margaret Lockwood 'had something with which every girl in the suburbs could identify herself'.[2] He ran a tight ship at Gainsborough, and was held in awe by the art directors. Harold Huth, too, was meticulous, claiming that 80 per cent of the material in their films reached the screen as planned.[3] R. J. Minney chose the novels on which the bodice-rippers were based. With *Madonna*, for example, 'the experts all said there wasn't a film in it. The subject had been rejected so often that it was regarded as voodoo. Minney quietly went to work, wrote his own script, planned the production, costed it.'[4] Minney was opposed to the notion of the quality film and thought that 'the commodity must be what the public wants, and what the public is at present educated enough to like.' Melodrama was the form which in Minney's view encapsulated popular culture; he preferred texts 'with blood and thunder' and thought that they should aim for 'a full-blooded story such as may be found in the pages of the Bible.' Documentary or realism could not fulfil the emotional needs of the audience.[5]

The management philosophy expressed itself on the studio floor in terms of careful pre-shooting costing and tight commodity control. Maurice Ostrer had attempted, in his work for the British Film Producers' Association, to inculcate such rigour.[6] He insisted to *Today's Cinema* on 4 January 1945 : 'I want the whole amount budgeted for the film to appear on the screen in the production, and not to have a large amount frittered away behind the scenes in extravagant and needless waste.' He wanted a cast-iron script, completed to the last detail, since the producer should be able to predict what his unmade film would look like, in terms not just of pictures, but of money.[7] There was very stringent analysis of the shooting diary of *The Wicked Lady*, and detailed inquests about any delay. There was very little location work, and a rigorous six-week schedule meant building sets at night. Ted Black even forbade personal phone calls and kept writing paper at a premium, with the result that the workforce sent each other notes written on toilet paper. Stars were sometimes required to work on two films at once. The studio insisted on star appearances, elaborate advertising, and negotiation of long bookings, to increase profits.[8] Stringent economies were exacted in the area of equipment. The only modern machinery at Gainsborough was the meteorological equipment, which could predict weather conditions and thus save expensive time.[9] Wind-machines and back-projection equipment were obsolete, and there was no illuminated footage counter. The sound department was unwillingly obliged to use British Acoustic equipment because it came from an Ostrer subsidiary company, instead of the RCA machinery they would have preferred. Maurice Ostrer insisted that this stringent system worked, as far as profit breakdowns were concerned.[10]

The studio workforce was structured in a classic Taylorist manner: all sections had separate meetings, and initially a union consciousness was difficult to establish. The management did not inform any group of the others' activities and there was a rigid separation between management and labour. The technical workforce rarely even saw Maurice Ostrer. The scriptwriters, however, were in a more privileged relationship to the producers. They were making a bid for higher status and intellectual power, and this was expressed by altering the class orientation of the original novels on which the films were based. Only the scriptwriters and the directors saw the rushes with the producers, and comments were filtered down privately to the technical workers. The intellectual chain of command meant that new script pages could be sent down at unusually short notice.

Up to and including *Jassy* (1947), Gainsborough's management philosophy made for a strong generic cycle. Tight economic control, a strongly hierarchical organisation, a privileged intellectual elite, an insistence that production values appear on the screen, were all combined with an awareness of key motifs in popular culture. But after 1945 Rank began to experience severe economic difficulties. He made unsuccessful attempts on the American market, and set up Independent Frame, an experimental method of pre-shooting preparation. In December 1946 he closed down Production Facilities (Films) Ltd., which had carried much of his administrative burden for Gainsborough.[11] In an attempt to fill the gap made when the Ostrers and Minney resigned, Rank had appointed Sydney Box as Head of Production in September 1946, because of his success with *The Seventh Veil*; Rank's difficulties were compounded by his urgent need to make more economic use of studio space.[12]

However, under Box there ensued an immediate crisis of staff morale. There was also a sharp increase in expenditure on costume films, probably because of new postwar conditions. A detailed comparison of the cost sheets of *The Man in Grey* (1943) with Box's *The Bad Lord Byron* (1948) is instructive.[13] A huge increase is evident in sets and location expenditure. The problem was that Box, skilled though he was in melodrama (*The Seventh Veil*), had no aptitude for costume films. He yearned for realism in art direction and costume design, and this was fatal to the tone of Gainsborough's enterprises. Box himself argued that the postwar audience wanted to identify with their own period rather than with the historical past.[14] His problems with costume films were exacerbated by the fact that many of the original Gainsborough scriptwriters left with Minney and the Ostrers, leaving Box to his own devices. Box had a perfectly good script for *Christopher Columbus*, which he proceeded to tear apart and rewrite with his wife and co-producer Muriel Box. *The Bad Lord Byron*, *Christopher Columbus* and *So Long at the Fair* also failed because of uncontrolled location spending, and because they did not address important class or sexual issues through the disguise of history; nor were they primarily aimed at a female audience.

The Gainsborough costume cycle, until and including *Jassy*, had been uncompromisingly slanted towards women. The studio publicists insisted on the gender bias of melodrama, and suggested that *Madonna of the Seven Moons* be marketed so as to redefine schizophrenia as a female ailment, with the headline 'Split-Mind Disorder Gives Idea for Year's Finest Romance!' Cinema managers were advised to appeal to 'curiosity, that great feminine characteristic. Trade on this!' *Picturegoer* followed the studio's lead on 23 June 1945 by printing an article on schizophrenia by a psychiatrist, which argued that cases like Rosanna/Maddalena were evidence that in women 'the normal personality is blanked out and the dark forces of the libido are released.' Gainsborough, from its producers down to its publicists, spared no effort to encourage libidinal release in its female audience, either by simulating the conditions of psychosis or by feminising the image of the male star. The poster for *Caravan* (1946), for example, displayed Stewart Granger in Valentino mode, with earrings, curls and lipstick. The Gainsborough film-makers and their publicists clearly intended that their films would usher women into a realm of pleasure where the female stars would function as the source of the female gaze, and where the males, gorgeously arrayed, would be the unabashed objects of female desire.

Gainsborough producers defined melodramas as the female equivalent of horse-racing or boxing – low-status anodynes which pleasurably and harmlessly defused aggression. Maurice Ostrer insisted that the films should produce a 'visual feast', 'pageantry' and 'romantic gaiety', which would solace the audience.[15] He argued in *Kinematograph Weekly* on 20 December 1945 that audience taste had followed the lead given by Gainsborough:

> It does seem that the public, which has always been intensely chary of costume spectacles, is now in full-blooded pursuit of them. Costume melodramas pack the box-office. I suggest that this is an escape from the drabness of this present-day world of clothes coupons and austerity.

Picturegoer recognised, on 14 October 1945, that the Ostrers were attempting to reorient popular cinema by stressing 'red-blooded love' which transported the audience 'back to the heyday of Valentino and Navarro'. A prominent director of Gainsborough melodramas, Leslie Arliss, also welcomed being called a 'women's director', arguing in *Picturegoer* on 3 April 1943 that the emotional inhibition which characterised British culture should be challenged by the screen: 'I am not afraid of sentiment, and am working to overcome this shyness and to put unashamed feelings on screen, rather than to depend on speed of action.' Arliss later argued that the success of the costume melodramas lay in their provision of a lascivious vitality with which female viewers could temporarily identify: 'They've got more colour and fire, and they're more human, too ... Wicked women excite you, even though you do not approve of them.'[16] The attractions of stylish villainy for female audiences were also discussed by Gainsborough stars. Margaret Lockwood noted that *The Wicked Lady*'s protagonist 'is even more ruthless than in the novel. They have given me an extra murder.'[17] *Picturegoer* noted on 3 September 1943 that female audiences were also drawn to the 'curved sensuous lips and dark compelling eyes' of the rascally heroes played by James Mason, and it was worried that 'this man makes villainy more attractive.' Even Lux Toilet Soap argued in its advertisements that its emollience worked best on 'the Bad, Bold and the Beautiful' like Lockwood.

It was doubtless Gainsborough's attention to female working-class audiences that prompted the critical opprobrium which the bodice-rippers attracted. The films did not conform to the criteria of good taste, since their lack of realism befitted a low-status audience. Time and again, critics from a wide range of journals attacked the films *because* they were aimed at working-class females. *Madonna of the Seven Moons* 'is a highly osculatory piece, comprising the kiss filched, the kiss rejected, the kiss paternal, the kiss devout, the kiss marital, the kiss passionate.' Stewart Granger 'sitting on an upturned barrel swigging rum and kissing Calvert with a passion only recognised as purple convinced me that there's a sadist in the Casting Department of Gainsborough Pictures.' *The Wicked Lady* was rejected as 'a carefully compounded bromide, the lines aiming no higher than *Mabel's Weekly*' in which 'highwaymen, doxies, poison cordials ... the heavy and the disagreeable are married with an infelicity rare even in costume.'[18] The *Daily Mail* noted that it was 'of the Twere and Werty School ("It is well that thou wert gone, my Lord") ... The attempt at credibility is atrocious.' Even for the critic of the *Dispatch*, the film 'was not my stoup of Romantic wine'. *Tribune* noted that 'because I am, by inclination at least, an historian, *The Wicked Lady* arouses in me a nausea out of all proportion to the subject.' This critic loathed 'this complete misunderstanding of Restoration England, this tatty Merry English roadhouse atmosphere, with the bowls of "daffies" on the gate-legged table.'[19] If possible, *Caravan* fared worse; it was 'not what is known as a critic's picture ... not for a moment compellingly realistic.'[20] Papers as different as *Tribune* and the *Graphic* expressed outrage: 'If Lady E. F. Smith's novel found a large public, this should certainly find a larger. It will certainly make lots of money', and 'To enjoy it, you need to have a mind that throbs to every sob of the novelette and a heart that throbs to every exposure of Stewart Granger's torso.'[21] The *Daily Mail* critic was worried about how 'the principal characters can exist for months in a cave, without visible washing facilities, preserving a spotless elaboration of dress.'[22]

Such broad displays of critical ill-temper were a sign that something important was afoot. Gainsborough bodice-rippers deeply offended pro-realism critics, who attempted to cleanse film culture of this supposed prurience. The critics were successful, in so far as these melodramas became invisible in cinema history until relatively recently. However, they are crucial in any mapping of British popular taste, and should be given major currency in debates about the cultural resources of the wartime and postwar period.

We should now turn to the verbal discourse of the Gainsborough costume melodramas. The films were based on a popular cycle of historical novels by women, with one exception; Manuel Konroff's 1941 *The Magic Bow* was also selected for adaptation, and it had stylistic similarities to the other adapted novels. The books all deployed a complex series of framing devices which put the reader at one remove from history, and this effect was not neutralised by the language, which was dense, metaphorical and opulent. All the novels featured groups on the boundary of the permissible – the higher aristocracy, gypsies, and libidinous women – and examined them for signs of social pollution. Such groups gained energy from their ambiguous poise, and the audience was encouraged to take pleasure in their excess. But coincidentally the novels impelled the reader to judge and to reject, so that creativity and complicity were inextricably mixed in the readership response demanded by the texts.

The novels all located the aristocracy with some care, balancing its negative against its positive qualities. It was the historical dimension that was responsible for the novels' popularity; books about the aristocracy in a modern setting did not appeal to the same mass readership, because they did not permit the fruitful elision of marginal groups. In the bodice-ripper novels,

123

gypsies also symbolise an exotic, sexual energy which is conveniently outside any class domain; any excessive qualities are safely neutralised by their ability to foretell the future. Passionate females, if linked to the aristocracy, are always categorised as dangerous, but they can be recuperated by marriage or death. Oriana's behaviour in the following passage from *Caravan* is exonerated by her later fidelity and death:

> Without a word, he got into bed beside her. And they made love with a fury, a violence, that left him exhausted ... he knew her then, for what she was, a sensual woman who had always wanted him. And as he embraced her, he remembered the sailors' talk of witch-women, of *sorcières* from which no man could escape. He lay there, indulging her wanton ways.[23]

Rosal in the same novel and Barbara in *The Life and Death of the Wicked Lady Skelton* sally forth in search of their heart's desire, and narrative pleasure ensues from their audacity; but such hubris is always corrected by the finale. The surviving females are always domesticated, and free from the inconveniences of desire.

The novels on which the Gainsborough cycle is based constitute the past as a series of intense sensual moments. These are scattered evenly throughout, so that there is no single cathartic release but a series of structured peaks. The narrators in the texts always appear alienated from the values of polite society. Interestingly, two of the novelists stressed their own social marginality. Lady E. F. Smith insisted on her own supposed gypsy blood.[24] Norah Lofts suggested that 'If we ever return to barbarism, I hope to be allowed to carry my mat from place to place and tell stories for copper coins ... One would thus always be one step ahead of the critics.'[25] In the novels, history is a country where female refugees from common sense can temporarily reside, but it is a place of banishment nonetheless; and there, gypsy, gentry and female excess are safely placed.

The structures of feeling contained within the Gainsborough scripts differed from the novels in important ways. The scriptwriters were a highly specialised and motivated group. Margaret Kennedy, Roland Pertwee, R. J. Minney, Leslie Arliss, and Frank Launder and Sidney Gilliat were the founding members of the Screenwriters Association (SWA) in 1937, and they maintained a continuity until the mid-1940s. These writers had a developed sense of their own institutional and industrial constraints, and they struggled to place themselves in a different market position from the original novelists.

There is little explicit material on authorship theory at Gainsborough. Roland Pertwee evinced a preference for stories that 'awaken an emotion'.[26] Margaret Kennedy expressed a contempt for the film audience as 'a community which never reads', and discouraged any novelist from adapting his own text, as he would 'break his heart on finding how anomalous his position is, and how small the chance that any fragment of his ideas will find its way to the screen.'[27] She proposed that the illiteracy of the audience enforced only two alternatives for the writer: to adapt a second-rate book for which one had no respect, or to become a director and editor.

Kennedy's strictures chimed in with studio practice at Gainsborough. The original novelists were rigorously excluded from filming. Minney, Arliss and director Arthur Crabtree specifically insisted on this. The technical staff were discouraged from reading the novels, and they felt in any case that 'it didn't do to get too involved like that, because you put all kind of emotions into it, and then the script would change a relationship or chop things, and then you'd be upset.'[28] The scriptwriters isolated themselves from the rest of the workforce as a kind of aristocracy of labour, and the Screenwriters Association fought for the free collective bargaining of a loose affiliation of individuals.[29] The SWA was contracted as a voluntary consultant by the MoI. It was able to oust the claims of the Association of Cine-Technicians (ACT) to act on behalf of script-writers, and Launder disingenuously noted that his members were 'neither reactionary conservatives nor reactionary unionists, but just simple, progress-ive, benevolent anarchists'.[30] The SWA had sufficient clout to defeat the Rank-backed Scenario Institute Limited of del Giudice, objecting to the monopolistic character of the venture, and it managed to co-opt Balcon to its cause. In spite of the hostility of the British Film Producers Association, the SWA set up an Ideas Committee, which reported to the MoI's Films Division on likely propa-ganda topics.[31]

The SWA was a combative, confident body, in which Gainsborough script-writers played a key role. The scripts they produced for the bodice-ripper cycle established the relationship between their professional theories and their ar-tistic practice. They tended to endorse their own class position and definitions of culture, and they clarified lines of class power. Although three scriptwriters were women, all the scripts imposed a normative morality upon deviant females. The original novels had addressed a middle-class readership, con-ceived as the equals of their authors; the scripts, addressing a largely working-class and female audience, shifted the 'marginal' groups in the novels into the danger zone. This profoundly affected the texts' ideological function.

The novels had complex framing devices, but the scripts all begin *in medias res*. The first *Wicked Lady* script begins with two modern tramps confronting the heroine's ghost, and it ends with the sound of 'thundering hooves' as her spirit exits; but both these scenes are removed from the final version. The script of *The Man in Grey* conceals the flashback effect, and that of *Caravan* contains a reprise which is similarly smoothed over. These scripts plunge the audience into history in a seemingly unmediated way.

The film scripts accorded more utterance to lower-class characters. Belinda in the novel *Jassy* is a mute; the script grants her speech. The role of Toby, the black servant in *The Man in Grey*, is greatly expanded, as is that of the gypsies in *Caravan* and *Madonna of the Seven Moons*, and the impover-ished characters in *The Magic Bow*. The film scripts also give crucial roles to middle-class males; the architect in *The Wicked Lady*, the librarian in *The Man in Grey*, the dispossessed farmer in *Jassy*, do not appear in the novels. Moreover, the scripts compare aristocratic excess with bourgeois professional-ism and restraint, to the latter's advantage. In the novel *Caravan*, Sir Francis is an amiable invalid. In the script, his villainy is outrageous; even whores remark that 'he's a beast – he's the worst of the lot!' The bourgeois hero then appropriates his whip and dispatches him to a gurgling death in a swamp. Similarly, in *The Man in Grey*, the aristocrat is transformed from the honest hero of the novel to a Byronic misogynist. The script has him announce that 'I've yet to meet a woman I don't despise', and makes him beat Hester to death.

125

The aristocratic father in *Jassy* and Lord Manderstoke in *Fanny by Gaslight* are similarly given a *grand guignol* treatment. The bourgeois hero in the script of *The Man in Grey* wonders what the gentry 'ever did to deserve all this', and in *Fanny* the protagonist suggests that 'a hundred years from now such class distinctions won't exist.' The scripts all present the aristocracy as the site of fascination, fear, and unspeakable dark sexuality.

Gypsies in the scripts no longer present an exotic wisdom as in the novels, but a social threat. In the novel *Madonna* the gypsies are a source of energy, whereas the script concentrates on their squalor; and the rape, which in the novel is perpetrated by the husband, is committed by a gypsy in the script. The *Caravan* script has gypsies assault and rob the hero, whereas the novel insists on their racial purity. Libidinous women are similarly removed from the ambiguous margins to the 'danger' category. Their relationships with each other are acrimonious – 'Wear *that*? I wouldn't be buried in it' – and their destruction ensues because of their position beyond the pale. The script of *The Man in Grey* notes ominously that Hester 'in her black dress, *does* look very like a witch.' *The Wicked Lady* script makes Barbara want 'a house and children, all the things I never thought would matter', as a restitution for her metonymous desires for 'a hundred mouths'. The rape by the returned Jackson is absent from the book, as is the sadistic nature of their verbal exchanges. And the split heroine in the film of *Madonna* has her double nature symbolised on her deathbed by the crucifix and the rose. Such sublime excess is absent from the novel.

Gainsborough scriptwriters, then, placed themselves in a different market relationship from the novelists. The latter had arrived, either by private research or instinct, at market dominance; Gainsborough scriptwriters desired instead an individualistic, quasi-guild authorship. Because of their scorn for the mass-culture factory in which they worked, they were unable to reproduce the novels' structures of social feeling. In the novels, marginal groups are dynamically poised in a sophisticated balance, and they offer a pleasing choice to the audience, whose anxieties they can defuse. In the scripts these groups are pushed headlong into a chasm where only fear resides. The audience is granted little creativity by the scripts, which present females as greedy and strange and the working class as culturally inferior. The institutional struggles faced by the scriptwriters were probably instrumental in causing them to draw the boundaries of class and gender more sharply. The novelists had an identity of interest with their target readers, since they too were middle-class and female; whereas the scriptwriters took refuge in a rhetoric of disdain towards their working-class female audience.

The lines of sexual morality and class power are strictly drawn by the Gainsborough scripts; but their message is at variance with that of the visual discourses of the films, which reside in the practices of art direction, costume design and body language. Different concepts of knowledge, history and pleasure are implicitly contained within these areas.

The art department at Gainsborough worked under conditions of extreme pressure but it attracted a number of expert period artists. There was strict control of over-spending; atmospheric 'overbuilding' was forbidden by Black, who dismissed the extravagant Walter Murton from *The Man in Grey* and insisted on dismantling his elaborate sets; Black then brought in the more economically minded art director Maurice Carter, who was at the beginning of his career. Location shooting was discouraged since the staff were then beyond studio control; the only example in the pre-Box cycle was the Welsh ('Spanish') countryside in *Caravan*. But such financial rigour contrasts with laxity in the area of historical interpretation. Maurice Carter commented that 'provided you could perform money-wise, and get the sets there on time, they [the executive producers] were reasonably happy. They didn't have much to say on the artistic side.' Carter suggested that he and John Bryan founded the Art Directors Guild as a direct consequence of what they had learned at Gainsborough. Certainly the practice there in the 1940s was far in advance of current theories of art direction.[32]

The art directors at Gainsborough constructed a past that was both familiar and sensually appealing. The audiences were implicitly positioned so as to feel confident in their own ability to fill in the gaps in the discourse; this was achieved by avoiding the conventional signs of authenticity. If documentation did appear in the films, it was personalised by a voice-over (as in Clarissa's diary pages in *The Man in Grey*) or it was so brief as to make only a ripple in the narrative (as in the newspaper cutting in *The Wicked Lady*). The spectacular aspects of *mise en scène* were foregrounded at Gainsborough, and they produced a vision of history as a place where only feelings resided; sociopolitical conflicts appeared merely in a disguised form.

The studio team had different backgrounds, which affected their styles. Maurice Carter had architectural and furnishing experience, and as Supervis-

The Wicked Lady

Caravan

ing Art Director he personally designed *Jassy*, *The Bad Lord Byron* and *The Man in Grey*. He and Vetchinsky, who was an architect by training, had long-term contracts. Andrew Mazzei was formerly a commercial artist, and designed *Madonna of the Seven Moons*. John Bryan, who had a theatrical background, designed *Fanny by Gaslight*, *The Wicked Lady* and *Caravan*. Gainsborough provided a site where art directors could flourish even if they had a commercial or applied arts background and were opposed to realism. The later careers of Carter and Bryan show a continuity with their Gainsborough style; Carter's *Anne of a Thousand Days*, Bryan's *Blanche Fury*, or *The Spanish Gardener* on which they collaborated, all avoided naturalist techniques. The influence of Continental art directors such as Andrejev, Bellan, Vincent Korda and Alfred Junge could clearly be seen at Gainsborough. They mediated expressionist traditions from Germany, and had a formative influence on Carter and Bryan, who tempered their influence with notions of craftsmanship.

John Bryan's work merits particular attention; he had a marked taste for asymmetrical composition and an interest in the picturesque aesthetic. His set work for *The Wicked Lady* displays considerable eclecticism. Each object is reproduced in a historically accurate way but it is placed in an unpredictable spatial relationship to other objects from different periods. The past is displayed not as a coherent whole but as a chaotic cornucopia of goods, whose meaning is uncertain but whose appearance is pleasurable. A Jacobean door, a baroque candleholder, an Elizabethan bed, a Puritan bible, a medieval fire-basket combine to form a dense visual texture. There were period advisers at Gainsborough, but their scholarship was used in *The Wicked Lady* so as not to alienate an uninformed audience. *Semper Fidelis* was the only Latin used in the film, appearing on a plaque between Patricia Roc and Griffith Jones as they affirm their love. Minney and Bryan use an accurate three-cornered gallows in the execution scene, but any heaviness which this accuracy might produce is lightened by first showing miniaturised toy versions of it.[33] Bryan's decor is sometimes ironical; when Lockwood lowers her eyes on her wedding night, a short dissolve compares her expression with the Madonna on her petit-point tapestry in the next scene.

Bryan avoided historicised decor when dealing with sexually explicit scenes. When Mason and Lockwood make love by the river, only mist, trees and water can be seen; no houses or accoutrements. Moreover, Lockwood in this scene wears a tailored blouse similar to severe 1940s fashion. History is concealed in order to suggest that sexuality is 'natural', without historical codes. Maurice Carter suggested that 'your instinctive reaction was to make the thing as rich as possible.'[34] But richness of decor is clearly seen as super-fluous when compared with the richness of desire.

Bryan's work on *Caravan* is also eclectic and idiosyncratic. The contrast between nature and culture is radically drawn; the Spanish scenery is an uncivilised wilderness where danger lurks, while the interiors display a dis-ordered amalgamation of culture. The interiors are crammed with exotica, and these are spasmodically concealed by darkness which gives them mystery. *Caravan*'s sets were extremely labour-intensive, and they were erected with remarkable speed.[35] But they present to the audience a set of locales of pleasure and narrative weight; the Victorian interiors, the gypsy cave and the sumptuous Spanish garden are all of equal cultural value. The audience is put at the same distance from all the historical locales and it is therefore given the illusion of making a free aesthetic choice. Bryan deploys the same technique in the earlier *Fanny by Gaslight*, where the shadowy recesses of the subterranean club 'Shades' are precisely replicated in the respectable family parlour above; a parallel is implicitly drawn which discomforts conventional morality.

The other art directors at Gainsborough displayed a similar avoidance of an aesthetic and historical hierarchy. Mazzei's work on *Madonna of the Seven Moons* suggests by tone and composition that the ruined garden, the Barucci interiors and the Labardi courtyard are equally full of symbolic resonance and picturesque wildness. His art direction for *The Magic Bow* also presents the past as a series of intense moments equidistant from the present. And Maurice Carter's designs for *The Man in Grey* combine surface accuracy with a concern for sensual arousal.

Until the arrival of Sydney Box in late 1946, visual style at Gainsborough presented the past as a site of physical pleasure; it was neither linear nor closed. Under Box's management, such expressionist (and relatively cheap) set work ceased. Expensive location work was undertaken for *The Bad Lord Byron*, and Carter was unwillingly obliged to use the poet's own furniture. Box was aware that the decor was a major selling point, and for *Jassy* Carter had a very large set budget in an attempt to replicate the success of *The Wicked Lady*. But this was a Technicolor film and new skills had to be learned by the art department. Box's interest in realism and 'status' production also influenced the decor in *Christopher Columbus*, where the costly location and replica work nullified any profitability.[36]

Until Box arrived, a set of managerial circumstances allowed a group of like-minded art directors to produce a visual aesthetic which undercut the class and moral position of the scripts. Their carefully costed expressionism permitted and encouraged fantasies which combined history and sexuality in a way which was paradoxically not unlike the original novels, and which also recalled the procedures of Korda in the 1930s. Historical costume design at Gainsborough paid minimal attention to accuracy or realism, but instead embedded, within the main discourse of the film, a 'costume narrative' whose provenance was sexual desire.

From *The Man in Grey* to *The Bad Lord Byron*, Elizabeth Haffenden's costumes celebrated sexual difference. The breasts were displayed to a greater extent, and the men's trousers were more tight-fitting, than in the actual historical period. Skirts were cut on the bias and with pleats so as to permit maximum freedom of movement; in *Fanny by Gaslight*, *The Wicked Lady*, *Caravan* and *Jassy*, they encouraged a broader body language with sinuous hip movements. This exploited the erotic potential of sound, with rustling fabric and tinkling bells. The frigid aristocratic wife in *Madonna of the Seven Moons* changes her kinesic behaviour once she glimpses the flowing gypsy clothes in the mirror; on her deathbed her respectability is signalled by the cut of her nightgown and, a desexualised mother once more, she is returned to polite society. Although government officials objected to the wasteful use of material in the 'drapes', the Costume Department stuck to its guns. It was using cloth itself as a symbol of revolt against official reality and respectable femininity. The marked preference of the female audience for the flowing clothes indicates that they could read the narrative inscribed into the non-verbal, 'unconscious' parts of the discourse.

The Wicked Lady is particularly fruitful for costume analysis. The audience is prepared for the failure of the Patricia Roc/Griffith Jones relationship by their early lack of sartorial consonance. Margaret Lockwood's first appearance links her with the gorgeous aristocratic male; her velvet, fur-trimmed coat is pulled back to reveal a silken interior. (Haffenden insisted that, though it was a black and white film, this silk *must* be scarlet.) The coat is swept back to form giant peplums which emphasise an opulent figure. The back view of this ensemble is significant. Fur and scarlet satin are held in place by a concealed fastening, and from the centre issue folds and pleats. This is hidden from the male, who approaches from the other side, but it is displayed to Roc and to the audience. This pattern is repeated in Lockwood's other clothes, and in her hairstyles, which radiate, either in plaits or curls, from a hidden vortex. Such stylised ensembles may be interpreted as symbolising female genitalia: the whorls and pleats covertly refer to the labia, vagina and clitoris. It has long been common practice in cinematic or literary criticism to hunt for (and indeed to admire) phallic symbols. Doubtless these have a function in male-centred genres. But it is entirely predictable that vulval symbolism should play a role in women-centred texts. *The Wicked Lady* makes an extended play with sexual symbolism; hence the private room with the secret passage to the freedom of the park, and the key held by the Puritan servant. Even the 'good girl' played by Patricia Roc experiences a change in her sexual

130

fortunes when she moves from austere stripes to frills and a vortex hairstyle, which the newly besotted Jones kisses from behind.

Lockwood is associated throughout with the mother-principle. Her extreme attachment to her mother is symbolised by the ruby brooch, which is redolent of blood. In a long insert, she cradles this jewel in her palm, which is contrasted with a later shot when Roc displays it in an unfeeling manner on the flat of her hand. The main identification thus offered to the audience is not with a sibling or friend. Such symbolic use of jewels, hairstyles and clothes is more feasible in a historical context, and clearly Elizabeth Haffenden, the designer of these and all other costumes in the cycle, was challenging the sexual stereotypes of the script.

Haffenden's early costume designs for theatre avoided naturalism. In the prewar and early war period her work attracted much critical opprobrium, since its expressionism was held to be un-English and therefore unpatriotic.[37] Haffenden's interest in symbolic and expressionist costume design could not be accommodated within the theatre, and after staging the 1939 costume pageants for de Gaulle's London visit she worked almost exclusively on Gainsborough period films from 1942 to 1949. Her occasional postwar work in the theatre gained praise for its 'heraldic magnificence'.[38]

From 1942, then, Gainsborough constituted a space for innovatory costume work. Minney encouraged such stylisation, arguing that 'one must not copy, one must adapt and evolve.'[39] The studio permitted historical models to be creatively altered. But such flexibility was banished by Box, who sent *The Bad Lord Byron*'s contemporary fashion plates to Haffenden for faithful copying.[40] Hitherto, her designs had been cost-effective; but when Box insisted on painstaking embroidery the costume department had problems. It had to compete for Ministry of Labour embroiderers, and as the latter were working on Princess Elizabeth's wedding dress the struggle was an unequal one. Box even studied the design of Byron's own shoes to make sure that Dennis Price got the limp right. Management style, therefore, minimised Haffenden's expressionism after *Caravan*; she also had to learn a colour language for the Technicolor *Jassy*, which limited the design range.

Other studios, such as Ealing and British Lion, used contemporary male couturiers who had higher status than their female counterparts at Gainsborough.[41] It was only with the period clothes that Gainsborough had any pretensions to style, as is shown by the frocks in *They Were Sisters* or *Love Story*. The relationship between Gainsborough period costume design and contemporary fashion was therefore a complex one. Crinolines could not 'service' the fashion industry as modern designs could.[42] Len England of Mass-Observation had already noticed the lack of consonance between costume texts and contemporary dress: 'Is there a trend towards bustles and brimmed hats? And yet surely such books as *Fanny by Gaslight* have been very popular this season.'[43]

In fact, the relationship between historical dress on screen and the sartorial imagination of the audience was not based on emulation or indeed on fashion as such. To be sure, Gainsborough carefully supervised Margaret Lockwood's wardrobe on her promotion tours. But direct audience imitation of the historical costumes was not the intention. Rather, historical clothes signalled an entry into a world of fantasy where freedom and pleasure were coterminous. The *Caravan* publicity material restricted possible fashion tie-ups to usherettes in gypsy uniform. That of *Madonna of the Seven Moons* suggested that cinema managers 'stir up feminine interest' by persuading a hat shop to exhibit a gypsy-like hat. The film had 'wide fashion appeal', and managers were urged to profit from this by setting up a dress design competition, judged by Haffenden, which combined modern and 'costume' elements. These were called 'elastic imitations'. The only direct area of suggested fit was in the film's hairstyles, which 'any girl can do herself'. Respectable underpinning was given by reference to Haffenden's creation of practical glamour 'with the minimum of coupons'. Cineguild, and American distributors, argued for a more straightforward relationship between costume film and fashion.[44]

But the arrival of the New Look changed the relationship between Gainsborough's period costumes and contemporary fashion. During the war, clothes rationing restricted the female wardrobe. Pretty underwear disappeared, heels over two inches high were banned, and Utility clothes were by law unembroidered, narrow-skirted and single-breasted. The female population was extremely unhappy about these conditions.[45] Consolatory hairdressing visits and heavier use of cosmetics were a result. The popularity of the Gainsborough costumes – tasteless, flared, exotic – was predicated in wartime on what was unavailable and forbidden. In this context, frills could have a talismanic significance and could symbolise a female sexuality denied expression through conventional signifying systems. For the Gainsborough histories which straddled the war and the postwar period the advent of the New Look in the Paris shows of Spring 1946 was therefore of great significance.

The New Look emphasised the waist, breasts and a swirling largesse of skirt, and had corsetry, tight bodices, layers of material, heavy embroidery and diamanté studs. It presented the body as a flowing mystery; an opulent, fecund femininity was implied. This style quickly became *de rigueur*, and not just among the wealthy; and it opposed utilitarian attitudes to the female body. Clearly, the mass aficionados of the Gainsborough costume films in the postwar period shared a definition of femininity with those who welcomed the New Look, and this was recognised by the studio. The *Caravan* publicity material suggested that Haffenden's success lay in her ability to predict the New Look; she

> is recognised in the fashion world as an excellent prophet of women's fashions, and in 1944 she forecast the swing over to glamour and what men call outrageous fashion. That she was correct is seen in the recent displays of garments in the big export houses.

Historical costume in Gainsborough films, then, could be interpreted as a debate, on a symbolic level, on female sexuality and the contemporary crisis of permission. The costumes presented history as a place of potential liberation rather than inevitable oppression. Up to and including *Jassy*, Gainsborough languages of costume and art direction displayed the past as a series of intense, illuminated moments, resonant with sensual meaning. The scripts were more rigorous in ascribing a class basis to social experience.

To return to the films themselves, the first two (*The Man in Grey* and *Fanny by Gaslight*) are structured by the critical juxtaposition of two female protagonists. In *The Man in Grey*, the contrast is between an amoral lower-class outsider and a naive aristocratic insider, but the clarity of that contrast is vitiated by the use of the framing device, at the beginning and end, of a modern story. This form of narrative construction does not recur; and in *Fanny by Gaslight*, both heroines have lower-class backgrounds. However, they are contrasted on a moral level: Phyllis Calvert is ardent and good, Jean Kent grasping and promiscuous. Both films appeared in the box office lists, probably because of the type of emotional release granted to the female audience. By way of the dramatic conflict between warring stereotypes the female viewer is encouraged to experience both forbidden and safe positions. This permits repressed desires to be articulated, and facilitates the identification of power with pleasure. In *Madonna of the Seven Moons*, this schism between sacred and profane females is more acutely presented, since both qualities exist in the same woman. Wolfenstein and Leites compared the presentation of good/bad girls in British and American films of the period, arguing that the films exemplify a major psychological problem of Western men, that of fusing desires for both good and bad women.[46] Inductive and idealist though such a position is, it might be appropriate if films were made for and enjoyed by men only. But this of course was not the case with Gainsborough. Films like *The Man in Grey* were successful because they addressed the *female* psychological constitution of the period. The notion of feminine contradiction is nuanced differently in varying historical periods. Through the disguise of costume, *Madonna of the Seven Moons* and other Gainsborough films claimed that it was the female, not the male, who was naturally quixotic.

During the war, then, Gainsborough costume films dealt at first with

The Man in Grey

psychosexual issues. These films were profitable. But *A Place of One's Own* was not, largely because of the mistaken casting of James Mason as an elderly and genial Yorkshireman. It was probably disconcerting for viewers to see their saturnine favourite transformed in this grizzled way. Moreover, wartime audiences were not fond of occult subjects, and the film dealt with ghosts and presented the past as a threat to the present. But with *I'll Be Your Sweetheart*, Gainsborough again appeared in the *Kinematograph Weekly* listings. On the face of it, the subject-matter (song copyright wars at the turn of the century) lacked allure. But the studio team transformed the material into a lively tale of music-hall history in which popular culture was robustly defended. The script insists that popular song is 'the life-blood of the people'. And Margaret Lockwood's musical numbers offer an interesting form of audience identification. In 'I'll Be Your Sweetheart' she takes a male role in the song's words and action. To a range of submissive admirers she sings 'When I'm a man, my plan will be to marry you.' And in 'You Are My Honeysuckle, I Am the Bee' she pollinates the female flower. Thus the proposed model of femininity is sensual and aggressive.

In the immediate postwar, pre-Box period, Gainsborough histories continued to combine the two themes of female wilfulness and popular culture. *The Wicked Lady* and *Caravan* have heroines who risk everything for emotional fulfilment. They die, finally; but the films suggest, in a high Romantic manner, that real life becomes an anticlimax once fantasy has been totally achieved. In *Jassy*, the good/bad heroine even survives; this film and *Caravan* feature wounded, vulnerable heroes whom the women succour. All these films implicitly place a high value on popular culture (consider the gypsy wedding in *Caravan*, or the Tyburn scene in *The Wicked Lady*). The defence of popular culture is also the main business of *The Magic Bow*. Here the violinist Paganini is emphatically a proletarian whose artistry is free of polite constraints. His vitality is celebrated in a key scene in which he is presented to the Pope, and Roman Catholic rituals cement his status. The crucial role played by Catholicism here is an extension from *Madonna of the Seven Moons*. In both films the faith represents a sort of siren of the senses; rational creatures can only withstand it if they are deaf, or strapped to the mast.

Such issues were alien to Box's Gainsborough. *The Bad Lord Byron*, for example, presents history as a place of querulous condemnation. The Regency period could be fruitful for popular historical film, as *The Man in Grey* (and Korda) had shown. And Byron himself, as a political radical, sexual omnivore and charismatic aristocratic artist, was a rich quarry. But Box insisted that the film be structured around the motif of a ghostly trial to determine whether Byron was really bad or not; and no one, particularly Byron's female fans, ever cared a fig about that. Consequently the film was not profitable.[47]

Pre-Box historical films at Gainsborough were never co-opted into a propaganda argument and were essentially native products, inappropriate for an international market. But with *Christopher Columbus*, Box attempted a reorientation. The American actor Fredric March was imported, and the film's script is essentially a paean to America. Moreover, the film has an elephantine pace, and is grimly silent on the key issues of popular culture and sexual pleasure. It was not a hit. Nor was the last Gainsborough costume film, *So Long at the Fair*. A comparison of this 1950 film with (say) the 1943 *Man in*

134

Grey is instructive. In the latter film, the site of dread is the excessive behaviour of the aristocracy and the lustful female; but in *So Long at the Fair*, dread resides within the male side of the bourgeois family. The heroine's brother has contracted the plague; a conspiracy is mounted to keep her in virginal ignorance. This is achieved by hiding a key, papering over a door and concealing a room – metaphors for the repression of knowledge and desire. In pre-Box histories such secret places are penetrated, to the delight of all parties.

From 1942 to 1947, then, a unique set of production circumstances resulted in the making of costume films at Gainsborough which were popular because they exploited key motifs in popular culture and because they gave a privileged role to female audiences. The next chapter examines that audience response in the wartime and postwar period.

10

WARTIME AND POSTWAR RESPONSES TO HISTORICAL FILM

There are problems with the assessment of audience response in the 1940s which are different from those of the 1930s. With the outbreak of war *Film Weekly* (so useful for its letter pages) ceased publication because of paper and manpower shortages, and the range of popular film journals was curtailed. Mass-Observation is of course a key resource for popular opinion, but the reliability of its findings was marred by the limitations of some of its observers, who displayed a peevishness in the face of historical contingency when they were unable to categorise such responses as 'I can't talk to you now, ducks, I've got no teeth – look!'[1] Middle-class Mass-Observation reporters were sometimes unable to interpret proletarian behaviour. And Sidney Bernstein, in his questionnaire, could not deal with respondents' irony; he recorded, with po-faced literalism, audience suggestions that latecomers should be hoisted to their seats by a mechanical crane.[2] Moreover, the findings of J. P. Mayer and other academic researchers may have been skewed by their hearty dislike of popular historical films. Another complicating factor is that there is far more evidence on responses to Gainsborough costume melodramas than on other historical films, and this, if not handled with care, may give overweening significance to Gainsborough. A further element in the assessment of cinematic taste is the degree to which quasi-official bodies were intervening. The British Film Institute and the Historical Association were still trying to temper the excesses of popular historical film throughout the war period. The middle and 'quality' ground of the debate may well have been influenced by them.

During the war the artistic establishment gave little priority to historical matters. An influential review of wartime theatre argued that historical plays were only acceptable if their realism had a minimal gloss.[3] *Penguin New Writing* placed no credence in non-contemporary settings, and more avant-garde literary publications rigorously eschewed the historical.[4] Certainly, novelists like Elizabeth Bowen and Rosamond Lehmann produced texts set in the Edwardian period. But these were exceptions in progressive practice. The work of the Artists' International Association was contemporary in orientation.[5] The Neo-Romantics' Arcadia was constructed so as to conceal its historical dimension.[6] Even historians of folk art tended to stress its immanent continuities rather than its traditionalism.[7] A range of middle-class autobiographies in the war period displayed a lack of interest in historical matters.[8] Male respondents to a 1943 Mass-Observation directive about reading habits were extremely hostile to historical novels; a taste for the 'mud, blood and midden school' was seen by men as an index of low status.[9]

By contrast, women readers of historical novels during and after the war defended the genre in the following terms:

> I am sometimes rather snobbishly ashamed of being seen with my current bromide, and would prefer to be reading Meredith.

> I take it as I do cigarettes – nothing so potent as a drug, merely a harmless bromide.

> When a novel has an historical interest, or deals with an economic or social problem, there is a reason for its existence, apart from its literary value.

> They help you to be patient; I found them particularly helpful earlier on in the war, when we were still adjusting our ideas to it.

> It's nice to be able to read about that sort of love and better-class people, because you don't notice things as much then.[10]

A sense of proportion, escapism, access to a vivid past – these were the alibis provided by women for the historical novel. It was the most heavily subscribed genre of light reading among female readers, and its popularity did not diminish after the war.[11]

It seems that the consumption of historical art tended to be a female prerogative in the wartime and postwar periods. The artistic establishment in different media avoided a period dimension, critics gave a privileged role to contemporary realism, and male readers scorned anything that smacked of costume fantasy. Only women evinced a preference for art located in the past. This pattern also held good for the cinema. Gainsborough costume films provoked an unprecedented assault from critics; writers upholding 'quality' took popular historical film as a proof of debased national taste. But evidence indicates that for female audiences these films provided a key site where their anxieties and desires could be addressed.

'Quality' cinema criticism sanctioned by the British Council, for example, gave extensive coverage to official and documentary film, but dismissed popular histories as 'cheaply romantic' and with a 'novelettish feeling'.[12] The Workers' Education Association expressed similar views in its film work.[13] The tendency for historical film to be more liberal in matters of sexual representation worried several bodies. The British Film Institute expressed anxiety on this score. So did Claude Mullins, Chairman of the Magistrates' Association and a leading figure in the Society for the Unmarried Mother and her Child, who campaigned against sleazy historical films which were inimical to family life. He made a direct correlation between the length of screen kissing (timed with a stopwatch) and 5,000 cases of marital trouble, concluding that 'such films are very dangerous. Many men select for courtship women who they think will give them these thrills. When married to them, they only too often find that they have married women who are rotten housekeepers and bad mothers.'[14] Similar anxieties were expressed by James Laver in his article in

Screen and Audience. Historical films permitted a greater sexual display: 'The couple in front of me did seem to be stimulated rather than appeased by the comparative liberality with which the producer had adorned his picture with cleavage.'[15] Other 'quality' critics, especially James Agate, tended to concentrate on the moral dangers of spectacle.[16] Even the *Penguin Film Review* was prescriptive and puritanical in its treatment of audience response and popular historical film.[17] The cultural conservatism of the British Film Institute was evident in attacks on popular historical film in *Sight and Sound* and the *Monthly Film Bulletin*. But writers with fewer intellectual pretensions took the same line. F. E. Baily, creator of such *chroniques scandaleuses* as *The Love Story of Lady Palmerston*, published *Film Stars of History* (1945), in which he claimed to give the real facts that should have appeared in such films as *Lady Hamilton*. He blamed 'feminine logic' for cinematic inaccuracy, and saw his chief function as enlightener of 'the great inarticulate mass of cinemagoers who, in a thousand cinemas, see historic characters butchered to make a Hollywood holiday'.[18] A similar position was taken by the right-wing critics the Robsons, who objected to historical films which encouraged 'marital double-crossings, venal murder, split-minded lunacies'. They required an accurate history that would raise the moral level of the audience. The Robsons also objected to the radical conservative use of the past in *A Matter of Life and Death*.[19]

It appears that to writers intent on upholding quality cinema, popular historical film was a cause for moral concern. There was no significant shift in this group's opinion from the wartime to the postwar period. Much can be gleaned, too, from statistical surveys on audience taste, provided we recognise the powerful filters at work. Some surveys are less useful because they did not quote respondents directly or because they had a naïve belief in the reality of statistics as such. For example, Moss and Box's 1943 *Wartime Social Survey: the Cinema Audience*, with a broad sample of 5,639 civilians, established that a high proportion of them were women and 'young workers' but failed to draw any conclusions about class and cinematic taste. Box's 1946 survey reiterated these findings, while asserting that 'age is a more important factor than sex.'[20] But nothing important was revealed about popular taste. The 1947 Bernstein Film Questionnaire reported that James Mason and Stewart Granger were favourite male stars and that Margaret Lockwood was the top female star. Drama was 'liked very much' by 66 per cent of respondents and historical films by 30 per cent. But there was no indication of the sex or class of respondents, so the results were inconclusive.

Other, more academic, studies are revealing. Barbara Kesterton's 1948 Ph.D. thesis on the effects of film on adolescents partially deployed Mayer's 'essay' method. Her work was premised on the notion that Secondary Modern schoolchildren were naturally more unintelligent, and visited the cinema because they lacked other 'healthy and stimulating recreations'. Kesterton demonstrated a strong gender difference in taste, indicating that the girls' preference for 'sentiment and pathos' in melodrama was due to social conditioning rather than inherent feminine bias. She also argued that the less educated girls had no taste for realism. Kesterton's research is illuminating on responses to Gainsborough films. *The Wicked Lady* featured strongly as a female favourite, which she saw as a film whose main appeal is to the sex-instinct. Yet it also has a lively, quick-moving story and picturesque gowns. It is probably these qualities that gave the film considerable appeal for girls. They, unlike the few boys who mentioned this production, concentrated on the costumes and the settings rather than on the 'bawdy' elements of the plot.

One 14-year-old Secondary Modern girl displayed an awareness of the more earthy elements of the tale: 'After she had been married to him for a few weeks she refused to sleep with him. Every night she meets Jackson who is a passionate lover.' So much for Kesterton's insistence that the children always displayed a 'natural' sense of moral values.

According to Kesterton's findings, Margaret Lockwood, James Mason, Stewart Granger and Patricia Roc took very high priority as stars among female respondents. Lockwood in particular operated as a powerful role model for the adolescent girls with lower academic attainments; a large proportion of them admitted to direct imitation (when they could) of her hairstyles and make-up. One 14-year-old noted that 'the beautiful dresses and hairstyles make me speechless with longing.' Gainsborough films in general, according to Kesterton's evidence, aroused emotions that were pleasingly contradictory. One young girl liked *Caravan* because the hero 'went back to his first wife, but Jean Kent loved him very much. It was sad but very nice.'[21]

Kesterton's work was part of a larger research programme at Birmingham University on adolescent responses to film. Predictably, therefore, her findings were consonant with those of Wall and Simpson, since they shared the same aims and methods, combining statistical interpretation with essay work.[22] Wall and Simpson's findings were significant. They established that female film stars exercised a formative influence over 13–15 year-old girls from lower educational groups in the areas of hairstyle and body language. From a sample of 2,000, they showed that historical melodramas constituted the overwhelming favourites among adolescent girls, and that this tendency was more marked with non-grammar school girls. Comments from essays are revealing. When retelling the story of *The Wicked Lady*, girls described the heroines as Margaret and Patricia, indicating the importance of star identification. *The Wicked Lady*, *Robin Hood* and *The Four Feathers* ranked sixth, fifth and seventh respectively as favourite films. But only male respondents endorsed the coercive moralism of the Gainsborough scripts: 'The film portrayed a wicked lady and her just end for her crimes', and 'She only started for a bit of fun but it soon became a habit.' Interestingly, these sharp gender differences in film taste were replicated in children's reading preferences.[23] Moreover, a postwar survey of children's taste commissioned by the Ministry of Education concluded that a liking for 'films of people in olden times' increased dramatically once audiences reached 14 and 15.[24] Gainsborough stars featured highly as role models. A very large number of the female sample preferred Lockwood, and named Mason as their favourite actor.

J. P. Mayer's *Sociology of Film* (1946) and *British Cinemas and Their Audiences* (1948) are, of course, a substantial resource, although they contain no statistical material and are encumbered by excessive references to Pascal, Malinowski and others. However, Mayer's documents are carefully located in place and class. In his first book, a set of nineteen essays from 15-year-old

Hampstead High School girls provides interesting material. The girls liked historical films *because* small liberties were taken with facts. A desire for 'realism' suffused some answers. But these middle-class girls shared some responses with less educated girls. They too gave a privileged role to visual pleasure. They admired and defended Lockwood's 'badness' in *The Man in Grey*. *Lady Hamilton* aroused sexual desire for the hero. And one girl's version of *The Scarlet Pimpernel* evinced a response consonant with Burke's definition of the Sublime: 'It seemed an awful pleasure of the French people to go and watch people guillotined with such joy on their faces even if the aristocrats were hated by the ordinary people of France.'[25]

Mayer also asked adults whether their dreams had ever been triggered by films. Only women responded in a significant way. One woman dreamt that she saw the Sign of the Seven Moons from *Madonna of the Seven Moons* being written on the mirror: 'It got bigger each time.' Another dreamt of *The Man in Grey*: 'I kept seeing the terrifying look on James Mason's face as he beat Hester to death. I could not get it out of my dreams for some time.' The same subject dreamed of a line from *Madonna of the Seven Moons*: 'It isn't possible, no one could be so lovely.' Another made love to Laurence Olivier in her dreams: 'I was always very forward in them, entirely unlike myself in real life.'[26] These extracts are extremely suggestive. In their dream-work, the women selected from the films passages which permitted them to confront repressed fears or desires: fears of male impassivity and violence, desire for self-knowledge and self-worth. Female respondents here also placed a high priority on the pleasures of historical costume: 'I wish we could go back a few centuries and the ladies wear beautiful crinolines, and gentlemen wear cavalier clothes.'[27]

Mayer's later book endorsed these findings. The sensual pleasures of historical costume were mentioned by a range of females, one 16-year-old hairdresser noting that

> I soon found out I enjoyed historical films, though I believe that the lovely costumes had a great deal to do with it, for I can often remember the times when I would come home and dream that I was the lovely heroine in a beautiful blue crinoline with a feather in my hair. I used to pray so hard for that crinoline.[28]

It was suggested by some respondents that period films permitted a greater laxity in the representation of sexual pleasure and in the encouragement of desire. A schoolboy noted that in *Fanny by Gaslight*, 'I could almost guarantee that every child over 14 knew what had been going on when the maid picked up the cufflinks from under her mistress's bed.'[29] One young woman described in detail her erotic sensations on viewing Granger's kissing in *Madonna of the Seven Moons*. According to this evidence, for female viewers costume films facilitated attention to that dark side of desire which is effaced by everyday common sense: 'I simply revel in seeing bold, bad men.'[30] Such films' presentation of male stars as charismatic objects of desire offended other men. One male student, feeling threatened by Granger, exploded in competitive spleen: 'I sincerely despise *showing off* in films.'[31]

Many of Mayer's respondents admitted to using historical films as an escape vehicle from the war:

I definitely go to the cinema to be taken out of myself and forget the cares of housework, rationing and the baby's nappies. Carry me back to the past with Laurence Olivier, Nelson Eddy, Greta Garbo and the rest, and I'm happy.[32]

But a range of alibis were presented by others for having enjoyed costume films. Two young women praised *Madonna of the Seven Moons* because it was realistic: 'The Italian backstreets were just as I imagine them to be.'[33] Other writers (of a slightly higher social stratum) discriminated between profitable costume drama and respectable historical films which had an exhortatory function; films like *Cavell*

> do much to inspire and to bring about the realisation that there have been, and always will be, men and women whose names will be handed down in history, and films are a sure way to keep these names evergreen in the minds of the community.[34]

Other respondents defended the usefulness of historical films in encouraging audiences to return to the original novels. It is rare, in Mayer's selection, to find attacks on historical inaccuracy.

Mayer's work, flawed though it may be in its premises and methodology, gives us access to important differences of taste between classes and genders. Mass-Observation material does not contradict these findings, though some of the gleanings are disappointingly thin. There was no research specifically on people's feelings about history; directives and projects on the Empire and the Royal Family look potentially fruitful, but in fact are not.[35] Mass-Observation commentators on cultural trends noted that Victorianism was on the increase in films and music halls, but could only conclude lamely that this was 'a new form of escape'.[36] Such conclusions were contaminated by many observers' bias against mass culture and popular forms: 'There has been a general decline in the spiritual and socially minded life, and a great increase in the amount of purely private, passive, uncreative use of leisure.'[37]

Nevertheless, Mass-Observation's basic material is valuable in the same way as Mayer's, in that it gives us access to the utterances of the audience, however selected and coded. Mass-Observation's archives provide comments such as this from one working-class wag:

> Each seat could be fitted with a moveable rod to which could be attached a large muzzle. By the mere pressure of a button the nearest victim of the talkative offender could move the muzzle onto the too industrious jaws.[38]

It gives us interpretations of the socio-economic meaning of cinema, such as this from a cinema manager:

> Take a man in a house at Sutton, say. He will come in, think of the weather, put another piece of coal on the fire, and settle down for the night. But a poor man will say, let's go to the pictures and save a shilling's worth of fuel.[39]

It can provide a mass of unsorted audience responses on the attractions of stars. It can indicate the way audiences would select elements within films which were appropriate to their own situation.[40] But Mass-Observation does not provide rich pickings on responses to historical film in wartime.

Only one directive is relevant, from November 1943: 'What films have you liked during the last year? Please list six films in order of liking and give your reasons for liking them.' This was not a 'priority' question, and it was the last of six, which must be taken into account. Replies are extant from 104 women and 116 men. Jeffrey Richards and Dorothy Sheridan suggest that the dissonance between Mass-Observation respondents' favourites and that of the nation (as indicated in *Kinematograph Weekly*) may be attributed to the composition of the sample, which was weighted towards more articulate types. Hence the presence of *Thunder Rock* in the Mass-Observation list, and the absence of such low-status musicals as *Hello, Frisco, Hello.*[41]

However, the November 1943 directive shows clear variations in taste according to gender. Men tended to prefer *The Life and Death of Colonel Blimp* because they saw it as an accurate representation of recent history. *The Young Mr Pitt* was praised by one sales manager for its historical probity: 'I am interested in history and for that reason I enjoyed this film ... Detail work and dialogue were well chosen and the historical data was paramount throughout.'[42] The very few men who mentioned *The Man in Grey* saw it literally as 'a page of history'. One teacher liked it because it provided a welcome return to sexual inequality: 'It is "escapist" and we forget the present to dwell in the past when young ladies were taught just what to say to men who asked for their hand in marriage, even though the latter were scoundrels.'[43] Female response differed interestingly. Very few women praised historical films for their accuracy, and if they did, they always provided additional reasons. Indeed, one typist liked *The Four Feathers* precisely because it was 'far-fetched'. A significant number of women praised *The Man in Grey* as 'a dramatic, well-produced film'; 'I enjoyed costumes and "Becky Sharpe" theme'; 'unusual plot and good acting'.[44] *Lady Hamilton*, too, was well received, but with no mention of its documentary history. One woman simply 'liked the style'. All these respondents were middle-class.

Mass-Observation shows how a taste for costume films could be gender-specific but not class-specific; middle-class women liked their allure, and valued historical films for reasons of visual style, narrative structure and star identification. Unlike male respondents, they did not place much credence in the nostrums of realism.

But it is crucial to recognise how bourgeois attitudes to the cinema were shot through and through with notions of class identity. Time and again, a contempt for the medium *as such* was expressed by middle-class respondents. A directive of August 1942 asked respondents how they envisaged social changes after the war, and included a form asking them to rate the influence on themselves of the cinema, radio, posters etc. A clear pattern emerges: the further up the social ladder the respondents were, the less they admitted to being influenced by the cinema. Conversely, the 'lower' respondents placed a higher value on film as a means of persuasion. Marginally more females than males admitted to being influenced by the medium. An earlier directive is even more revealing. In June 1939, respondents were asked which class they belonged to, and also 'what priced seats do you use in the cinema and why?' The replies are remarkable for two reasons. Firstly, middle-class replies displayed extensive class antagonism towards those 'below' and were hypersensitive to class distinctions; one woman managed to discriminate between twenty-eight different class fractions.[45] Secondly, the cinema was a site of dread to many bourgeois respondents, since it encouraged undue class mixing. *All* working-class respondents of whatever sex simply went to the best seats they could afford, and thought that the entertainment was excellent value for money. Middle-class patrons, by contrast, displayed great contempt for the medium, and the replies to this 1939 directive contain the following comments:

> I will not pay more as I think no film merits it.
> 3/6 seems too much to pay for a film, even if in French.
> The seats at more than two bob are not worth the rubbish that one sees.
> I begrudge paying more for a pleasure that means very little to me.
> I don't think the average movie is worth more.

Such remarks were equally spread between male and female respondents, as was the expression of physical disgust toward denizens of the ninepenny seats:

> I avoid the stink of unwashed humanity.
> The ninepennies are for common people.
> I go medium price, as suited to my station.
> You might have someone eating an orange beside you, or laughing like this – ooah! – down the back of your neck.
> Often they smell.
> I do not choose the cheaper seats because you are apt to pick up strange company and the humour of these seats does not appeal to me.
> I do not use the cheapest because I am afraid of picking up fleas.

Where you sat, and what you enjoyed, were important markers of class superiority for many middle-class patrons.

The Mass-Observation method of class allocation was quite precise, and care was taken not to allocate a woman's class automatically according to her husband's occupation. According to evidence in this 1939 directive, the cinema was for the middle classes a means of enforcing class distinction, rather than being a democratising influence. It was a ritual means whereby difference and identity were symbolically enacted, in order to increase self-confidence. Sometimes snobbery and *nostalgie de la boue* coincided nastily. One medical student wrote:

> I prefer to sit next to working-class or lower-middle-class women, as their comments are generally most amusing. For example, to me familiar with Oxford, the way in which *A Yank at Oxford* was swallowed as complete truth was most amusing.

Mass-Observation material shows us that wartime taste was rigidly divided along the axis of class as well as of gender, and that responses to historical films were probably a matter of status, class mobility and cultural competence.

Finally, there are the letter pages in the key film journal of the war and postwar period, *Picturegoer*. Less precise conclusions can be drawn from this than from Kesterton, Mayer and Mass-Observation, since *Picturegoer* writers rarely located themselves in any class and often did not indicate their sex. First we should analyse the Mass-Observation collection of unpublished 1941 letters to *Picturegoer*, compiled at the behest of Len England, who conducted a rough-and-ready survey. He concluded that 50 per cent of the sample were about film stars, and 60 per cent of women's letters addressed this topic.[46] Certainly, very many of the letters debated the merits of Deanna Durbin and her angora cardigans; but there was a significant number of letters about historical film, and they displayed clear gender differences. Male letters praised realism and parallelism: 'The history of this world is reflected by the great men of each country. In the main we have been given historical reminders.'[47] Women's letters differed significantly. One 'proud factory hand' objected to the way girls of her class were represented in historical films. Many women strongly defended the historical genre as such, and praised its pleasures.[48] One female respondent alluded to 'the colour and thrill of those historical dramas. I don't think it is such a bad thing for audiences to be reminded that even in the so-called "good old days" ordinary folk were up against it, just as we are today.'[49]

The letters printed in *Picturegoer* during the war and in the postwar period differed from those of the 1930s. Writers displayed fewer preoccupations with the probities of historical film. Editorial policy was rigorously critical of poetic licence in historical film, and throughout the war consistently praised 'quality' historical films with an accurate gloss, such as *This England* and *The Great Mr Handel*. *Thunder Rock* was pushed hard on 26 December 1942: 'We can turn out fine pictures if the picturegoers prove they want them. So in the end it's up to you.'

Readers, however, proved resistant to such special pleading. A 1944 ballot gave the Gold Medal to James Mason for *The Man in Grey* (Olivier had won it the year before for *Lady Hamilton*), and this was clearly part of a general boredom (in women at least) with war films. There were many suggestions, mainly from women, about possible historical films: on Cromwell, Gladstone, Paine, Byron and Messalina (played by Lockwood).[50] One woman argued on 22 July 1944 that films about Empire history were the most efficacious form of popular art. A range of letters, mainly from women, stoutly resisted accuracy as a *sine qua non*; one wrote of *The Prime Minister*:

> Of all the squawks and praise about this picture, nobody seems to pause in the search for inaccuracy to say whether they thought it entertaining ... Providing a film is not glaringly inaccurate, I can enjoy it thoroughly without worrying, if it is interesting. I want pictures first and history second for my entrance money, but if historical accuracy and entertainment value go together, then it is indeed a movie.[51]

More remarkable was the flood of (mainly female) responses to Gainsborough historical films. These gave rise to analyses of the significance of the costume genre.[52] They made readers rethink the relationship between book and film and consider the films' representation of national culture.[53] They stimulated one man to connect the rituals of Catholicism with the decoding practices required by costume melodrama. In a letter printed on 20 July 1946, he accounted for the success of Roman Catholic themes in Gainsborough films thus: 'The Roman Catholic religion is so colourful. The beautiful images, the candles, the pictures, the chanting of the hymns in Latin ... appeal to the cinema and more especially to the feminine side of it.' A substantial number of female writers commented in extremely positive terms about Margaret Lockwood and Gainsborough histories in general.[54] They praised acting style and narrative structure. Very few critical letters were printed. A male writer won the editor's prize on 4 June 1947 for suggesting that *The Private Life of Henry VIII*, *King Solomon's Mines* and *Lady Hamilton* were all inaccurate, and that *The Magic Bow* was 'the greatest historical travesty since Tyrone Power built the Suez Canal'. Editorial policy may have favoured a more sober realism; but in general readers resisted *Picturegoer*'s frequent attacks on Gainsborough histories.[55]

This was because many female readers chose to co-opt historical melodrama into a broader debate about female pleasure and sexual difference. In the immediate postwar period, *Picturegoer* readers (again, mainly women) used Gainsborough histories as the starting-point of a reassessment of traditional ideas of feminine virtue and artistic identification. One woman, on 6 January 1945, urged Lockwood to continue as a 'vixen' because good parts were not sympathetic. Another added, on 3 August 1946, that 'those naughty wenches have their female fans. Men want to meet them and women to be like them. Women of doubtful character hold a fascination for the average person because their lives are never dull.' Glumly, the editor added that following Lockwood's 'portrayal of a vicious female, her fan mail went up by thousands.' Other women debated the phenomenon, arguing that Lockwood was acting out the repressed desires of the audience: humdrum filmgoers liked highway robbery because 'such things don't happen to ordinary people.'[56] Advertisers in the postwar *Picturegoer* recognised the draw of powerful, corrupt heroines from the past, using such figures as Catherine the Great to promote Grossmith's perfume. These should be compared with the 1930s 'historical' advertisements from *Film Weekly*, which were devoid of such resonance. Indeed, the public conception of female taste as being naturally inclined to 'bad' women was a post-1945 development. During the war, critical debates about female taste were still premised on the ideal of feminine probity.

Of course, *Picturegoer*'s postwar policy wanted to clean up such dangerous trends; the magazine argued on 26 October 1946 that 'good girls will always be welcome, but so will bad girls be, as long as they keep within the tenets of good taste.' But the widening gender difference in taste had to be addressed, especially if historical films appeared to be sanctioning female licence. *Picturegoer* published several articles on psychoanalysis and film, and it printed a range of pieces on female taste, at least one of which was viciously misogynistic.[57] The journal institutionalised the difference between male and female taste in a series of articles entitled 'Sally and I'. These took the form of disagreements on films between a husband and wife, and indicated the degree to which such splits were now common sense. On 6 June 1946, for example, the husband disliked *Caravan* whereas his wife Sally found Granger 'every inch a matador'. Sally also loved *The Magic Bow*, though on 7 December 1946 she was aware that 'to live happily with a musician, a girl would have to be tone deaf.' She displayed an awareness that the 'good old days' were repressive to females and that films deliberately concealed this.[58] So by 1946 there was a clearly recognised female taste, and the popularity of Gainsborough films was accounted for by some commentators as the result of a consonance between star styles and audience needs.

But more was at issue. From evidence in *Picturegoer*, historical melodramas also permitted women to question traditional images of male sexuality. Much earlier than the comments on 'bad women', *Picturegoer* contained letters from women in praise of a more robust and less civilised masculinity. One woman thought, on 11 June 1941, that fashions in males could be altered by a different type of historical film: 'Here's to a bit more aggressive masculinity on the part of our screen heroes.' Another noted that 'we seem to prefer bad men because their more good-living brothers are often fearful bores.'[59] James Mason's phenomenal popularity dated from his 'bad' roles in Gainsborough, and audience taste for his 'exquisite brutality' made *Picturegoer* editors uncomfortable.[60] But it can be interpreted as a shrewd response by Gainsborough producers (and also by Sydney Box, who produced and co-scripted *The Seventh Veil*) to newly articulated female desires. It seems likely that female film taste for domineering, sadistic males was strong and deep-seated between about 1942 and 1947, and that films such as *The Man in Grey* and *Jassy* allowed female viewers to look head-on at what they both feared and desired. But this masochistic trend in the films was always balanced out and resolved by the presence of dominant, sometimes sadistic, females.

Picturegoer, then, produced some useful insights into the audience taste for historical melodramas. But after about 1948, its debate about historical 'badness' and accuracy lost steam. Letters from both male and female readers were printed that denigrated historical spectacle, and no positive letters were selected. The magazine's policy towards historical film had shifted to such an extent by 1949 that it commissioned a special series of articles by Kate Quinlan which analysed the role of women in British costume films, but from a very conservative perspective. The Gaiety Girls in *Trottie True* were dismissed as 'past masters in the art of ensnaring men'. *The Idol of Paris* was disgusting because 'there is always something slightly sickening about the spectacle of a couple of women fighting.' Even *Madame Bovary* was savaged because its heroine was not like that of *Brief Encounter*.[61]

The crucial break in audience taste did not occur between the war and the postwar period, but between pre-Gainsborough and post-Gainsborough histories. A consonance of taste among female viewers between 1943 and 1948 was evident, although the female taste for 'badness' in history was more pronounced in the working-class and the younger audience. Official, 'quality' and masculine attempts to discredit this trend met with considerable resistance, and were in the end counter-productive.

11

THE POSTWAR PERIOD

CONTEXTS AND CONSTRAINTS

After Labour's victory in the 1945 election, new government policies were implemented in every area of public life. But socialist policies were in the habit of going askew, especially in the areas of culture and imports. The film industry was badly affected by mismanagement at the Board of Trade. A prohibitive ad valorem tax was imposed on film imports in 1947, and this led to a damaging embargo by the American conglomerates. However, we cannot account for changes in historical feature film as a straightforward consequence of government policies.

What is certain is that there was a general liberalisation of attitudes towards the uses of history in the postwar period. *Picture Post* produced a broad but instrumental deployment of historical perspective.[1] Harry McNicol's *History, Heritage and the Environment* influentially argued that 'it is high time that the hold of the generation which idolised Dizzy and Mr. Gladstone' be broken.[2] Critical books began to appear which took a more permissive view of the deployment of history in fictional texts.[3] From 1945 until 1951 the BBC produced historical plays which were largely populist in tone.[4] It also continued its radical approach to historical programmes for schools. And the Bureau of Current Affairs took an extremely liberal position, arguing that the masses had an abiding passion for learning their own history and that popular historical film was the main index of this.[5] Even popular educational textbooks on film argued that history need not be literally purveyed.[6] Such views would have been unthinkable during the late 1930s or the war period; after 1945, the widespread 'unfixing' and freeing of historical interpretation was accompanied by a greater pluralism in the production of historical feature films.

However, such flexibility and permissiveness on film and history was not evident in official thinking after 1945. During the war, quite separate theories of culture had obtained at the MoI, the Foreign Office and the British Council, and these differences had been evident in the historical films they sponsored. After the war, the British Council, as the cultural arm of the Foreign Office, attempted to take over all the overseas work of the MoI. The intention was to obviate any MoI/British Council overlap, and to produce for overseas consumption a politically more radical image of Britain, in which history would have a significant role as it had done in the wartime British Council films. But too many conflicting opinions scuppered the project. The ill-feeling produced by the high-handed behaviour of the British Council's Films Committee during the war still rankled with some influential figures, and encouraged their non-co-operation in the postwar scheme to 'show Britain as a tourist centre' with its heritage well to the fore.[7] Other Ministries also had axes to grind.[8] Various specialist bodies were keen to get a piece of the action. Private squabbles among film directors thwarted the Council's proposed Shakespeare films.[9] And the British Film Producers Association objected strongly to the Council's instrumentalist views of history and culture.

Finally, the Foreign Office was forced to abandon its film ambitions. In mid-1946 it conceded that all its overseas material would be made by the Central Office of Information (COI), which was a postwar version of the MoI. Foreign Office personnel had maintained that the British Council's cultural and film work should embrace 'all aspects of British life, thought and history'.[10] But this perspective had to be narrowed to appease MoI pressures. Ultimately the Foreign Office was forced to present its film aims in terms of the way Britain spread 'social democracy and individual liberty and welfare throughout the world'.[11] By 1947 the British Council was reduced to arranging showings of the historical documentary *Market Town* to French school-teachers. Since the Council's domestic film production had also been taken over by the COI, its defeat was complete. And so its views on the uses of history had no platform; the Foreign Office, which had partially informed those views, was outmanoeuvred. A long trajectory had come to an end.

How did the MoI, and later the COI, locate history in their postwar productions? History's importance for the MoI declined fast after 1943, and so it would be unrealistic to expect the past to play a privileged role in the postwar period. Moreover, officials recognised that there was a serious staffing problem if they wished to produce instructional films with even a tiny amount of historical information.[12] The difficulty was that the personnel the COI wanted (like Carol Reed, Eric Ambler, Edgar Anstey) were all employed elsewhere, and some were not convinced of the government's policies. And COI staff were not really convinced either; they thought that 'the whole country is not behind the present methods of tackling the aftermath ... Every audience has a large proportion of cynics, doubters, the bored and the frankly antagonistic.'[13]

Historical films produced by the COI shared a pessimistic view of the past; this is clear from advice offered by COI personnel to those engaged in official film-making. The impression given by *Houses in History* and *Local Government* was that the past was an unpleasantness best left behind.[14] COI films were politically conservative in their interpretation of the past. *The History of Writing* suggested that writing originated merely as a need to mark property. *Robinson Charley* presented the sum of human achievement as 'paying one's own way'. And *The House of Windsor* showed royalty as 'not our only trump card, but the one with which we are always sure of taking a trick'.[15]

Such conservatism was carried through into the COI's definitions of Englishness. *Dim Little Island* constructed national identity through the music of Vaughan Williams and the painting *The Last of England*.[16] The compilation film *Picture of Britain* presented 'the nation rich in heritage, where the past is written in the mellowed walls of its stately mansions ... woven together in a rich tapestry of tradition is the pageantry of Britain, history come alive.'[17] Particularly revealing is the material pertaining to the 1947 *A Yank Looks at*

Britain. COI staff experienced the utmost difficulty in complying with government policy, since their own definitions of history and national culture were not consonant with socialism. Tritton of the COI complained:

> The best thing to do to get a feeling of unity in this country is for the Prime Minister to tell Mr Shinwell, Sir Hartley Shawcross, and others who advocate class warfare, to keep quiet about it, and for the cabinet to follow Mr. Morrison's advice instead. It makes me angry when we are told to make a United British film when ministers and responsible Labour men are doing their best to disunite the country.[18]

In general, then, late MoI and COI films were marked by a pessimism about history and indeed about the whole process of instructional film. In a nutshell, official film-sponsors had lost their nerve. This had a profound effect upon commercial producers. During the war, they had responded with varying degrees of enthusiasm to MoI initiatives on history and other propaganda issues. But now there was a vacuum where before there had been a coherent policy. One way of accounting for the pluralism of postwar historical films would be to see them as a messy and energetic attempt to fill that vacuum.

However, the commercial producers of historical film were subject to other external constraints than the MoI and the COI. The Board of Trade had its favourite producers; it also had its own prejudices, many of which were encapsulated in the remark, 'Most of the people engaged in the industry are rogues of one kind or another.'[19] Some officers at the Board were also opposed to Rank's attempts on the American market. A memo noted that

> *Henry V* was the only film which is really bringing substantial sums from America to the British film producers, and this is due to the fact that 'Del' [del Giudice] arranged for special exploitation through the Theatre Guild It is *no use* sending to America the films of the mass product based on a stereotyped formula of entertainment. The Americans have better ones of that type.[20]

The unidentified writer went on to say that Rank's labours were 'just wasted' and that the government should instead foster companies like del Giudice's Two Cities and Pilgrim.

The problem was that different groupings within the Board of Trade championed different producers. Rank had his opponents but he also had his supporters. The President of the Board of Trade argued in late 1945 (probably before the various interested parties had got to him) that Rank should be left as unencumbered as possible.[21] Del Giudice, as we shall see, aroused both admiration and ire among members of the Board. Only Korda had unqualified support.[22]

The British Film Producers Association, therefore, was in a complex situation vis-à-vis the government. The Board of Trade's machinations caused producers to vie with each other for government funding. The run-up to the 1948 Cinematograph Films Act brought profound anxiety, according to Association minutes, and when the distributors' quota was reduced by that Act, it had an immediate effect on the number of films produced: a great many cheap historical films were abandoned. In addition, the industry was assailed by rising costs. The BFPA's Export Committee was particularly hostile to government policy. It found the COI impossibly naïve in its attitudes, and it bewailed the fact that the Foreign Office was no longer to be relied on to intervene in a sensible way. It concluded that 'little assistance was to be expected from the Board of Trade'.[23] And later, despite government indifference (or even downright hostility) to the issue of history, the Committee chose to give a very high priority to historical films. When a series of films was chosen as an index to foreign audiences of British producers' competence, historical films featured prominently.[24]

Similarly, the BFPA's Cinematograph Films Act Committee was suspicious of the government's intentions towards the industry. The unlikely triumvirate of Korda, Balcon and Rank banded together to resist government views. The Executive Council, on the urgent advice of Korda, chose Hugh Gaitskell to be Vice-President of the Association, presumably in order to spike the government's guns.[25] But to little avail: producers were not naturally inclined to perceive the advantages of socialism, especially when administered in a maladroit fashion. And so the Executive Council wasted much energy on acrimonious internal debates, instead of formulating a policy. Grumbling also took up abundant time; there were complaints about the misalliances between government departments, about the BBFC, about film critics, and more. But there are few records that anything got done – the Association gave the impression of querulous truculence. Of course, particular producers like Korda and del Giudice had their own private arrangements with the government; but in a period which saw a huge boom in historical feature films, the BFPA appeared to be without a coherent plan.

The producers were still subject to the British Board of Film Censors. As in wartime, some producers consulted the BBFC before filming while others did not trouble until later. The BBFC personnel were the same as before; the somnolent Col. Hanna ruled and Mrs Crouzet still maintained her propensity for outrage. The Board's cultural politics now appeared more conservative in the context of the new Labour government. Throughout the postwar period strong hostility was expressed by the Board towards popular forms, and towards any political system likely to celebrate these forms. Particular scorn was reserved for figures like Old Mother Riley and Frank Randle who appealed to a working-class audience. A Randle film was excoriated in the Scenario Notes of 1945: 'The whole of the business of pouring beer into the ear-trumpet which is inserted into the waistband of the man's trousers is extremely vulgar, coarse, and not a bit funny.' In 1947 a Gainsborough film about a working-class football pools winner was discouraged:

> That the pools should be counted as co-equals with racing is giving them an illusory status. Racing benefits the nation, and the breeding of English blood stock is an important asset. But the pools only benefit a few prize-winners and the promoter, and incidentally the GPO.

Easy Money was made nonetheless, and with no significant change in nuance, because the Board was expressing an opinion rather than issuing a downright veto. Only thus could it directly affect films, since as a pressure group it was toothless. But, using its official status, the Board warned the producers about the dangers of violence in films, on the grounds that it encouraged the populace's natural lawlessness.[26]

The BBFC's political conservatism inevitably extended to its views on history. The script readers were morbidly sensitive to the feelings of surviving relatives of the aristocracy. Of *Princess Fitz*, a proposed film about the morganatic marriage of the Prince Regent, the censors wondered in the 1947 Scenario Notes whether it was 'just possible that the present Lady Jersey may resent the part played by her ancestors'. The film was made anyway, and in the original format proposed by the studio. Another film about the Regency, mooted in the same year, was 'unfortunate in that the references to the German princess underline the German ancestry of our Reigning House.' There is little evidence that producers paid attention to the Board's strictures. In general, the BBFC thought history should be well laundered before its lessons could be learned; its more brutal aspects should be expunged. So in 1946 it wanted the riot scene in *Fame is the Spur* to be 'reduced to the minimum', because it was as inflammatory as the Odessa steps sequence in *Battleship Potemkin*.

The BBFC failed to recognise that times had changed, and it became progressively marginal to contemporary cultural concerns, huffing away against a proposed film of 'the deification of the scandalous Wilkes'. The only successful stand taken by the BBFC was on a proposed film on Elizabeth I, which the Board assaulted as 'an example of unauthenticated, quasi-historical muck-raking'.[27] The film was never made, probably because both government and public knew that the Second Elizabethan Age would begin one day and they wished to protect the first against depredation. The BBFC was most likely expressing a common-sense position rather than instigating a veto.

The ineffectiveness of the BBFC is most clearly evident in the case of the Gainsborough costume melodramas. These films should not be seen as arising out of a more permissive censorship atmosphere, but rather as a deliberate defiance of official guidance. For example, in 1945 the Board recommended a restrained version of the Papal Court in *The Magic Bow*. While a dialogue between the Pope and Paganini was discouraged, 'I do not think any exception would be taken to a distant view of the ceremonial entrance of the Pope into the concert hall of the Vatican, or a quick close-up of his reception and reaction to the music, or of his conferring a title on Paganini.' In fact, this scene was the most gorgeous in the film, the Pontiff was seen long and close and Vatican ceremonies were explicit. Similarly, in the 1945 Scenario Notes on *The Wicked Lady*, the Board requested a deletion of a Bible verse, a lightening of a sex scene, the removal of 'cheap though she looks', and the toning down of the hanging scene; but all this was ignored. It was the same with *Caravan*. Studios like Ealing and Two Cities, which were circumspect in their use of the past, gained the Board's praise.

So from 1945 the BBFC persevered with its old standards, but these were no longer accepted by the producers, who followed their noses attempting to predict popular taste. In the postwar years, historical films constituted a much larger proportion of the total output than in the prewar or wartime period (15 per cent of the total as against 7 per cent), but this trend fell off dramatically after about 1950.[28] How, in broad terms, are we to account for this? One possibility is that historical films provided a symbolic means by which both public and producers could come to terms with the war. The war had a formative role in definitions of national identity and social unity, but it was not until the 1950s that films dealing directly with the war captured a mass market. *The Cruel Sea* was the top moneymaker for 1953, *The Dam Busters* for 1955, and *Reach for the Sky* for 1956. But from the end of the war until the 1951 Festival of Britain there were few such war films, and a relatively large number of historical films with a wide range of periods and political orientations. Historical films were clearly performing an important function, possibly of a cathartic type; they were dealing indirectly with the past, in a way in which other genres could not. On a symbolic level, they were thus allaying important postwar anxieties.

There are, of course, other possible interpretations of the postwar history boom. One is political: producers felt that the political climate was more conducive to popular history. Another is cultural: the 'quality' critics were finally influencing producers to base their efforts on prestigious novels and plays. Neither interpretation completely answers the case, because neither takes into account the complexity of textual and production patterns. But first we should consider which historical films were profitable.

According to *Kinematograph Weekly*, *The Wicked Lady* was the outstanding success of 1946, with *Caravan* and *The Magic Bow* also doing extremely well. Josh Billings mentioned *Caesar and Cleopatra* as bringing good returns. Other profitable films deployed the 'Enoch Arden' theme of the returned lover, which clearly addressed emotional readjustments after the war.[29] The popular films of 1947 displayed a different pattern. The biggest box-office success was *The Courtneys of Curzon Street*, and other 'notable attractions' were *Nicholas Nickleby*, *Jassy*, *Captain Boycott*, *Great Expectations* and *Man About the House*. *A Matter of Life and Death* was also a 'notable attraction'. The popularity of historical films declined in 1948. Neither of the two *Kinematograph Weekly* winners was historical (*The Best Years of Our Lives* and *Spring in Park Lane*), although *Oliver Twist* and *Hamlet* were runners-up. So was *Forever Amber*. 'Notable successes' included *Blanche Fury*; *Anna Karenina* and *The Greed of William Hart* were modest successes. By 1949 historical films had declined again; the box-office favourite was Carol Reed's *The Third Man*, with *The Blue Lagoon*, *Easter Parade* and *Scott of the Antarctic* as runners-up. The only historical 'notable attractions' were *Trottie True* and the American *Three Musketeers*. Josh Billings suggested that *Elizabeth of Ladymead* and *The Case of Charles Peace* were modestly successful. By 1950, the decline of historical film was almost complete. Public taste had shifted; Ealing's police drama *The Blue Lamp* was the box-office favourite, along with the schooldays comedy *The Happiest Days of Your Life*. The American *Treasure Island* and *The Black Rose* were also reasonably successful.[30] Some producers and distributors felt aggrieved at Billings's methods of assessment; his influential list could affect a studio's reputation. But *Kinematograph Weekly* insisted that his system was based on a scientific analysis of box-office returns.

Of course, these results were skewed by the extraordinary market conditions of 1947. At first, British audiences were completely deprived of American films, then they flooded the market. Meanwhile many historical British films were made, and *Gone With the Wind* was re-released in 1948. The ultimate effect of the American embargo was to bewilder the audience with an embarrassment of riches. Even so, it is possible to chart a development in taste. Gainsborough costume films had peaked in popularity by 1947, and gave way to the 'quality' literary adaptation and to different class arrangements, as in *The Courtneys of Curzon Street* and *Trottie True*. Other popular historical films were residual throwbacks to earlier forms.

12

MONOPOLY AND HISTORY

RANK FILMS 1945–50

J. Arthur Rank had little confidence in his own cultural judgments and was liable to be captivated by such flamboyant entrepreneurs as Filippo del Giudice and Gabriel Pascal. Thus historical films as diverse as the sumptuous *Caesar and Cleopatra* and the sober *Captain Boycott* owed their genesis to Rank's intellectual neutrality. His brand of laissez-faire financing provided an 'umbrella' for a range of independent producers who had various approaches to cultural politics and history. They were both provided for and shaken loose by Rank's semi-monopoly. To be sure, he reorganised his empire after the war; John Davis masterminded the enterprise, and was skilled in setting everyone's teeth on edge.[1] But there is little evidence that Rank interfered on the studio floor of independent producers under his patronage. Rank's acceptance of lavish studio expenditure brought him assorted enemies; Korda, R. J. Minney and the Robsons all castigated him.[2] The débâcle of his attempt on the American market brought him little sympathy. To Bernard Miles he complained that 'one of the greatest difficulties is to make films which are in the English taste and tradition and at the same time have a world-wide appeal. I think producers in this country are grappling with the problem.'[3] His formulation was naïve. But his masterly cultural inactivity was, paradoxically, a blessing for historical feature film.

Del Giudice had enormous financial support from Rank, because of the winning streak inaugurated by the Noël Coward-David Lean naval drama *In Which We Serve* and Carol Reed's Army propaganda film *The Way Ahead*. During the war del Giudice's output was primarily contemporary, with the notable exception of *Henry V*, but he was responsible for a number of postwar historical films. *Beware of Pity* was released in June 1946, followed by *Carnival* (October 1946), *Hungry Hill* (January 1947), *Fame is the Spur* (September 1947), *The Mark of Cain, Vice Versa* (January 1948). *Hamlet* (June 1948) was the last Two Cities film del Giudice planned. *Uncle Silas*, which was released in September 1947, is difficult to attribute. It was made within del Giudice's period at Two Cities, yet unlike the others it did not bear his name as overall producer but that of Josef Somlo, the next studio head. Somlo produced *The History of Mr Polly* (February 1949), *Cardboard Cavalier* (April 1949), *Trottie True* (July 1949) and *The Reluctant Widow* (April 1950). Two Cities' output was heterogeneous, which may be partially accounted for by the fact that it had no core of staff like Gainsborough, and every film had to have technicians, cast and story hire separately negotiated. But another reason for the films' lack of coherence was the eclecticism of del Giudice, who was inclined to extreme enthusiasms.

Harold Wilson, the President of the Board of Trade, was bombarded in 1948 with fulsome tributes from del Giudice:

> Your visit of yesterday was like a tonic to my brain, and a source of inspiration to my firm determination to serve this British film art until the last day of my life. If you only knew how good conversations like that of yesterday are for my brain and soul, I am sure that you would spare me a few hours from time to time.

The more cynical Woodrow Wyatt mocked del Giudice's style in a memo to Wilson: 'I gather we are both the most remarkable people ever to have been in the House of Commons.' But del Giudice's past performance and his developing notion of the 'quality film' had significant support from within the Board of Trade. Harold Wilson was privately advised that he should 'consider Del's films as a reserve for British film art and treat them as you would treat the Old Vic, for pride and prestige of the country, but with Del's showmanship and financial soundness added.'[4] The terminology and valuation precisely replicated an earlier memo by del Giudice himself. Someone in government was taking him on his own terms.

What was del Giudice's notion of 'quality', and what were its implications for his historical films? He argued in *Kinematograph Weekly* on 14 January 1943 that the public 'is much cleverer and more endowed with common sense than we think.' This public could best be served by superior scripts; and in 1942/3 del Giudice inaugurated his Scenario Institute Ltd to achieve this. This Institute was an attempt at a quasi-university setting for scriptwriters. In order to raise film standards from an industrial to an artistic practice, he proposed to snap up the rights of high-quality novels before they were even published. Of course, the Screenwriters' Association scotched this plan. But it was an important clarification of del Giudice's aims, which he refined throughout the postwar period. He mounted attacks on the declining taste of the mass audience and those who pandered to it:

> The masses are unfortunately more inclined to enjoy a *Wicked Lady* than one of our pieces of art which have brought such a credit to the British film industry ... My contention is that if we make a film comparable to Cartiers' jewels we ought to sell it only in specialised shops like Cartiers.[5]

Del Giudice was deeply opposed to the ideas of Maurice Ostrer and Leslie Arliss on historical film, and he castigated *The Idol of Paris* as immoral and mass-produced.[6] He argued that films which aspired to artistic quality should have different distribution patterns, such as long bookings, word-of-mouth contact and the co-option of leading intellectuals.[7] Del Giudice's position led to a rigorous separation of business from intellectual labour: 'People connected with the commercial side of the business cannot possibly understand what is meant by art.'[8] This was clarified in his 1947 'Technical Testament', which was privately circulated. Here he argued that an *Administrator* should first select the story, and 'create the atmosphere in which an artistic product can be brought to life.' The *Creator* should be a director committed to 'the art and dignity of film making.' The Administrator leaves the Creator unhampered, but 'the cleverest Directors generally consult me because they respect me.' *Sales* of exhibition and distribution should be the slave of Creation and Administration.[9]

Of course, these opinions rendered it well-nigh impossible for del Giudice to work comfortably with Rank. Del Giudice's ideas became identified with those of actor, producer and director Bernard Miles, who had made *Tawny Pipit* and went on to make *Chance of a Lifetime*. Two Cities began to experience managerial problems, probably because del Giudice was preoccupied with his and Miles's ideas. They set up Pilgrim Pictures in 1947, and Two Cities was then headed by Josef Somlo and Earl St. John. Del Giudice continued to lobby everyone; but in the mind of the National Film Finance Corporation there was little room for his bitterness, naïvety and elitism. He was given nothing, and had a dramatic reconversion to Catholicism instead.

Del Giudice wanted to produce films which were both 'hopeful' and 'tasteful'.[10] How were these aims met in Two Cities' historical films, and what was the audience response? *Hamlet* was a critical and popular success, and *Trottie True* appeared in the *Kinematograph Weekly* list. But that is a small proportion of the studio's overall historical output. There was clearly some mismatch between the producer's and the audience's taste. *Beware of Pity*, for example, has considerable cultural pretensions. It is based on a Stefan Zweig novel, and the script gives ample hints of the producer's intentions. The dialogue is 'deliberately written in a stylised manner', so as to redeploy Zweig's own florid words and to 'add to the grace and sense of period.' The decor should be 'a little larger than life, florid, very rococo', with a huge number of sets which would 'enable us to have some spectacular riding and drilling on horseback.' But the narrative deals with a crippled girl who falls hopelessly in love with an insensitive chuckle-head, and the film is profoundly depressing. The publicity material suggests why: 'The theme of this story goes down to the roots of a very human failing. Haven't we all caught ourselves ... rousing false hopes and telling white lies?' The position thus offered to the male audience was one of shamefaced clumsiness, and to women only helpless misery. So although the film had a quality gloss and displayed its Zweig source well to the fore, no one liked it except the Russians, whose gloomy national temperament it perhaps suited.[11]

Del Giudice's next historical film, *Carnival*, which he produced personally, was also an interesting failure. This too was based on a well-known novel (by Compton Mackenzie), and the revised shooting script contained extensive hints about the desirability of a sumptuous visual texture. But the film was advertised with a lyrical pretentiousness: 'Jenny's fate is sealed from the beginning. "To the birth of a columbine!" toasts the old clown. "Think before you condemn your child to everlasting damnation", declares an aunt.' The ballerina heroine, deprived of her career, marries a dour Cornish farmer who kills her in jealousy. But the main problem is the film's script, by Eric Maschwitz and Peter Ustinov. It has neither period sense nor the energetic panache of (say) a Gainsborough script, and the characterisation and idiom are coarsely handled: 'I am the prey of a woman who has surrendered to the foul dictates of the flesh and the devil.' The film displays a contempt for its audience, and the *grand guignol* is clumsy when compared to *Hatter's Castle* or *Gaslight*. Again, it did not do well, probably because of the awkward way it quoted high culture.

Del Giudice credited films under his personal supervision as 'F. del Giudice in Charge of Production', and his next historical enterprise marketed thus was Daphne du Maurier's *Hungry Hill*, an Irish family saga spanning forty years. Two Cities' publicity material betrayed the film's pretensions. Margaret Lockwood would not be seen 'as a wicked lady, but as girl, wife, and mother'. Dennis Price came 'from the role of villain in *Caravan* to the sympathetic Greyhound Johnnie in *Hungry Hill*'. The film was supposedly superior to Gainsborough tastelessness; 'extensive research was necessary to ensure that everything was in period', down to ducks and chickens. The studio commissioned Arthur Pann, who had painted a famous Churchill portrait, to produce two pictures because of the status he conferred. But the studio was not above cashing in on the stars' reputation, with the film's poster showing Price leering across a supine Lockwood. Since the film contains little sex, audiences were bound to be chagrined.

Again, conspicuous cultural consumption was attempted, and again the enterprise was scuppered by a maladroit script. Terence Young and Du Maurier herself did not improve on the original; rather, they made it more leaden. There is no coherent characterisation, and the protagonist's undisciplined behaviour is lazily attributed to poor parenting. The script clumsily compares past and present: a picnic is 'an opportunity to give real production values – the cold hams, goose and other necessities of life – from which we have been so long separated'. The Irish are conventionally handled, as 'a strange, illogical people, perhaps because they're less worldly than most.' A less fey, more radical approach to the Irish problem could be popular, as *Captain Boycott* showed; but *Hungry Hill* appeared to please no one, especially not the critics.

John and Roy Boulting's *Fame is the Spur* was del Giudice's next historical enterprise. Anthony Aldgate has indicated that the film (a thinly veiled biography of Ramsay MacDonald) was a critical but not a popular success, and he suggests it failed because its critique of a moribund Labour tradition could not exploit any significant audience discontent with the Labour government, which was then handling its problems with aplomb.[18] What should also be stressed is that the Boultings' partnership was far stronger than any del Giudice had so far encountered, and that there are more similarities between this film and their *Thunder Rock* and *I'm All Right Jack* than there are with other Two Cities films. To be sure, *Fame is the Spur* conforms to the 'quality' canon in so far as it is artistically made and requires considerable cultural competence. But it fails to use history in a mode appropriate for audience concerns of 1947. Firstly, the past could not be profitable in films if it was shown as unrelieved oppression and gloom; and secondly, as the leader comment in *Tribune* on 17 October 1947 suggested, 'no members of the present cabinet are liable to fall victim to the steadily decreasing temptations and charms of the Conservative social set ... Today, other dangers loom ahead.'

The next two historical enterprises to bear del Giudice's name were *Vice Versa* and *The Mark of Cain*. Both films were based on well-known novels, were critically assaulted, and were box-office failures. *Vice Versa* is about a Victorian schoolboy and his father who change places with the help of a magic stone. Visually, it is cramped and chaotic. The studio's publicity material suggests that the film was 'a burlesque of that period of English life when there was a strict dividing line between what was and what was not "done" ... Exaggeration of characteristics is the keynote throughout the production.' The problem was that del Giudice had given Peter Ustinov great licence during production, and an undisciplined text resulted, in which everyone was playing in the hyperbolic Crummles style.

Vice Versa was an attempt at comedy; *The Mark of Cain* was a stab at melodrama. Two Cities attempted to upgrade the film by advertising it as a dignified oil painting within an ornate frame, and by emphasising its 'classic' features. The publicity material contained what must be history's most down-beat account of adultery: 'Discouraged by her husband's lack of appreciation, Sarah makes Richard her confidant.' But these tasteful aims accorded ill with the original Joseph Shearing novel, which dealt luridly with hanging, poison-ing and fratricide. Shearing was really Marjorie Bowden, who was adept at producing novels about Victorian heroines faced with patriarchal oppression.[13] But *The Mark of Cain* deploys the melodrama mode in an uneven manner, perhaps because those working on the production were either inexperienced in the genre or despised it.

So far, then, del Giudice's attempts to produce 'hopeful' and 'tasteful' historical films were a failure. The use of high culture in the films was often mismanaged. Del Giudice's tendency to give inexperienced or wilful personnel their head meant that Two Cities produced no coherent historical opus, and there were no box-office hits until *Hamlet*, which was a major success. It won great critical acclaim and also Academy Awards, including Best Film, Best Art Direction, Best Actor, and Best Black-and-White Photography. *Hamlet* did well, too, in the *Kinematographic Weekly* listings. On 1 February 1949, *Picturegoer* produced an interesting analysis of audience response in Birmingham, where the film had had elaborate pre-run publicity campaigns. *Picturegoer* suggested that this hard sell was more productive for middle-class audiences, who saw their enjoyment of the film as an index of their cultural status. But working-class patrons were more severe:

> I thought Hamlet was supposed to be mad all the way through. Give me a good musical any day.

> There were too many steps all over the place.

> The ghost was too tin canny.

> I'd prefer to see a good musical. It's all right for some, but I'm too rough and ready. Still, fair's fair; I've never seen anything by Shakespeare before.

> Give me a nice human drama. My favourite stars are Joan Fontaine and Burt Lancaster.

Clearly, the success of *Hamlet* was predicated not on the film's artistic quality but on the parish of belief it evoked. It was made and presented in such a way as to encourage audiences with a modicum of cultural nous to feel confident about their ability to decode high art. The previous Olivier/del Giudice collab-oration, *Henry V*, had functioned similarly, but with the added benefit of the wartime relevance of the topic. In fact, *Hamlet* is mannered and stagey, and Olivier's production foregrounds the misogynistic aspects of the play. The direction of the Gertrude/Hamlet relationship forces an Oedipal interpretation, and the Hamlet/Ophelia scenes are unduly full of sexual loathing. Moreover, Olivier depoliticises the play. Rosencrantz and Guildenstern are excised, as, more importantly, is Fortinbras. With them go much of the play's political cutting edge. Of course, Olivier and his captive critics justified this in terms of textual economy and audience stupidity.[14]

Hamlet was a well-documented result of del Giudice's intervention. But there are problems of attribution with Two Cities' next historical film, an adaptation of Sheridan Le Fanu's *Uncle Silas*. This was a Gothic story with an ornate literary style, which the film emulated by expressionist visual methods. Elizabeth Haffenden, usually at Gainsborough, did the costumes, and the production was designed by Laurence Irving. According to him, *Uncle Silas* encountered extreme costing difficulties because of its style ('to artificial smoke, £2,000') and it failed to break even. It received extensive critical vituperation; the *Tribune* reviewer thought Jean Simmons like 'the old Laurel and Hardy gag about standing round waiting to be hit'. For the *News of the World*, it was 'the most preposterous production it has ever been my misfortune to see'.[15] Other critics were equally savage.

However, *Uncle Silas* constituted a marked shift in Two Cities' orientation, which should lead us to attribute it to Somlo's influence and not del Giudice's. It quotes high culture ironically, and its witty sense of play with established forms constitutes a different kind of Gothic idiom from that of *The Mark of Cain*. *Uncle Silas* is not played for laughs, but it displays a sophisticated awareness of literary and visual convention, combined with a tendency to push every situation and gesture to the limit. It is experimental and eccentric in style, narrative and characterisation, and its extremism and unexpected lightness of touch probably alienated both critics and audience.

It is that same lightness which also characterised later Two Cities histories. *The History of Mr Polly* compares interestingly with the 1941 H. G. Wells film, *Kipps*. This was an uncomfortable film, thanks to an overload of different embarrassments and to the unease with which lower-middle class ethics were presented. But *Mr Polly*, which was produced by John Mills, was more coherent. Two Cities' publicity material presented the film as anarchically critical of Victorian certainties. *Mr Polly* displays lower-middle class experience as a depressing panorama of spitefulness, ugliness and misplaced affection; it attempts to mediate this with slapstick comedy and visual quotations from Chaplin films. This combination of modes confused some critics: 'The presenting of the period as though it were a turn in a review destroys the verve and springs of character.'[16]

Indeed, the combination of period setting with comedy was rarely successful in British film of the period. Nonetheless, Two Cities next produced *Cardboard Cavalier*, an appalling farrago which scotched the company's reputation as a producer of 'quality' histories. This starred comedian Sid Field and featured Margaret Lockwood as Nell Gwyn, trading on her (by now rather tired) décolleté allure. Walter Forde, the director of *Cardboard Cavalier*, recalled his exclusion by Somlo from any production or scripting decisions, and that he had not wanted to make the film anyway.[17] Two Cities advertised the film like an MGM multi-star vehicle, but the design of the posters was so lacklustre as to appear tatty; the array of stars looked dumbstruck. The main problem with *Cardboard Cavalier* is that the parallels between Cromwellian England and postwar shortages are laid on with a trowel ('the cheddar is for export only'), and the language is uneven ('zounds, stone a crow'). The film's populist politics are incoherent, even though Sid's favourite mouse is called Henry VIII and the bad rat Cromwell. *Cardboard Cavalier* was trounced horribly.

However, Two Cities produced one popular history in its post-Giudice period. *Trottie True* appeared in the *Kinematograph Weekly* listings, in spite of mixed reviews. The lowbrow papers praised it, and the film's poster emphasised this popular orientation; the raised, frilly skirts of the Gaiety Girl filled the frame, and her legs were spread at right angles. *Trottie True* succeeded not because it was based on a famous book (the novel by Brahms and Simon was not a bestseller) but because of the class liaisons it supported. Trottie is a Gaiety Girl who, spurning the attentions of an amorous balloonist, marries into nobility and becomes a Duchess. En route, the film celebrates the vitality of working-class culture, and suggests that an aristocracy of style is available to all; it also criticises the narrow-minded bourgeoisie. This structure of feeling replicates that of Korda's earlier films and also Gainsborough's, and it indicates the enduring fertility of the theme. But there were some important changes. The script insists that Trottie is a 'good girl', which contrasts with the earlier, more permissive morality; and radical class values are more overtly stated. Trottie's dowager mother-in-law suggests 'You are a born Duchess. You are never afraid of doing something that others might consider wrong, or in bad taste, and subsequently you are an aristocrat and entirely free of vulgarity.' In addition, the film displays its rich pictorial values brightly, and they scorch the eyeball.[18]

In the late 1940s, then, there was still an audience appreciative of a more radical history and of vivid celebrations of lower-class fun. Two Cities' success with *Trottie True*, though, must be interpreted as a lucky freak rather than a deliberate stratagem. The last historical film from the studio was *The Reluctant Widow*, which attempted a different tack. It was based on a Georgette Heyer novel, which was hardly quality fare, but it was conceived as an accurate, respectable enterprise. The publicity material stressed that 'real' campaign sheets of the Peninsular War were used, 'and some small shells used in the battle of Copenhagen'. But such painstaking literalism accord ill with the narrative, which contains forced marriages, syphilitic deathbed scenes, and quasi-rapes. The script is unable to reconcile these conflicts, and is an unhappy mixture of burlesque and respectability.

Two Cities' historical output varied considerably according to the producer. Under del Giudice a 'quality' history was attempted, but high culture was laid on with too heavy a hand and, in spite of studio efforts at reform, the scripts were poorly crafted. *Hamlet* succeeded because of del Giudice's hard sell and distribution pattern, and also because the consumption of such a text conferred status. Under Somlo, Two Cities abandoned its 'quality' image, but its hit-and-miss methods were unable to substitute a coherent alternative.

However, there were other independent producers within the Rank network who could deploy history in a more profitable way. Cineguild produced

duced *Great Expectations* (released December 1946), *Blanche Fury* (February 1948), *Oliver Twist* (July 1948) and *Madeleine* (February 1950). The first three films appeared in the *Kinematograph Weekly* listings, and the Dickens films did very well indeed, winning a number of awards. Cineguild was formed in 1943 by Ronald Neame and Anthony Havelock-Allan, to produce Coward's *This Happy Breed* and, later, *Brief Encounter*. David Lean directed all the above historical films except *Blanche Fury*, and was associated with the company from the beginning. Neame was originally a cameraman and, besides being interested in the minutiae of production control, had considerable technical competence. But he was no technocrat and he had intellectual ambitions: 'I was always considered the Art House type director.'[19] In the postwar period, there was great scope for 'art house' history. Neame applied to the cinema Bevin's remark about Britain's artisanal excellence:

> We have never been able to compete with Americans in mass-producing articles. But when it comes to hand-made articles, everyone turns to Britain ... Let our films also be good hand-made articles, each individual and special in its own way.[20]

Cineguild histories attempted to be such 'hand-made articles'.

Anthony Havelock-Allan was a more contentious personality. His obstreperous approach delayed Cineguild's inclusion into the British Film Producers' Association.[21] Once admitted, he made nitpicking demands which necessitated the constitution of a new committee.[22] A letter from Havelock-Allan to the Board of Trade in 1948 clarifies his position. He argued that all the best films were made by producers 'not conditioned by the needs and notions of the front office of a major company'. In order to make films that were 'artistically and culturally of the highest importance', producers needed 'the minimisation of the speculative element in independent production'. Only thus could quality films attain a world market. But this was not a politically radical position. Havelock-Allan attacked attempts at creative collaboration by the unions: 'To extend this participation in control to the so-called creative functions of picture-making cannot but lead to confusion ... The creative function is one that cannot be shared beyond the customary triumvirate of writer, producer, and director.'[23] David Lean made exactly the same point in 1947.[24] For him, the chief benefit conferred by Rank was that directors were enabled to please themselves. Clearly, Cineguild's policy was elitist. Its production conditions were unlikely to encourage a 'family atmosphere' like Ealing's, or even to permit the elaboration of different narrative languages by the workforce, as at Gainsborough. Rather, Cineguild films exhibited a homogeneity of tone and approach in a period when these were in short supply; and this, combined with great visual flair and a compellingly reconstructed notion of realism, doubtless accounted for their popularity.

Great Expectations received remarkably good reviews from all critics. It was an immediate success; the *Daily Mirror* noted on 3 January 1947 that '120,000 people saw it in the West End in a fortnight. It has scooped the pool, and drawn crowds that beat even that box-office miracle, *The Wicked Lady*.' It won American Academy Awards for its photography, art direction and interior design. Cineguild's publicity material advertised *Great Expectations* as a re-

Great Expectations

alistic film and puffed the accuracy of its costumes, which would 'uphold, both in texture and in form, the inherent spirit of the times'. But it advocated a naturalism modified by narrative demands: 'Any who profess an interest in history and, in particular, admirers of Dickens' genius will be enthralled by this visual conception of an England of a hundred years ago. No diminuendo in the tempo of the story has been allowed to creep in by any insistence on authenticity.' This was a significant shift from the tiresome insistence on accuracy which was evident in material from the more ambitious and academic Ealing or Two Cities.

Great Expectations was successful on a popular and critical level for a number of reasons. The post-production script strongly emphasised the importance of a coherent point of view, and gave instructions to film such objects as trees, banisters and Estella's muff 'from Pip's eyeline'. Its visual style is a refined expressionism, more respectable than Gainsborough's and less idiosyncratic than Powell and Pressburger's. John Bryan designed the production, and his customary interest in asymmetry and the picturesque inform the whole film. The visual narrative of *Great Expectations* offers the audience a wide variety of pace and texture. It does not attempt to replicate the novel via the *mise en scène*. Rather, the film's style *reinterprets* the Dickens text, and makes it more markedly Gothic. The novel was a turning-point in Dickens's output, since it exemplifies a more restrained approach, and contains few of the caricatures which were his trademark hitherto. The original ending (the one preferred by Dickens and overruled by the popular novelist Bulwer-Lytton) is a masterpiece of understatement. Lean's film expands the grotesque element, producing in effect a more conventional reading of Dickens.

This is consonant with Dickens's peculiar role in popular literary culture. Dickens's novels were pirated in cheap versions and dramatisations immediately after their publication, and his profitable public readings of sensational extracts may be interpreted as an aspect of melodramatic theatre. One cannot imagine George Eliot wrapping-paper or tea-towels; but both exist for Dickens, whose ideological function was (and is) of a skilled though lurid caricaturist. The state of Dickens scholarship was fairly advanced in the 1940s. But Cineguild ignored this and instead reproduced the 'folk' Dickens, with a crucial quality gloss. *Great Expectations* and *Oliver Twist* were classic texts from the past, but that past was given a populist interpretation by the films, which was probably not the conscious intention of their makers.

Predictably, *Oliver Twist* had much in common with *Great Expectations*. Again, it received very favourable reviews and appeared in the *Kinematograph Weekly* ratings. Again, the studio's publicity material presented the film as broadly naturalistic, although the sets were not copied from any actual building – they quoted images from the cartoonists Cruikshank and Doré. And again, the script had a consistent mode of address and an expressionist bias.[25] But *Oliver Twist* was from an earlier stage in Dickens's career, and was firmly within the *grand guignol* style usually associated with him; and so the Cineguild film had less reconstructive work to do. *Oliver Twist* fitted better into the desired mould.

Cineguild, then, successfully recuperated two Victorian classics which are generally held to belong to the realist canon. There has been much doctrinaire discussion on realism since the late 1970s, and it has been fashionable to berate the realist novel for having a 'hierarchy of discourses' and 'textual closure'. Such assertions simplify the complexity of Victorian literary culture, and they are unhelpful when we attempt to formulate the means whereby realism can be recycled in subsequent periods. Victorian realism had four premises. First, it deployed familiar and sometimes residual languages which did not bamboozle its readers (Thackeray's *The History of Henry Esmond* or Bulwer-Lytton's *Pelham*). Second, realist writers were acutely aware that their texts were commodities, and were constantly fine-tuning (Dickens's *David Copperfield* or Gaskell's *North and South*). Third, the species of reflectionalism used by Victorian novelists was predicated on the desirability of 'mirroring' not a material world, but a series of subjective perceptions of it (Eliot's *Middlemarch* or Brontë's *Wuthering Heights*). Fourthly, realist novels foregrounded the relationship between the individual and society, but rarely represented this predictably (Mrs Craik's *John Halifax, Gentleman* or Kingsley's *Alton Locke*).

If we define Victorian realism thus, we can see why it was so compelling for Cineguild, and why, alone among its competitors, it managed to revamp and popularise it. Within the realist mode, the Gothic was perfectly permissible, as was overt quotation and authorial intervention. Lean and his producers clearly knew this, and could pick their way with marvellous flexibility between the poles of allusiveness and contemporary relevance. Another example of Cineguild's realist flair was *Blanche Fury* (1948), which was made between the two Dickens films. This may be interpreted as an attempt to rewrite Marjorie Bowden's 1939 novel as a Victorian *Bildungsroman*. Its appearance in the popularity lists indicates that the enterprise was well-judged, although it had poor reviews.

Blanche Fury had script problems. The first draft script presented the heroine positively; the themes of land management and gypsy symbolism were heavily foregrounded in this version, and the hero, Philip Thorne, bore no guilt for the death of the female heir. The pre-final shooting script still laid no blame on the heroine, who dies an old maid; she witnesses the hubris of Philip, but does not share it. A later addition exonerates her: 'His dark masculine beauty instantly and strongly affects Blanche.' But by the final filmed version Blanche's villainy is established and psychologically convincing. She is passionate and predatory, but the audience is encouraged from the outset to identify closely with her, by the use of distorted point-of-view shots and privileged flashbacks.

In its components (gypsies, aristocrats and libidinous females) *Blanche Fury* has some similarity to Gainsborough costume melodramas. But what we must take into account is the radically different *manner* of the Cineguild film. *Blanche Fury* is soberly Gothic, and more restrained than its original; its structures of feeling are recognisably those of classic Victorian novels such as *Jane Eyre* and *Daniel Deronda*. Its narrative depends on techniques of justification, so that everyone has clear motivations, even the gypsies and the doomed protagonists. The film's publicity material suggested that the film trod warily on the ground between blame and exoneration. Visually, it teeters between reality and illusionism.

Blanche Fury

Blanche Fury derived its coherence from its complex relationship with Victorian realism, something it shared with *Great Expectations* and *Oliver Twist*. All three films succeeded because they combined a degree of sensationalism with more respectable literary pleasures. Cineguild's next historical film, *Madeleine*, could not duplicate this pattern. Like *Blanche Fury*, it was based on a Marjorie Bowden novel, and had sets designed by John Bryan. But it was produced by Stanley Haynes, who clearly had a less coherent view of the past than Neame or Havelock-Allan. *Madeleine* deals with the case of a woman tried for poisoning her lover; the publicity material reproduced the official synopses of the trial. The film handles its symbolism clumsily, and the glacial manner of the heroine (Ann Todd, then married to David Lean, the film's director) is inappropriate. Visually, *Madeleine* is less seductive than its Cineguild precursors. And the original trial had been a *cause célèbre*, so the real-life notoriety of the subject matter hampered the film's imaginative trajectory. Lean clearly thought that the original court's verdict of 'not proven' should be dealt with by sitting on the fence – Madeleine's villainy or innocence is never indicated in the film. But contemporary audiences liked female wickedness to be more explicit, and they booed the film.[26]

In the wake of its earlier successes, then, Cineguild deployed the Rank umbrella to develop a compelling version of the past. This was popular so long as the films combined visual sumptuousness with a subtly reworked realism; the history thus produced was securely embedded in recognised forms. With *Madeleine*, Cineguild faltered because its realism was insufficiently tempered and because its production methods no longer fitted the case. Of course, one could argue that Cineguild's coherent performance in historical film was largely due to the directorial influence of David Lean. Certainly 1940s critics thought so.[27] But Lean's subsequent career leaves room for doubt. There is no visual, emotional or intellectual continuity between the Cineguild films and blockbusters such as *Dr Zhivago*, *Lawrence of Arabia* or *A Passage to India*, although it is entertaining to see modern critics attempting to argue the reverse. Rather, we should attribute Cineguild homogeneity to the successful production concepts of Neame and Havelock-Allan, and to Lean's artistic skill in interpreting them.

The Rank empire was deployed to quite different effects by Two Cities and Cineguild. Two Cities produced an incoherent body of historical films, with unpredictable popularity; Cineguild had more homogeneity. But there were other histories produced with Rank's support. *Caesar and Cleopatra* was a notable eccentricity. Since it reputedly cost £1,500,000, it had no chance of recouping its losses; but its box-office returns encouraged Josh Billings to place it among the popular films of 1946, and another *Kinematograph Weekly* journalist noted that it played to packed houses on its release.[28] *Caesar and Cleopatra* had uniformly bad reviews, which mainly stressed the tastelessness of its spectacle, the ponderousness of Shaw's script, and the possibility that such extravagance could bankrupt the industry.[29]

Caesar and Cleopatra was produced and directed by Gabriel Pascal, who had a very good relationship with Shaw; the book of the film is prefaced by mutual dedications in which the pair laud each other's genius.[30] Pascal was an obsessive with a passion for self-justification. His autocratic production

165

Caesar and Cleopatra

methods led to mass protests by his workforce.[31] Pascal's perfectionism was one of the film's selling points; the publicity material boasted that 'a small model of the Sphinx was constructed at Denham and transported to the desert. It weighed eight tons.' At Pascal's behest, 1,000 battle shields were varnished with an authentic fish-glue, which seemed delicious to the 250 horses, who ate them. These were expensive mistakes, but Pascal was scornful of Rank's financial worries: 'He can sell a few more bags of flour.'[32] Rank was reportedly scared of Shaw. He was certainly intimidated by Pascal, and was distracted by his desire to foster quality films for the world market.

    Caesar and Cleopatra could not recoup its costs but it was significant nonetheless, and in unpredictable ways. The audiences who flocked to the film in late 1945 and 1946 did so, I suggest, not to view conspicuous consumption but to revel in the visual pleasures the film offered. John Bryan was loaned from Gainsborough at Pascal's special request, and he was aided by Hein Heckroth, who produced such outstanding set work for Powell and Pressburger. *Caesar and Cleopatra*'s set and costume work presented the audience with a historical past which was saturated in the visual style of popular Victorian painters such as Lord Leighton and Sir Lawrence Alma-Tadema. This style was echoed in the highly coloured pictures which adorned every cheap illustrated Bible from 1900.

166

The Alma-Tadema view of the ancient world was one of blue skies and white marble, where carefully placed artefacts attest both to the alien quality of the past and to the continuity of 'human nature'. Sensual and imperious maidens in drapes and thongs seem to muse on the nature of erotic power. In such Victorian historical painting the past is a series of brightly lit moments, redolent of strangeness and desire. This was precisely replicated in the set work of *Caesar and Cleopatra*, where the organisation of space and light has both clarity and mystery. Moreover, the film has two stars, Vivien Leigh and Stewart Granger, whose physical charms are well displayed. I suggest that whatever success *Caesar and Cleopatra* enjoyed was due to the way it evoked images that were well assimilated into common-sense culture. It also owed much to the sexual charisma of its stars. Shaw's wordy script was, in a sense, irrelevant to the meanings the audience probably chose to decode.

Rank's Independent Producers group also contained Individual Pictures and Wessex Film Productions, who each made one historical film. Frank Launder and Sidney Gilliat had joined Rank in late 1944, and their Individual Pictures had been responsible for *The Rake's Progress* and *I See a Dark Stranger*. *Captain Boycott*, released in 1947, was the only historical film they produced, though they had scripted *Jamaica Inn*, *Kipps* and *The Young Mr Pitt*. *Captain Boycott* deals with landlord tyranny in nineteenth-century Ireland, and it was moderately successful; Josh Billings included it in the 'notable attractions' of 1947.

Captain Boycott was conceived as a modest enterprise by Launder and

Captain Boycott

167

Gilliat, with a bias towards the eponymous landlord. But contributions from the Rank organisation radically altered the film's orientation. Stewart Granger was offered for the 'rebel' role, and his star status shifted the script's sympathies away from the absentee Boycott. Moreover, the liberal location money obviated any sense of urgency – on wet days the Wicklow extras would sing, 'Everytime it rains, it rains Pennies from Denham.'[33]

Captain Boycott had mainly good reviews, many of which concentrated on its factual history. However, it seems unlikely that historical accuracy was the reason for the film's modest success. It was filmed in such a way as to wring the maximum picturesque effect from the scenery: the final shooting script insisted that the castle ruins 'should be situated on a piece of rising ground, so that the broken walls stand out in sombre contrast to the evening sky.' In spite of frequent shifts of angle and point of view, the film foregrounds the romantic energy of the rebel Granger. More importantly, the script includes radical comments on oppression and an arguably socialist interpretation of historical events. *Captain Boycott* combines picturesque and star values within a coherent political framework. The original intentions of Launder and Gilliat were subverted, with unexpected effects, by their place in the Rank structure.

Esther Waters, released by Wessex films in September 1948, was produced and directed under the Rank umbrella by Ian Dalrymple. It is an interesting case: superbly made, a highly literate adaptation of a naturalist novel, and a critical and box-office disaster.[34] Wessex's publicity material for the film indicated an unusually painstaking approach: even the race-cards were facsimiles, correct flags flew on the grandstand, and the interior of a mansion was reproduced life-size. If this were all, *Esther Waters* would be tiresome indeed; but the film is shot with a marvellous fluidity, and the unjust sufferings of the heroine are very moving.

Esther Waters

Of greater interest is the film's creative response to literary naturalism. Novelists of the 1890s such as George Gissing, Mark Rutherford, Arthur Morrison and George Moore (on whose novel the film was based) exhibited three major characteristics. They rendered the surface detail of the material world with regard only to its formal dimensions. Secondly, they were preoccupied with determinism and Zolaesque heredity, in a rather mechanical way. Thirdly, they appropriated the language of social investigators of the period such as Charles Booth, and inserted it into fictional works.

Ian Dalrymple's film is an innovative attempt to create a visual correlative of literary naturalism. It presents the world of objects and class idiolect as both powerful and mystifying. Esther's illiteracy and religiosity cause her exclusion from racing jargon, below-stairs culture and upper-class discourses. But this exclusion is conveyed visually, via composition within the frame, facial expression, editing, and body language. Secondly, the film's script proposes social deprivation (rather than heredity) as the major determinant of consciousness; indeed it excises Esther's family altogether.[35] Thirdly, the film has a patina of visual reference to the documentary movement, not all that surprising given Dalrymple's former leadership of the Crown Film Unit.

Esther Waters was an extraordinary attempt to respond to a naturalist novel. Looking at the opening passages of book and film, we can see that Dalrymple deployed very subtle methods of visual equivalence. But the problem was that naturalism had been an avant-garde phenomenon which was never thoroughly assimilated into the mainstream of cultural life, as classical realism was. British audiences had a distaste for the avant-garde, especially when tainted with a documentarism ineluctably linked to the hardships of war. Moreover, *Esther Waters* presented history as the site of female sacrifice.

The Rank empire had varied and unpredictable effects on historical feature film. It facilitated important innovations in the field, not all of which were popular. Independent producers outside Rank's aegis did make the occasional hit, but they deployed trusted methods which appeared fossilised. Korda, Wilcox, Arliss, Box, British-National and even the redoubtably gory Tod Slaughter were still trying, but with varying degrees of success.

13

A FOSSILISED HISTORY

INDEPENDENT PRODUCERS 1945 – 50

Immediately after the war Alexander Korda was extremely active in the British Film Producers' Association, and, through subtle manipulation, won most of his battles.[1] But he was not so successful in making popular historical films in the postwar period. He was responsible for five such films: *An Ideal Husband* (release date January 1948), *Anna Karenina* (March 1948), *Bonnie Prince Charlie* (November 1948), *Gone to Earth* (September 1950) and *The Elusive Pimpernel* (November 1950). The last film was the only one to appear in the *Kinematograph Weekly* listings. Korda gave some figures to the Board of Trade in 1948. He showed that *Anna Karenina* cost £495,000, and that its British takings were only £200,000. *Bonnie Prince Charlie* cost £550,000 to make, but box-office takings in Britain were only £250,000.[2]

Although these were unimpressive figures, Korda's supporters in government rallied to his aid. In April 1948, Korda cunningly addressed a memo to the Board of Trade, feeding its by now strong reservations about Rank; he presented the Board with the alternative of 'the Charybdis of the great monopoly and the Scylla of a possible American monopoly'. Unless companies like London Films were supported, he suggested, 'pictures would lose their Englishness'.[3] This was a potent argument. Korda then approached the Treasury direct with his financial plight, and was there so often that Sir Wilfred Eady came to feel that 'there is some advantage in having someone like Korda knocking around the office.'[4] He also haunted the Board of Trade. R. C. Somervell wrote to Eady that Korda had 'poured out his troubles to me at great length' and that he (Somervell) feared an imminent crash: 'I have been thinking very anxiously what could be done to avert this.'[5]

Of course, Korda was calling in his 'markers' in the moment of desperation. The authorities owed him some favours for his wartime work, both known and covert. Even though there was now a Labour government, there was still a sense of official continuity. Korda had set up the independent distribution company British Lion in 1946, and it was this body that the government attempted to help. For a variety of complex reasons, it took some time before Korda was 'loaned' £3 million from the Film Fund.

An Ideal Husband, directed by Korda himself, was visually sumptuous. Korda's old colleagues were in evidence: Cecil Beaton designed the stylish costumes, Vincent Korda the heavily decorated sets, and Georges Périnal the complex camera set-ups. The film's prologue indicates that historical *mise en scène* was a priority: 'The naughty Nineties crowds upon the screen/VICTORIA

Anna Karenina

reigns – but FASHION is the Queen.' But the visual representation of the past
was sorely at odds with that contained within the script. Korda's old standby
Lajos Biro produced a lacklustre script (it was his last before his death in
1948), and in any case *An Ideal Husband* was Oscar Wilde's least witty play.
The film had very mixed reviews; it was called 'a spectacle for jaded house-
wives' and 'a bowl of wax fruit'.[6] The most interesting comments came from
Picture Post on 16 August 1947. It featured profuse illustrations from the film,
but remarked that

> behind it all, the reality was otherwise. The old values were going to the
> devil. The working man still touched his cap, but he was in his union now.
> The world of the Lady Windermeres was a dream world ... cloud cuckoo
> land is a great place for a film setting.

These were astute remarks. *An Ideal Husband* probably failed because it did
not recognise the increased confidence of the working class after 1945. Korda
addressed himself to that class as he had always done; but the image of the
past needed certain adjustments if it was now to succeed with that audience.
Stupendous visual undertakings were not enough.

The same mistakes were made with *Anna Karenina*. Korda intended it
for the international market, and he accordingly chose Jean Duvivier to direct,

Henri Alekan to photograph and Jean Anouilh to script the film. The script meetings were extremely acrimonious. Korda clearly had his own ideas on the adaptation, which conflicted with those of Anouilh and Guy Morgan, who was co-opted later. The final script clarifies the novel's adultery theme by omitting most of the Levin story. But in Tolstoy's original, Levin and his philosophical crises are a vital counterbalance to the frivolous Anna. The script's excision of Levin throws undue weight on the Anna/Vronsky relationship, which suffers from the inadequacies of the protagonists' performances. Anna's 'ruin' is presented as a pleasurable event. Lightning symbolises sexual passion, and afterwards she remarks, 'I should feel ashamed, but I don't.' In the novel, of course, the seduction is presented as a dreadful act, and Tolstoy never allows his heroine to experience sexual pleasure.

Korda's *Anna Karenina* attempts to provide the tale with a modern sexual relevance. However, this is obscured by the film's mannered visual style, which offended the critics. *Anna Karenina* comes to grief through its use of history; it is a dark, painterly prison, which punishes refugees from convention. The film's keynote is joylessness, albeit aesthetically done. But after 1945 historical films which were more in touch with popular taste (such as *Caravan* or *Trottie True*) presented history as a place where oppressed groups could achieve a modicum of pleasure.

Korda was fast becoming the poet of failure and of the inefficacy of desire. *Bonnie Prince Charlie* shows history as a muddy field, which swallows winsome Flora MacDonald and the Prince, who wears an ill-fitting yellow wig. The film had a chaotic production history, which could not this time be redeemed by

Bonnie Prince Charlie

172

set work.[7] The pace is leaden, and the camerawork clumsy and uninspired. Korda took the (for him) unusual step of insisting on historical accuracy. *Bonnie Prince Charlie*'s publicity material suggested that it was scholarly and realistic, and Korda even took a two-page advertisement to allay any suspicions that the film might not resemble the real thing.[8] But such claims of verisimilitude enraged the press. The 1745 rebellion, like the Roundheads and Cavaliers, was always a tender spot in British consciousness. Korda had assailed it with a club.

Korda's next historical venture, *Gone to Earth*, was made jointly with Selznick and was directed by Powell and Pressburger. The débâcle of the film is well known; Selznick objected to the finished product, and had Mamoulian reshoot part of it in America, where it was released as *The Wild Heart*.[9] Absurdly enough, the film encountered opposition from the anti-blood sports lobby, and fear of reprisals caused the British Field Sports Society to refuse permission to any Master of Hounds to lead a pack for the final scene.[10] Dogged by misfortune, *Gone to Earth* had appalling reviews too; *The Times* noted on 22 September 1950 that there was 'a gasp of shocked incredulity' from the audience.

But with *Gone to Earth*, Korda was partially responsible for a (then unrecognised) masterpiece. Heckroth's sets attempted 'a sculptural approach to film design', which provided a visual texture of fairy-like insubstantiality.[11] The inventive use of colour and the sexual charisma of Jennifer Jones and David Farrar produce an image of the past which is both sensual and dangerous. Powell and Pressburger's scenario is a very intelligent version of Mary Webb's novel. But by 1950, her type of fey ruralism was unfashionable. *Gone to Earth*, artistically brilliant though it is in every way, is thoroughly residual; it duplicates cultural themes of the 1920s and earlier. And it is also formally innovatory: a fatal combination for postwar taste.

As noted earlier, *The Elusive Pimpernel* was Korda's only historical film of the postwar period to appear in the *Kinematograph Weekly* listings, albeit in a minor way. This too was a Powell and Pressburger film, which they deemed 'a disaster'. Powell had wanted to make it as a musical, but Korda wanted much of the original story line duplicated. This was doubtless because he recalled the triumphs of the Pimpernel films of the 1930s, in which Sir Percy had negotiated his way through the discourses of Dandy and Corinthian and inculcated a general class confidence. The stylish decor of the 1930s films deployed the Regency as a key site of changes in class power.

The 1950 *Pimpernel* successfully duplicated these characteristics. Heckroth's sets again eschew realism. The hero again displays charisma, and competence in different registers. Of course, *Pimpernel* had bad reviews. But by now this seemed to be standard for Korda's historical films. The modest success of the film indicated either that the audience had very long memories or that the Orczy novels still had an important job to do, ideologically speaking. But this potential could not be fully exploited. The problem was that Korda was now in financial crisis, and powerless in the face of demands being made by Sam Goldwyn, one of his chief backers for the film. According to Powell, 'Goldwyn wanted all the old, creaky, theatrical scenes restored to the film.'[12] Korda was both unwilling and unable to take on Goldwyn, or to resist his bribes.

We can conclude that in the postwar period, Korda was unable to repeat his earlier triumphs in historical film. He produced one masterpiece (*Gone to Earth*) which was out of kilter with popular and critical taste; and in any case, this film's artistic success can be attributed to Powell and Pressburger. The rest of Korda's late histories duplicated the structures of feeling of his earlier ones, but without their conviction; he was no longer able to deploy the aristocracy/proletarian theme to any effect. Possibly Korda's financial problems hindered his artistic and popular success. Yet his *The Fallen Idol* (1948) and *The Third Man* (1949) were box-office hits. It seems that Korda had lost his flair with the deployment of history.

Herbert Wilcox also continued after 1945 to deploy history, and the films have a clear trajectory from his earlier work. Wilcox was a trimmer. When costume romps were in vogue, he supplied them (*Nell Gwyn*); when stern endorsements of the monarchy were ideologically sound, he produced them (*Victoria the Great*); when pro-American and pro-monogamy propaganda was needed, he made it (*I Live in Grosvenor Square, Piccadilly Incident*). Wilcox had only one abiding principle: that his wife Anna Neagle should star in his projects, however unsuitable she was.

After the war Wilcox continued the mixture as before, with careful adjustments for social change; and because his company and his methods were less ambitious he made profits more easily than Korda.[13] He released *The Courtneys of Curzon Street* in May 1947, and it was the biggest box-office success of the year according to *Kinematograph Weekly*. The film is a family saga encompassing the Boer War and World War II, dealing with the marriage of an Irish servant (Neagle) to the aristocratic Courtney (Michael Wilding). She becomes a music-hall star, and inspires troops in both World Wars. Neagle's Irish accent is extremely erratic, and the aquiline Wilding connotes nobility by wearing a glazed expression and hunching his shoulders up round his ears. But these faults did not detract from the film's success. *The Courtneys of Curzon Street* was a hit because of its arrangement of class values. It welds the aristocracy to the working-class by the 'glue' of sexual desire and popular art. The Courtney marriage is structured in such a way as to be irresistible to all females; the husband remains romantically passionate, the wife magically unwrinkled.

This is, then, a film of lyrical improbabilities, in which historical class tensions are resolved by love and art, but without altering social composition one iota; Courtney's career in both the army and the City are applauded by his wife and the status quo is simply reconstituted.[14] Visually, the film is competent if unremarkable. The publicity material, in a display of fancy footwork, presented the film as both escapist and patriotic. The reviews were all outstanding; the *Daily Mirror* noted that 'this film winner will make women cry and like it.' The *Evening News* argued that 'Mr Wilcox is content to tell a tale simply, in scenes which cannot fail to be grasped by the humblest of mental equipment.'[15]

Wilcox had discovered a potent mix for the postwar period; and he proceeded to use the same ingredients for his next film, but in a modern context. He teamed Neagle with Wilding for the musical *Spring in Park Lane*, released in April 1948 and the top moneymaker for its year. It deals with a Lord who

174

poses as a footman to gain the heart of a rich female. Again, class mobility is the ostensible theme, while in reality the status quo is endorsed with a new vigour; and again, music is the 'glue' which holds the transaction together.

Wilcox was nothing if not persistent. For *Elizabeth of Ladymead*, his last historical film of the period, he again redeployed the concepts of *The Courtneys of Curzon Street*. *Elizabeth* takes four wives from the same family from the Crimean and Boer Wars, and from World Wars I and II, and shows the difficulties experienced when war encourages female independence. Wilcox modulates changes in women's experience so that they can be recuperated within a rhetoric of democracy and sexual difference. Each woman's struggle for autonomy shows the modern heroine that 'our past shapes our futures, and that what women have battled for is the right to a say in that future.'[16]

This was by now common-sense reformism, and was well received by the critics; audiences, too, approved of *Elizabeth of Ladymead*, which was a modest success at the box office. Clearly Wilcox refurbished his earlier insights and produced a view of history which took profitable account of postwar ideological conditions. But he later reverted completely. His 1951 biopic of Florence Nightingale, *The Lady With the Lamp*, was a gross misjudgment, since it contained explicit visual quotations from the *Victoria* films.

Another independent producer, Anatole de Grunwald, was responsible for two historical features in 1949: *The Queen of Spades* and *The Last Days of Dolwyn*. During the war, de Grunwald had produced *The Demi-Paradise* and *The Way to the Stars* and had developed a more rigorous theory of quality film than del Giudice's, but one which equally misunderstood popular taste:

> How much better to be an artist than a loud-mouthed exhibitionist; how much better to believe wholeheartedly in what you are doing than to turn out rubbish ... The public – our masters – are no longer prepared to tolerate films which are 'empty', films with no thought behind them.[17]

The Queen of Spades, directed by Thorold Dickinson, was an attempt to produce such a film, with the marks of its 'thought' clearly displayed. De Grunwald behaved in a very autocratic manner throughout, over both the script and the direction, and the film became a *cause célèbre* in the Law Courts.[18] Visually, it was a masterpiece, with a virtuoso range of camera and editing techniques. Certainly, *The Queen of Spades* should be interpreted as art-house history *par excellence*. The producer's publicity material had a crusading tone: 'With fashion in film-making swinging almost completely towards the realistic, the factual, it seemed to Anatole de Grunwald that the time had come to attempt something more imaginative ... a pictorial quality seldom equalled in a British picture.' The cultural competence required to decode *The Queen of Spades* was extensive, and the visual skills evoked were not those of popular cinema.

De Grunwald's *The Last Days of Dolwyn* had elements in common with the Dickinson film. Korda financed the film and provided the technicians but took no part in the production himself; it was written and directed by Emlyn Williams, who also starred. Since Williams was inexperienced in the minutiae of film-making, Korda arranged for de Grunwald to act as his mentor. *The Last*

Days of Dolwyn, about a dam project in a Welsh village in the 1890s, was not a commercial success. The publicity material indicated that de Grunwald was much in evidence on set. The film was shot on location, with strict attention to a 'quality' appearance.[19] The style was restrained, and it pleased the film critics. But artistically and culturally, it did not please anyone else.

Other independent producers were also persevering with historical film. Sydney Box still had interests in independent companies whilst head of Gainsborough, and in 1947 his Triton Films produced *The Man Within*. Box appointed a range of Gainsborough personnel: Bernard Knowles as director, Andrew Mazzei as art director, Elizabeth Haffenden as costume designer and Jean Kent as star. The film, about smuggling in the 1820s, was based on a Graham Greene novel. All these components augured well; but *The Man Within* moved stiffly, as did most scripts by Sydney and Muriel Box. Its focus on revenge, sadism and male bonding meant that it failed to reproduce earlier Gainsborough *élan*.

Other Gainsborough refugees attempted to recapture the market. Ted Black and Leslie Arliss released *Man About the House* in August 1947, made for British Lion. Korda had no hand in the production and was keen for his name to be kept out of the enterprise, even after it made profits. *Man About the House* was a 'notable success', according to *Kinematograph Weekly*. This was because of the frank way the film dealt with sexual repression. Based on a well-known novel by Frances Brett Young, the script is about two spinsters in 1907 Italy. One of them falls in love with and marries their handsome but mercenary butler, who dies after attempting to murder her; but she never finds out, and lives on in affectionate regret.

The publicity material for *Man About the House* stressed two selling points: the visual pleasures of the Italian local colour and 'the kindling of the fire of love in the sex-starved Agnes'. This was a potent combination, and rendered well-nigh irresistible by the casting of Kieron Moore, who was directed, according to the *Daily Worker*, so as to 'display a torso that rivals Mr Granger's'. The film had excellent reviews, many of which stressed Arliss's experience in directing blockbusters.[20]

Man About the House succeeded because of its exotic settings and its handling of female desire. But Arliss could not retrieve that formula for his next historical film, *Idol of Paris*, which he made with Maurice Ostrer and R. J. Minney for Premier (Warner Bros.). On the face of it, *Idol of Paris* should have succeeded – an experienced team and a colourful story about a ragman's daughter who becomes a titled courtesan and fights a famous duel (with whips) with a rival for the favours of Napoleon III. The script, by Minney and Norman Lee, is competently crafted.[21] The costumes and decor are spectacular, and the film's posters emphasised 'the team which made *The Wicked Lady*'. Moreover, the film was completed cheaply two weeks ahead of schedule by using rigorous methods of preparation.[22]

Idol of Paris faltered for two reasons. Firstly, Arliss lost his nerve; the sublimely tacky story is vitiated by an uncharacteristic attack of morality. Madame Whip is presented as history's most unlikely virgin, since this 'Queen of the Half-World' is supposedly unsmirched. No audience could suspend that amount of disbelief, since the heroine's performance displays that bemused abstraction which always betokens sexual excess. Secondly, *Idol of Paris* was subjected to quite unprecedented attacks from critics. It is never possible to predict the effects of reviews; critical attacks could not dissuade audiences from Gainsborough melodramas, nor could high praise persuade them to visit *The Queen of Spades*. But *Idol of Paris* was a special case. The *New Statesman* remembered 'the Berlin bookshops full of flagellation pictures shortly before Hitler's rise to power', and the *Daily Express* reviewer was 'shocked and angry'. All other reviews objected to the whipping, and in loudly immoderate terms – a piquant reminder of national hypocrisy, given that flagellation is generally held to be *le vice anglais*.[23] A moral panic scotched *Idol of Paris*, although its view of history was no less compelling than, for example, *Caravan*'s. The film careers of Arliss, Minney and Ostrer never recovered.

So far, the postwar careers of independent producers of historical film showed clear continuities, not always profitable, from their earlier work. Smaller production companies also produced histories as before. British-National, for example, released *The Laughing Lady* in November 1946, *The Ghosts of Berkeley Square* in September 1947 and *Mrs. Fitzherbert* in November 1947. During the war, British-National's historical films had no consistent class position. This pattern was repeated after the war. None of these films appeared in the listings. *The Laughing Lady* is an Anne Ziegler and Webster Booth musical set in the Regency period, which utterly fails to capitalise on its setting. *The Ghosts of Berkeley Square* is another whimsical venture, which deals episodically with a haunted house and its royal connections over 200 years. The film is referentially witty and has an outstanding

Idol of Paris

177

cast, but it lacks a coherent narrative structure, and it sank without trace. *Mrs. Fitzherbert* deals with the morganatic bride of the Prince Regent, but British National again failed to deploy the rich material to full effect and the film resembles a Madame Tussaud's display. All these films were produced by Louis Jackson, who lacked a delicate touch and trumpeted his own 'cheese-paring' and 'rush methods'.[24]

The Associated-British Picture Company (ABPC) produced two historical films in 1950, *The Dancing Years* and *Portrait of Clare*. Neither made much impact. *The Dancing Years* is a Viennese musical based on an Ivor Novello play which had been extraordinarily popular in World War II, particularly with women. The camerawork is by Stephen Dade, and the Technicolor is well managed. All this should have augured well. But Dennis Price playing the lead looked like an ill-intentioned scoutmaster in his lederhosen; and anyway the appeal of Ruritania had declined. The residual and ossified nature of the film was exactly caught by the *Sunday Times* critic: 'a near-antique which evokes nowadays the shuddering nostalgia of a junk-shop full of Diamond Jubilee mugs and pictures of kittens peeping from old boots.'[25] *Portrait of Clare* is similarly ill-conceived. Directed by Lance Comfort, it deals in a lacklustre manner with a woman's three marriages. The film's poster was tactless. It showed a giant female holding three homunculi in her hand, but this was inappropriate for the sexual politics of 1950. ABPC clearly had no competence in historical film.

There were many histories made by smaller British production companies. Only two were modestly successful, according to *Kinematograph Weekly*: *The Greed of William Hart* (Bushey/Ambassador, 1948) and *The Case of Charles Peace* (Argyle/Monarch, 1949). *The Greed of William Hart* starred Tod Slaughter, whose quasi-Victorian villains had been stalking the screens since the 1930s; it tells, with ghoulish relish, the story of a body-snatcher who 'sometimes by-passed the cemetery altogether'.[26] *Charles Peace* dealt with the nefarious life and execution of the famous bigamist and murderer. The trial and execution scenes were obsessively detailed.[27] Both these films chimed in with a change in popular taste. Gory historical films did not do well in wartime – there was enough physical horror in real life. But in the postwar period, symbolic transgression of social norms by violent and bloody films had an important cathartic function, and *William Hart* and *Charles Peace* were examples of this. Hammer Films, set up in 1947, was soon to respond in similar vein. Its *Room to Let* is about an escaped lunatic thought to be Jack the Ripper. The publicity material suggested, in a combination of the sinister and the prurient which was later to become a Hammer trademark, that 'if anyone else were to stumble on the truth, he would surely be content, in the interests of moral justice, to keep it to himself.' Hammer also produced *The Fall of the House of Usher*, which was the only film to receive an 'H' certificate in 1950. But neither of these films were particularly successful, probably because Hammer had not yet found its touch.

Other small British companies attempted more light-hearted histories. Excelsior's 1947 *Meet Me at Dawn* featured duelling and the songs of Stanley Holloway. Butcher's produced Frank Randle in *When You Come Home*, a comedy about the early days of music hall. The film was billed as 'family fare' which 'presented a new Frank Randle'. The problem was that the old Frank

Randle was a Silenus-like figure whose coarseness could not easily be refined, and the combination of history and comedy was a difficult one at the box office.

Some small companies attempted more serious historical films, but with little success. New Realm produced *Jim the Penman*, about a famous forger whose work was 'a matter of court record'. But courtroom verisimilitude required other elements for audience appeal. Holbein Films made *Master of Bankdam*, a Yorkshire family saga about woollen weaving in the nineteenth century. Walter Forde directed, and visually the film is competent enough, with varied textures and editing by Terence Fisher. But examination of the script shows that the film's arrangement of class values is devoid of creative tension and its narrative is unenterprisingly constructed. Family sagas had had their day, for the time being.

American production companies also financed historical features in Britain, which complicated the overall map. American histories in the prewar and war periods were generally unremarkable, and rarely filled any important gap in popular or critical taste. However, conditions in the postwar British film industry were more conducive to American intervention, particularly after 1948 when recession increased job insecurity.[28] Certainly, two American-financed histories found significant audience favour in 1950: *Treasure Island* and *The Black Rose*. Why was this, and why did other competent American efforts fail to please British audiences?

One example of this failure was Warners' 1946 *Gaiety George*, which was produced and directed by George King, an old MGM hand from the 1930s. A musical, it deals with the vicissitudes of an Irish stage producer, has an excellent cast, but is handicapped by a leaden script which has no period sense and poor narrative construction. Kay Struesby, one of its authors, thought that scriptwriting was a tiresome headache, which hardly indicated professional commitment.[29] *Gaiety George* was not aimed at sophisticated audiences, and critics savaged it. The *Tribune* critic complained on 28 June 1946 that it was 'torture ... I can well believe that it will make money outside the West End.'[30] But there is no record that it did, probably because British-backed films had thoroughly exploited this medium during the war. *Variety Jubilee*, *Champagne Charlie* and *I'll Be Your Sweetheart* had saturated the market for music-hall sagas.

The same fate attended Columbia's 1948 *The First Gentleman*, which dealt with the Prince Regent's family problems. This was directed by Cavalcanti, whose talents were not best suited to period work. Elizabeth Haffenden designed the costumes. The film's publicity material indicated that it was a 'quality' production which gave accurate insight into the Regency. But the problem was that popular cinematic representations of this period were by now habitually spectacular. The *Pimpernel* films and *The Man in Grey* had deployed the Regency as a lustrous space in which to rehearse debates about aristocracy/proletariat alliances. There was simply no room for other types of Regency period films.

Paramount's 1948 *So Evil My Love* suffered similarly. It was based on a Joseph Shearing novel about a missionary's widow who became a wicked lady. Well-known stars (Ann Todd and Ray Milland) played the leads, Edith Head designed the dresses, and Sir Robert Vansittart loaned his country estate for some exterior shots, according to the publicity material. But the script is subdued, and its assertion that wickedness was 'as universal as love' lacks conviction. Moreover, *So Evil My Love* was designed by Tom Morahan, whose work was always realistic, and the decor was lacklustre and unable to raise the emotional temperature of the film. *So Evil My Love* merely duplicated the job done by *The Wicked Lady*, *Jassy* and *Blanche Fury*, but without their expressionist flair.

Jean Negulesco directed two historical films for Fox, *Britannia Mews* and *The Mudlark*, in 1949 and 1950. But by this time, considerable hostility was being expressed towards American representations of British history. Dana Andrews starred in *Britannia Mews*, and the *Observer* spoke for many other critics when it argued that he had been 'brought over here to play in a film of alleged British life, which might have been made far more expeditiously and just as badly in Hollywood.'[31] So although the film was lit by Périnal and designed by Andrejev, it was handicapped in Britain. A significant controversy raged around *The Mudlark*. This deals with an urchin who raises the spirits of the mourning Queen Victoria, played by the American Irene Dunne. *The Mudlark* was chosen as the Royal Command Performance film, which enraged critics, viewers and actors. Clearly, British sensibilities were injured by the apparent annexation of their national history. *The Mudlark* could not fulfil any significant cultural function, however artistically competent it was.

It seems that American production companies could not produce historical films which were popular with British audiences if they replicated the work of the British studios. In any case, the latter were more conversant with national preoccupations and motifs. American studios could only please British audiences when they broke with the British historical mould and returned to their own methods. It is in this light that we can account for the presence of *The Black Rose* and *Treasure Island* in the *Kinematograph Weekly* listings. *The Black Rose*, produced in 1950 by Fox and directed by Henry Hathaway, received appalling reviews, to be sure. But it was advertised as 'A Great Adventure Sweeping You From the Castles of Medieval England to the Secret Strongholds of Far Cathay'. The film's poster displayed a turbanned Tyrone Power and a mandarin Orson Welles, and the whole film is redolent of such eastern extravaganzas as *Shanghai Express* and *The Garden of Allah*. *The Black Rose* evokes the exotic, and it is swiftly paced. *Treasure Island* was produced by Disney and directed by Byron Haskin with enormous flair; Stevenson's novel was intelligently adapted, the script foregrounding local colour and eccentric protagonists. One critic described the film as 'yo-ho-ho and some fine old ham'.[32] But this ham was tasty and well-cured.

In general, independent producers outside the Rank network experienced problems with historical film in the postwar period. For Korda and Wilcox, it was the mixture as before, with varying success. Other independent studios produced films which were generally residual and old-fashioned in their approach. American efforts like *The Black Rose* heralded a new, more vigorous style of historical adventure, which was to include such later films as *Ivanhoe* and *Captain Horatio Hornblower*. The indigenous historical film had had its day. It was giving way to international historical epics financed by the Hollywood majors.

CONCLUSION

This book has charted three separate histories: that of official institutions and attitudes, that of production patterns, and that of audience taste. Although there is a demonstrable unevenness of evidence, the most suggestive areas for investigation are where the three different histories conflict and coalesce. This conclusion, therefore, will initially provide a shorthand version of a complex narrative; such enterprises are usually unsatisfactory since they often give the reader a sense of 'after such knowledge, what forgiveness?' But I shall also generalise from the detailed evidence, and attempt to establish precisely how the historical film changed in its social function and meaning over the whole period.

If we first address official responses to historical feature films, it is clear that as a genre it was of the greatest significance to some government bodies and establishment institutions, for specific reasons and for limited periods. The Historical Association, sometimes working for the Board of Education under the disguise of the British Film Institute, made an innovatory attempt to redirect public opinion on the issue of historical film. It generated a 'moral panic' about historical film, and convinced middle-class audiences and middle-brow critics with its arguments about moral probity and national culture. The Association also affected official and documentary historical film, and probably convinced Michael Balcon and Wilcox in his later films. But the Historical Association's polemic had little positive effect on mass audiences and most commercial producers; indeed, it may even have had a negative one, in confirming producers and mass audiences in their own tastes and causing them to resent the notion that the function of historical film was to reflect official realities. In the wake of the Association's pressures, some producers did indeed appoint historical advisers, but they also greeted the BBFC's strictures with less than enthusiasm.

The Historical Association's influence declined during the war. This was probably for two reasons: firstly, because the class fraction it encouraged (gentry and old Tory) was habitually represented in a less explicit way in British culture. The aristocracy/proletariat alliance was a key theme in popular historical film, but it was nuanced in a way that emphasised its *symbolic* status. The Historical Association urged its quasi-gentry position with an offensive directness. The second reason for the decline of the Association's influence was that during the war its voice could no longer be heard above that of the MoI. The Films Division of the Ministry initially insisted on an instrumentalist approach to history, and gave this quite a high priority; but after 1942 it discouraged those wishing to use history for propaganda purposes.

The reasons for this were twofold. Firstly, the Films Division was largely staffed by middle-class intellectuals, many of whom were sympathetic to the documentary tradition. They mistrusted the taste of mass audiences and displayed some puritanism in artistic matters; they also favoured contemporary subjects. Secondly, the Ministry of Information was engaged in a secret war of its own with the Foreign Office. The subtext of most exchanges between the two bodies during the war and in the postwar period is that of a fight to the death for control over government film policy. The Ministry meant to wrest all control in film matters away from the Foreign Office and the British Council. These two bodies had given a high priority to supporting historical films throughout the 1930s; indeed the Foreign Office, which was catholic and sophisticated in its tastes, had covertly done much to raise the overseas status of historical film, and it had favoured the work of Korda. Hence *Lady Hamilton*, with its implicit message that a confident aristocratic style could be the property of all classes, can be seen as a film made *on behalf of* the Foreign Office. This is certainly borne out by documentary evidence from Sir Robert Vansittart, Lord Lothian and official American files.

However, such were the institutional clout of the Ministry of Information and the conditions of national emergency prevailing at the time that the Foreign Office and the British Council were routed in matters of film policy. The MoI wanted its revenge, and historical film was the chief hostage it took. Consequently, after the war official film-makers attached to the COI lost their nerve where history was concerned; a preoccupation with it was no longer perceived as expedient.

So historical film was marshalled into a variety of notions of national interest from 1933 to about 1946. No other genre of film operated in this way, since none was held to be so vitally concerned with cultural politics. Clearly, government institutions wished to deploy historical film as an agency of social influence and control; official bodies differed in the intensity and duration of their interest. The struggle between institutions may well have depleted their involvement in the topic and hampered the long-term efficacy of the costume genre as a form of class symbolism. In any case, official bodies confused social control with box-office success; they failed to recognise that popular film was such precisely because it was a tactful negotiation between the audience's desires and its sense of actuality. Commercial producers, however, were aware of this.

So if we turn to our second narrative, that of commercial production, it is clear that a very wide range of historical representation obtained in feature films of the 1930s and 1940s. The profit motive alone cannot provide an explanation for the rich variety of historical films. It was not simply desire for high returns which motivated (say) Michael Balcon or Powell and Pressburger in their historical enterprises; rather, history was the most vital persuasive tool then at their disposal, which they deployed in an attempt to gain an audible voice in the prevailing babble of cultural forms. Moreover, producers right across the board clearly saw historical films as a genre with special properties. The non-historical films of Wilcox, Korda and others simply did not address the issues of class and gender with the same degree of subtlety and resonance.

Let us first re-examine the efficacy of Raymond Williams's dominant/ residual/emergent paradigm in the light of the larger perspective now at our disposal. I have noted that Williams categorised cultural forms into symbolic representations of existing, fossilised or new social forces. Firstly, producers espousing a radical political position (whether left or right) generally tended to use historical topoi which were recognisably part of the dominant symbolic system; that is to say, Korda or R. J. Minney at Gainsborough would select the potent aristocracy/proletariat alliance, or periods like the Regency or the Restoration which were deeply embedded in the popular historical imagination. From that position of security, they could attempt to push their audiences into acceptance of their radical views about class and pleasure. Habitually, they deployed spectacular visual styles to do this.

Secondly, producers espousing a reactionary position tended to use symbols or themes which were so residual as to run the risk of seeming stale. For example, Herbert Wilcox's *Victoria* films deployed narrative methods of characterisation which had *no status* because of their old-fashioned air; and the historical films of British-National or BIP sought to make their audiences feel secure by encouraging them to acknowledge that fossilised modes of thought could still have modern relevance. Significantly, no American production companies deployed residual elements appropriately. It may have been that they lacked the requisite cultural nous, but it may also have been because they recognised that elements residual in British culture were irrelevant to the needs of the international mass audience.

Thirdly, producers espousing an entrepreneurial position on class tended to deploy emergent and potentially avant-garde definitions of culture. For example, Michael Balcon's work at Gaumont-British and Ealing concentrated on the competence of the middle class; the confidence of its various fractions was premised on the desirability of struggle. Discomfort and difficulty in protagonist and audience was part of the meaning of the text. The films of Thorold Dickinson, del Giudice or de Grunwald were also of this type, and encouraged the audience to celebrate their own cleverness in penetrating the labyrinth of the work of art. *Status* is a key concept in films of this type; normally, emergent groups such as the lower-middle class require its bolstering effect in order to mask their insecurities.

So far so good. This model does enable us to make broad distinctions between producers within an overall map; it helps us to see who was securely within the hegemonic process and who was not. The problems with the dominant/residual/emergent paradigm are many, however. Firstly, it does not allow us to predict or explain films' popularity. In the 1930s, a dominant film could be popular (*The Scarlet Pimpernel*), but so could a residual one (*Victoria the Great*) and an emergent one (*Rhodes of Africa*). A similar list for the 1940s would be *Lady Hamilton*, *Trottie True* and *Scott of the Antarctic*. A different means of theorising the popular historical film is required, and I shall sketch this out in due course. Secondly, this paradigm does not permit us to address the key issue of gender, and again I shall deal later with this issue. Thirdly, the dominant/emergent paradigm, while differentiating between films in a neat way, does not permit a strong sense of period to develop. I shall now attempt to redress this.

In the prewar period, there were inevitable disjunctions between the class origin of producers/directors and the class fraction they gave prominence to in their films. That is to say, Korda and Wilcox had no *personal* interest in alluding to aristocracy or royalty; but that disposition of meanings was necessary for them to construct a coherent and recognisable position. In the 1930s, producers' eclecticism with regard to history is noteworthy, but there was a clear attempt across the whole field to develop a consistent studio style. For example, Julius Hagen at Twickenham, Max Schach at Capitol and Basil Dean at Associated Talking Pictures each placed a characteristically personal stamp on their historical films, and in all cases this was based upon an exclusive preoccupation with class but not with gender. In the costume films of Basil Dean or Julius Hagen, for example, the minutiae of historical surfaces were rigorously categorised according to class; but at no stage did sexual matters interrupt or complicate the narrative flow.

This is where we can draw a sharp distinction between smaller production companies and the big triumvirate of Korda, Balcon and Wilcox. Each of these three producers gave a vital role to the consideration of gender issues in their historical films of the 1930s, and each nuanced the purity/danger axis differently. Korda gave a privileged role to the senses; his earlier histories inculcated a sense of *confidence* towards the past for repressed groups such as women or the working class, so that a flash of pleasure and recognition was evoked. The *Pimpernel* films contained a hero who, possessing both masculine and feminine qualities, permitted the audience to enjoy, in a covert manner, those aspects of sexuality denied expression in more respectable cultural forms. *The Four Feathers* functioned similarly. In his 1930s work, and of course in the later *Lady Hamilton*, Korda gave class themes an irresistible resonance by combining them with the celebration of sexual love.

Balcon's 1930s historical films addressed specifically masculine preoccupations. In such films as *Rhodes of Africa*, *King Solomon's Mines* and *Jew Süss*, concerns with Empire and acquisitiveness are tempered by nostrums on male superiority. Balcon drew the lines of acceptability with a rigorous hand; on the 'danger' side was female unreliability, produced by the feminine propensity for pleasure. On that side too was sensationalism and spectacular style. On Balcon's 'purity' side resided realism, gruff masculinity and middle-class values.

With Herbert Wilcox, we have a producer with no firm views of his own who possessed an outstanding sense of the *anxieties* of a conservative populace plunged into radical change. The *Victoria* films should be interpreted as a measured response to crises temporarily experienced because of high unemployment and the abdication. Wilcox resolved these panics symbolically, by placing in the seat of power a woman both fecund and chaste. The old order was powerfully reasserted, by emphasising the vitality of monarchical and familial systems. The female element was crucial in Wilcox's enterprises. One crown is as good as another, symbolically speaking; but imagine how differently a royal hagiography would function if based on the life of a chaste *male* monarch. Only females could be used to insist on moral probity because only they could carry the required metaphoric and iconographic weight.

In the 1930s, therefore, the major producers combined class and gender elements in their historical films, and this combination allowed them to provide different symbolic resolutions of the social tensions they perceived. The main thing to understand about historical film production during the war and in the postwar period is that there were as many important continuities as there were radical breaks. Throughout the 1940s, Korda, Balcon and Wilcox continued along their earlier trajectories; they made little adjustment to changed social conditions, and this accounted for the vicissitudes they experienced at the box office. Korda's *Lady Hamilton* and his last Pimpernel film replicated the structures of feeling of his earlier work; but he lost his sense of the urgent relevance of history, and such films as *Anna Karenina* and *Bonnie Prince Charlie* are a testament to that loosening grasp. Balcon also continued the same 1930s paean to bourgeois probity in his historical films at Ealing, and he replicated his earlier production methods. But he too met with declining success in the historical field, because the parish of belief he had evoked with such 1930s films as *Tudor Rose* had been the indirect result of moral panics generated by official bodies. Of the triumvirate, only Wilcox managed to deploy history in a profitable way in the later period. This was because, although he still endorsed the sexual politics of the *Victoria* films, he managed to conceal them with a flattering gloss in such works as *The Courtneys of Curzon Street*.

However, other producers did respond more immediately to changed social conditions in the post-1939 period. The MoI and American-backed companies inculcated into a number of historical films war messages that were drawn with a firm hand; even Rank entered the propaganda fray with *The Great Mr Handel*, and British-National with *This England* and *Penn of Pennsylvania*. But it is important to notice how shallow-rooted such enterprises were, culturally speaking. They were a purely temporary phenomenon, and did not draw on the geological strata of cultural history. By contrast, the two production companies that did use history in an innovatory way during the war (Gainsborough and The Archers) shared important characteristics. Firstly, they both drew on deep-rooted topoi, deploying the aristocracy in order to inspire marginal groups. Secondly, they both exemplified production methods which were highly structured. Thirdly, they both displayed a version of expressionist style, cheap and flamboyant at Gainsborough, Continental and expensive at The Archers. Fourthly, they both addressed changes in female mores, and celebrated the erotic.

Powell and Pressburger's wartime films presented history as a place where elite groups could operate as a vital conduit, through which a sense of the past could flow for the whole of society. Their wartime films, formally innovatory though they were, won a significant slice of the box-office market. Gainsborough's bodice-rippers, of course, dominated that market from 1943 to 1947. The reasons for this were complex; but it was primarily because the social arrangements of the films encouraged marginal groups (women and the working class) to experience a sense of social ease, albeit in imagination only. This was achieved by two means: by foregrounding the aristocracy and allowing them to function as the symbol of a whole complex of repressed social needs, and by foregrounding 'free' women and allowing them to run the gamut of the sacred and the profane, sexually speaking. Gainsborough films were a key example of the way in which popular texts can function hegemonically; they provided a temporary imaginary location where marginal groups could experience that pleasure and confidence which were normally the prerogative of those who made the rules.

Otherwise, the story of historical film production in the postwar period is a chaotic one. Historical films increased as a proportion of the whole output, as I have shown; but the prodigality of period films attested to producers' general unease about the appropriate way to the postwar settlement. Del Giudice's 'quality' solution was scuppered by maladroit scripts which quoted high culture awkwardly, and *Caesar and Cleopatra* only achieved a modicum of success because of its visual style. Cineguild recuperated Victorian realism in 'classic' adaptations which were securely within literary Gothicism. In general, after about 1947 producers of historical film began an assault upon supposed female excess. Female unchastity was rigorously punished in a range of films, from *The Idol of Paris* to *Saraband for Dead Lovers*. Historical films gradually became the site of humiliation for the group at which they had initially been aimed.

So by 1950 the structures of social and sexual feeling which had been so finely drawn in the historical films of the 1930s had become vitiated and blurred. However, there is some evidence that audiences often chose to interpret films 'against the grain'. In order to establish the nodes where producers' intentions and audiences' interpretations intersected and sometimes conflicted, a third and final narrative is required, that of popular taste and audience response. It is worth reiterating that evidence on audience taste is based on box-office returns, Mass-Observation material, academic surveys and letters to journals; we do not know directly what audiences felt but have to infer it from secondary evidence.

Bearing this proviso in mind, we can first cut the 'cake' of popular taste in the 1930s in a vertical manner. Different producers represent variously sized slices of the cake. Korda deployed the aristocratic topos; Balcon reinstated bourgeois respectability: and Wilcox opportunistically played both sides against the middle. This model proposes that most audiences were rigorously segmented according to class, and that those who chose a Balcon film were somehow in revolt against Korda; it also implies that the audiences predicted the product from the reputation of the studio, and chose accordingly. This model grants major prominence to the *Victoria* films, and it suggests that audiences judged films according to producer or director. This is reinforced by the letter pages of film journals.

But the cake can also be cut another way. Lateral slices may display a linear progression in audience taste, which can be related to the economic and social conditions of audiences at different times. It is possible to interpret patterns of popularity so that class and gender themes can be seen to have a definable ebb and flow. If we consider historical films of the 1930s in terms of their release dates and appearance in the popularity lists, it becomes apparent that there were three distinct phases.

The first phase lasts from 1933 to mid-1935, and comprises *The Private Life of Henry VIII, Catherine the Great, The Scarlet Pimpernel* and *Nell Gwyn*. These were all politically liberal, sexually permissive and visually sumptuous, and in their various ways they foregrounded female desire and constructed the bourgeoisie as the enemy.

The second phase lasts from mid-1935 to mid-1937, and comprises *Jew*

Süss, Tudor Rose, Rhodes of Africa, Victoria the Great and *King Solomon's Mines.* These films all constructed history as the site of painful struggle. All were politically conservative, and all warned against excess. *Peg of Old Drury,* which appeared in the popularity listings for this period, was really a hangover from phase one.

The third phase lasts from mid-1937 until late 1939, and comprises *Under the Red Robe, Dr Syn, Return of the Scarlet Pimpernel* and *The Four Feathers.* This represents a partial return to the principles of phase one. All phase three films, which were from a variety of production backgrounds, gave a privileged role to visual pleasure. They all provided a place for females, while eschewing realism and espousing a quasi-aristocratic code. *Sixty Glorious Years,* which appears in the popularity lists for this period, was really a hangover from phase two.

This has interesting implications. We can argue that phase two films developed as a *reaction* against phase one, and that they also represented a nervous response to volatile social conditions. Audience taste reacted accordingly, and deployed such films as *Victoria the Great* as a means of neutralising anxiety about national and international events. But it is crucial to notice how *temporary* the change is. If we take a longer perspective forward into the war and the immediate postwar years, we can see that mass audiences had an abiding taste for spectacular and inaccurate histories, which celebrated female pleasure and the aristocratic/proletarian alliance. *Lady Hamilton* and *Hatter's Castle* did well in 1942; from 1943 Gainsborough costume melodramas dominated the market; and The Archers' films did well. The reissues of *Lady Hamilton* and *The Private Life of Henry VIII* were also profitable later in the war. In the post-1947 period another change was evident; more respectable literary adaptations were in vogue, and Wilcox's *Courtneys of Curzon Street* was very popular. But there was still considerable call for historical films which foregrounded subordinate groups, such as *Trottie True* or *Captain Boycott.* By 1949, the débâcle of historical films was almost complete in the popularity listings.

We can conclude from this that the 1930s successes of Balcon and the later Wilcox were really a temporary 'blip' in a longer trajectory. The successes of films like *Victoria the Great* should not lead us into thinking that the British audience had finally concurred with official views of history. Such films as *Victoria the Great* were attempting to function consensually, but in the last analysis could not. The mass audience chose to allay its anxieties in a similar way with *The Young Mr Pitt* at a crucial stage of the war; but there is overwhelming evidence to suggest that it was the spectacular costume dramas which mainly pleased mass audiences from 1943 to 1947. The successes of *Henry V* and *Hamlet* should be attributed to their 'hard sell' and to the status granted by their consumption.

Responses to historical films show a sharp schism between middle-brow and mass taste from about 1936, and between male and female taste from about 1942. The genre was initially viewed as one which catered for mass views of history, indeed dangerously so; and it was increasingly seen by critics and audiences as a female prerogative. Therein lay its threat and its charm. Popular historical films permitted their audiences to address the past confidently, and to claim it as their own; and there is ample evidence to suggest that female and working-class respondents mounted a lively resistance to official blandishments about the so-called pleasures of accurate historiography. Historical film was a key arbiter of one's role vis-à-vis popular memory. For the middle classes, it was a means of enforcing class distinctions in cultural matters; but for the working classes, and probably also for women of that class and the lower-middle class, it was a means of imaginative liberation. It encouraged them to conceptualise social and sexual relations in a pre-industrial landscape. Popular historical films required considerable audience creativity, and that is the key to understanding mass taste, which is never simply the prisoner of common sense.

I suggested earlier that an appropriate metaphor for the culture of historical film was that of the patchwork quilt. This still holds good; patterns of production and audience taste are composed out of fragments of different political colours. There may be one overall colour which dominates, but the 'quilt' is held together by important fragments from earlier periods or ways of seeing. I also proposed another metaphor appropriate for film culture, that of geological strata which owe their existence to different stresses in the historical process. Some 'fossils' become buried by accident; others are forced to the surface by social pressures, or by the continuity of the role they play in the social formation. Historical film played a particularly crucial part in the composition of film culture in Britain in the period 1933–50; indeed I would argue that it played an important part in cultural life as a whole. It permitted notions of national consciousness to be perceived in a new and vital way. It reassessed certain historical periods and recuperated them for new purposes, and it captured the past as the site of fantasy in a period where other 'fantastic' modes were not markedly successful. It never reflected history, but produced symbolic readings of it which were always, as it were, at a tangent from reality.

Historical film in Britain ended in a minor key. From about 1948, the narrative is one of steady decline. The fertile gentry/proletarian topos no longer answered the case in popular culture. It became the business of film texts to punish and repress female desire. Key producer-authors in the genre all died, left, or went into artistic decline. In addition, the difficulties of the British film industry, and the increasing dominance of the American system, played a part in the process. The burgeoning industry of mass television had little space for history, and where it did appear, it was stereotypical and stultified. It was not until the late 1950s that Hammer studios initiated a return to costume films, and not until the 1960s that television deployed the past in a popular way.

But for a relatively short period, historical films had been tailored to the demands of British audiences, and they had played an important role in the constitution of a pleasurable sense of the past. Some film-makers had established a common parish of belief with their viewers, and they had drawn from, and contributed to, key historical motifs in popular memory and mass culture.

NOTES

Notes to Introduction

1. A. Gramsci, *The Modern Prince and Other Writings* (New York: International Publishers, 1957), p. 59.
2. P. Bourdieu, *The Field of Cultural Production* (London: Polity Press, 1993).
3. Popular Memory Group, 'Popular Memory: Theory, Politics, Method', in Centre for Contemporary Cultural Studies, *Making Histories* (London: Hutchinson, 1982).
4. See Raymond Williams, 'Forms of English Fiction in 1848', in F. Barker *et al.*, (eds.), *The Sociology of Literature 1848* (University of Essex, 1978), and 'Base and Superstructure in Marxist Cultural Theory', in his *Problems in Materialism and Culture* (London: Verso, 1980).
5. Mary Douglas, *Purity and Danger* (London: Routledge, 1966); *Natural Symbols* (London: Barrie and Rockliff, 1970); *Implicit Meanings* (London: Routledge, 1975).

Notes to Chapter 1: Political Constraints

1. House of Commons Debates, 16 March 1927, 5s, cols. 203, 214.
2. House of Lords debate on the Cinematograph Films Bill, 28 November 1927, pp. 284, 288, 290.
3. *The Times*, 4 January, 25 January, 9 August 1926, 19, 21, 22, 26 January 1927.
4. S. Craig Shafer, *Enter the Dream House: the British Film Industry and the Working Classes in Depression England 1929–39*, University of Illinois PhD thesis, 1981, pp. 29–39. Shafer bases his figures on D. Gifford's *The British Film Catalogue 1895–1985* (London: David and Charles, 1986).
5. *Kinematograph Weekly*, 8 January 1931.
6. See J. Richards and D. Sheridan, *Mass-Observation at the Movies* (London: Routledge, 1987).
7. BBFC Scenario Reports, 1933 (in British Film Institute library). The film was not made.
8. PRO HO 45/23091. All subsequent references to the PRO indicate documents held in the Public Record Office, Kew.
9. J. Richards and J. Hulbert, 'Censorship in Action: the Case of *Lawrence of Arabia*', *Journal of Contemporary History*, vol. 19, 1984, pp. 153–70.
10. See, for example, House of Commons Debates, 5s., 301, col. 3, on the possibly deleterious effects of *Lives of a Bengal Lancer* on British-Indian relations, and 5s. 342, col. 2153 on *The Siege of Lucknow*.
11. See J. C. Robertson, '*Dawn* (1928), Edith Cavell, and Anglo-German Relations', *Historical Journal of Film, Radio and Television*, vol. 4, no. 7, 1984, and H. Wilcox,

189

25,000 Sunsets (London: Bodley Head, 1967). See also House of Commons Debates, 214, col. 13–19, and 214, col. 413.

12. See I. Colvin, *Vansittart in Office* (London: Gollancz, 1965); R. Vansittart, *Even Now* (London: Hutchinson 1949) and *Lessons of My Life* (London: Hutchinson, 1943). See also Winston Churchill, *The Gathering Storm* (London: Cassell, 1948).

13. PRO FO 395/615. The film in question was *Victoria the Great*.

14. PRO PREM 1/272, memo from Vansittart, 28 May 1938.

15. Ibid., memo from Chamberlain, 29 May 1938. See also memos from the Treasury on 24 June 1938 and from the FO on 2 June and 23 June 1938.

16. PRO FO 395/496, memo to FO, 18 December 1933. The 'bumph' remark comes from an undated FO memo here.

17. PRO FO 395/504.

18. Ibid., FO memo, 2 January 1933.

19. PRO FO 395/486, Leeper to Vansittart, 6 January 1933.

20. Ibid., Leeper to Courtauld, 22 May 1933.

21. PRO FO 395/487, British Library of Information to FO, 6 January 1933. See also memo from Madrid Legation to FO, 6 December 1933, taking the same view on *Cavalcade*, and FO reply agreeing, 16 December 1933.

22. PRO FO 395/487, memo from Haigh, 20 January 1933.

23. Ibid., FO memo, 16 September 1933. The FO even sent round a set of photographs to Gaumont-British to help them make selections of workers and styles.

24. PRO FO 395/519, FO to Ostrer, 3 July 1934.

25. PRO FO 395/487, British Library of Information to FO, 20 October 1933, and resultant FO memos.

26. PRO FO 395/487, Legation at Stockholm to FO in London, 7 December 1933.

27. PRO FO 395/504, quotes from memo from Leeper, 23 April 1934. See also Leeper to Woods, 12 February 1934, and Leeper to Treasury, 29 January 1934.

28. PRO FO 371/18368, Vienna Legation to FO, 7 November 1934.

29. Ibid., FO memo, 3 January 1935. See also FO minute, 7 September 1934.

30. Ibid., Leeper to Guedalla, 18 October 1934.

31. For material on Peru, see PRO FO 395/516. For material on Japan, see PRO FO 371/18194.

32. PRO FO 371/17764, exchange of notes between FO and Berlin embassy, March 1934.

33. Ibid., Federation of British Industry to FO, 21 March 1934, and Federation of British Industry to the Reichsfilmkanzler, 16 and 28 March, and 24 April 1934.

34. PRO FO 395/517, British Library of Information to Leeper, 9 March 1934. The British Library (and indirectly the FO) were now being frequently consulted on British historical details for American films, according to a note of 7 September 1934.

35. PRO FO 371/17587, FO memo, 15 June 1934.

36. PRO FO 395/515, DoT report on cinema business overseas, 27 October 1934. This also reports on the popularity and value of *Cavalcade*.

37. PRO BW 2/213, FO to British Council, 9 December 1935.

38. See PRO FO 395/530. The two quotations are dated 8 and 23 April 1935 respectively. For defence of the film from foreign criticism, see PRO FO 371/19329, letter from Peking legation to FO, 16 July 1935.

39. PRO BW 2/213, J. Croom-Johnson to Council 20 March 1936: Regina Evans at Conservative Central Office is referred to as 'a personal friend of mine. She guarantees that any requirements of this sort with the Council will be granted with the minimum of fuss.'

40. PRO BW 2/213, memos of November 1936.

41. PRO BW 2/213, exchange of letters between FO and British Council, March 1938.

42. PRO FO 395/621, FO memos of August 1938. See Federation of British Industry to FO, 24 November 1938.

43. PRO FO 371/23301, London Films to FO, 18 March 1939, and FO to Chancery, 8 May 1939.
44. PRO FO 371/21839, FO memo of 30 August 1938.

Notes to Chapter 2: Korda and Balcon

1. *Film Weekly*, 7 November 1936. For *Film Weekly*'s criticism of Korda, see the issues of 20 June 1936 and 2 January 1937. See also the *Observer*, 22 January 1937 and the *Sunday Chronicle*, 14 March 1937 for similar attacks on Korda. For other examples of Korda's views on historical film, see *Film Weekly*, 23 February and 28 September 1934, 12 July, 17 August and 23 November 1935, and *Picturegoer*, 26 January and 10 August 1935.
2. *Picturegoer*, 18 January 1936. See also *Morning Post*, 18 June 1936, for his views on film and the Empire.
3. A. Korda, 'British Films Today and Tomorrow', in C. Davy (ed.), *Footnotes to the Film* (London: Lovat Dickson, 1937), pp. 163, 165, 166, 168.
4. *Daily Worker*, 23 December 1933; *Tribune*, 19 July 1948; M. Wasey, 'The Influence of Alexander Korda', *Millgate Monthly*, April 1936.
5. *Film Weekly*, 22 September 1933.
6. *Picturegoer*, 24 March 1934. Wimperis was, like Korda, opposed to censorship: 'There is not much chance for historical film, if you cannot refer to the countries concerned', he wrote, in *The Star*, 30 September 1933.
7. E. Betts, *The Private Life of Henry VIII* (London: Methuen, 1934); *Cinema Quarterly*, Winter 1935; and Betts' reply in *Cinema Quarterly*, Spring 1935. See also C.A. Lejeune's contribution to the debate in the *Observer*, 2 December 1934.
8. M. Dickinson and S. Street, *Cinema and State: the Film Industry and the British Government 1927–84* (London: British Film Institute, 1984), pp. 76, 86. The figures given here are that *Catherine* cost £127,868 and netted £127,000 by March 1937; *Don Juan* cost £114,239 and made £53,700; *Scarlet Pimpernel* cost £143,521 and netted £204,300; *Rembrandt* cost £138,945.
9. The controversy is aired in the *Daily Telegraph* on 30 September, 14 and 25 October, 3, 6, 7 and 8 November 1933.
10. *The Times*, 25 October 1933; *Week-End Review*, 25 October 1933; *Spectator*, 27 October 1933; *Country Life*, 4 November 1933; *New Age*, 2 November 1933; *New Britain*, 30 May 1934; *The Sphere*, 17 November 1934; *Era*, 13 February and 8 May 1935.
11. *The Times*, 17 April 1937. Accounts of the trial also appeared on 9, 13, 14, 16 and 28 April 1937.
12. *Observer*, 11 February 1934; *Daily Express*, 7 February 1934. Interestingly, two papers from opposite ends of the political spectrum attacked the film: see *New Britain*, 21 February 1934, and *New Clarion*, 3 March 1934.
13. *Sunday Times*, 24 December 1934; *Observer*, 23 December 1934; *Sunday Telegraph*, 24 December 1934; *Daily Telegraph*, 21 December 1934; *Morning Post*, 22 December 1934.
14. See *Daily Telegraph*, 11 August 1934, and *Picturegoer*, 8 September 1934 ('Of all the periods in English history, the Regency is one of the most picturesque ... the men's clothes had colour and femininity'). Press books and publicity material for all the films are located in the British Film Institute library.
15. *Film Weekly*, 12 October 1934. In this article Orczy enumerates the desirability of 'subconscious' or 'inspirational' attitudes by the creators of popular texts.
16. *Picturegoer*, 27 November 1937.
17. *Film Weekly*, 25 July and 8 August 1936.
18. *Evening Standard*, 17 February 1937.

19. See 'Ajax', 'On Location: Film-Making in the Sudan', *Royal Engineers Journal*, March 1940, pp. 86–7.
20. R. C. Sherriff, *No Leading Lady* (London: Gollancz, 1968), p. 293.
21. See extensive props list at the end of the Final Shooting Script, dated July 14 1938, with revisions, in BFI library. All scripts referred to in the book are located here.
22. M. Balcon, *Michael Balcon Presents ... a Lifetime of Films* (London: Hutchinson, 1969), pp. 92–5.
23. See Basil Dean papers, John Rylands University Library, Manchester, letter from Balcon to Dean, 22 February 1928, in which Balcon remarks, ' Even in these times of talk about technique, treatment and the other things, I feel the basis will always remain the same, story-telling and acting.
24. *Picturegoer*, 12 May 1934, interview with A. Beverley Baxter, Director of Public Relations at Gaumont-British.
25. *Sunday Dispatch*, 6 January 1936. This was apropos of *Rhodes*.
26. *Cambridge Review*, 24 April 1936.
27. *Film Weekly*, 29 December 1933, 13 April and 5 October 1934. For information on the production, see D. Farnum and A. Rawlinson, *Jew Süss: Scenario of a Film* (London: Methuen, 1935).
28. *Saturday Review*, 13 October 1934. See also *Film Weekly*, 24 November 1933, 4 May 1934, 12 October 1934 and 11 January 1935.
29. *Sunday Referee*, 7 October 1934; *Spectator*, 12 October 1934.
30. *Picturegoer*, 14 April 1934; *Film Weekly*, 28 July and 3 November 1933.
31. George Arliss, *My Ten Years in the Studios* (Boston: Little, Brown and Co., 1940), p. 240. See also pp. 242, 255.
32. *The Times*, 13 April 1936. See Viertel's obituary in *The Times*, 26 September 1953, where his time with the Vienna Volksbühne is described. See also *Film Weekly*, 3 May 1935, in which Viertel insists that his work should be seen within a European non-naturalist perspective.
33. Natalie Barkas, *Thirty Thousand Miles for the Films* (London: Blackie, 1934), pp. 133–4. See also Clifford Hornby, *Shooting Without Stars* (London: Hutchinson, 1940), pp. 119–77.
34. *The Times*, 12 March 1936; *Daily Herald*, 13 March 1936. See *Daily Telegraph*, 16 March 1936, for a detailed account of Weigall's speech after a lunch in honour of the film.

Notes to Chapter 3: Dean, Wilcox and Others

1. There is some material on foreign receipts. See PRO BT 55/4, Doc. 30, Table L. This is a list of receipts from overseas distribution of films during the twelve months ending 31 March 1936, and shows that London Films made £202,000; Wilcox's British and Dominions made £50,920; Butcher's made £2,000; Gaumont-British made £12,000 from the Empire and £9,000 from other foreign sales, excluding the US; ATP had exactly the same figures as Gaumont; Twickenham made £4,748.
2. See *Kinematograph Weekly*, 12 July 1934; *Cinema Quarterly*, Autumn 1934; *Film Weekly*, 24 August 1934; *Picturegoer*, 22 December 1934; *Film Pictorial*, 22 December 1934. See especially *Observer*, 2 October 1934: 'I hardly ever remember seeing a film which brought such an electric response from an audience.'
3. Quotation from *Picturegoer*, 27 October 1934. See also N. Lee, *Log of a Film Director* (London: Quality Press, 1949), p. 16.
4. See *Picturegoer*, 4 May 1935, where Mycroft tells 'The Inside Story of Royal Cavalcade'. See also *Film Weekly*, 22 March 1935 and 25 January 1936.
5. *Daily Telegraph*, 4 March 1935. Here Dixon notes that Max Schach and Karl Grune 'resolved to stake everything on this one big picture' and that 'the men chiefly

responsible for this brave and distinguished essay in the history of yesterday are all exiles from Germany.' Hans Eisler was responsible for the music, and Otto Kanturek for the photography; both were distinguished artists. For further information, see Kevin Gough-Yates, *The European Film-Maker in Exile in Britain, 1933–45*, unpublished PhD thesis, Open University, 1991.

6. *Empire News*, 19 May 1935. The *News of the World*, 19 May 1935, noted that 'it successfully recreates those spacious days of England when we were proud to think ourselves superior to all the "foreign dogs".' The *Evening News*, 20 May 1935, praised the film because 'it is not afraid to be patriotic ... the good people of this country are in the mood for flag-waving.'

7. *Morning Post*, 6 and 9 July 1934; *Picturegoer* 18 January 1936 and 2 January 1937; *British Film Reporter*, January 1934.

8. *The Times*, 29 May 1936, found the representation of the landed classes stimulating. The *Evening Standard*, 25 May 1936, noted that the film presented the view that 'there were some aristocrats who could see injustice'. *Picturegoer*, 20 June 1936, praised the film for the way in which it showed 'a small community where the presiding aristocrat is loved by the people over whom he exercises a benevolent autocracy.'

9. *Film Weekly*, 21 December 1935, noted with distaste that Grune was 'an intellectual. Fortunately, that does not mean that historical films are not good entertainment.' *Picturegoer*, 9 November 1935, mocked Grune's zeal for verisimilitude, and the fact that the production team 'took a guillotine to France, not being confident they could purchase one locally.' See also *Kinematograph Weekly*, 4 June 1936, which suggested that, although it was an offering only for 'the better-class audience', Grune's intellectualism marred the film.

10. Basil Dean, *Mind's Eye* (London: Hutchinson, 1972), pp. 220, 224–5.

11. *New Age*, 3 August 1933, calls him 'an evil genius', and on 1 March 1934 attacked the way he 'irons out all spontaneity' of the actors. The *Referee*, 20 August 1933, criticised his 'barking and drilling'. See also *Film Weekly*, 14 February 1934.

12. Basil Dean papers, John Rylands University Library, Manchester, Dean to John Drinkwater, 31 March 1927. All subsequent references to Basil Dean papers are located here.

13. See accounts of his attempts in *Daily Telegraph*, 25 September and 10 October 1935; *Daily Express*, 11 October 1935. See also the attack on Dean in *Sunday Referee*, 13 October 1935, which argues that 'the working classes do not look for education', and *Evening Standard*, 28 September 1935, where a cartoon shows Shakespeare as a film star 'over to make a picture for my old buddy Basil Dean'.

14. *Filming England*, 1929 (unpublished mimeo), Basil Dean papers.

15. See interview in the *Northern Mail*, 10 February 1934. See also *Meet the British Talking Picture*, undated, but probably early 1930s, in John Rylands Library. See also *Talking Films*, 1929; *Whither Cinema?*, 1937; *25 Years of British Films*, 29 March 1935, all in mimeo form in Basil Dean papers.

16. This is from a handwritten lecture to be given on St George's Day, undated, but probably mid-1930s, in Basil Dean papers.

17. *The Question of Censorship*, undated, probably early 1930s, in Basil Dean papers.

18. See exchange of letters between Dean and Drinkwater in Basil Dean papers. See also Dean to Galsworthy, 2 and 7 January 1930, 16 January 1931 and Dean to Shaw, 8 August 1930.

19. Dean to Vansittart, 24 March 1936, in Basil Dean papers. Here Dean notes that visits to such a historical and cultural film by British diplomats 'might not be injudicious at this time'.

20. Dean to Vansittart, 7 May 1935: 'I must thank you for all you have done for us,' he wrote, of *Whom the Gods Love*. See also in Basil Dean papers, Dean to Vansittart, 11 July 1935. Here Dean was asked to accept an Austrian decoration for the film and

asked Vansittart, 'Will you tell me what I should do?' Vansittart was still recommending Dean for official FO work in 1939; see his note dated 15 February 1939.

21. See letter from Stephen Courtauld to Dean, 1 March 1933, in Basil Dean papers. See also Minutes of ATP Directors' meeting, 3 June 1934.

22. See letter from Dean to Reg Baker, 18 February 1934, in Basil Dean papers.

23. See Dean to Baker, 24 August 1934, on the film's financial difficulties, in Basil Dean papers. See Baker to Dean, 24 August 1934, on the inability to pay scriptwriters, and the extravagance of the location group.

24. See *Film Fashionland*, July 1934, for the use of 'actual surroundings rather than recreated artificial theatrical atmosphere'. See also *Western Morning News*, 3 August 1934; *Daily Film Renter*, 22 August 1934; *Western News*, 7 September and 13 October 1934. Of the studio scenes, see *Film Weekly*, 28 September 1934, on the farmyard with 'six highly atmospheric pigs'.

25. Dean to Stephen Courtauld, September 1935, in Basil Dean papers.

26. Typescript of talk by Dean for Australian radio, dated 1935, in Basil Dean papers.

27. See Anthony Kimmins, *Half-Time* (London: Heinemann, 1947). On pp. 9–13 Kimmins describes aspects of his own early life at sea which coincide extraordinarily with some of the events in *Midshipman Easy*.

28. See Reg Baker to Basil Dean, 12 July 1935, in Basil Dean papers. Baker pleads 'for the love of Mike get Mozart within its budget'.

29. Dean to Courtauld, December 1935, in Basil Dean papers.

30. Drinkwater, quoted in the *Morning Post*, 21 September 1936.

31. See material in PRO BT 64/100. The Home Office memo in the file is dated 11 June 1937. The whole file is invaluable since it gives details of payment for a range of personnel and shows the labyrinthine corporate structures (and often scams) involved in American-owned subsidiaries. The Board of Trade originally became involved because there was a dispute about the nationality of the films' personnel, particularly Conrad Veidt. Seventy-five per cent of the payees had to be British for a film to qualify as British quota. It is rare for this degree of detail about payment to be available. P. T. Kane, the American producer, was paid £5,000, Sjöström £3,000, Biro £3,000, Wimperis £866 and Veidt (the star) £4,700 plus a percentage of takings.

32. H. Wilcox, *25,000 Sunsets* (London: Bodley Head, 1967), pp. 95, 115 and 121. See also *Film Weekly*, 12 July 1935, and *Daily Mail*, 26 August 1935, where Wilcox maintains that 'utterly unreal' costume films could never be popular. See *Evening Standard*, 16 August 1937, for Wilcox's attack on Hollywood methods.

33. The Hays Office objected to the cleavage, but more importantly to the fact that Nell was a mistress who did not get her comeuppance. See Anna Neagle, *There's Always Tomorrow* (London: W. H. Allen, 1974), pp. 78–9. See *Era*, 8 May 1935, on Quigley's objections to *Nell*. See *Everyman*, 10 May 1935, and *Daily Mirror*, 10 May 1935, where indignation is expressed that 'the true history of Nell Gwyn must be distorted in the case of morality'.

34. The *Birmingham Evening Post*, 16 August 1934, admired its 'lusty humour, animation, and historical warranty' and asked 'Is that history? It does not matter much, for it makes for fine drama.' *Reynolds News*, 20 September 1934, suggested that historical films could totally alter perceptions of the past, and in a positive way.

35. As I have indicated, *Nell* gained third place in the *Film Weekly* listings. Wilcox discusses its popularity in Wilcox, *25,000 Sunsets*, pp. 103–4. See also the *Daily Telegraph*, 11 September 1935, for reports of the huge crowds at the cinema in Leicester Square where it was first shown. See also *Picturegoer*, 20 March 1937, where Wilcox claims that *Nell* was seen by 5 million people and *Peg* by 5,180,000.

36. Neagle, *There's Always Tomorrow*, p. 84.

37. See Wilcox, *25,000 Sunsets*, pp. 111–21; and Neagle, *There's Always Tomorrow*, pp. 88–110. See the *Star*, 11 December 1937, where it is noted that seats were block-booked for schools in groups of 350.

38. Wilcox, *25,000 Sunsets*, pp. 111, 115.
39. *Teacher's World and Schoolmaster*, 8 October 1937.
40. Wilcox, *25,000 Sunsets*, pp. 120–1, and Neagle, *There's Always Tomorrow*, pp. 104–10. See also *Picturegoer*, 20 August 1938, on the 'amazing official co-operation'.
41. Dickens is (wrongly) presented by the script as a radical writer who 'lives among the people he writes about'. Tennyson's 'Charge of the Light Brigade' is (wrongly) instanced as a paean to victory. Browning's 'Grow old along with me / The best is yet to be' is taken out of context in order to celebrate the ceremony of Royal afternoon tea. Kipling's 'Lest we forget, lest we forget' is used as a valediction to the old Queen.
42. *Evening Express*, 16 July 1938.
43. *Weekly Illustrated*, 1 October 1938.

Notes to Chapter 4: Lowbrow and Middlebrow

1. See *Evening News*, 7 June 1934, and *Evening Standard*, 7 June 1934. See *Sunday Referee*, 26 June 1936, bewailing the fact that American audiences would be able to see Victoria in *David Livingstone* whereas British audiences would not, given the then legal prohibition.
2. *Daily Herald*, 18 September 1933 and *Sunday Referee*, 1 October 1933. See also *Daily Mirror*, 21 December 1934, which sees Korda's historical films in terms of their continuity with popular tradition, and *The Bookman*, September 1934, which argued that *Henry VIII* gave rise to 'monarchical fervour' in British cinema.
3. The *Daily Dispatch*, 12 February 1934, suggested that 'spectacular history' was what the British excelled at. See also *Everyman*, 16 February 1934, which argued that Korda had 'created the best kind of historical novel'. See especially *Evening News*, 28 March 1934, which contains an interview with Sir Max Pemberton, where he argues that since history itself is 'a lying jade', British cinematic liberties with history may be excused.
4. See *Yorkshire Post*, 15 October 1935, which contains a defence of 'familiar legends, fleshing them up either by means of spectacular settings, or by giving the dialogue a modern twist'. See also *Daily Mail*, 3 July 1935, which contains a defence by the historical novelist Sabatini of the moral improvements wrought by historical films.
5. The *Morning Post*, 10 May 1937, prints a letter on the hairstyles in *Tudor Rose* and the dances in *Romeo and Juliet*. The *Star*, 19 July 1937, objects to sidewhiskers in *Parnell*; so does the *Sunday Graphic*, 18 July 1937. The *Daily Herald*, 28 August 1936 and the *Glasgow Evening Times*, 24 July 1936, object to the sartorial blunders in *Mary Queen of Scots*.
6. *News of the World*, 8 July 1934. See also *Film Pictorial*, 13 January 1934; the *Star*, 9 August 1934; *Film Fashionland*, February 1935. *Picturegoer*, 24 March 1937, contains an interview with Schiaparelli. See especially *Film Pictorial*, 30 December 1933, where the writer describes the attractions of 'silken, rustling dresses, white shoulders, and men in slimly-fitting thigh-high riding boots'.
7. *Film Weekly*, 30 November 1935. See also 7 December 1935, where it is argued that 'women deep down really love romantic chivalry'. See also *Picturegoer*, 4, 11, 18 and 25 February; 4 and 11 March 1939. Here romantic and historical short stories, clearly aimed at women, are included in the main body of the journal.
8. Incorporated Society of British Advertisers, *The Readership of Newspapers and Periodicals in Great Britain*, 1936. Certainly this Home Counties orientation is evidenced in the geographical origin of letters printed in the magazine. However, material on cinematic taste in the north of England does not contradict my *Film Weekly* findings; see J. Poole, 'British Cinema Audiences in Wartime', *Historical Journal of Film, Radio and Television*, vol. 7 no. 1, 1987.
9. *Film Weekly*, 7 July 1933. See also editorial article of 11 August 1933, where it is

argued that specifically cinematic histories should be made which had no reliance on the theatre.

10. *Film Weekly*, 3 March 1933 on Disraeli; 30 June 1933 on Nightingale; 14 July 1933 on Tussaud's, Drury Lane, the Tower, and Napoleon; 29 December 1933 on the Borgias and Richard III; 9 March 1934 on Napoleon and Nelson; 22 June 1934 on Hereward; 28 September 1934 on Byzantium; 19 July 1935 on Captain Scott; 16 August 1935 on George IV. The suggestions trail off after 1935.

11. See *Film Weekly*, 24 November 1933 on plucked eyebrows; 23 March 1934 on 'Germany' in *Henry VIII*. See also 11 May 1934, where a reader asserts that the *ancien régime* 'had sangfroid, but the film [*Voltaire*] is as clamorous as a fish market'. See 6 June 1936 on incorrectly cropped dogs' ears.

12. *Film Weekly*, 15 December 1933, where the real 'historical figure of Turpin is of no importance. Ainsworth's novel is properly followed in the film.' See 14 September 1934, on the irrelevance of scholarly views on the two Catherine films. See 21 December 1934; 10 May 1935; 20 September 1935; 11 October 1935; 14 January 1939; 6 May 1939. See also 21 June 1935, where it is forcefully argued that filmgoers do not want realism.

13. *Film Weekly*, 12 January 1934. A letter on 13 June 1934 argues that the cycle is 'created by public opinion'. For other letters of praise, see 6 July 1934; 19 October 1934; 23 November 1934; 1 and 8 February 1935; 11 January 1936; 14 and 21 March 1936. These last two letters defend Korda's historical films from *Film Weekly* editorial criticism. For further letters of praise, see 13 June 1936; 12 September 1936; 15 May 1937; 4 December 1937; 11 March 1939; 13 May 1939; 10 June 1939; 5 August 1939. The last three are very enthusiastic about *The Four Feathers*.

14. *Picturegoer*, 22 December 1934. See 27 January 1934: 'There is a kind of faith to be kept with the past.' See 14 July 1934: 'Is there no end to this costume boom?'

15. *Picturegoer*, 28 October 1933. See also 25 March 1933; 23 March 1935; 13 April 1935; 4 January 1936. See 19 September 1936, saying that Britain should specialise in historical film. See also 28 September 1935, for an attack on DeMille's *Crusades*. There is a clear awareness of the relevance of historical film for national propaganda; see 4 November 1939, two letters.

16. *Picturegoer*, 30 May 1936 on Greek and Norse myths; 4 July 1936 on Windsor; 20 February 1937 on the Boer War; 6 March 1937 on Tolpuddle; 6 September 1939 on the War of the Roses. The last writer asks, 'Are we waiting for the Americans to pick the plums from our historical orchard?'

17. *Picturegoer*, 10 April 1937. Here a teacher says historical films have a lot of damage to undo. See 26 August 1939, signed 'Historian'. See also 24 April 1937 and 27 February 1937. These last two deny that historical film can ever be educational.

18. J.P. Mayer, *Sociology of Film* (London: Faber, 1946), pp. 195, 197, 230.

19. J.P. Mayer, *British Cinemas and Their Audiences* (London: Dennis Dobson, 1948), p. 22 (age 16, hairdresser), p. 29 (age 30, housewife), p. 30 (age 27, typist), p. 31 (age 30, housewife), p. 107 (age 18, typist), p. 184 (age 18, female textile worker).

20. Ibid., p. 53, housewife, age 26.

21. Ibid., p. 69, clerk, age 19. See also p. 84, clerk, age 22; and p. 178, accounts clerk, age 16.

22. J. Richards and D. Sheridan, *Mass-Observation at the Movies* (London: Routledge, 1987), pp. 34–6. Historical film comes third with women and fourth with men. It rates quite highly across a range of different cinemas.

23. Ibid., p. 65.

24. Ibid. See also p. 80, from a male: 'Historical films should be authentic in outline without too much divergence from the actual story.'

25. Hugh Griffith, 'Films and the British Public', *The Nineteenth Century*, August 1932.

26. *United Empire*, April 1933.

27. See H. Blundell, 'Films and the Fight for Peace', *Congregational Quarterly*, October

1935, and H. Waring, 'Documents of Democracy', *The Millgate*, May 1935. But see S. H. Cole, 'The British Industry Film', *Socialist Review*, July 1933, which criticises the 'sweated' nature of British film production but is more tolerant towards the melodramatic aspects of popular historical films.

28. *Socialist Review*, July 1933, unsigned note on p. 226. See also J. L. Walsh, 'The Movies and History', *The Commonweal*, 20 July 1934; *The Independent*, 12 January 1934.

29. *The Times*, 6 March 1934, for references to the Yousoupoff case. See 9 March 1934, on the desirability of a film about *The Odyssey*. See 13, 14, 15, 16 March 1934 for letters on this proposal. Many of them include Greek quotations. See also *Teacher's World*, 28 February 1934, which contains a jokey piece on the 'committee of reconciliation' for history teachers and film producers.

30. *London Mercury*, October 1934. The Dumas Method is 'the use of historical events as a means of escape to an imaginary world of rhetoric and romance'. The Strachey Method consists of 'debunking history from a knowing standpoint of modern disillusion'.

31. *Listener*, 6 November 1935.

32. *Spectator*, 30 August 1935, and 'The Middle-Brow Film', *Fortnightly Review*, March 1936. See Greene's attack on popular film in the *Spectator*, 8 May 1936: 'This is the dark ages of scholarship.' See also Greene's article in *Night and Day*, 23 December 1937, where he attacks 'dialogue written in the conventional rhetoric of the middle-brow historical novelist'.

33. See James Agate in the *Tatler,* 6 July 1936, where he argues that 'cherchez la femme' is the only real subject of historical film.

34. *Hansard*, House of Lords debate, 9 December 1936, pp. 700, 703, 706.

35. See James Agate in the *Tatler*, 29 September 1937. *The Times* attacked the vulgarity of American histories (12 April 1937), but showed, with the reissue of *The Scarlet Pimpernel*, a subtle awareness of the distinctions between history and popular forms, on 20 December 1937: 'In so essentially a romantic story, the colours of popular fiction should not be allowed to fade.'

36. *Cinema Survey*, Blue Moon Press, 1937.

37. J. Betjeman, 'Settings, Costumes, Backgrounds', in Charles Davy *et. al.*, *Footnotes to the Film* (London: Lovat Dickson, 1937), p. 92.

38. *Cinegram Preview: A British Magazine Devoted to Outstanding Films*, 22 November 1939.

39. *The Scotsman*, 23 August 1937; *Daily Telegraph* 16 and 17 January 1938, and 9 January 1939, *Teacher's World and Schoolmaster*, 8 October 1937

40. D. Sharar, 'Should Historical Films be Accurate?', *Great Britain and the East*, 30 September 1937.

Notes to Chapter 5: Highbrow Interventions

1. H. Temperley, *Foreign Historical Novels* (London: G. Bell, 1929), p. 5.

2. D. Dymond, *A Handbook for History Teachers* (London: Methuen, 1929), p. 221. Miss Dymond's collaborators were Professor Hearnshaw, Rachel Reid and H. Gerred.

3. PRO ED 121/144, Board memorandum, 30 November 1938. See also PRO ED 121/143, exchange of letters between Board of Education and Historical Association, 19 April 1935, 2 May 1935, and PRO ED 121/145.

4. C. MacInnes, *The Empire and the War* (London: G. Bell, 1941). See Historical Association Minutes for 3 January 1941, and Historical Association Annual Report for 1942, p. 19. These are located in the Historical Association archive.

5. BBC Archive, Caversham, R16/421/1, C. M. MacInnes to BBC, 2 January 1942. All subsequent references prefixed by R are from this archive.

6. Historical Association, *Why We Study History* (London: P.S. King, 1944), p. 15. See also 'The Value of Historical Studies in Wartime', *History*, March 1940.

7. F. J. C. Hearnshaw, 'History on the Film', *Fortnightly Review*, June 1936. See also his articles in *Sight and Sound*, Summer 1937 and Spring 1938.

8. F. J. C. Hearnshaw, *Conservatism in England* (London: Macmillan, 1938), p. 45. See also *The Socialists' New Order* (London: Society of Individualists, 1941).

9. Historical Association Council Minutes, 2 February 1932, 9 July 1932.

10. F. Consitt, *The Value of Films in the Teaching of History* (London: Carnegie Trust, 1931), pp. 7, 13–14. For working-class visual literacy, see pp.136–7, 141, 203–4, 329–30. Consitt was granted a Ph.D. for the text, and subsequently became head of the Avery Hill teacher training college.

11. PRO ED 121/144. According to this file, Hankin represented the Board at meetings on education at the League of Nations. He was also the Board's spokesman at a key conference on postwar schooling; see R16/370/8, Hankin to Arnfeldt, 8 February 1942.

12. PRO HO 45/20169, Howard Smith to Hankin, 24 January 1933.

13. R16/370/3, Hankin to Gibbs, 1 January 1939.

14. R16/370/2, file 1b, memo from Hankin, 2 April 1939.

15. R16/370/1, Hankin to Gibbs, 7 April 1938.

16. R16/370/2, file 1b, Hankin to Gibbs, 10 November 1938.

17. R16/44, report by Hankin on education conference.

18. PRO ED 121/143, Board of Education memo 5 December 1934, and Hankin to Richards, 11 November 1934. See also ED 121/282, memo 29 April 1936.

19. PRO ED 121/282, Board of Education memo 29 April 1939.

20. PRO ED 121/282, Hankin to Board, 5 July 1935.

21. PRO ED 121/282, Hankin to Board, 5 July 1935. For Hankin's views on *Sight and Sound*, see PRO ED 121/279, Hankin to Board, 2 January 1937. For the *Monthly Film Bulletin*, see Hankin to Richardson, 26 November 1936. On his opinion of the BFI in general, see PRO ED 121/279, Hankin to Board, 23 March 1937.

22. PRO ED 121/282, Dance to Hankin, 12 July 1935.

23. PRO HO 45/20169, memo from Hankin, 16 November 1937. Hankin recommended the pamphlet to an unenthusiastic BBC; see R16/730/3, Hankin to BBC, 1 January 1939.

24. Historical Association Council Minutes, 29 September 1945.

25. Sir C. Petrie, *Chapters of Life* (London: Eyre and Spottiswood, 1950), pp. 83, 151, 153, 281–2. For Petrie's anti-socialism, see his 'The Position in the Mediterranean', *The Nineteenth Century*, July 1936, pp. 12, 22.

26. PRO ED 121/279, Minutes of Education Panel, 22 February 1935.

27. Petrie, *Chapters of Life*, p. 308.

28. Sir C. Petrie, 'The Historical Film', *The Nineteenth Century*, May 1935, pp. 613–17, and 'The Historian and the Educational Film', *Educational Film Review*, April 1935, pp. 13, 22.

29. F. Wilkinson, 'Can History Be Taught By the Film?', *Sight and Sound*, Autumn 1933, and 'New Historical Films', *Sight and Sound*, Autumn 1936.

30. Mary Field, 'Making the Past Live: Inaccuracy in Historical Films', *Sight and Sound*, Autumn 1933, and 'The Scope and Production of Educational Film', in J. A. Lauwerys (ed.), *The Film in the School* (London: Christopher's, 1935), pp. 98–111. See also her *The Child-Mind and the Screen* (London: British Film Institute, 1946), p. 4; *Good Company* (London: Longman's, 1952), pp. 32, 65, 139, 152; 'Can the Film Educate?', in R. S. Lambert (ed.), *For Film Fans Only: The Intelligent Film-Goer's Guide to the Film* (London: Faber, 1934).

31. R. Reid and J. M. Toyne, *The Planning of a History Syllabus for Schools* (London: Historical Association, 1944), p, 10.

32. R16/370/8, Dobson to Steele, 2 July 1946. See also R16/370/7, Historical Association

to BBC, 27 February 1944, on the Wireless Committee of the Association, at which Reid had been very vocal on accuracy. See also R16/370/2, file 1b, Reid to BBC, 4 August 1938.

33. Arthur Bryant, *The Spirit of Conservatism* (London: Methuen, 1929), p. 75; *The English Saga* (London: Collins, 1940), pp. 92–100.

34. A. Bryant, *The Art of Writing History*, English Association Presidential Address, July 1946, pp. 2, 9, 10, 11.

35. *History Teaching Films* (London: British Film Institute, 1937).

36. *Daily Mirror*, 10 May 1937, and *Manchester Guardian*, 14 May 1937.

37. *The Freethinker*, 16 May 1937.

38. *Cork Examiner*, 12 May 1937; *Glasgow Evening Citizen*, 7 May 1937; *Dundee Evening Telegraph*, 6 May 1937; *Greenock Telegraph*, 6 May 1937; *Edinburgh Evening Post*, 6 May 1937.

39. The article appeared in (among others) *Newcastle Evening Chronicle*, 7 May 1937; *Manchester Evening Chronicle*, 7 May 1937; *North-Eastern Daily Gazette*, 7 May 1937.

40. *The Times*, 7 May 1937; *Morning Post*, 6 May 1937; *News Chronicle*, 16 December 1936; *British Weekly*, 20 May 1937; *Northern Whig*, 6 May 1937; *The Schoolmaster*, 13 May 1937; *Journal of Education*, June 1937.

41. The Moyne Report, HMSO 1936, pp. 127, 130. GB-Instructional, and Mary Field, were very well thought of by the British Council; see PRO BW4/2, British Council to GBI, 26 May 1943.

42. *Educational Film Bulletin*, March 1947.

43. *Sight and Sound*, Summer 1936; PRO ED 147/111, Beales to Ministry, 29 October 1947; PRO HO 45/24945, Home Office memo, 15 July 1937. See also R. S. Lambert (ed.), *For Film Fans Only*, pp. 12, 20.

44. PRO BW 4/15. Neville Kearney of the British Council, in a memo dated 27 October 1941, found it 'much too gloomy and depressing in its historical sequences ... One would think that the whole of our civilization was based on the selfishness and greed of a few, which is not true.'

45. *Monthly Film Bulletin*, February 1944 and March 1944.

46. F. Cross, 'Historical Films', *Sight and Sound*, Winter 1939; J. Laver, 'Dates and Dresses', Spring 1939.

47. C. Beard, 'Why Get It Wrong?', *Sight and Sound*, Winter 1934.

48. W. George, *The Cinema in Schools* (London: Pitman, 1935), p. 101; D. C. Ottley, *The Cinema in Education* (London: Routledge, 1935), pp. 21–2, 97–8; F. Fairgreave, 'The Film in the Classroom', in Lauerys (ed.), *The Film in the School*, pp. 65 6.

49. *Educational Film Review*, October 1935; *Educational Outlook*, Spring 1936; R. M. Findlay, 'The Teaching Film', *Contemporary Review*, April 1936. See also L. E. C. Hughes, 'The Classroom Film', *Discovery*, 1936, and 'Education by Talkie', *Times Educational Supplement*, 17 August 1935.

50. R910, Rhoda Power Talks 1, 12 July 1937. See also R910, Rhoda Power Talks 3, April 1939, and R910, Rhoda Power Talks 1, 1 May 1935. For earlier work of Power, see Rhoda Power Talks 1, letter from Power, 11 May 1935: 'Can you invent an authentic Hebridean folk air?' See Rhoda Power Talks 2, Power to BBC, November 1937, on the fall of Constantinople: 'Is there no legend connected with it?' Of particular interest, considering the 1936 GB-I film on the subject, is a memo in this file from Power, 12 July 1937, on a script about Laxton: 'It is dull as it stands so we shall have to get a little more zip into it.'

51. See R19/1173, where *Sir Guy of Warwick* 'should be treated definitely as a legend', in a memo from Rose to Read, 16 March 1936. See also R19/710, the 1937 *Last Trial and Death of Mary Queen of Scots*, especially memo dated 7 October 1937: 'What we are trying to do is to present an historical actuality from sources in both countries and at the same time to produce a script that has entertainment value.' See es-

pecially R19/157, on the difficulties encountered by the 1938 *The Chartists' March*. An undated memo complains that the script is 'too Bloomsbury'.

52. R16/421/1, file 1, memo 18 March 1942. Scriptwriters were encouraged to use literary texts as 'real historical relics of the period' (memo 19 November 1941). The BBC also disagreed with the Association's Wireless Committee on matters of historical value; see R16/370/7, exchange of letters between BBC and HA, February 1944.

53. R16/421/8, memo 8 April 1949.

54. R19/451, memo 10 October 1940. A programme on the Elizabethans was presented as a 'celebration of the common man' (R19/301, memo 5 December 1945) and sensational topics such as the Borden Murders were encouraged (R16/102).

55. BFI Annual Report, 1935. See also a Governor of the BFI in *Public Opinion*, 8 August 1935.

56. In *BFI Newsletter*, July 1937, pp. 8, 17. *Fire Over England* and *Drake of England* were much more suitable for boys, because 'adventurous'.

57. *Daily Telegraph*, 6 May 1939; *Home Movies*, March 1939; *Country Life*, 10 June 1939; *Sunday Times*, 7 May 1939. The BFI was allied with the British Folklore Association and the British Folk Dance Association in this project.

58. *Stockport Express*, 23 July 1936, and letter to *Yorkshire Post*, 2 January 1937.

59. *Kinematograph Weekly*, 12 January 1939. See also Bell's 'Sociological Aspects of the Cinema', *Nature*, 16 September 1939.

60. W. Ashley, *The Cinema and the Public: A Critical Account of the Origin, Constitution, and Control of the British Film Institute* (London: Nichols and Watson, 1934), pp. 7, 15, 22, 30.

61. PRO HO 45/20169, Treasury memo 9 January 1934; HO 45/24964, Home Office memo January 1934; ED 121/279, Board of Trade memo 13 June 1935; HO 45/29964, record of Privy Council meeting, 9 October 1936.

62. PRO HO 45/24964, Board of Education report, 2 February 1934.

63. PRO ED 121/279, Board memos dated 11 December 1935 and 2 July 1936.

64. PRO ED 121/280, HMI reports 17 October 1935 and 22 November 1935.

65. PRO ED 121/280, Dance to Hankin, 11 March 1937.

66. PRO ED 121/279, Board memo 4 December 1936; ED 136/143, Board memo 1 December 1936; ED 22/197, Board memo 27 October 1936.

67. PRO INF 619/3, memo 19 January 1940, and PRO BW 4/62, minutes of Films for Overseas Publicity Committee, January 1940.

68. PRO BW 4/2, Council memo 24 July 1942.

69. PRO BW 4/18, Council to BFI, 18 February 1943, and PRO BW4/2, Council to Board of Education, 16 April 1943.

70. PRO BW4/2, exchange of letters between Reid, Bell and Kearney, July and August 1942.

71. PRO BW 4/28, memo from Film Library Committee, 30 April 1945, and Council to Bell, 17 January 1946.

72. O. Bell, 'Wartime Uses of the Film', *Journal of the Royal Society of the Arts*, 5 April 1940, p. 468.

73. Ibid., p. 478, and O. Bell, 'Government and Films', *Journal of Contemporary Legislation*, 1942, 3rd series, part 24, pp. 42–4.

74. PRO INF 1/615, MoI memo 13 March 1940.

75. PRO INF 1/615, letter from Duff Cooper to BFI, 4 February 1941.

76. PRO INF 1/615, BFI to MoI, 29 March 1940; Bell to Board of Trade, 17 January 1940; Elton to Bell, 13 March 1944.

77. PRO HO 45/24945, Ministry of Education memo, undated but certainly 1946, and Treasury to Home Office, 22 January 1946.

78. Ibid., minutes of Treasury meeting 23 January 1947, Treasury memo 13 January 1947, and Home Office memo 28 February 1948.

79. *Radcliffe Committee Report* (HMSO, 1948), and *Today's Cinema*, 31 December 1947 and 28 April 1948.
80. In PRO ED 147/112, the Ministry of Education's list No. 5/241 had only four historical films out of thirty-five. A Provisional Catalogue in this file, dated April 1949, had no historical films at all.

Notes to Chapter 6: Official Histories in the War Years

1. R19/454, correspondence dated 15 November 1939.
2. PRO INF 1/724, 1 June 1939, nos. 28, 29, 31.
3. PRO INF 1/723, Home Publicity Enquiry, May 1939.
4. PRO INF 1/724, MoI memo 1 June 1939; INF 1/249, Minutes of Planning Committee.
5. F. Bartlett, *Political Propaganda* (Cambridge University Press, 1940).
6. PRO INF 1/318, unsigned note from MoI, 1 May 1940. See a long memorandum from Glover, dated September 1940. This took the view that people's emotions are symmetrically distributed at any one time along a negative axis of anxiety, discontent, depression, rage and indifference.
7. PRO INF 6/430, on *This Was Britain*. Only films which emphasised historical progression were to be supported: 'It was for ordinary people that all these things were done.'
8. PRO INF 1/199.
9. PRO INF 1/849, Policy Committee Minutes, 26 June 1940.
10. Ibid., Policy Committee Minutes, 8 June 1940.
11. PRO INF 1/196, exchange of letters between Clark and the Director-General.
12. PRO INF 1/867, Policy Committee document, undated but from internal evidence, January 1940.
13. PRO INF 1/849, Policy Committee Minutes, 26 June 1940.
14. PRO INF 1/196, undated MoI memo, from internal evidence early 1940.
15. PRO INF 1/615, Kenneth Clark to Sir William Brass, 8 April 1940.
16. Ibid., Arthur Elton to Bell, 13 March 1940.
17. PRO INF 1/196, Director of Broadcasting Relations to BBC, 6 March 1940.
18. R910, Rhoda Power Talks 4, MoI to Power, January 1940.
19. R16/421/1, memo from Bourdillon, 19 November 1941.
20. R19/815.
21. R19/451.
22. PRO INF 1/196, memo from Hargreaves to Williams, 18 April 1941: INF 1/251, MoI memo 27 May 1941.
23. *Motion Picture Herald*, 25 January 1941. See PRO FO 371/26184 for Foreign Office attacks.
24. R19/174/3; *Today's Cinema*, 13 January 1943, for an account of a radio adaptation of *Victoria the Great*.
25. PRO INF 1/867, Feature Films Policy, March 1943.
26. PRO 1/615, draft by Beddington for UNESCO, November 1945.
27. PRO INF 12/260, INF 6/377, and Jacquetta Hawkes, 'The Beginnings of History: a Film', *Antiquity*, June 1946. Hawkes notes on p. 82 of her article that the film was made for the top 10 per cent of the population, 'since they are the inspiration for all the rest'.
28. PRO INF 1/635. The film was never made.
29. See *The American Speeches of Lord Lothian, July 1939 to December 1940* (Oxford University Press, 1941). The book shows enormous intellectual flair and a radical (though conservative) view of the uses of history.
30. PRO FO 371/22839, Lord Lothian to FO, 28 September 1939. See also Lothian to Sir

F. Whyte, 2 October 1939, suggesting a range of means whereby British propaganda performance in America could be improved.

31. Ibid., memo from Vansittart 21 October 1939. See FO 371/24232 for a letter dated 24 September 1940, from the British Library of Information to Beddington, praising Korda's propaganda work.

32. PRO FO 371/24227, memo from Lord Lothian to FO, 11 February 1940.

33. PRO FO 371/22840, British Library of Information, New York, to FO, 3 October 1939.

34. PRO FO 371/24227, FO memo 24 January 1940, FO telegram to Lord Lothian 25 January 1940. The MoI instead favoured working with RKO; see letter from Head of American section of MoI to Lothian, 1 January 1940. See FO 371/24228, for a plan by J. Walter Thompson to aid British propaganda through the FO.

35. PRO FO 371/24230, British Embassy in Washington, 13 January 1940.

36. PRO FO 371/26183, FO memo 13–16 February 1941.

37. PRO FO 371/34386, MoI and Political Warfare Executive, 23 June 1943. The same executive had also noted on 24 May 1943 that 'we should lay particular emphasis on our positive achievements and war-time advancements, not the past'.

38. See PRO BW2/218, Council memo 30 June 1939 on Korda's efficacy. See BW 2/214, Council account of a meeting with the Royal Empire Society 16 August 1938, and memos 11 November 1938 about historical country houses; BW 2/215, Council memo 18 January 1939 on the usefulness of American historical features; BW 4/62, Council memo February 1939 on the desirability of a film on the history of the British monarchy.

39. PRO BW 2/216, Guedalla to Clark, 9 April 1940.

40. PRO FO 371/23161, MoI memo 8 December 1939.

41. PRO BW 4/20, Kearney's notes on meeting with Beddington, 19 July 1940.

42. Ibid., memos from Kearney, 4 November and 9 December 1940.

43. PRO INF 1/598, MoI memo 20 June 1940.

44. PRO BW 4/23.

45. PRO FO 371/24263, Duff Cooper to Churchill 6 May 1941, Churchill to Eden 18 May 1941, Eden to Churchill 20 May 1941.

46. PRO BW 4/17, Bell to Council, 8 November 1941; Kearney memos March and October 1941. Council film-makers liked such extravaganzas as *The Man in Grey*, as 'a creditable imitation of Hollywood': see BW 4/18.

47. PRO BW 4/17, report from HMSO and BFI, February 1942. They thought, like the Council, that there was a place for films about 'the traditional heritage of the people'.

48. PRO BW 4/21, MoI memo July 1942.

49. PRO FO 370/715, MoI to FO, 16 February 1943; Council to FO, 6 October 1943; Guedalla to FO, 30 August.

50. PRO FO 924/164, memo from FO to Council, 19 April 1945.

51. PRO BW 4/6, MoI to Council, 28 April 1944.

52. PRO BW 4/45.

53. E.g. P. Guedalla, *Essays of Today and Yesterday* (London: Harrap, 1926), *The Duke* (London: World Books, 1931), and *The Liberators* (London: Hodder, 1942).

54. PRO BW 4/40, Holmes to Bundy, 18 August 1944.

55. *Today's Cinema*, 18 September 1942 and 11 July 1947.

56. PRO LAB 26/35, Minutes of Ministry of Labour conference on concerts in factories, 3 March 1941: BW4/18, Select Committee memo 28 December 1942.

57. Letter from Bernard Miles to Rank, dated 8 August 1945, in Bernard Miles papers, BFI library. See also Roy Boulting, *New Year's Choice*, a Light Programme piece transmitted on 19 November 1949, and *The Boulting Brothers Ask; Whatever Happened to British Film Production*, undated mimeo, both in BFI library. Both pieces evince a commitment to highbrow views.

58. Bernard Lewis, *Always and Everywhere*, unpublished manuscript in BFI library,

p. 171. Boulting says here that they were released from the services for six months to make the film.

59. Ibid., p. 172.

60. PRO FO 924/494.

61. R19/173/3, Bower to William Walton, 2 October 1942.

62. Dallas Bower, *Plan for Cinema* (London: Dent, 1936), p. 23; *Cinema Quarterly*, Autumn 1934, p. 46.

63. J. W. Young, 'Henry V, the Quai D'Orsai, and the Well-Being of the Franco-British Alliance', *Historical Journal of Film, Radio and Television*, vol. 7 no. 3, 1987.

64. 'Three Interviews on the Work of Roger Furse', in J. Cross and A. Rattenbury, *Screen and Audience* (London: Saturn Press, 1947), p. 76.

65. *Kinematograph Weekly*, 9 August 1945: *Today's Cinema*, 18 and 31 July, 2 October, 20 November 1945. See discussion of children's taste in the Bernstein Film Questionnaire, *Kinematograph Weekly*, 19 December 1947.

66. *Commonweal*, 21 July 1946; *New Statesman*, 2 December 1944 and 7 July 1945; *Spectator*, 1 December 1944; *Guardian*, 23 November 1944. See also R. J. Minney's criticisms in *Kinematograph Weekly*, 18 December 1947.

67. *Boston Post*, 7 April 1946. *Hollywood Quarterly*, in October 1946, commissioned a professor to analyse the 'official' input into the film.

68. US Senate, 77 Congress, Senate Library Vol. 684, September 9–26, 1941, pp. 346–7, 354, 371, 378. See also pp. 112, 338–9.

69. Interview with Dickinson in *Film Dope* 11, January 1977.

70. PRO FO 371/43326.

71. *Daily Mail*, 4 July 1942. The speaker was Francis Hartley, head of the British side of Fox.

72. See *Kinematograph Weekly*, 30 October and 6 November 1941, and *Cavalcade*, 5 November 1941. The film is here said to have cost £250,000, with sets a much higher percentage of the total than was usual.

73. G. Brown, *Launder and Gilliat* (London: British Film Institute, 1977), p. 150.

74. *Manchester Evening Guardian*, 10 December 1941.

75. PRO BT 64/117, memo from S. Gates to Sir W. Venning, 11 August 1942.

76. According to Josh Billings in *Kinematograph Weekly*, 8 January 1942, the film was a close runner-up to *The 49th Parallel* in the overall popularity figures for 1941. See also M. Korda, *Charmed Lives* (London: Penguin, 1980), pp. 73, 153, and K. Kulik, *Alexander Korda: the Man Who Could Work Miracles* (London: W. H. Allen, 1975), p. 249, for other references to the film's popularity.

77. R. C. Sherriff, *No Leading Lady* (London: Gollancz, 1968), p. 321.

78. L. Olivier, *Confessions of an Actor* (London: Weidenfeld, 1982), p. 91.

79. Churchill was reputed to have written some of the speeches. For comments on Churchill and Korda in this period, see *Charmed Lives*, p. 251; *The Man Who Could Work Miracles*, pp. 249–50; Sheridan Morley, *Tales From the Hollywood Raj* (London: Weidenfeld, 1983), p. 168; E. Betts, *This Film Business* (London: Allen and Unwin, 1973), p. 152.

80. PRO FO 371/26184, memo from British Library to FO, 23 April 1941. Korda made *The Biter Bit* for the British Council in 1943: see PRO BW4/22, memo from MoI to Council, 13 September 1943.

81. PRO FO 371/36921, letter from Mrs Robson to FO, dated 18 August 1943.

82. US Senate, 77 Congress, 1st Session, S. Res. 152, September 9–26, 1941, US Govt Printing Office, 1942.

83. R. C. Sherriff, 'Writing for the Films', in *Uncommon Pleasures* (London: Contact Publications, 1949), pp. 22–4.

Notes to Chapter 7: Commercial Film Production and History 1939–45

1. A. L. Rowse, *The Use of History* (London: Hodder & Stoughton, 1946), p. 11, and 'Mr. Churchill and English History', in his *The English Spirit* (London: Macmillan, 1944), pp. 1–22.
2. See G. H. Cole, *Chartist Portraits* (London: Macmillan, 1941); *British Working-Class Politics* (London: Routledge, 1941); *The British Working Class Movement* (London, Gollancz, 1944). See R. H. Tawney, *Why Britain Fights* (London: Macmillan, 1941), and *Harrington's Interpretation of His Age* (the Raleigh lecture) (London: Humphrey Milford, 1942). A. L. Morton's *People's History of England* had been published in 1938 by the Left Book Club, and Cole and Postgate's *The Common People* had been published by Methuen in 1938.
3. See Sir H. Butterfield, *The Englishmen and his History* (Cambridge University Press, 1944), and L. Namier, *Conflicts: Studies in Contemporary History* (London: Macmillan, 1942).
4. A. Toynbee, *A Study of History* (ed. Somervell) (Oxford University Press, 1946), 1949 edn., pp. 215–16.
5. H. V. Morton, *I Saw Two Englands* (London: Methuen), first came out in 1942. It went through a number of editions very quickly.
6. Collie Knox, *For Ever England* (London: Cassell, 1943). The material is selected so as to reconstruct the past in a very conservative light. It should be compared with J. B. Priestley's *Our Nation's Heritage* (London: Dent, 1939).
7. Arthur Mee, *Nineteen-Forty: Our Finest Hour* (London: Hodder, 1941), p. 41.
8. Arthur Bryant, *The Years of Endurance* (London: Collins, 1942), pp. 5–6, and *English Saga* (London: Collins, 1940), pp. 328–31.
9. See H. Roberts, *British Rebels and Reformers* (London: Collins, 1942), and N. Carrington and C. Hutton, *Popular English Art* (London: Penguin, 1945). See especially E. L. Woodward's very radical *British Historians* (London: Collins, 1943). Arguably Gordon Childe in his *What Happened in History* (London: Penguin, 1942) also offered a radical view of the historical process; but this was concealed beneath an analysis of pre-history and archaeology. See also F. D. Klingender, *Russia, Britain's Ally 1812–1942* (London: Harrap, 1942), which used the Napoleon/Hitler comparison beloved of the MoI, but in a more radical way. For a children's history which used quasi-cinematic techniques and had a quite liberal interpretation, see Dorothy M. Stuart, *Historic Cavalcade* (London: Harrap, 1943).
10. *Picture Post*, 3 December 1938. See also 4 March 1944, where there is a debate between Lord David Cecil and Raymond Postgate on the usefulness of the aristocratic family tradition in politics. See 18 March 1944 for readers' response to the debate, in which a surprising number defend the aristocracy. See also 2 July 1944 for a very positive article about the Cromwell Association.
11. *Picture Post*, 13 May 1939. See also 25 February 1939 on 'The Good Old Days'. On fashion and history, see 5 November 1938, 'The Crinoline Comes Back'; 11 February 1939 on the return of the wimple; 8 April 1938 on 'Grandmother's Hat Comes Back'. See especially 15 April 1939, where Antonia White argues that the rather chaotic return to historical elements in dress signals that 'fashion is protesting against totalitarian states with their uniform shirts and uniform ideas.' For other articles on history, see 22 and 29 April 1939, 13 May 1939.
12. *Picture Post*, 29 April 1939.
13. *Picture Post*, 23 March 1940. This is quoted from E. Hulton, 'Is History Important?'.
14. See *Picture Post*, 13, 20, 27 January, 3, 10, 17, 24 February, 2 March 1940, on the history of weaponry. See 27 April 1940 for parallels between Bismark and Hitler. See 2 November 1940 for parallels between France 1870 and 1940. See 16 November 1940 for Byron's fight for Greek independence. See 11 January 1941 on the history of the kilt as a fighting uniform. See 5 July 1941, 'There's Nothing New in War', with

reference to 1783 and 1885. See 16 August 1941, extract from Napoleon's letters on the retreat from Moscow. There is relatively little on history after this.

15. See *Picture Post*, 20 April 1940 on *Gaslight*; 14 May 1942 on *The Great Mr. Handel*; 30 May 1942 on *Thunder Rock*; 20 February 1942 on the pageant in *The Demi-Paradise*; 14 October 1944 on *I'll Be Your Sweetheart*; 24 February 1945 on *Henry V*; 15 December 1945 on *Caesar and Cleopatra*. All these stress the work of the films' designers.

16. Sir John Marriott, *English History in English Fiction* (London: Blackie, 1940). Marriott was based on, but surpassed, A. Tresidder Sheppard, *The Art and Practice of Historical Fiction* (London: Humphrey Toulmin, 1930), and E. A. Baker's *A Guide to Historical Fiction* (London: Macmillan, 1914).

17. Lady E. F. Smith, *The Man in Grey* (London: Hutchinson, 1941); *Caravan* (London: Hutchinson, 1943); *Magic Lantern* (London: Hutchinson, 1944); Magdalen King-Hall, *Lord Edward* (London: Peter Davies, 1941); *The Life and Death of the Wicked Lady Skelton* (London: Peter Davies, 1944); Joseph Shearing (Marjorie Bowden), *The Fetch* (London: Hutchinson, 1942); Norah Lofts, *Jassy* (London: Michael Joseph, 1944). The publishers I managed to contact could not give figures, but could only comment that novels of this low-status type were 'very, very popular'. My sense of these books' popularity is taken from Mass-Observation material, from the novelists' autobiographical writings, and from publishers' comments when advertising at the back of books, some of which contain sales figures. Also of use are reports in *The Author*, *Books and Bookmen* and *The Annual Register*.

18. *Today's Cinema*, 6 January 1943.

19. *Kinematograph Weekly*, 14 January 1939.

20. *Kinematograph Weekly*, 14 January 1943.

21. *Kinematograph Weekly*, 11 January 1940.

22. Letter to J. Arthur Rank from F. del Giudice, dated 8 August 1943, in Bernard Miles papers.

23. Letter from Bernard Miles to J. Arthur Rank, 13 March 1944, in Bernard Miles papers. In this letter Miles suggests that British film should 'use the full riches of our national life, tradition, character and culture'. This includes popular culture, and films linked to this tradition should display 'visual mastery'.

24. *Kinematograph Weekly*, 20 December 1945. See also 11 January 1945, where Ostrer argues for 'Romance and Gaiety', 'to fill the void in the hearts of the people'. See an interesting difference of opinion between Ostrer and Balcon on 8 January 1942, where Ostrer and Reg Baker say the public are tired of war themes and Balcon insists they are not.

25. BFPA Executive Council Minutes, 6 March 1940, and 2 October 1941.

26. BFPA Executive Council Minutes, 19 March 1942. See also 23 December 1941 and 6 January 1942. Interestingly, it is noted in the minutes for 15 January 1942 that the Screenwriters' Association was 'the body mainly responsible for setting up the Ideas Committee'.

27. Letter from Bernard Miles to Ernest Bevin, 14 January 1944, in Bernard Miles papers. Here Miles claims that 'it is the first time the Film Industry has drawn upon Progressive History in order to point a lesson for the future.'

28. *Kinematograph Weekly*, 11 January 1940, 9 January 1941, 8 January 1942, 14 January 1943, 13 January 1944, 11 January 1945, 19 December 1946.

29. *Sunday Times*, 17 November 1941: it is melodramatic, but 'Wuthering Heights would win no prizes at the scenario show ... the masterpiece confers its own vitality on the story.' See also *New Statesman*, 15 November 1941: 'The period provides the distance that lends enchantment to melodrama.' See *Observer*, 16 November 1941, where C. A. Lejeune praises Robert Newton's performance: 'Only a bad actor would have played it down, tried to soften the film's melodrama with subtlety.'

30. Tania Modleski, *Loving With a Vengeance* (London: Methuen, 1982), p. 66.

31. For material on Corfield, see *Kinematograph Weekly*, 19 December 1940, and *Picture-goer,* 10 February 1940. Corfield had been attached to the Foreign Office and was a personal friend of Lady Yule.

32. *Time and Tide*, 14 September 1945. See also *The Times*, 8 July 1945: 'The pair have just spent an hour or two by the old duck-pond leaning on the balustrade and bawling into each other's larynxes.' The *Daily Herald*, 7 July 1945, suggests that it is 'one of the Perhapsburgers'.

33. I. Christie, 'Blimp, Churchill and the State', in Christie (ed.), *Powell, Pressburger and Others* (London: British Film Institute, 1978), pp. 105–20: Jeffrey Richards and Anthony Aldgate, *Best of British* (Oxford: Blackwell, 1983), pp. 61–74; N. Pronay and J. Croft, 'British Film Censorship and Propaganda Policy During the Second World War', in J. Curran and V. Porter (eds.), *British Cinema History* (London: Weidenfeld, 1983), pp. 144–63: Michael Powell, *A Life in Movies* (London: Heinemann, 1986), pp. 398–419.

34. Powell, *A Life in Movies*, p. 491.

35. Ibid., pp. 455–6.

36. E. E. and M. M. Robson, *The World is My Cinema* (London: Sidneyan Society, 1947), pp. 63, 75; R. Durgnat, *A Mirror for England* (London: Faber, 1970), pp. 29–31; N. Pronay, 'The Projection of Peace Aims in Britain', in K. R. M. Short (ed.), *Film and Radio Propaganda in World War II* (London: Croom Helm, 1983), pp. 51–77; I. Christie, *Arrows of Desire* (London: Waterstone, 1985), p. 78.

37. Sue Harper and Vincent Porter, 'A Matter of Life and Death: the View from Moscow', *Historical Journal of Film, Radio and Television*, vol. 9 no. 2, 1989.

Notes to Chapter 8: A Middle-class View of History

1. PRO BW2/218, Council memo, 30 June 1939.

2. M. Danishewsky (ed.), *Michael Balcon's 25 Years in Films* (London: World Film Publications, 1947), pp. 23–7. See also M. Balcon, *Michael Balcon Presents: a Lifetime in Films* (London: Hutchinson, 1969).

3. See *Picturegoer*, 10 May 1941, in which Balcon attacked a number of British filmmakers who remained in Hollywood. On 7 June 1941, readers' letters give strong support to Balcon's position.

4. PRO BT 64/117, Minutes of Meeting of Cinematographic Films Council, Trade Committee, 7 August 1942. An account of Balcon's isolation on the Controller issue is given in Minutes of a Films Council Meeting on 3 December 1941: 'His own views were not endorsed even by other film producers.'

5. The Second Draft Script (S41) in the BFI library shows the mining village of Leybourne; it includes a pit disaster. There is nothing on mining in the final version. In S41, Queen Victoria listens to one of the 'seditious' songs and notes that it is 'an appeal for reform, which, as a constitutional monarch, we cannot command, but can only encourage and commend.' This rather radical interpretation of the monarchy is also removed from the final version.

6. Stanley Holloway, *Wiv a Little Bit o' Luck* (London: Leslie Frewin, 1967), p. 263.

7. Peter Bailey, 'Champagne Charlie: Performance and Ideology in the Music Hall Song', in J. S. Bratton (ed.), *Music Hall: Performance and Style* (Milton Keynes: Open University Press, 1986), p. 67.

8. Interview with Harry Watt, reprinted in BFI fiche on *Fiddlers Three*.

9. The *Daily Herald*, 12 July 1947, found it 'as thrilling as cold mutton'. The *Daily Graphic*, 13 June 1947, noted that 'she returned disconsolately to her muttons'. The *Observer*, 15 June 1947, noted that Withers 'kept her wool on'.

10. See a circular on the film by the Christian Cinema and Religious Film Society, urging the recipients to see *Scott* because it deals with gallant self-sacrifice which we

should all emulate. Seeing the film is itself presented as striking a blow against 'undesirable' film texts. This letter is with the film's publicity material in the BFI library.

11. BBFC scenario notes, 25 July 1947.
12. BBFC scenario notes on *Scott*, 15 August 1947, suggest that the script is 'magnificent ... a monumental story', and even the word 'bloody' is explicitly permitted.
13. See script of *Saraband*, S237, in BFI library.
14. See Louis Levy, *Music for the Movies* (London: Sampson Low and Marston, 1948).
15. Helen Simpson, *Saraband for Dead Lovers* (London: Heinemann, 1935), p. 37. The book emphasises the extremely dissolute past of Königsmark, which the film purifies. But the film does maintain the misogynistic treatment of Platen (Flora Robson), and lifts the line 'I shan't be a woman much longer'. The Princess's final imprisonment is much less harsh in the book than in the film. A. E. W. Mason had also written a novel on the same topic, *Königsmark*, in 1937. But his version was much more liberal and sensational, and doubtless that was why it was not chosen as a basis for the film.
16. T. Morahan, 'Modern Trends in Art Direction', *British Kinematography*, vol. 18 no. 3, March 1951.
17. *Saraband for Dead Lovers: the Film and its Production at Ealing Studios* (London: Convoy Publications, 1948). On p. 87, Rembrandt, Van Dyke and the Elder Brueghel are adduced as 'an object lesson in colour control' for the film.
18. *Sunday Chronicle*, 12 September 1948.

Notes to Chapter 9: History and the Working Class

1. Alan Wood, *Mr Rank* (London: Hodder & Stoughton, 1952), p. 123. See also 'J. Arthur Rank: un Minotier anglais', in *Réalités*, February 1947.
2. Wood, *Mr Rank*, p. 146.
3. *Kinematograph Weekly*, 21 March 1946. Huth claimed here that because of tight planning the rough-cut of *They Were Sisters* was only 625 feet longer than the final version.
4. Norman Lee, *Log of a Film Director* (London: Quality Press, 1949), pp. 34–5.
5. R. J. Minney, *Talking of Films* (London: Home and Van Thal, 1947), pp. 19, 43. Minney was himself, of course, no mean writer. He produced a very interesting novel (dedicated to Maurice Ostrer 'for his constant encouragement'), *A Woman of France* (London: Macdonald, 1945). This text has a marvellous sense of structure and visual detail. Minney's concern was that the language and local colour should not be naturalistic or in any way avant-garde; this is documented in J. L. Hodson, *The Home Front* (London: Gollancz, 1944), pp. 246–7. Minney also wrote many non-fictional texts.
6. See BFPA Executive Council Minutes, which reveal that Ostrer and Black were co-opted on 17 November 1939. See also Minutes of 23 December 1941 and 6 January 1942, where Ostrer is active on the costume front and critical of the government.
7. *Kinematograph Weekly*, 19 April 1945. Here Ostrer also displays his contempt for highbrow critics.
8. *Kinematograph Weekly*, 20 December 1945. Here Mark Ostrer insists that star appearances are 'a means of creating a more intimate link between patrons and the names behind the screen'. See also the issue of 14 January 1943, which contains interviews on studio organisation with Ted Black and Maurice Ostrer. For careful studio supervision of promotion tours, see Margaret Lockwood, *Lucky Star* (London: Odhams, 1955), pp. 112, 135.
9. B. Woodhouse, *From Script to Screen* (London: Winchester Publications, 1947), pp. 63–4.

10. *Kinematograph Weekly*, 19 April 1945. Here Ostrer notes that *Fanny* cost £90,000 and grossed £300,000. *Love Story* cost £125,000 and grossed £200,000. *Madonna* cost £125,000 and was expected to gross more than £300,000. He also gives a very interesting detailed rundown of the cost-sheet for *The Man in Grey*, which cost £95,000 to make. Predictably, the sets take up an enormous 16 per cent of the budget. See also *Kinematograph Weekly*, 4 February 1942 and 20 December 1945, on profits.

11. See an unpublished mimeo, *Production Facilities (Films) Ltd.*, by F. L. Gilbert, c. 1984, in the BFI library.

12. *Today's Cinema*, 7 August 1946. On floor-space problems, see Woodhouse, *From Script to Screen*, p. 11.

13. See *Daily Herald*, 2 March 1948.

14. S. Box, 'More British Films', *Cinema and Theatre Construction*, June 1946. Here he argues that 'the public wants a few films about the people who live as they do.' See also his article 'I Challenge the Critics', in *Picturegoer*, 1 January 1949. For an account of his production methods, see 'The Evolution of a Feature Film', in J. Cross and A. Rattenbury, *Screen and Audience* (London: Saturn Press, 1947), pp. 8–17. See also Adrian Brunel, *Film Script* (London: Burke Publishing, 1948), pp. 171–82, on a Box script.

15. *Kinematograph Weekly*, 11 January 1945; *Today's Cinema*, 5 January 1944.

16. *Picturegoer*, 10 November 1945.

17. *Picturegoer*, 14 April 1945. See also Stewart Granger, *Sparks Fly Upwards* (London: Granada, 1981), pp. 71 ff., and James Mason, *Before I Forget* (London: Hamish Hamilton, 1981), pp. 185–7.

18. *Sunday Times*, 17 December 1944; *Time and Tide*, 23 December 1944; *News Chronicle*, 19 November 1945; *Sunday Times*, 18 November 1945.

19. *Daily Mail*, 16 November 1945; *Dispatch*, 16 November 1945; *Tribune*, 23 November 1945.

20. *News of the World*, 14 April 1946.

21. *Tribune*, 12 April 1946; *Graphic*, 14 April 1946.

22. *Daily Mail*, 14 April 1946.

23. Lady E. F. Smith, *Caravan* (London: Hutchinson, 1943), p. 97.

24. Lady E. F. Smith, *Life's a Circus* (London: Longman, 1939), pp. 5–7.

25. S. Kunitz and H. Haycroft (eds.), *Twentieth Century Authors* (New York: H. W. Wilson, 1942), p. 842.

26. Roland Pertwee, *Master of None* (London: Peter Davies, 1940), p. 251.

27. Margaret Kennedy, *The Mechanical Muse* (London: Allen and Unwin, 1942), p. 29. However, Kennedy's is an advance on other extant theories of film authorship, such as Ursula Bloom's 1939 *ABC of Authorship*.

28. S. Aspinall and R. Murphy (eds.), *Gainsborough Melodrama* (London: British Film Institute, 1983), p. 53.

29. The SWA won the fight for higher basic payments, for the creation of a jointly owned 'story fund', and for the freedom of radio film-critics. See Draft Constitution, 11 March 1937, especially Resolution 14, formerly in the archives of the Society of Authors. The SWA papers have been acquired by the British Library.

30. Letter from Launder to the Screenwriters' Guild, June 1947, in SWA files.

31. See letters from Del Giudice to Secretary of the SWA, 10 and 14 November 1942, in SWA files. See also *Kinematograph Weekly*, 1 January 1943, and Wood, *Mr Rank*, pp. 134–7. See BFPA Executive Council Minutes, 29 January 1942, where the SWA admits that it is the sole sponsor of the Ideas Committee.

32. See interview by the author with Maurice Carter in Aspinall and Murphy (eds.), *Gainsborough Melodrama*, p. 58. For examples of contemporary writing on art direction, see E. Carrick, *Designing for Films* (London: Studio Publications, 1949, first published 1941); A. Mayerscough-Walker, *Stage and Film Decor* (London: Pitman,

1940); T. Morahan, 'Modern Trends in Art Direction', *British Kinematography*, March 1951.

33. R. J. Minney, *The Film-Maker and his World: A Young Person's Guide* (London: Gollancz, 1964), p. 86.

34. Interview in Aspinall and Murphy (eds.), *Gainsborough Melodrama*, p. 59.

35. *Kinematograph Weekly*, 16 August 1945.

36. See *The Cinetechnician*, November/December 1948.

37. *Illustrated London News*, 11 March 1939, dismissed Haffenden's designs as 'travesties' using 'alien methods, rather loosely called expressionist, [which] are not interesting or impressive'. *The Bystander*, 8 March 1939, noted that her costumes were 'nothing more than our old friend Expressionism repeating its well-worn tricks.'

38. *Tatler*, 26 June 1946. See also *Picture Post*, 26 March 1945. All her postwar theatrical work had period settings, and was non-naturalistic. Haffenden subsequently went to Hollywood and won an Oscar for her costume work on *Ben Hur*.

39. Minney, *The Film-Maker and His World*, p. 91.

40. S. Box and V. Cox, *The Bad Lord Byron* (London: Convoy, 1949), pp. 88–9.

41. These male couturiers were Hartnell, Strebel, Messel and Molyneux. Haffenden was helped in her period work at Gainsborough by Joan Ellacott. The modern-dress films were designed by Yvonne Caffin and Julie Harris. See a later (and very interesting) article by Julie Harris, 'Costume Designing', in *Films and Filming*, November 1957.

42. See, for example, Hedda Hopper, 'Clothes and the British Film Industry', *Kinematograph Weekly*, 27 June 1946.

43. Mass-Observation File no. 485, 7 November 1940.

44. The publicity material for *Blanche Fury*, in the BFI library, suggests that special blouses and 'Fury Red' lipstick be marketed. The American distributors of *The Wicked Lady* (material in BFI library) encouraged managers to give away handkerchieves: 'Have some woman embroider 'The Wicked Lady' on each. The workmanship need not be of the best.'

45. See Mass-Observation File no. 728, 'Changes in Clothing Habits', 9 June 1941.

46. M. Wolfenstein and N. Leites, 'An Analysis of Themes and Plots in Motion Pictures', in W. Schramm (ed.), *Mass Communications* (University of Illinois, 1960), p. 385. See also M. Wolfenstein and N. Leites, *Movies: a Psychological Study* (New York: Hafner, 1971), pp. 295–6.

47. See *Picturegoer*, 28 February 1948, for Dennis Price's account of his 'realistic' construction of Byron's character.

Notes to Chapter 10: Wartime and Postwar Responses to Historical Film

1. Mass-Observation Box 15, 'London Town' survey, from the unnumbered collection of loose papers at the back. See also M-O File 1775, Box 1, observer's report, 14 February 1948.

2. The *Bernstein Film Questionnaire*, 1947, p. 18a.

3. Peter Noble, *British Theatre* (London: British Yearbooks, 1946), p. 163.

4. Alex Comfort and John Bayliss (eds.), *New Road 1943* (Billericay: Grey Walls Press, 1943). On p. 1, 'progressive' work is defined as that which is not historical.

5. Lynda Morris and Robert Radford, *The Story of the AIA 1933–53* (Oxford: Museum of Modern Art, 1983).

6. D. Mellor (ed.), *A Paradise Lost: the Neo-Romantic Imagination in Britain 1935–55* (London: Barbican Art Gallery, 1987).

7. Noel Carrington and Clarke Hutton, *Popular Art in Britain* (London: Penguin, 1945); Enid Marx and Margaret Lambert, *English Popular and Traditional Art* (London: Collins, 1946); Margaret Lambert and Enid Marx, *English Popular Art* (London: Batsford, 1951).

8. For example, F. Howard Lancum, *Press Officer Please!* (London: Crosby Lockwood, 1946); J. A. Hammerton, *Other Things Than War* (London: Macdonald, 1943); F. Partridge, *A Pacifist's War* (London: Hogarth Press, 1978); Lord Elton, *Notebook in Wartime* (London: Collins, 1941); Trevor Evans, *Strange Fighters We British!* (London: Robert Hale, 1941).

9. Mass-Observation Archive, directive of October 1943. Questions about the historical romance prompted the following male responses: a commissionaire, 19, said they 'fairly turn me up'; a schoolboy hated 'the mud, blood, and midden school'; a commercial traveller, 35, asserted that 'real history is more interesting than fiction about it'; an Education Inspector, 36, noted that 'a novel dealing with the aristocracy bores me'.

10. Ibid., female press agent; File 2018 p. 85, C class female; ibid., p. 92, housewife; ibid., p. 93, female clerk; File 2537, p. 34.

11. See Mass-Observation File 2018, p. (ix), and 'Reading in Tottenham', p. 37. See also Mass-Observation File 46, 'Book Reading in Wartime', File 1332, 'Books and the Public', 1942, and File 947, 'Wartime Reading'. We should not make any automatic assumptions about working-class reading habits. Those readers often patronised 'twopenny libraries' or informal ones in newsagents, for which there is no documentary evidence. For differences in class taste in reading matter, it is worth consulting *The Press and its Readers* (London: Art and Technics, 1949).

12. Dilys Powell, 'Films since 1939', in *Since 1939: Ballet, Films, Music, Painting* (London: Longman, for The British Council, 1948), p. 91.

13. See S. B. Carter, *Ourselves and the Cinema* (London: Workers' Education Association, 1948).

14. Claude Mullins, 'Marriage à la Mode', in J. Cross and A. Rattenbury, *Screen and Audience* (London: Saturn Press, 1947), p. 37.

15. *Screen and Audience*, pp. 33–6.

16. See, for example, James Agate, *Around Cinemas* (London: Home and Van Thal, 1946), and *Around Cinemas (Second Series)* (London: Home and Van Thal, 1948). There is a particularly interesting piece of evidence in Agate's *Ego 9* (London: Harrap, 1948), pp. 97–9. This is the script of a radio programme on historical film. Agate had no time to prepare the script himself, but his extreme views on historical film were so well known that he could persuade Roy Plomley (a fellow member of the Savage Club) to do it on his behalf. See also Roger Manvell, *Film* (London: Penguin, 1944), and Ernest Lindgren, *The Art of the Film* (London: Allen and Unwin, 1948). See also B. Woodhouse, *From Script to Screen* (London: Winchester Publications, 1947), p. 163, and the collection of Richard Winnington's writings of the period in *Film: Criticism and Caricatures 1943–53*, ed. Paul Rotha (London: Paul Elek, 1975). A classic articulation of a 'quality' position may be found in Peter Dyer, 'In Praise of Ourselves', *Picturegoer*, 2 March 1946.

17. See, for example, C. de la Roche, 'That Feminine Angle', and A. L. Vargas, 'British Film and Their Audiences', in *Penguin Film Review*, no. 8, 1949. See J. MacLaren-Ross, 'A Brief Survey of British Feature Films', in *Penguin New Writing* (London: Penguin, 1947).

18. F. E. Baily, *Film Stars of History* (London: Macdonald, 1945), p. 5.

19. E. W. and M. M. Robson, *Bernard Shaw Among the Innocents* (London: Sidneyan Society, 1945), p. 18. See also their *The World is My Cinema* (London: Sidneyan Society, 1947), pp. 63, 75, and *The Film Answers Back* (London: Bodley Head, 1939), pp. 142–50. A similar position is expressed in A. Crooks Ripley, *Spectacle: a Chronicle of Things Seen* (London: Brownlee Nineteen Forty-Two, 1945), pp. 46–9.

20. K. Box, *The Cinema and the Public: an Enquiry into Cinema Going Habits and Expenditure* (London: Crown, 1946), p. 5.

21. B. Kesterton, *The Social and Emotional Effects of the Recreational Film on Adolescents of 13 and 14 Years of Age in the West Bromwich Area*, University of Birmingham Ph.D., 1948, pp. 72, 102, 99, 208.

22. See accounts of this work in W. D. Wall and W. A. Simpson, 'The Effects of Cinema Attendance on The Behaviour of Adolescents as Seen By Their Contemporaries', *British Journal of Educational Psychology*, vol. XIX, part I, 1949, pp. 53–61, and 'The Film Choices of Adolescents', in Vol. XIX, no. 2, 1949, pp. 121–36.

23. See A. J. Jenkinson, *What Do Boys and Girls Read?* (London: Methuen, 1940). From the lists given, it appears that historical novels are again a female preference, and adventure tales a male one.

24. J. W. Ward, *Children and the Cinema: the Social Survey* (Central Office of Information, 1949), pp. 37, 42–3, 58.

25. J. P. Mayer, *Sociology of Film* (London: Faber, 1946), p. 103.

26. Ibid., pp. 201–2, 213, 239.

27. Ibid., p. 183.

28. J. P. Mayer, *British Cinemas and Their Audiences* (London: Dennis Dobson, 1948), p. 22. For similar references to costume, see pp. 81, 107, 184. All these are from young women in lower-class employment.

29. Ibid., p. 43.

30. Ibid., p. 73. This is a 17-year-old clerk. See also p. 180, where a female prefers Lockwood in her 'bad girl' parts.

31. Ibid., p. 192.

32. Ibid., p. 37. See also pp. 30, 176.

33. Ibid., pp. 22, 189. See also p. 184, where a female textile worker of 18 says *Fanny* and *The Man in Grey* 'are unpretentious but they have an atmosphere of realism of England and English life that Americans cannot get.'

34. Ibid., p. 43. This is a typist aged 23. See also p. 84, where a female clerk aged 22 says of *Sixty Glorious Years* and similar films that 'they give me an exultant pride in my own country and her achievements'.

35. Mass-Observation 878, 'What Does Britain Mean to You?' (1940), contains a range of responses which are very critical of traditional British values. M-O 1364A, 'The Future' (1942), also contains a very wide range of views arguing that the old class system should be swept away. Most interestingly, M-O 247, 'The Royal Family' (1940), showed a marked lack of interest in royalty. One working woman argued that 'I think it's all a bit silly, Kings and Queens in wartime. I don't think they're wanted. Now it's up to us all, not Kings and Queens'.

36. Mass-Observation 485, 'Victorianism in Films and Music Hall' (1940).

37. Mass-Observation 835/4, 'Social Change' (1941).

38. Mass-Observation, Box 5, File C.

39. Mass-Observation, Box 4, interview with manager of cinema in Granada chain, 28 December 1939.

40. Len England's 1940 Report on 'Audience Preferences in Film Themes' (Mass-Observation 57) shows that audience response to the reissued *Things to Come* was different from that on its original release; shots of air raids and gas-masks were much more intensely considered.

41. J. Richards and D. Sheridan, *Mass-Observation at the Movies* (London: Routledge, 1987), p. 221.

42. Ibid., p. 237.

43. Ibid., p. 231.

44. Ibid., p. 278, WAAF, obviously middle-class; p. 263, a teacher; p. 262, a teacher.

45. Mass-Observation directive, June 1939. To very many respondents, the working class is defined by its taste for tripe, winkles and cockfighting. One lower middle-class writer nicely defines the middle class as one which contains 'the well bred dog, the wife who always notices pregnancies in others, sportsmen who go into religion, cultured homosexuals, people slumming'.

46. Mass-Observation Box 5, File A, note from Len England, 13 January 1941.

47. Mass-Observation Box 5, File A. For other male letters in this file, see 5 December

1940, on the desirability of making a film of *Thunder Rock*; 10 November 1940, on the desirability of a film on the life of Disraeli; 29 September 1940, on nefarious Hollywood producers stealing 'our great and glorious history'. See File D, two male letters (one undated, one dated 4 September 1940) praising the realism of *Nell Gwyn*.

48. See ibid., File A, female letter on Anna Neagle, 7 January 1941; File E, female letter, 19 September 1940; File C, female letter, 3 January 1940 on the desirability of a film about Mary Wollstonecraft; File C, female letter, 8 December 1940; File B, female letter, 28 December 1940, wanting films on the lives of the Romantic poets; File A, female letter, 14 November 1940 on a film on Byron ('He died for Greece, and Greece is in the news'); File A, female letters, 31 October 1940 and 10 November 1940, on the importance of fantasy in historical film. For letter from 'proud factory hand', see undated letter in File A.

49. Ibid., File D, letter dated 6 November 1940.

50. *Picturegoer*, 8 March 1941, for Cromwell and Gladstone; 6 January 1945, for Paine; 7 December 1946, for Byron. There are several letters on this topic, one from 'three ardent Byron fans'. For Messalina, see 5 January 1946.

51. *Picturegoer*, 26 April 1941. See 4 October 1941, on the irrelevance of historical inaccuracies in *Lady Hamilton*. See 2 February 1946, on the stupidity of critics' rejection of *Caesar and Cleopatra*.

52. *Picturegoer*, 27 May 1944; 8 June 1946; 3 August 1946; 24 May 1947.

53. *Picturegoer*, 25 May 1946, where one reader (m/f) finds the film of *Madonna* a very accurate version of the book, and another (m/f) does not find *The Wicked Lady* disgusting, because 'it was England at that period and that is the saving grace as far as I am concerned'. See also 28 September 1946, where another reader has diligently sought for (and found) another literary source for *The Wicked Lady*.

54. *Picturegoer*, 16 May 1942; 8 and 22 January 1944; 17 March 1945; 21 July 1945; 15 and 29 September 1945; 27 October 1945.

55. *Picturegoer* attacked Gainsborough notions of history on 26 November 1946 and 12 April 1947.

56. *Picturegoer*, 14 September 1946. Others discuss different scopic drives; see 30 August 1947, where a letterwriter (m/f) argues that 'biological urges make females prefer romance'.

57. *Picturegoer*, 17 February 1945, 'Freud and the Films', and 12 May 1945, 'Hypnosis on the Screen'. For an account of female taste, see 2 August 1947. Here Inman Race attacks 'polluting' females: 'woman is the noisy sex'. See 4 August 1945, where John Stapleton notes that 'women always find great interest in stars, while men concern themselves with stories. Men complain when love stories interfere with historical films.' See also Stapleton on 7 June 1947, where he bemoans the fact that 'I know three typists who went to see it [*Caesar and Cleopatra*] for one reason alone – Stewart Granger.'

58. *Picturegoer*, 4 January 1947. The comments on *The Wicked Lady* on 19 January 1945 are hilarious. The husband rebukes Sally that she and her females friends give 'a shudder of delight' on seeing Mason: 'You'd be scared to death to meet him on a dark night, yet you queue up in your thousands to see him in a dark cinema.' Sally retorts that 'for a woman of Lady Skelton's temperament, Sir Ralph [her husband] must have been very slow going'.

59. *Picturegoer*, 1 February 1941. See similar letter, 21 March 1942, and an article on Mason, 22 July 1944, noting that 'there's nothing wrong with a good old villain now and then.'

60. *Picturegoer*, 26 October 1946. Here the editor says he has a 'huge mailbag' praising Mason in these roles. See also female letter, 5 August 1944.

61. *Picturegoer*, 8 and 22 October 1949. See 5 November 1949, on *Madame Bovary* versus *Brief Encounter*.

Notes to Chapter 11: The Postwar Period

1. See *Picture Post*, 1 June 1946, for the history of the British in India. See 4 January 1947 for material on coal shortages in history. See 1 February 1946 for the history of cold winters. The magazine also began to deal with women's history; see 10 March 1945, for example.

2. H. McNicol, *History, Heritage, and Environment* (London: Faber, 1946), p. 65. This was a widely discussed attempt to inculcate the more liberal aspects of history teaching as contained in the Board of Education's *Handbook of Suggestions for the Consideration of Teachers* (HMSO, 1944). See E. J. Boog-Watson and J. I. Carruthers, *History Through the Ages: a Teacher's Companion* (Oxford University Press, 1949), and Lionel Elvin, 'History Teaches Us', in *The Highway*, November 1946.

3. See F. Alan Walbank, *England Yesterday and Today in the Works of the Novelists 1837–1938* (London: Batsford, 1949), and R. J. Cruikshank, *Roaring Century* (London: Hamish Hamilton, 1946). See also C. B. Andrews, *The Theatre, the Cinema and Ourselves* (London: Clarence House Press, 1947), pp. 8–11.

4. See, from Caversham Archive, the 1946 *The Elizabethans*, for example, in R19/301. This play, by D. Cleverdon, presented the entire period 'from the point of view of the common man'. Other historical plays of the same type are *The Great Governor* (R19/453), *March of the 45* (R19/701), *Marco Polo* (R19/703), *Famous Trials* (R19/344), *Guy Fawkes* (R19/349), *Boswell* (R19/104), *Kingcraft* (R19/536), *Tutenkhamun* (R19/1342), and *St. Joan* (R19/589).

5. J. Hampden Jackson, *What is History?* (Bureau of Current Affairs, 1949), pp. 5–7.

6. See Andrew Buchanan, *Going to the Cinema* (London: Phoenix House, 1947). On pp. 62–4, he argues that 'history presented in moving pictures is so much more vivid than in any other form.' See also O. Blakeston (ed.), *Working for the Films* (London: Focal Press, 1947). Both these books were for children.

7. PRO FO 924/164.

8. PRO FO 930/494, minute of meeting of Films Committee, 26 July 1946, where John Strachey, the Minister of Food, took exception to FO plans for film.

9. PRO FO 924/474.

10. PRO INF 12/499.

11. FO 930/494, memo from FO, dated 16 July 1946. According to an FO memo of 10 July 1946, the COI was commissioned to make twelve films for that year. Not one of them had any historical content.

12. PRO INF 12/562, COI memo, 25 January 1947.

13. PRO INF 12/564, memo from Forman.

14. PRO INF 6/691. *Houses in History* was made in 1947 for the Ministry of Education. Material on *Local Government* is in PRO INF 6/770.

15. For *The History of Writing*, see PRO INF 6/737. For *Robinson Charley*, see PRO INF 6/549. For *The House of Windsor*, see PRO INF 6/1351.

16. PRO INF 6/545. This was made in 1948.

17. PRO INF 6/35. This was completed in 1951, and bears the imprimatur of the Crown Film Unit. It was aimed at American audiences.

18. PRO INF 12/544. This film stressed the necessity of the Anglo-American alliance, and used a conservative interpretation of history. See also PRO INF 12/545 for more information on the politics of this film.

19. PRO BT 64/2366. An undated memo, probably to Harold Wilson from one of his civil servants.

20. Ibid., Board of Trade memo dated 4 May 1948. To judge from the trouncing reviews of Rank's films by the American *Motion Picture Herald*, the Board of Trade was correct. See 14 February 1948, on James Mason's lack of appeal; 7 February 1948, on

the failures of *San Demetrio London*; 7 June 1948, for *The Man in Grey*; 11 October 1948, for the 'four Bronx cheers' merited by *A Matter of Life and Death*.

21. PRO BT 64/4139, memo from the President, 19 November 1945. There was quite a strong body of support within the Board of Trade for Rank's Independent Frame because it would supposedly save money and personnel; see PRO BT 64/2366, memo dated 4 February 1949.

22. See PRO BT 64/4139, Board of Trade memo, 24 March 1946; here the acrimonious feelings between Rank and Korda are described purely in terms of the former's jealousy and inefficiency. Balcon and Box, it is said here, had to throw in their distribution lot with Rank because they were not clever enough to do so with Korda.

23. Minutes of the BFPA Export Committee meeting on 16 July 1946.

24. Minutes of the BFPA Export Committee meeting of 12 April 1949. Here, out of a total of twenty-two films selected for French distribution, and intended to show the best British producers could do, eight were historical: *Hamlet, Saraband for Dead Lovers, Scott of the Antarctic, Eureka Stockade, Cardboard Cavalier, The Queen of Spades, The Elusive Pimpernel, Bonnie Prince Charlie*. A later list of twenty-three films was selected for broader foreign distribution which contained ten histories: *Saraband for Dead Lovers, Hamlet, Scott of the Antarctic, Eureka Stockade, Cardboard Cavalier, The History of Mr. Polly, The Bad Lord Byron, Christopher Columbus, Trottie True, Madeleine*.

25. Minutes of Executive Council, 27 August 1945; 26 September 1945; 9 January 1946.

26. PRO HO 45/23091, letter dated 19 May 1948.

27. BBFC Scenario Notes, 25 February 1945, which also say: 'Nobody with even a rudimentary knowledge of the Tudors could take this seriously, but to those who know no history, it could do infinite harm ... It is known that some American films have twisted or adapted OUR history to suit THEIR ends, but it would be reprehensible if a British production followed suit ... It is a book to be shunned, especially as we are within sight of the reign of Queen Elizabeth II.'

28. If we extend the definition of 'historical' to encompass costume films, as I suggested in the Introduction and Chapter One, Gifford's *The British Film Catalogue 1895–1985* indicates that there were 86 historical films made between 1933 and 1939, out of a total of 1,428. This is 6 per cent. For 1940–45, there were 25 out of a total of 357 (7 per cent). For 1946–50, there were 74 historical films out of a total of 482 (just over 15 per cent).

29. *Kinematograph Weekly*, 19 December 1946. 'Enoch Arden' is my term for films which deal with a loved one who is presumed dead and returns home unexpectedly. Three of these films appeared in the *Kinematograph Weekly* list: Sydney Box's *The Years Between*, Wilcox's *Piccadilly Incident* and RKO's *Tomorrow is Forever*. 'Enoch Arden' films were popular because they enabled audiences to rehearse a number of responses in the postwar period. They could admit fears that those who returned from the war would be permanently changed; they could recognise the desire that those who were dead would return home in a stranger's guise; and they could enjoy the provision of an alibi for having loved strangers, in that they might thereby have been entertaining angels unawares.

30. *Kinematograph Weekly*, 18 December 1947; 16 December 1948; 15 December 1949; 14 December 1950.

Notes to Chapter 12: Monopoly and History

1. F. L. Gilbert, 'Production Facilities (Films) Ltd.', unpublished mimeo, 1981, in the BFI library. See *Kinematograph Weekly*, 16 December 1948, for a large spread on Davis.

2. For Korda's criticism of Production Facilities (Films), see BFPA Council Minutes,

1 May 1946. For Minney's objections to Rank's expenditure, see *Kinematograph Weekly*, 18 December 1947: 'Hollywood, despite a far larger assured market, rarely indulges in such extravagance.' For the Robsons, see *Bernard Shaw Among the Innocents* (London: Sidneyan Society, 1945), and *The World is My Cinema* (London: Sidneyan Society, 1940). See also Ralph Bond, *Monopoly: the Future of British Films* (ACTT, 1944). See also *Kinematograph Weekly*, 25 December 1945, where Maurice Ostrer is very critical of Rank's policies and distribution practices.

3. Unpublished letter from Rank to Bernard Miles, 9 December 1947, in Bernard Miles papers, in the BFI library.

4. PRO BT 64/2366, letter from Del Giudice to Harold Wilson, 4 June 1948; memo from Woodrow Wyatt to Wilson, 7 June 1948; unsigned memo to Wilson, 10 June 1948, marked 'Private'.

5. Unpublished letter from Del Giudice to Bernard Miles, 12 November 1947, in Bernard Miles papers.

6. See letter from Del Giudice to Miles, 12 March 1948, in Bernard Miles papers. It is worth quoting at length: 'This morning I was distressed to read in the "Kinematograph Weekly" an article where Maurice Ostrer tries to prove that it is much better to produce films like "The Idol of Paris" (unanimously proclaimed by the critics to be the worst and most sadistic film ever produced) in order to save the industry from "bankruptcy". I was very distressed to see that such a statement was allowed, whilst bankruptcy has nearly been provoked by mass production.'

7. *Leader Magazine*, 21 June 1947. See also, in Bernard Miles papers, a letter from Bernard Miles dated 8 August 1948: 'Del's idea is that foreign markets are only open to those British films which are based on a story founded on classicism or realism (either historical or topical) but their success is only possible if they are exploited in a different way from the ordinary routine.'

8. Memo from Del Giudice to Alan Jarvis, 15 December 1948, in Bernard Miles papers. See also *Kinematograph Weekly*, 18 September 1947.

9. Del Giudice, 'Technical Testament', unpublished mimeo, in Bernard Miles papers.

10. For the need for 'hopeful' films, see letter from Del Giudice to Walter Greenwood, 20 December 1948, in Bernard Miles papers. For the desirability of 'tasteful' films, see letter to Alan Jarvis, 15 September 1948.

11. See a report on the film (in the publicity material in the BFI library) from the Film Officer, HM Embassy, Moscow: 'The fact that the novel is known well here is a great point in its favour. Some of the more highbrow Russians criticized it for a certain artificiality of treatment; but by the great majority this was not regarded as a defect. The elegance of the settings and costumes had a great appeal; and the combination of this elegance with a theme which is fundamentally serious is likely to make this film a favourite among the Russians; it has style, in which the present Russian films are so conspicuously lacking; whilst at the same time it cannot be dismissed as entirely frivolous.'

12. Jeffrey Richards and Anthony Aldgate, *The Best of British* (Oxford: Basil Blackwell, 1983), pp. 75–86.

13. See *Picturegoer*, 22 May 1948, where Bowden discusses the success of films based on her books.

14. See Alan Dent (ed.), *Hamlet: the Film and the Play* (London: World Film Publications, 1948), pp. 10, 25–6. See especially Olivier's account of the cuts on pp. 3–4. On p. 4, he mentions the 'generous instigation' of Del Giudice.

15. *Tribune*, 17 October 1947; *News of the World*, 12 October 1947.

16. *The Times*, 10 February 1949. Other critics liked the film but were similarly thrown by the combination of period setting and comedy.

17. Geoff Brown, *Walter Forde* (London: British Film Institute, 1977), p. 52. But Forde had always been opposed to the influence of producers in costume films; see *Picturegoer*, 14 July 1934.

18. In the film's script, dated 12 July 1948 (in the BFI library), there are some interesting directives about decor which are followed in the finished film. One interior is described thus: 'There is now and then a touch of the baroque to indicate continental culture. There is, for example, a cabinet in "pietra dura", with its inlaid and encrusted designs in marble and semi-precious stones.'

19. Remark by Neame in his own biographical material, in the BFI library. For an account of Neame's and John Bryan's break with Rank, see *Daily Mail*, 18 December 1957. See also 'Production Facilities (Films) Ltd.', for information on Cineguild's place in the Rank organisation.

20. *Kinematograph Weekly*, 18 December 1947. See also 1 March 1945, for his article 'Where Britain May Outstrip America'.

21. Minutes of BFPA Finance and General Purposes Committee, 11 October 1944. For details of Havelock-Allan's career, see *Today's Cinema*, 7 April 1948; *Kinematograph Weekly*, 8 April 1948.

22. BFPA Executive Council Minutes, 1 May 1946. He wanted the subject matter of a film, rather than its title, to be registered as a company's property.

23. PRO BT 64/2366, letter from Havelock-Allan to the Board of Trade, 28 February 1948. He was still vociferously making the same point in *Picturegoer*, 12 March 1949.

24. David Lean, 'The Film Director', in O. Blakeston, *Working for the Films* (Focal Press, 1947), pp. 27–37. See also Lean's *'Brief Encounter'*, in *Penguin Film Review*, no. 4, October 1947.

25. See Draft Script, dated 12 April 1948, in the BFI library. Here a sequence is described thus: 'The following shots are intended to be impressionistic ... they should give the idea of the boys passing through a human rabbit-warren.' One locale is described as 'the windows are windows no more, the doors are falling into the street, with holes from which to look upon the slime beneath.'

26. *Daily Express*, 17 February 1950. A large number of critics were unenthusiastic about the film's ambiguity.

27. See B. Ford (ed.), *Film Since the Second World War* (Cambridge University Press, 1988), D. Forman, *Films 1945–50* (London: Longman, 1952), and Simon Harcourt-Smith, 'David Lean', in J. Cross and A. Rattenbury (eds.), *Screen and Audience* (London: Saturn Press, 1947). See also Catherine de la Roche, *The Director's Approach to Film-Making: David Lean*, BBC pamphlet, 1948, in the BFI library.

28. *Kinematograph Weekly*, 27 December 1945. The reporter noted that this success 'confounded the critics'.

29. The *Tribune* critic, 14 December 1945, suggested that it was difficult to 'draw a mean between my own rather "highbrow" reactions, and the impact of a given picture on the one-and-ninepennies', and argued that the film's appeal was predicated on sex: 'Mr. Granger's handsome person gives pleasure to thousands normally. And here it is bared as never before.'

30. Marjorie Deans, *Meeting at the Sphinx* (London: Macdonald, 1946), pp. vii, viii. See also *The Times*, 31 December 1945, which contains a letter from Shaw justifying the film.

31. See *Daily Express*, 9 April 1946, where Pascal is censured by the ACT for the length of time spent on set and location. See also *Daily Mail* and *Daily Telegraph*, 29 April 1946.

32. A. Wood, *Mr. Rank* (London: Hodder and Stoughton, 1952), pp. 165, 166.

33. Geoff Brown, *Launder and Gilliat* (London: British Film Institute, 1977), p. 121.

34. *Esther Waters* was Dirk Bogarde's first film, and he indicates in his autobiography that it was widely known to be a complete box-office débâcle; see his *Snakes and Ladders* (London: Triad Grafton, 1979), p. 151.

35. See the First Draft Shooting Script, in the BFI library. In the novel, Esther's mother is particularly important in establishing a sort of matriarchal pattern. Other im-

portant differences between novel and script are the film's lack of the harrowing childbirth scene and its greater celebration of sexual ('pagan') pleasure. The novel's Esther is rather prim, but she does articulate her own oppression: 'A woman can't do the good she would like to do in this world. I've my husband and my child to look to. Them's my good.' In the script, this crucial statement is uttered by a man. The final draft shooting script (in the BFI library) obscures the fact that the son is forced to be a soldier, and that all Esther's efforts produce is 'fodder for powder and shot'.

Notes to Chapter 13: A Fossilised History

1. Executive Council Minutes of the BFPA, 1 May 1946, on nomenclature; 7 August 1946, on Association attitudes to the Hays Office, and on the necessity of co-operating with the *Mail*'s Silver Star awards; and 4 September 1946, on the necessity of limiting foreign directors.
2. PRO BT 64/2366, memo of a meeting at the Board of Trade on 7 July 1948. Korda said he made a loss on *Call of the Blood* and *Mine Own Executioner* as well.
3. Ibid., memo from Korda to the Board of Trade, dated April 1948. Korda had an increasingly acrimonious relationship with Del Giudice: see letters from Korda to Del Giudice, 8 April 1948, and 15 December 1948.
4. Ibid., memo from Eady to Somervell, 19 April 1948. See also a Treasury memo dated 15 June 1948, in which it is argued that Korda should be rewarded because 'he is not excluding other people's talents'.
5. Ibid., memo from Somervell to Eady, 2 July 1948. Somervell noted in another memo of the same day, 'I am very worried about Korda's present position.'
6. *Sunday Graphic*, 16 November 1947; *Daily Mail*, 14 November 1947.
7. K. Kulik, *The Man Who Could Work Miracles* (London: W. H. Allen, 1975), pp. 304–5, notes that the film was first initiated by Ted Black. Korda took over when he died. Leslie Arliss was the original director; he was replaced by Anthony Kimmins, then Korda himself, then Robert Stevenson. A whole string of writers attempted to give form to the script. David Niven recalled that Korda ordered another battle whenever the actors ran out of script pages; see *The Moon's a Balloon* (London: Coronet, 1973), pp. 258–9.
8. For Korda's advertisement, see *Manchester Guardian*, 12 November 1948. See also a letter from Korda to *Daily Telegraph*, 2 November 1948: 'There was no loss of authenticity.'
9. I. Christie, *Powell, Pressburger and Others* (London: British Film Institute, 1978), pp. 39–40. Powell here notes that the film was 'a disaster'. See also M. Powell, *Million Dollar Movie* (London: Heinemann, 1992), pp. 61–83.
10. See Powell's letter on this to *The Times*, 31 October 1949.
11. According to the film's publicity material, in the BFI library, Heckroth claimed to have abolished solid set construction and to have used 'a canvas cyclorama which completely encircles the stage. Against this is built the minimum of lath and plaster sets.' He argued that the main advantage was greater mobility for the camera crew.
12. Powell, *Million Dollar Movie*, pp. 59–60.
13. See PRO BT/2366, where, at a meeting with Eady on 7 July 1948, it is revealed that *The Courtneys of Curzon Street* cost £280,000 and that its takings were £390,000 in Britain alone. *Spring in Park Lane* cost £220,000 to make, and the takings were £405,000. These figures are very much better than Korda's, as indicated in the same file.
14. The official 'book of the film' makes this point quite clearly. See Kit Porlock, *The Courtneys of Curzon Street* (London: World Film Publications, 1947).
15. *Daily Mirror*, 7 May 1947; *Evening News*, 8 May 1947.

16. There is no available script of this film. The quotation is from W. Mannon, *Elizabeth of Ladymead: the Book of the Film* (London: World Film Publications, 1949), p. 64.
17. A. de Grunwald, 'Workmanship, or Cash? Ousting the Know-Alls With Only Cheques', in *Kinematograph Weekly*, 14 January 1943. De Grunwald had been strongly associated with Terence Rattigan and Anthony Asquith.
18. Rodney Ackland and Elspeth Grant, *The Celluloid Mistress, or the Custard Pie of Dr. Caligari* (London: Allan Wingate, 1954), pp. 208–28.
19. See an article by Williams on the film's production in the *Listener*, 23 June 1949. See also Williams's script for a radio talk on the film's production, dated 8 June 1949, in the BFI library.
20. *Daily Worker*, 4 October 1947. See also *News of the World*, 5 October 1947, which says that 'Arliss is competent at knowing exactly what you, the paying public, want ... For the expenditure of £380,000 (*Love Story, The Man in Grey, The Wicked Lady*) Mr. Arliss has persuaded you customers to part with a sum of about £1,250,000.'
21. *Idol of Paris* was well constructed and tightly characterised. See an account of the film's genesis in Norman Lee, *Log of a Film Director* (London: Quality Press, 1949), p. 50. The producers originally negotiated with Marlene Dietrich for the title role. Lee says that Minney worked on the script, but the credits mention Henry Ostrer.
22. See Leslie Arliss, 'The Only Real Way to Cut Costs is to Cut Time' in *Kinematograph Weekly*, 30 October 1947.
23. *New Statesman*, 13 March 1948; *Daily Express*, 5 March 1948; *Observer*, 7 March 1948; *Sunday Chronicle*, 7 March 1948; *Daily Mail*, 5 March 1948; *Sunday Graphic*, 7 March 1948; *News of the World*, 7 March 1948; *Reynolds News*, 7 March 1948 ('I am disgusted by this stupid film'); *The Times*, 8 March 1948 ('bad enough to be important'); *Daily Mirror*, 5 March 1948; *Sunday Times*, 7 March 1948; *Daily Herald*, 5 March 1948; *Sunday Express*, 7 March 1948.
24. Louis Jackson, 'Planning for Production', *Film Industry*, January 1947.
25. *Sunday Times*, 9 April 1950. See also *Observer*, 9 October 1950: 'like strawberries and cream, to which some people are passionately addicted and others violently allergic.'
26. See the film's publicity material, in the BFI library. Tod Slaughter had made a historical melodrama in 1946, *Curse of the Wraydons*. See the publicity material, in the BFI library, which claimed that the film was based on 'the famous melodrama Spring-heeled Jack the Terror of London'.
27. See, in the film's publicity material in the BFI library, a letter from the advertising agents to cinema managers saying that 'the whole production is based on factual and authentic records, including Police reports and newspaper cuttings of the trial, published at the time.'
28. See Peter Baker, 'Over 2,000 Studio Employees Have Lost Their Jobs', in *Kinematograph Weekly*, 31 March 1949.
29. *Kinematograph Weekly*, 18 December 1947.
30. *Tribune*, 28 June 1946.
31. *Observer*, 27 February 1949. See also *Picturegoer*, 16 December 1950, for a savage review of American histories made in Britain.
32. *Evening News*, 22 June 1950. See *Daily Graphic*, 20 June 1950, which contains a piece by Disney on 'Why I Filmed *Treasure Island*'.

SELECT BIBLIOGRAPHY

Primary sources have been fully referenced in the footnotes or in the text. Those wanting more detailed bibliographical information should consult my Ph.D. thesis, *The Representation of History in British Feature Film 1933–50*, Polytechnic of Central London, 1990. The following bibliography lists secondary sources since 1960.

Books

All books published in London, unless otherwise indicated.

Aldgate, A. and Richards, J., *Britain Can Take It*, Oxford, Basil Blackwell, 1986.
Anderegg, M., *David Lean*, Boston, Twayne Press, 1984.
Aspinall, S. and Murphy, R. (eds.), *Gainsborough Melodrama*, British Film Institute, 1983.
Attridge, D., Bennington, G. and Young, R. (eds.), *Post-Structuralism and the Question of History*, Cambridge University Press, 1989.
Balcon, M., *Michael Balcon Presents . . . A Lifetime of Films*, Hutchinson, 1969.
Barr, C., *Ealing Studios*, Newton Abbot, David and Charles, 1977.
Barr, C. (ed.), *All Our Yesterdays*, British Film Institute, 1986.
Barsacq, L., *Le Décor du Film*, Paris, Seghers, 1970.
Betts, E., *This Film Business*, Allen & Unwin, 1973.
Bogarde, D., *Snakes and Ladders*, Triad Grafton, 1979.
Bourdieu, P., *Outline of a Theory of Practice*, trans. R. Nico, Cambridge University Press, 1977.
Box, M., *Odd Woman Out*, Leslie Frewin, 1974.
Brown, G., *Launder and Gilliat*, British Film Institute, 1977.
Brown, G. (ed.), *Walter Forde*, British Film Institute, 1977.
Butler, I., *To Encourage the Art of the Film*, Robert Hall, 1971.
Callow, S., *Charles Laughton: a Difficult Actor*, Methuen, 1987.
Canary, R. and Kozicki, H. (eds.), *The Writing of History: Literary Form and Historical Understanding*, University of Wisconsin Press, 1978.
Christie, I., *Powell, Pressburger and Others*, British Film Institute, 1978.
Christie, I., *Arrows of Desire*, Waterstone, 1985.
Clarke, T. E. B., *This Is Where I Came In*, Michael Joseph, 1974.
Colvin, I., *Vansittart in Office*, Gollancz, 1965.
Curran, J. and Porter, V., *British Cinema History*, Weidenfeld & Nicholson, 1983.
Dean, B., *Mind's Eye*, Hutchinson, 1972.
Dickinson, M. and Street, S., *Cinema and State: the Film Industry and the British Government 1927 91*, British Film Institute, 1984.
Douglas, M., *Purity and Danger*, Routledge, 1966.
Douglas, M., *Natural Symbols*, Barrie and Rockcliff, 1970.
Douglas, M., *Implicit Meanings*, Routledge, 1975.
Dukore, F., *The Collected Screenplays of George Bernard Shaw*, George Prior, 1980.
Durgnat, R., *Films and Feelings*, Faber, 1967.
Durgnat, R., *A Mirror for England*, Faber, 1970.
Elley, D., *The Epic Film: Myth and History*, Routledge, 1984.

Ellwood, D. W. (ed.), *I Mass Media e la Storia*, Bologna, RAI, 1986.

Ferro, M., *The Use and Abuse of History*, Routledge, 1984.

Fraser, G. MacDonald, *The Hollywood History of the World*, Michael Joseph, 1988.

Geduld, H., *Filmguide to Henry V*, Bloomington, Indiana, 1973.

Gifford, D., *The British Film Catalogue 1895–1985*, David and Charles, 1986.

Granger, S., *Sparks Fly Upwards*, Granada, 1981.

Grenville, J. A. S., *Film and History: the Nature of Film Evidence*, University of Birmingham Press, 1971.

Higham, C., *Charles Laughton: an Intimate Biography*, W. H. Allen, 1976.

Holloway, S., *Wiv a Little Bit o' Luck*, Leslie Frewin, 1967.

Jarvie, I., *Hollywood's Overseas Campaign: The North Atlantic Movie Trade, 1920–1950*, Cambridge University Press, 1992.

Jones, S. G., *The British Labour Movement and Film, 1918–1939*, Routledge, 1987.

Korda, M., *Charmed Lives*, Penguin, 1980.

Kulik, K., *Alexander Korda: The Man Who Could Work Miracles*, W. H. Allen, 1975.

Lant, A., *Blackout: Reinventing Women for Wartime British Cinema*, Princeton University Press, 1991.

Leese, E., *Costume Design in the Movies*, Isle of Wight, B.C.W. Publishing, 1977.

Longmate, N., *How We Lived Then: a History of Everyday Life During the Second World War*, Arrow Books, 1973.

Lowenthal, D., *The Past is a Foreign Country*, Cambridge University Press, 1987.

McArthur, C., *Television and History*, British Film Institute, 1978.

MacFarlane, B., *Sixty Voices*, British Film Institute, 1992.

MacLaine, I., *Ministry of Morale*, Allen & Unwin, 1979.

Macnab, G., *J. Arthur Rank and the British Film Industry*, Routledge, 1993.

Mason, J., *Before I Forget*, Hamish Hamilton, 1981.

Mellor, D. (ed.), *A Paradise Lost: The Neo-Romantic Imagination in Britain, 1935–55*, Barbican Art Gallery, 1987.

Miles, P. and Smith, M., *Cinema, Literature and Society*, Croom Helm, 1987.

Mills, J., *Up in the Clouds Gentleman Please*, Weidenfeld & Nicholson, 1980.

Minney, R. J., *The Film-Maker and His World: a Young Person's Guide*, Gollancz, 1964.

Minney, R. J., *'Puffin' Asquith*, Leslie Frewin, 1973.

Modleski, T., *Loving With a Vengeance: Mass-Produced Fantasies for Women*, Methuen, 1984.

Moorhead, C., *Sidney Bernstein: a Biography*, Jonathan Cape, 1984.

Morley, S., *Tales From the Hollywood Raj*, Weidenfeld & Nicholson, 1983.

Morris, L. and Radford, R., *The Story of the A.I.A. 1933–53*, Museum of Modern Art, Oxford, 1983.

Moss, R. T., *The Films of Carol Reed*, Macmillan, 1987.

Murphy, R., *Realism and Tinsel*, Routledge, 1989.

Neagle, A., *There's Always Tomorrow*, W. H. Allen, 1974.

Niven, D., *The Moon's a Balloon*, Coronet, 1973.

O'Brien, M. and Eyles, A., *Enter the Dream House*, British Film Institute, 1993.

Olivier, L., *Confessions of an Actor*, Weidenfeld and Nicholson, 1982.

Pascal, V., *The Disciple and his Devil*, Michael Joseph, 1980.

Powell, M., *A Life in Movies*, Heinemann, 1986.

Powell, M., *Million Dollar Movie*, Heinemann, 1992.

Pratley, G., *The Cinema of David Lean*, Tantivy Press, 1974.

Pronay, N. and Spring, D. W. (eds.), *Propaganda, Politics and Film 1918–45*, Macmillan, 1982.

Richards, J., *Visions of Yesterday*, Routledge, 1984.

Richards, J., *The Age of the Dream Palace: Cinema and Society in Britain 1930–39*, Routledge, 1984.

Richards, J., *Thorold Dickinson: The Man and His Films*, Croom Helm, 1986.

Richards, J. and Aldgate A., *The Best of British: Cinema and Society 1930–1970*, Oxford, Basil Blackwell, 1983.

Richards, J. and Sheridan, D., *Mass-Observation at the Movies*, Routledge, 1987.

Robertson, J. C., *The BBFC: Film Censorship in Britain 1897–1950*, Croom Helm, 1985.

Rollins, C. B. and Wareing, R. J., *Victor Saville*, British Film Institute, 1972.

Sherriff, R., *No Leading Lady*, Gollancz, 1968.

Short, K. R. M. (ed.), *Feature Film as History*, Croom Helm, 1980.

Short, K. R. M. (ed.), *Film and Radio Propaganda in World War II*, Croom Helm, 1983.

Silver, A. and Ursini, J., *David Lean and His Films*, Leslie Frewin, 1974.

Silverman, S., *David Lean*, André Deutsch, 1989.

Solomon, J., *The Ancient World in the Cinema*, New Jersey, A. S. Barnes, 1978.
Sorlin, P., *The Film in History: Restaging the Past*, Oxford, Basil Blackwell, 1980.
Smith, P., *The Historian and Film*, Cambridge University Press, 1976.
Sussex, E., *The Rise and Fall of the British Documentary*, Berkeley, University of California Press, 1975.
Swann, P., *Hollywood Feature Film in Postwar Britain*, Croom Helm, 1987.
Taylor, P., *The Projection of Britain*, Cambridge University Press, 1981.
Taylor, P. (ed.), *Britain and the Cinema in the Second World War*, Macmillan, 1988.
Thorpe, F. and Pronay, N., *British Official Films in the Second World War*, Oxford, Clio Press, 1980.
Wilcox, H., *25,000 Sunsets*, Bodley Head, 1967.
Williams, R., *Problems in Materialism and Culture*, Verso, 1980.
Winnington, R., *Film: Criticism and Caricatures, 1943–53*, Paul Elek, 1975.
Wolfenstein, M. and Leites, N., *Movies: a Psychological Study*, New York, Hafner, 1971.
Wood, L., *British Films 1927–39*, British Film Institute, 1986.
Wood, L., *The Commercial Imperative in the British Film Industry: Maurice Elvey, a Case Study*, British Film Institute, 1987.
Wright, P., *On Living in an Old Country*, Verso, 1985.

Articles

Arnold, R., 'The Architecture of Reception', *Journal of Film and Video*, Winter 1985.
Badder, D., 'Powell and Pressburger: the War Years', *Sight and Sound*, Winter 1978.
Barr, C., 'War Record', *Sight and Sound*, Autumn 1989.
Bawden, L.A., 'Film and the Historian', *University Vision*, no. 2, 1968.
Beck, P., 'Historicism and Historism in Recent Film Historiography', *Journal of Film and Video*, Winter 1985.
Bourdieu, P., 'Outline of a Sociological Theory of Art Perception', *International Social Science Journal*, vol. 20, no. 4, 1968.
deCordova, R., 'Film History as Discipline', *Camera Obscura*, September 1988.
Dollimore, J. and Sinfield, A., 'History and Ideology: the Instance of *Henry V*', in J. Drakakis (ed.), *Alternative Shakespeares*, Methuen, 1985.
Duckworth, J., 'History on the Screen', *Teaching History*, February 1981.
Ellis, J., 'Made in Ealing', *Screen*, vol. 16, no. 1, 1975.
Gans, H. J., 'Hollywood Films on British Screens: an Analysis of American Popular Culture Abroad', *Social Problems*, vol. 1, no. 4, 1961.
Grenville, J. A. S. and Pronay, N., 'The Historian and Historical Films', *University Vision*, no. 1, 1968.
Highet, G., 'History and the Silver Screen', in I. and H. Dear (eds.), *The Popular Arts: A Critical Reader*, Charles Scribner, New Jersey, 1967.
Holderness, G., 'Agincourt 1944: Readings in the Shakespearean Myth', *Literature and History*, Spring 1984.
Hollis, T., 'The Conservative Party and Film Propaganda Between the Wars', *English Historical Review*, April 1981.
Isenberg, M., 'A Relationship of Constrained Anxiety: Historians and Film', *The History Teacher*, vol. 6, no. 4, 1973.
Isenberg, M., 'Towards an Historical Methodology for Film Scholarship', *The Rocky Mountain Social Science Journal*, vol. 12, no. 1, 1975.
Jarvie, I., 'Seeing Through Movies', *Philosophy of the Social Sciences*, no. 8, 1978.
Jowett, G., 'The Concept of History in American Produced Films', *Journal of Popular Culture*, 1973.
Poole, J., 'Independent Frame', *Sight and Sound*, Spring 1980.
Poole, J., 'British Cinema Audiences in Wartime', *Historical Journal of Film, Radio and Television*, vol. 7, no. 3, 1987.
Porter, V. and Litewski, C., '*The Way Ahead*: the Case of a Propaganda Film', *Sight and Sound*, Spring 1981.
Richards, J. and Hulbert, J., 'Censorship in Action: the Case of *Lawrence of Arabia*', *Journal of Contemporary History*, vol. 19, 1984.
Richards, J., 'Korda's Empire: Politics and Film in *Sanders of the River*, *The Drum* and *The Four Feathers*', *Australian Journal of Film Theory*, nos. 5–6, 1979.

221

Roads, C. R., 'Film as Historical Evidence', *Journal of the Society of Archivists*, vol. 3, no. 4, October 1966.

Robertson, J. C., *'Dawn* (1928): Edith Cavell and Anglo-German Relations', *Historical Journal of Film, Radio and Television*, vol. 4, no. 1, 1984.

Rosen, P., 'Securing the Historical and the Classical Cinema', in Mellencamp, P. and Rosen, P. (eds.), *Cinema Histories, Cinema Practices*, American Film Institute Monograph, 1984.

Schwarz, B., 'The Communist Party Historians Group 1946–56', in Centre for Contemporary Cultural Studies, *Making Histories: Studies in History-Writing and Politics*, Hutchinson, 1982.

Short, K. R. M., *'That Hamilton Woman* (1941): Propaganda, Feminism and the Production Code', *Historical Journal of Film, Radio and Television*, vol. 11, no. 1, 1991.

Street, S., 'Alexander Korda, Prudential Assurance and British Film Finance in the 1930s', *Historical Journal of Film, Radio and Television*, vol. 6, no. 2, 1986.

Summerfield, P., 'Education and Politics in the British Armed Forces in World War II', *International Review of Social History*, vol. 26, part 2, 1981.

Wildy, T., 'From the MoI to the CoI: Publicity and Propaganda in Britain, 1945–51', *Historical Journal of Film, Radio and Television*, vol. 8, no. 1, 1986.

Williams, R., 'Forms of English Fiction: 1848', in F. Barker *et al., The Sociology of Literature 1848*, Colchester, University of Essex, 1978.

Young, J. W., *'Henry V*, The Quai d'Orsay and the Well-Being of the Franco-British Alliance', *Historical Journal of Film, Radio and Television*, vol 7, no. 3, 1987.

Unpublished Theses

Gough-Yates, K., *The European Film-Maker in Exile in Britain, 1933–45*, Open University, 1991.

Wood, L., *Low Budget Production and the British Film Industry, with Particular Reference to Julius Hagen and Twickenham Film Studios 1927–38*, M.Phil., Polytechnic of Central London, 1989.

FILMOGRAPHY

HISTORICAL FEATURE FILMS 1933 – 50

Information adapted from D. Gifford, *The British Film Catalogue 1895–1985* (London: David and Charles, 1986).

Abbreviations

d   –   Director
p   –   Producer
ap –   Associate Producer
s   –   Story
sc –   Scenario or script

Release date	*1933*
March	**Soldiers of the King**, Gainsborough, reissue 1939. *p* – M. Balcon. *d* – M. Elvey. *s* – Douglas Furber. *sc* – W. P. Lipscomb, J. O. C. Orton, Jack Hulbert. Period musical with Hulbert/Courtneidge.
July	**Bitter Sweet**, British and Dominions. *p/d* – Herbert Wilcox. *s* – L. Hayward, H. Wilcox, from Noël Coward's operetta. *sc* – L. Hayward, H. Wilcox, M. Hoffe. Neagle musical; Vienna, 1875.
	The Veteran of Waterloo, National Talkies, Paramount. *p* – Harry Rowson. *d* – A. V. Bramble. *s* – play, A. Conan Doyle. Recall of Waterloo adventures.
August	**A Royal Demand**, Moorland Productions. *p* – Mrs. C. Williams. *d* – Gustave Minzenky. *s* – Jane Moorland. Royalist Lord poses as Roundhead in 1645.
	The Private Life of Henry VIII, London (UA), reissue 1946. *p* – A. Korda, L. Toeplitz. *d* – A. Korda. *s* – L. Biro, A. Wimperis. *sc* – A. Wimperis. Wives of Henry.
September	**The Girl from Maxim's**, London (UA). *p* – A. Korda, L. Toeplitz. *d* – A. Korda. *s* – play by Feydeau. *sc* – A. Wimperis, H. Graham. Paris comedy 1905.
November	**Dick Turpin**, Stoll-Stafford. *p* – Clyde Cook. *d* – John Stafford, Victor Hanbury. *s* – Harrison Ainsworth, *Rookwood* (novel). *sc* – V. Kendall. Highwayman tale.
	A Dickensian Fantasy, Gee Films. *p* – D. MacKane. *d* – Aveling Genever. *s* – Dickens, *A Christmas Carol*. Characters from novel come to life.
	The Wandering Jew, Twickenham. *p* – Julius Hagen. *d* – Maurice Elvey. *s* – play by E. Temple Thurston. *sc* – H. Fowler Mear. Jew lives through the ages.

	1934
January	**Colonel Blood**, Sound City (MGM). *p* – Norman Loudon. *d/s* – W. P. Lipscomb. Irish patriot steals crown jewels in 1670.
	Catherine the Great, London (UA), reissue 1943. *p* – A. Korda, L. Toeplitz. *d* – P. Czinner. *s* – play, M. Lengyel, L. Biro (*The Czarina*). *sc* – L. Biro, A. Wimperis, M. Deans. Empress in Russia, 1745.
	Waltzes from Vienna, Tom Arnold, reissue 1942. *d* – A. Hitchcock. *s* – play, *Walzerkrieg*, by H. Reichart, E. Marischka, A. M. Willner. *sc* – A. Reville, G. Bolton. Vienna 1840; musical.

March	**The Unfinished Symphony**, Cine-Allianz. *p* – A. Pressburger. *d* – W. Forst, A. Asquith. *s* – W. Reisch. *sc* – W. Forst, B. Levy. Schubert's love life; Vienna 1820.

March   **The Unfinished Symphony**, Cine-Allianz. *p* – A. Pressburger. *d* – W. Forst, A. Asquith. *s* – W. Reisch. *sc* – W. Forst, B. Levy. Schubert's love life; Vienna 1820.

April   **Those Were the Days**, BIP–Wardour, reissue 1938. *p* – W. Mycroft. *d* – T. Bentley. *s* – play, Pinero, *The Magistrate*. *sc* – F. Thompson, F. Miller, F. Launder, J. Jordan. Comedy, 1890.

August   **Nell Gwyn**, British and Dominions, reissue 1941, 1948. *p/d* – Herbert Wilcox. *s* – M. Malleson. *sc* – M. Malleson. King's love for cockney actress.

Blossom Time, BIP–Wardour. *p* – W. Mycroft. *d* – P. Stein. *s* – F. Schulz. *sc* – J. Drinkwater, R. Burford, P. Perez, G. Clutsam. Musical, Vienna 1826; Schubert gives up girl he loves to virile dragoon.

Java Head, Associated Talking Pictures, reissue 1944. *p* – Basil Dean. *d* – J. W. Ruben. *s* – novel by J. Hergesheimer. *sc* – M. Brown, G. Wellesley. 1850; Bristol shipbuilder marries Manchu girl.

September   **The Private Life of Don Juan**, London (UA). *p/d* – A. Korda. *s* – L. Biro, F. Lonsdale, from play by H. Bataille. *sc* – L. Biro, F. Lonsdale. Spain 1650; ageing lover attempts comeback.

October   **Jew Süss**, Gaumont. *p* – M. Balcon. *d* – L. Mendes. *s* – D. Farnum, A. R. Rawlinson, from novel by L. Feuchtwanger. *sc* – D. Farnum, A. R. Rawlinson. Jews in Württemberg 1730.

December   **The Old Curiosity Shop**, BIP–Wardour. *p* – W. Mycroft. *d* – T. Bentley. *s* – Dickens novel. *sc* – M. Kennedy, R. Neale. Little Nell and Quilp.

1935

January   **Lorna Doone**, Associated Talking Pictures, reissue 1945. *p/d* – Basil Dean. *s* – novel by R. D. Blackmore. *sc* – D. Farnum, M. Malleson, G. Wellesley. Exmoor adventure, 1625.

The Scarlet Pimpernel, London (UA), reissues 1942, 1947. *p* – A. Korda. *d* – Harold Young. *sc* – R. Sherwood, S. Berman, A. Wimperis, L. Biro, from novel by Baroness Orczy. Fop dons disguise in French Revolution.

The Iron Duke, Gaumont. *p* – M. Balcon. *d* – Victor Saville. *s* – H. Harwood. *sc* – Bess Meredyth. Duke of Wellington in 1816.

D'Ye Ken John Peel, Twickenham. *p* – Julius Hagen. *d* – Henry Edwards. *s* – C. Cullum. *sc* – H. Fowler Mear. Musical, 1815.

The Rocks of Valpré, Real Art (Radio). *p* – Julius Hagen. *d* – Henry Edwards. *sc* – H. Fowler Mear, from novel by Ethel M. Dell. Crime; Belgium 1860.

February   **The Triumph of Sherlock Holmes**, Real Art. *p* – Julius Hagen. *d* – Leslie Hiscott. *sc* – H. Fowler Mear, C. Twyford, from novel by A. Conan Doyle. Holmes and Moriarty.

The Dictator, Toeplitz, reissues 1943, 1947, 1955. *p* – L. Toeplitz. *d* – Victor Saville, A. Santell. *sc* – H. Lustig, H. Wilhelm, M. Logan, B. Levy. Denmark 1776; doctor usurps power of king.

March   **The Immortal Gentleman**, Bernard Smith (EB). *d/s* – Widgey Newman. *sc* – J. Quin. Shakespeare discusses his work with friends.

April   **Abdul the Damned**, BIP–Wardour. *p* – Max Schach. *d* – Karl Grune. *sc* – A. Dukes, W. Chetham Strode, R. Burford, from novel by Robert Neumann. Turkey 1900; opera star joins harem.

Royal Cavalcade, BIP–Wardour. *p* – Walter Mycroft. *d* – Thomas Bentley, Herbert Brenon, Norman Lee, Walter Summers, Will Kellino, Marcel Varnel. *s* – Val Gielgud, H. Marvel, E. Maschwitz. *sc* – Marjorie Deans. History of George V's reign.

Maria Marten, or the Murder in the Red Barn, George King (MGM), reissue 1940. *d* – George King. *sc* – R. Faye. Folk tale; squire kills mistress.

May   **The Case of Gabriel Perry**, British Lion, reissue 1939. *p* – Herbert Smith. *d* – Albert de Courville. *sc* – L. DuGarde Peach, from play, *Wild Justice*, by James Dale. Crime 1885; JP kills local woman.

Mimi, BIP–Wardour. *p* – Walter Mycroft. *d* – Paul Stein. *sc* – C. Grey, P. Merzbach, J. Davies, D. Waldock, from novel by Henri Murger, *La Vie Bohème*. Poor girl helps playwright, then dies.

June   **Drake of England**, BIP–Wardour. *p* – Walter Mycroft. *d* – Arthur Woods. *sc* –

C. Grey, A. Tolnay, M. Deans, N. Watson, from play by Louis Parker. Drake and the Armada.

The Divine Spark, Allianza Cinematografica Italiana (GB). *p* – A. Pressburger. *d* – Carmine Gallone. *sc* – Emlyn Williams, R. Benson. *s* – W. Reisch. Musical, Naples; romantic vicissitudes of composer.

August   **Me and Marlborough**, Gaumont. *p* – M. Balcon. *d* – Victor Saville. *s* – W. P. Lipscomb, R. Pound. *sc* – I. Hay, M. Gaffney. Comedy, Flanders 1709; woman poses as her soldier husband.

Scrooge, Twickenham, reissues 1947, 1951. *p* – Julius Hagen, Hans Brahm. *d* – Henry Edwards. *sc* – S. Hicks, H. Fowler Mear, from Dickens's *A Christmas Carol*. Miser undergoes reform.

The Student's Romance, BIP–Wardour. *p* – Walter Mycroft. *d* – Otto Kanturek. *sc* – C. Grey, N. Watson, R. Hutter. From play by B. and N. Neumann, *I Lost my Heart in Heidelberg*. Musical, Austria 1830; princess poses as poor girl.

Peg of Old Drury, British and Dominions, reissues 1941, 1948. *p/d* – Herbert Wilcox. *sc* – Miles Malleson, from play by T. Taylor and C. Reade, *Masks and Faces*. Peg Woffington and Garrick in 1740.

September   **Flame in the Heather**, Crusade (Paramount). *p* – Victor Greene. *d/sc* – D. Pedelty, from novel by E. Maule, *The Fiery Cross*. Scotland, 1745; English spy saves chieftain's daughter.

October   **Invitation to the Waltz**, BIP–Wardour. *p* – Walter Mycroft. *d* – P. Merzbach. *sc* – P. Merzbach, C. Grey, R. Burford, from radio play by E. Maschwitz, H. Marvel, G. Posford. Musical 1803; British ballerina becomes Duke's mistress.

Midshipman Easy, Associated Talking Pictures. *p* – B. Dean, T. Dickinson. *d* – C. Reed. *sc* – A. Kimmins, from novel by Captain Marryat, *Mr. Midshipman Easy*. Vicissitudes of lad at sea.

November   **I Give My Heart**, BIP–Wardour. *p* – Walter Mycroft. *d* – Marcel Varnel. *sc* – F. Launder, R. Burford, K. Siodmak, P. Perez, from opera, *The Dubarry*, by J. M. Welleminsky, P. Knepler. Musical, France 1769; milliner weds count to become king's mistress.

The Mystery of the Marie Celeste, Hammer. *p* – H. Fraser Passmore. *d/s* – Denison Swift. 1872; mad sailor kills shipmates.

Hyde Park Corner, Grosvenor. *p* – Harcourt Templeman. *d* – Sinclair Hill. *sc* – D. Wyndham-Lewis, from play by W. Hackett. Duelling death of 1780 repeats itself in 1935.

1936

January   **The Amateur Gentleman**, Criterion (UA). *p* – Marcel Hellman, Douglas Fairbanks Jnr. *d* – T. Freeland. *sc* – C. Dane, E. Knoblock, S. Nolbandov, from novel by J. Farnol. Regency boxer poses as 'buck'.

February   **Whom the Gods Love**, Associated Talking Pictures, reissue 1949. *p/d* – Basil Dean. *s* – Margaret Kennedy. Mozart's wife rebuffs amorous prince.

Faust, Publicity Picture Productions–National Interest. *p* – F. Swann. *d* – A. Hopkins. *s* – opera by Gounod. Period musical; Faust sells his soul.

When Knights Were Bold, Capitol, reissues 1942, 1947. *p* – Max Schach. *d* – J. Raymond. *sc* – A. Parker, D. Furber, from play by C. Marlow. Lieutenant is transported in dreams to medieval times.

March   **Sweeney Todd, the Demon Barber of Fleet Street**, George King (MGM), reissue 1940. *d* – George King. *sc* – F. Hayward, H. F. Maltby, from play by G. Dibdin-Pitt. Barber recycles clients into pies.

Wedding Group, Fox (British). *p* – L. Landau, *d* – A. Bryce, C. Gullan, from radio play by P. Wade. Scotland, 1855; minister's daughter becomes nurse in the Crimea.

Rhodes of Africa, Gaumont. *p* – Michael Balcon. *d* – B. Viertel, G. Barkas. *sc* – M. Barringer, M. Malleson, L. Arliss, from novel *Rhodes* by S. Mullin. Diamond miner becomes Prime Minister of Cape.

The Cardinal, Grosvenor. *p* – Harcourt Templeman. *d* – Sinclair Hill. *sc* – D. B. Wyndham-Lewis, from play by L. N. Parker. 16th-century Roman Cardinal feigns madness to clear brother of crime.

May   **Tudor Rose**, Gainsborough, reissue 1948. *p* – M. Balcon. *d/s* – Robert Stevenson.

225

sc – R. Stevenson, M. Malleson. 1553; young Queen executed after reign of nine days.

June **The Marriage of Corbal**, Capitol, reissue 1942. *p* – Max Schach. *d* – Karl Grune. *sc* – S. Fullman, from novel by R. Sabatini, *The Nuptials of Corbal*. France 1790; deputy loves aristocrat and makes her marry Marquis to escape revolution.

July **A Woman Alone**, Garrett-Klement Pictures (UA), reissues 1942, 1947. *p* – R. Garrett, O. Klement. *d* – E. Frenke. *s* – F. Otzep. *sc* – L. Lania, W. Chetham Strode. Russia, 1896; married soldier has affair with peasant and frames her fiancé.

September **As You Like It**, Inter-Allied (20th). *p* – J. Schenk, P. Czinner. *d* – P. Czinner. *sc* – J. M. Barrie, R. Cullen, from play by Shakespeare. Duke's daughter poses as a man; Bergner vehicle.

Spy of Napoleon, JH Productions. *p* – Julius Hagen. *d* – M. Elvey. *sc* – L. DuGarde Peach, F. Merrick, H. Simpson, from novel by Baroness Orczy. France 1852; dancer poses as emperor's bastard to foil assassination plot.

November **David Livingstone**, Fitzpatrick Pictures (MGM). *d* – James Fitzpatrick. *s* – W. Williamson. Africa 1871, Livingstone found by Stanley. Contains cameo of Victoria.

Rembrandt, London (UA). *p*/*d* – A. Korda. *s* – K. Zuckmayer. *sc* – L. Biro, J. Head. Amsterdam 1642–69; life of painter.

December **Conquest of the Air**, London (UA), reissue 1944. *p* – A. Korda. *d* – Z. Korda, A. Esway, D. Taylor, A. Shaw, J. Saunders. *s* – J. Saunders. *sc* – H. Gray, P. Bezencenet. Man's attempts to fly, from AD 57 to date.

Toilers of the Sea, Beaumont (Columbia). *p* – L. Beaumont. *d* – S. Jepson, T. Fox. *s* – novel by Victor Hugo. *sc* – S. Jepson. Guernsey 1824; seaman salvages the first steamship.

Did I Betray?, UFA (Reunion), reissue 1938 as **Black Roses**. *d* – P. Martin. *s* – P. Martin, C. Brown, W. Supper. *sc* – J. Heygate, P. Macfarlane. Finland 1900; Russian ballerina becomes mistress of Tsarist governor to save her radical lover.

1937

January **The Mill on the Floss**, Morgan, reissue 1948. *p* – J. Clein. *d* – T. Whelan. *s* – novel by George Eliot. *sc* – J. Drinkwater, G. Weston, A. Melford, T. Whelan. Family politics in 19th-century Lincolnshire.

Fire over England, London–Pendennis (UA), reissue 1949. *p* – E. Pommer, A. Korda. *d* – W. K. Howard. *s* – novel by A. E. W. Mason. *sc* – C. Dane, S. Nolbandov. Armada foiled by young lieutenant in 1580.

February **Auld Lang Syne**, Fitzpatrick Pictures (MGM). *p*/*d* – J. Fitzpatrick. *s* – W. Williamson. Scotland 1780; life of Robert Burns.

May **The Vicar of Bray**, JH Productions. *p* – J. Hagen. *d* – H. Edwards. *s* – A. Dyer. *sc* – H. Fowler Mear. Charles I's ex-tutor persuades him to pardon prisoner. Contains cameo of Cromwell.

July **King Solomon's Mines**, Gaumont, reissue 1942. *ap* – G. Barkas. *d* – R. Stevenson, G. Barkas. *s* – novel by Rider Haggard. *sc* – M. Hogan, R. Pertwee, A. Rawlinson, C. Bennett, R. Spence. Exiled African chief helps explorers find diamond mine.

Under the Red Robe, New World (20th Century-Fox), reissues 1943, 1945, 1948. *p* – R. Kane. *d* – V. Sjöström. *s* – novel by S. Weyman. *sc* – L. Biro, P. Lindsay, J. Hodgson, A. Wimperis. France 1612; Cardinal's emissary falls in love with revolutionary's sister.

The Lilac Domino, Grafton-Capitol-Cecil (UA). *p* – M. Schach, I. Goldschmidt, L. Garmes. *d* – F. Zelnick. *s* – play by R. Bernauer, E. Gatti, B. Jenbach. *sc* – B. Mason, N. Gow, R. Hutter, D. Neame. Ruritanian musical.

September **Victoria the Great**, Imperator (Radio), reissue 1950. *p*/*d* – Herbert Wilcox. *s* – play by Laurence Housman. *sc* – M. Malleson, C. de Grandcourt. Life of Queen Victoria.

The Bells of St. Mary's, Fitzpatrick Pictures (MGM). *d* – J. Fitzpatrick. *s* – W. Williamson. Devon 1880; chorister trains in Rome and returns to marry sexton's daughter.

November **The Return of the Scarlet Pimpernel**, London (UA), reissue 1943. *p* – A. Korda,

226

A. Pressburger. *d* – Hans Schwarz. *s* – novel by Baroness Orczy. *sc* – L. Biro, A. Wimperis, A. Brunel. Paris 1797; fop again dons disguise to save wife from guillotine.

December **Remember When**, Embassy. *p* – George King. *d* – David Macdonald. *s* – H. Fowler Mear. 1879 comedy; solicitor helps blacksmith to win cycle race.

1938

January **Georges Bizet, Composer of Carmen**, Fitzpatrick Pictures (MGM). *p/d* – James Fitzpatrick. *s* – W. Williamson. Musical; starving composer dies after new opera fails.

The Life of Chopin, Fitzpatrick Pictures (MGM). *p/d* – James Fitzpatrick. *s* – W. Williamson. Jilted composer becomes lover of George Sand.

March **Governor Bradford**, AIP (Columbia), *p* – W. Newman. *d* – H. Parry. *s* – pageant by H. Parry. Persecution causes pilgrims to set sail in *Mayflower*.

John Halifax Gentleman, George King (MGM), reissue 1940. *d* – George King. *s* – novel by Mrs Craik. *sc* – A. R. Rawlinson. Apprentice inherits mill in 1790 and marries above himself.

June **The Challenge**, London-Denham (UA), reissue 1944. *p* – G. Stapenhorst, A. Korda. *d* – M. Rosmer, L. Trenker. *sc* – E. Pressburger, P. Kirwan, M. Rosmer. Matterhorn, 1865; English climber wrongly suspected of killing friends.

We're Going to be Rich, 20th Century Productions. *p* – Robert Kane, Samuel Engel. *d* – Monty Banks. *s* – James Grant. *sc* – R. Siegel, S. Hellman. Gracie Fields vehicle; singer in Africa, 1880.

October **Sixty Glorious Years**, Imperator. *p/d* – Herbert Wilcox. *s* – R. Vansittart, M. Malleson. *sc* – C. de Grandcourt. Events during Queen Victoria's reign.

November **Marigold**, ABPC. *p* – Walter Mycroft. *d* – Thomas Bentley. *s* – play by C. Garvice, A. Harker, F. Prior. *sc* – Dudley Leslie. Scotland, 1842; girl flees from father and discovers mother was an actress.

December **A Royal Divorce**, Imperator. *p* – Herbert Wilcox. *d* – Jack Raymond. *s* – novel by J. Thery. *sc* – M. Malleson. Love of Napoleon and Josephine.

1939

April **The Face at the Window**, Pennant, reissue 1942. *p/d* – George King. *s* – play by B. Warren. *sc* – A. R. Rawlinson, R. Faye. Crime in Paris, 1880; fake revival of corpse.

May **Jamaica Inn**, Mayflower, reissues 1944, 1948. *p* – E. Pommer. *d* – A. Hitchcock. *s* – novel by D. du Maurier. *sc* – S. Gilliat, J. Harrison, J. B. Priestley. Cornwall adventure; government agent poses as wrecker.

The Four Feathers, London (UA), reissues 1943, 1948. *p* – A. Korda, I. Asher. *d* – Z. Korda. *s* – novel by A. E. W. Mason. *sc* – R. C. Sherriff, L. Biro, A. Wimperis. Coward redeems himself by posing as Arab.

June **The Good Old Days**, Warner Bros. *p* – J. Jackson. *d* – R. W. Neill. *s* – R. Smart. *sc* – A. Melford, J. Dighton. Comedy 1840; Max Miller saves Lord's son from chimney sweep.

August **Young Man's Fancy**, Ealing, reissue 1944. *ap* – S. C. Balcon. *d/s* – Robert Stevenson. *sc* – Roland Pertwee, R. Ackland, E. V. Emmett. Comedy 1868; Lord elopes with human cannonball.

1940

February **Crimes at the Dark House**, Pennant–British Lion, reissues 1944, 1947. *p/d* – George King. *s* – novel by Wilkie Collins, *The Woman in White*. *sc* – E. Dryhurst, F. Hayward, H. Maltby. Crime 1850; impostor kills rich wife.

May **Gaslight**, British-National. *p* – John Corfield. *d* – Thorold Dickinson. *s* – play by Patrick Hamilton. *sc* – A. R. Rawlinson, Bridget Boland. Crime 1880; bigamist attempts to drive wife insane.

1941

March **The Prime Minister**, Warner Bros. *p* – Max Milder. *d* – Thorold Dickinson. *s* – Brock Williams, M. Hogan. Parliamentary and private life of Disraeli.

This England, British-National. *p* – John Corfield. *d* – David Macdonald. *s* – A. R. Rawlinson, Bridget Boland. Landowner and labourer fight for their heritage across a range of historical periods.

June   **Lady Hamilton**, Alexander Korda Films, made in Hollywood. *p/d* – A. Korda. *sc* – W. Reisch and R. C. Sherriff. Vicissitudes of Nelson's mistress.

August   **Kipps**, 20th Century Productions, reissue 1944. *p* – Ted Black. *d* – Carol Reed. *s* – novel by H. G. Wells. *sc* – S. Gilliat. Shop assistant inherits wealth.

Penn of Pennsylvania, British National. *p* – Richard Vernon. *d* – Lance Comfort. *s* – book by C. Vulliamy, *William Penn*. *sc* – A. de Grunwald. Persecution of Quakers leads to founding of Pennsylvania.

November   **Hatter's Castle**, Paramount British, reissue 1947. *p* – Isadore Goldsmith. *d* – Lance Comfort. *s* – novel by A. J. Cronin. *sc* – Paul Merzbach, R. Bernauer, R. Ackland. Scotland, 1879; tyrannical hatter goes mad.

1942

June   **The Young Mr. Pitt**, 20th Century Productions. *p* – Ted Black. *d* – Carol Reed. *s* – Viscount Castlerosse. *sc* – Frank Launder, Sidney Gilliat. Rise of Earl's son to become Prime Minister.

September   **The Great Mr. Handel**, IP-GHW. *p* – J. Sloan. *d* – Norman Walker. *s* – radio play by L. Du Garde Peach. *sc* – G. Elliott, V. MacClure. Composer wins royal favour by writing *The Messiah*.

Thunder Rock, Charter (MGM). *p* – John Boulting. *d* – Roy Boulting. *s* – play by Robert Ardrey. *sc* – Wolfgang Wilhelm, Jeffrey Dell, Bernard Miles, Anne Reiner. Writer peoples his lighthouse with victims of 1849 shipwreck.

1943

March   **Variety Jubilee**, Butcher's, reissues 1945, 1949. *p* – F. W. Baker. *d* – Maclean Rogers. *s* – Mabel Constanduros. *sc* – Kathleen Butler. Love behind the scenes in a music-hall from the Boer War to the present day.

When We Are Married, British National. *p* – John Baxter. *d* – Lance Comfort. *s* – play by J. B. Priestley. *sc* – Austin Melford, Barbara Emery. Yorkshire, 1890; three couples celebrating their silver weddings learn that their marriages are invalid.

June   **The Life and Death of Colonel Blimp**, Archers, reissue 1948. *p/d/s* – Michael Powell and Emeric Pressburger. Life of a professional soldier from 1902 to present day.

July   **The Man in Grey**, Gainsborough, reissues 1946, 1950. *p* – Ted Black. *d* – Leslie Arliss. *s* – novel by Lady E. F. Smith. *sc* – Margaret Kennedy, Leslie Arliss, Doreen Montgomery. Regency; Marquis's unloved wife is killed by female friend.

1944

May   **Fanny by Gaslight**, Gainsborough, reissues 1945, 1948. *p* – Ted Black. *d* – Anthony Asquith. *s* – novel by Michael Sadleir. *sc* – Doreen Montgomery, Aimée Stuart. Minister's illegitimate daughter is saved from lustful Lord.

August   **Champagne Charlie**, Ealing, reissue 1956. *p* – Michael Balcon. *ap* – John Croydon. *d* – Alberto Cavalcanti. *s* – A. Melford, A. Macphail, J. Dighton. Feud between rival music-hall singers in 1880s.

Fiddlers Three, Ealing, reissue 1948. *p* – Michael Balcon. *d* – Harry Watt. *s* – Diana Morgan, Angus Macphail. Sailors save Wren from Nero's orgy when lightning transports them back to Ancient Rome.

1945

January   **Henry V**, Two Cities. *p/d* – Laurence Olivier. *s* – play by Shakespeare. *sc* – Laurence Olivier, Alan Dent. Henry leads army to win at Agincourt in 1415.

March   **A Place of One's Own**, Gainsborough, reissue 1949. *p* – R. J. Minney. *d* – Bernard Knowles. *s* – novel by Osbert Sitwell. *sc* – Brock Williams, Osbert Sitwell. Companion of old couple is possessed by spirit of murdered girl in 1900.

June   **I'll Be Your Sweetheart**, Gainsborough, reissue 1948. *p* – Louis Levy. *d* – Val

228

Guest. *s* – Val Guest, Val Valentine. Musical, 1900; problems with musical piracy bring about Copyright Act.

July **Waltz Time**, British National. *p* – Louis Jackson. *d* – Paul Stein. *s* – H. James, Karl Rossler. *sc* – Montgomery Tully, Jack Whittingham. Musical; Empress poses as her masked friend in Vienna to win Count's heart.

November **Latin Quarter**, British-National. *p* – Louis Jackson, Derrick de Marney. *d* – Vernon Sewell. *s* – play by Pierre Mills, C. de Vylars. Crime, Paris 1893; mad sculptor kills wife and puts her in statue.

The Wicked Lady, Gainsborough, reissue 1949. *p* – R. J. Minney. *d* – Leslie Arliss. *s* – novel by Magdalen King-Hall. *sc* – Leslie Arliss, Aimée Stuart, Gordon Glennon. 1683; orphan weds nobleman and becomes highway robber as a diversion.

Pink String and Sealing Wax, Ealing, reissue 1949. *p* – Michael Balcon. *d* – Robert Hamer. *s* – play by Roland Pertwee. *sc* – Diana Morgan, Robert Hamer. Brighton 1880; publican's wife blackmails chemist by involving his son in her husband's murder.

1946

January **Caesar and Cleopatra**, IP-Pascal, reissue 1948. *d* – Gabriel Pascal. *s* – play by G. B. Shaw. *sc* – G. B. Shaw, Marjorie Deans, W. P. Lipscomb. Egypt 45 BC; Roman conqueror falls in love with young queen.

February **Gaiety George**, Embassy (WB), reissue 1953. *p/d* – George King. *s* – Richard Fisher, Peter Cresswell. *sc* – Katherine Struesby, Basil Woon. Musical 1900–20; Irish producer's show business vicissitudes.

April **Caravan**, Gainsborough, reissue 1949. *p* – Harold Huth. *d* – Arthur Crabtree. *s* – novel by Lady Eleanor Smith. *sc* – Roland Pertwee. Spain 1840; novelist marries gypsy girl and dispatches noble rival.

June **Beware of Pity**, Two Cities. *p* – W. P. Lipscomb. *d* – Maurice Elvey. *s* – novel by Stefan Zweig. *sc* – W. P. Lipscomb, Elizabeth Baron, Margaret Steen. Crippled girl realises that lieutenant's love is merely pity.

September **The Curse of the Wraydons**, Bushey. *p* – Gilbert Church. *d* – Victor Gover. *s* – play, *Spring-Heeled Jack the Terror of London*. *sc* – Michael Barringer. Mad inventor in Napoleonic period. Tod Slaughter melodrama.

October **The Magic Bow**, Gainsborough. *p* – R. J. Minney. *d* – Bernard Knowles. *s* – novel by Manuel Komroff. *sc* – Roland Pertwee, Norman Ginsbury. Paganini's musical and amatory successes.

Carnival, Two Cities, reissue 1949. *p* – John Sutro, William Sassoon. *d* – Stanley Haynes. *s* – novel by Compton Mackenzie. *sc* – Stanley Haynes, Peter Ustinov, Eric Maschwitz, Guy Green. Ballerina loves artist but marries farmer.

November **The Laughing Lady**, British National. *p* – Louis Jackson. *d* – Paul Stein. *s* – play by Ingram d'Abbes. *sc* – Jack Whittingham. French artist will be spared the guillotine if he steals English Lady's pearls.

December **Great Expectations**, Cineguild, reissue 1948. *p* – Anthony Havelock-Allan, Ronald Neame. *d* – David Lean. *s* – novel by Charles Dickens. *sc* – Ronald Neame, Kay Walsh, Cecil McGivern, Anthony Havelock-Allan. Orphan becomes a gentleman.

1947

January **Hungry Hill**, Two Cities, reissue 1948. *p* – William Seastrom. *d* – Brian Desmond Hurst. *s* – novel by Daphne du Maurier. *sc* – Daphne du Maurier, Terence Young, Francis Crowdy. Irish family feud over three generations.

February **Meet Me at Dawn**, Excelsior, reissue 1953. *p* – Marcel Hellman. *d* – Thornton Freeland. *s* – Anatole Litvak, Marcel Archaud's *Le Tueur*. *sc* – James Seymour, Lesley Storm, Maurice Cowan. Paris 1900; duellist loves editor's daughter.

March **Nicholas Nickleby**, Ealing, reissue 1953. *p* – Michael Balcon. *ap* – John Croydon. *d* – Alberto Cavalcanti. *s* – novel by Charles Dickens. *sc* – John Dighton. 1831 adventures of young teacher.

When You Come Home, Butcher's, reissue 1951. *p/d* – John Baxter. *s* – David Evans, Geoffrey Orme, Frank Randle. Randle comedy set in 1908.

We Do Believe in Ghosts, WW British. *p/d* – Walter West. Ghosts of Charles I and Anne Boleyn.

April **The Man Within**, Production Film Services, reissue 1948. *p* – Muriel and Sydney Box. *d* – Bernard Knowles. *s* – novel by Graham Greene. *sc* – Muriel and Sydney Box. Smuggling adventures in Sussex in 1820.

May **The Courtneys of Curzon Street**, Imperadio, reissue 1950. *p/d* – Herbert Wilcox. *s* – Florence Tranter. *sc* – Nicholas Phipps. 1899–1945 family saga, based on union between Irish maid and nobleman.

June **The Loves of Joanna Godden**, Ealing. *p* – Michael Balcon. *ap* – Sidney Cole. *d* – Charles Frend. *s* – novel by Sheila Kaye-Smith. *sc* – H. E. Bates, Angus Macphail. Loves of female sheep-farmer.

August **Jim the Penman**, Frank Chisnell. *d* – Frank Chisnell. *s* – radio play. *sc* – Terry Sanford, Edward Eve. 1870 tale of barrister who turned to forgery.

A Man About the House, BLPA. *p* – Ted Black. *d* – Leslie Arliss. *s* – novel by Francis Brett Young. *sc* – Leslie Arliss, J. B. Williams. Italy, 1907; handsome butler plans to kill two rich English spinsters.

Jassy, Gainsborough, reissue 1948. *p* – Sydney Box. *d* – Bernard Knowles. *s* – novel by Norah Lofts. *sc* – Dorothy and Campbell Christie, Geoffrey Kerr. Psychic gypsy weds gambler in 1830s in exchange for his house.

Master of Bankdam, Holbein. *p* – Nat Bronstein, Walter Forde, Edward Dryhurst. *d* – Walter Forde. *s* – novel by Thomas Armstrong, *The Crowthers of Bankdam*. *sc* – Edward Dryhurst, Moie Charles. Yorkshire 1854–1900; three generations of mill-owners.

September **Captain Boycott**, Individual, reissue 1954. *p* – Frank Launder and Sidney Gilliat. *d* – Frank Launder. *s* – novel by Philip Rooney. *sc* – Frank Launder, Wolfgang Wilhelm, Paul Vincent Carroll, Patrick Campbell. Ireland 1880; persecuted farmers ostracise landlord's agent.

Fame is the Spur, Two Cities. *p* – John Boulting. *d* – Roy Boulting. *s* – novel by Howard Spring. *sc* – Nigel Balchin. Political career of Manchester socialist, 1870–1935.

Uncle Silas, Two Cities. *p* – Josef Somlo. *d* – Charles Frank. *s* – novel by Sheridan Le Fanu. *sc* – Ben Travers. Guardian plots to kill young heiress in 1890.

The Ghosts of Berkeley Square, British National. *p* – Louis Jackson. *d* – Vernon Sewell. *s* – novel by Caryl Brahms and S. J. Simon, *No Nightingales*. *sc* – James Seymour. Comedy about two eighteenth-century ghosts doomed to haunt house until Royalty visits.

Mrs. Fitzherbert, British National. *p* – Louis Jackson. *d* – Montgomery Tully. *s* – novel by Winifred Carter, *Princess Fitz*. Prince Regent's marriage to Catholic widow.

December **Comin' Thro' the Rye**, Advance. *p* – Arthur Dent. *d* – Walter Mycroft. *s* – Gilbert McAlister. Life and loves of Robert Burns.

1948

January **The Mark of Cain**, Two Cities. *p* – W. P. Lipscomb. *d* – Brian Desmond Hurst. *s* – novel by Joseph Shearing. *sc* – W. P. Lipscomb, Francis Crowdy, Christianna Brand. Jealous man kills his younger brother in 1900.

Vice Versa, Two Cities. *p* – Peter Ustinov, George H. Brown. *d* – Peter Ustinov. *s* – novel by F. Anstey. *sc* – Peter Ustinov. Fantasy 1907; magic stone makes father and son change places.

An Ideal Husband, London. *p/d* – Alexander Korda. *s* – play by Oscar Wilde. *sc* – Lajos Biro. Comedy; viscount foils blackmailing widow.

February **Call of the Blood**, Pendennis Pictures. *p* – John Stafford, Steven Pallos. *d* – John Clements, Ladislas Vajda. *s* – novel by Robert Hitchens. *sc* – John Clements, Akos Tolnay, Basil Mason. Sicily 1900; tourist seduces villager and is killed by her father.

Blanche Fury, Cineguild, reissue 1950. *p* – Anthony Havelock-Allan. *d* – Marc Allegret. *s* – novel by Joseph Shearing. *sc* – Audrey Erskine Lindop, Hugh Mills, Cecil McGivern. Governess weds landowner in 1860; he is killed by ambitious steward.

	Idol of Paris, Premier (WB). *p* – R. J. Minney. *d* – Leslie Arliss. *s* – novel by Alfred Shirkauer, *Paiva Queen of Love*. *sc* – Norman Lee, Stafford Dickens, Harry Ostrer. Queen of the demi-monde in 19th-century Paris gains notoriety without actual unchastity. Contains female fight with whips.
March	**So Evil My Love**, Paramount British. *p* – Hal B. Wallis. *d* – Lewis Allen. *s* – novel by Joseph Shearing. *sc* – Leonard Spiegelglass, Ronald Millar. Crime in 1886; artist involves missionary's widow in blackmail and murder.
	The First Gentleman, Columbia British. *p* – Joseph Friedman. *d* – Alberto Cavalcanti. *s* – play by Norman Ginsbury. *sc* – Nicholas Phipps, Reginald Long. Prince Regent tries to make his daughter marry Prince of Orange.
	Anna Karenina, London Films. *p* – Alexander Korda. *d* – Julien Duvivier. *s* – novel by Tolstoy. *sc* – J. Duvivier, Jean Anouilh, Guy Morgan. Adultery in Russia in 1870s.
	The Greed of William Hart, Bushey. *p* – Gilbert Church. *d* – Oswald Mitchell. *s* – John Gilling. Tod Slaughter melodrama about resurrectionists who kill half-wit and sell his corpse to anatomist.
June	**Hamlet**, Two Cities, *p/d* – Laurence Olivier. *s* – play by Shakespeare. Murdered king's ghost inspires son to revenge.
July	**Oliver Twist**, Cineguild. *p* – Anthony Havelock-Allan. *d* – David Lean. *s* – novel by Dickens. *sc* – David Lean, Stanley Hayes. Workhouse foundling is trained as a pickpocket.
September	**Saraband for Dead Lovers**, Ealing. *p* – Michael Balcon. *ap* – Michael Relph. *s* – novel by Helen Simpson. *sc* – John Dighton, Alexander Mackendrick. Hanover 1689; romantic intrigues of prince's wife.
October	**Esther Waters**, Wessex. *p* – Ian Dalrymple. *d* – Ian Dalrymple, Peter Proud. *s* – novel by George Moore. *sc* – Michael Gordon, William Rose, Gerard Tyrrell. Maid is seduced in 1870s and brings up her son alone.
November	**Bonnie Prince Charlie**, London Films. *p* – Edward Black. *d* – Anthony Kimmins. *s* – Clemence Dane. Scotland 1745; pretender fails in his bid to restore Stuarts to the throne.
December	**Scott of the Antarctic**, Ealing. *p* – Michael Balcon. *ap* – Sidney Cole. *d* – Charles Frend. *s* – Ivor Montagu, Walter Meade, Mary Hayley Bell. Expedition to South Pole ends in death.

1949

January	**Eureka Stockade**, Ealing. *p* – Michael Balcon. *ap* – Leslie Norman. *d/s* – Harry Watt. *sc* – Harry Watt, Walter Greenwood, Ralph Smart. Australia 1850; revolt of gold diggers.
	Elizabeth of Ladymead, Imperadio. *p/d* – Herbert Wilcox. *s* – play by Frank Harvey. *sc* – Frank Harvey. Four generations of husbands return from war to find their wives have become independent.
February	**The History of Mr. Polly**, Two Cities. *p* – John Mills. *d/sc* – Anthony Pelissier. *s* – novel by H. G. Wells. Draper rebels against his wife in 1900.
March	**The Bad Lord Byron**, Triton. *p* – Aubrey Baring, Sydney Box. *d* – David Macdonald. *s* – Terence Young, Anthony Thorne, Peter Quennell, Laurence Kitchin, Paul Holt. Life and loves of Lord Byron.
	Britannia Mews, 20th Century. *p* – William Perlberg. *d* – Jean Negulesco. *s* – novel by Margery Sharpe. *sc* – Ring Lardner Jnr. Period romance; girl marries artist, and after his death marries his double.
	The Case of Charles Peace, Argyle, reissue 1952. *p* – John Argyle. *d* – Norman Lee. *s* – Doris Davidson, Norman Lee. Crime 1870; true story of picture-framer who became burglar.
April	**The Cardboard Cavalier**, Two Cities. *p/d* – Walter Forde. *s* – Noel Langley. Comedy 1658; barrow-boy gets involved with plot against Cromwell.
	The Queen of Spades, ABPC–World Screenplays. *p* – Anatole de Grunwald. *d* – Thorold Dickinson. *s* – novel by Pushkin. *sc* – Rodney Ackland, Arthur Boys. Russia 1806; poor captain wrests Devil's winning card from Countess.
May	**The Last Days of Dolwyn**, London BLPA. *p* – Anatole de Grunwald. *d/s* – Emlyn Williams. Wales 1892; old woman tries to stop industrialist flooding village.

June	**Christopher Columbus**, Gainsborough. *p* – A. Frank Bundy, Sydney Box. *d* – David Macdonald. *s* – Cyril Roberts, Muriel and Sydney Box. Columbus discovers the New World.

June   **Christopher Columbus**, Gainsborough. *p* – A. Frank Bundy, Sydney Box. *d* – David Macdonald. *s* – Cyril Roberts, Muriel and Sydney Box. Columbus discovers the New World.

    Kind Hearts and Coronets, Ealing. *p* – Michael Balcon. *ap* – Michael Relph. *d* – Robert Hamer. *s* – novel by Roy Horniman, *Israel Rank*. *sc* – Robert Hamer, John Dighton. Period comedy; disinherited man kills eight relatives to inherit dukedom.

July   **Trottie True**, Two Cities. *p* – Hugh Stewart. *d* – Brian Desmond Hurst. *s* – novel by Caryl Brahms and S. J. Simon. *sc* – C. Denis Freeman. Music-hall girl loves balloonist in 1900 but marries Lord.

October   **Diamond City**, Gainsborough. *p* – A. Frank Bundy. *d* – David Macdonald. *s* – Roger Bray. *sc* – Roger Bray, Roland Pertwee. Diamond digging in 1870 Africa.

1950

February   **Madeleine**, Pinewood–Cineguild. *p* – Stanley Haynes. *d* – David Lean. *s* – Stanley Haynes, Nicholas Phipps. Glasgow 1857; girl may have poisoned her blackmailing lover.

March   **Room to Let**, Hammer. *p* – Anthony Hinds. *d* – Godfrey Grayson. *s* – radio play by Margery Allingham. *sc* – John Gilling, Geoffrey Grayson. 1904 reporter discovers Jack the Ripper.

April   **The Reluctant Widow**, Two Cities. *p* – Gordon Wellesley. *d* – Bernard Knowles. *s* – novel by Georgette Heyer. *sc* – Gordon Wellesley, J. B. Boothroyd. Governess weds dying Lord and saves papers from Napoleon's spies.

    The Dancing Years, ABPC. *p* – Warwick Ward. *d* – Harold French. *s* – play by Ivor Novello. *sc* – Warwick Ward, Jack Whittingham. Vienna 1910; composer loves opera star.

May   **So Long at the Fair**, Gainsborough. *p* – Betty Box. *d* – Anthony Darnborough, Terence Fisher. *s* – novel by Anthony Thorne. *sc* – Hugh Mills, Anthony Thorne. Paris 1889; English girl's brother and his room vanish from hotel.

June   **Treasure Island**, Walt Disney (RKO). *p* – Perce Pierce. *d* – Byron Haskin. *s* – novel by R. L. Stevenson. *sc* – Lawrence E. Watkin. Widow's son finds pirate treasure.

    The Fall of the House of Usher, GIB Films, reissues 1955, 1961. *p/d* – George Ivan Barnett. *s* – story by Edgar Allan Poe. *sc* – Kenneth Thompson, Dorothy Catt. Period horror; Lord's sister survives premature burial.

July   **Bitter Springs**, Ealing. *p* – Michael Balcon. *ap* – Leslie Norman. *d/s* – Ralph Smart. *sc* – W. P. Lipscomb, Monja Danischewsky. Australia 1900; sheep farmer fights Aborigines.

August   **Portrait of Clare**, ABPC. *p* – Leslie Landau. *d* – Lance Comfort. *s* – novel by Francis Brett Young. *sc* – Leslie Landau, Adrian Arlington. Romance 1900; woman weds three husbands.

    The Black Rose, 20th Century, reissue 1954. *p* – Louis Lighton. *d* – Henry Hathaway. *s* – novel by Thomas Costain. *sc* – Talbot Jennings. Saxon scholar saves captive girl from Mongol chief in 1260.

    Shadow of the Eagle, Valiant-Tuscania. *p* – Anthony Havelock-Allan. *d* – Sidney Salkow. *s* – Jacques Companeez. *sc* – Doreen Montgomery, Hagar Wilde. Venice 1770; envoy falls in love with Princess.

September   **Gone to Earth**, London–BLPA–Vanguard. *p* – David O. Selznick. *d/sc* – Michael Powell, Emeric Pressburger. *s* – novel by Mary Webb. Country girl prefers fox to Squire.

November   **The Mudlark**, 20th Century. *p/sc* – Nunnally Johnson. *d* – Jean Negulesco. *s* – novel by Theodore Bonnet. 1876; urchin breaks into Windsor Castle, humanising the mourning Queen.

    The Elusive Pimpernel, London–BLPA–Archers. *p* – Samuel Goldwyn, Alexander Korda. *d/sc* – Michael Powell and Emeric Pressburger. *s* – novel by Baroness Orczy. English fop dons disguise in order to save French aristocrats from the guillotine.

INDEX

234

235

237

238